W9-CWX-020

BRITISH POLICY IN THE SOUTH PACIFIC

BRITISH POLICY IN THE SOUTH PACIFIC

(1786-1893)

A study of British policy in the South Pacific
islands prior to the establishment of Governments
by the Great Powers

By

JOHN M. WARD, M.A., LL.B.

Challis Professor of History, University of Sydney

With a Foreword by
Professor S. H. ROBERTS
Vice-Chancellor, University of Sydney.

GREENWOOD PRESS, PUBLISHERS
WESTPORT, CONNECTICUT

Library of Congress Cataloging in Publication Data

Ward, John M
   British policy in the South Pacific (1786-1893).

   Reprint of the 1950 ed. published by Australasian Pub.
Co., Sydney.
   Bibliography: p.
   Includes index.
   1. Oceanica--Foreign relations--Great Britain.
2. Great Britain--Foreign relations--Oceanica. 3. Great
Britain--Colonies--Oceanica--Administration. 4. Great
Britain. High Commission for Western Pacific Island.
I. Title.
DU40.W3 1976   327.41'09   76-10622

ISBN 0-8371-8821-0

FOREWORD

THE revival and extension of Pacific studies during recent years have stimulated interest in the history of the islands of the South Pacific. The present work is a pioneer study in British policy in this region. Great Britain, Australia and New Zealand now administer the greater part of the island world; but hitherto even the most obvious questions as to the growth of British interest in the islands have been left both unasked and unanswered.

Looking back to-day, three questions stand out very prominently about island history. Why was Great Britain, for long the paramount Power in the South Pacific, so reluctant to seek territories there? What was the official British policy towards British traders, missionaries and planters who resorted to the islands in the years before they passed under the control of modern Powers? What was the relationship between the development of British policy in the islands and the growth of Australian and New Zealand interest in the South Pacific region? All of these questions need consideration; the first has been partly answered by previous authors; in the main, the second and the third break new ground. Mr. Ward set out in this book to answer all three questions. In doing so he found himself confronted with a fascinating (and unusually diverse) body of material. His book traces British policy in the islands from 1786 to 1893. During this lengthy period there were times of swift and feverish action, times of dullness, times of slow and steady development in which policy was catching up with the efforts of British missionaries, traders and planters to spread themselves throughout the entire island world.

The book opens with a limited canvas. In 1786 when the British Government was deciding to plant a penal colony at Botany Bay, the islands came into the picture as possible sources of food, livestock and flax. There is an interesting account of how the British Government, believing in the barrenness of New South Wales, called in the resources of the islands to redress the deficiencies of the continent. Within a few years of the settlement of New South Wales traders, whalers and sealers from New South Wales, Great Britain and America were pushing their way throughout the islands. So far as British subjects were concerned, these activities ran directly counter to the monopoly rights of the East India Company. This book traces in detail the often intricate, but important, story of how the East India Company's monopoly was whittled down piece by piece and British subjects allowed freedom to trade and navigate in the South Pacific.

At this point the story enters into island history as it is ordinarily understood. The record is one of extraordinary complications and unexpected points of interest. British colonial policy and foreign policy were important, but so was the growth of New South Wales from a penal colony to a colony of settlement. The ambitions of France, the United States of America and Germany at times exercised a decisive influence in shaping island affairs, but in the long term the activities of the Powers were probably less important than the gradual economic and social transformation which took place in islands developed by European and American planters and traders and the growth of sea and cable communications across the Pacific. Mr. Ward has shown that international rivalry was a much less important factor in the opening up of the islands than has sometimes been imagined. The attempts of the Royal Navy to maintain law and order amongst British subjects in the islands, the British recognition of the sovereignty of some native rulers and the extraordinary position of consuls who found themselves called on to act as judges, legislators and administrators because of the lack of effective government amongst Europeans in the islands, have all been examined for the first time. An interesting chapter discusses some of the attempts made by British subjects to erect their own governments in the islands, usually in the form of native kingdoms with British subjects exercising real power behind the scenes. As a culminating event Mr. Ward describes the establishment of the new Western Pacific High Commission in 1893, through which Great Britain, after a century of resistance to acquiring territories in the island world, set up an authority to regulate her numerous colonies and dependencies in Southern Oceania.

Some parts of the record are of course better known than others. For example, the reasons for the British acquisition of New Zealand have been investigated by many scholars. Mr. Ward's return to this subject is, however, justified because his consideration of the broad picture of British activity in the islands has led him to suggest a very considerable re-interpretation. His conclusions show some interesting departures from those of Marais, Harrop and Williams. He has also presented the kanaka trade problem

vi

from a new viewpoint while the accounts of British policy towards Fiji up to the cession and of Anglo-French negotiations over Tahiti and the Society Islands have much of an original character to record. By contrast, the history of Samoa, which has been so thoroughly investigated by Sylvia Masterman, G. H. Ryden and J. W. Ellison, has provided less opportunity for the later research worker. Accordingly, assessment of the Samoan record has been confined in the present work to those aspects of British activity which are of significance in British policy as a whole.

By far the greater part of the book, however, is concerned, not with re-interpretation, but with the opening up of a new subject. In examining British policy towards British subjects in the islands prior to annexation, Mr. Ward has entered a largely untrodden field. The conclusions that he has reached attribute more importance to the general island scene and to the development of the Australasian colonies as factors in British policy than has been suggested in the past.

It may be said, as the author himself has stated at several points in his book, that South Pacific history will be subject to still further re-interpretation when the general economic and social history of the main island groups throughout the nineteenth century has been adequately investigated. This is a subject to which Mr. Ward's work has certainly drawn attention as one promising really important results. Similarly, some of the special aspects of the British record referred to in the following pages need more detailed treatment than could be afforded them in a work such as this, whose main function is to open the field. It is to be hoped that others will not be slow to work in and extend the field to which this book has made so fine a contribution.

S. H. ROBERTS.

University of Sydney,
November 12th, 1947.

AUTHOR'S NOTE

I am delighted to have my first book reprinted, because much has changed since I wrote it thirty years ago. I include here my own later assessment of it, which appeared in R. W. Winks (ed.), *The Historiography of the British Empire - Commonwealth,* Duke University Press, 1966.

John Manning Ward of the University of Sydney built directly on the foundations laid by Benians and Brookes when he wrote *British Policy in the South Pacific, 1783-1893* (Sydney, 1948).

Ward's book, confessedly a pioneering study, was the work of a young scholar who used only the sources available in Sydney and Canberra. It tried to trace British policy toward the South Pacific Islands before they were brought under the rule of the powers. Ward managed to blaze a rather rough trail, usually in the right direction, but leaving formidable tasks of rectification and discovery to his successors. From 1786, when Britain decided to found a colony in eastern Australia, giving the governor power over the "adjacent" islands in the Pacific, down to 1893 when the Western Pacific High Commission was formally reconstituted, British policy toward the islands was as likely to be formulated in legal terms (such as acts of Parliament, orders in council, and official memoranda on problems of international law) as in any other way. Using this kind of evidence, Ward was able to find great continuity in British policy than any other historical working on the same subject.

CONTENTS

LIST OF MAPS

ABBREVIATIONS USED IN THE TEXT
(See also page 333)

H.R.A.: Historical Records of Australia (with number of series, volume and page).

H.R.N.S.W.: Historical Records of New South Wales (with number of volume and page).

H.R.N.Z.: Historical Records of New Zealand (with number of volume and page).

PP.: British Parliamentary Papers (with session, number of paper and volume and page).

S.M.H.: Sydney Morning Herald.

W.P.H.C.: Western Pacific High Commission.

PREFACE

THE aim of this book is to trace the development of British policy in the South Pacific islands during the period prior to their passing under the control of the Great Powers. Despite its obvious interest, the subject has previously attracted little systematic attention. Individual parts of it have been examined with great thoroughness, but, apart from a valuable chapter by Dr. E. A. Benians in the *Cambridge History of the British Empire,* the over-all picture has not been drawn. As a result, the detailed surveys of particular aspects of British policy have suffered from the lack of adequate research into broad trends. The subject has been tackled piecemeal so that, despite contributions of most distinguished merit, the main outlines of long-term developments have not been made clear.

The period covered in the present book is a long one. Commencing with the references to the islands occurring in the plans of 1786 for a settlement in New South Wales, the record proceeds up to the reconstitution of the Western Pacific High Commission in 1893. As the aim has been to blaze a trail throughout the period, the character of the story varies most extensively. But British policy, whether it were confined to trifling matters like obtaining flax and food from the islands for New South Wales, or whether it related to vital matters like annexation, native government and peace and war, was always one of the dominant factors in island affairs. The purpose of this book is to trace the growth of that policy, to determine the island influences which went to its making and its significance in relation to South Pacific history.

The subject touches on many fields. No one could speak or write with authority on all of them, ranging as they do from the decay of the East India Company's monopoly to the emergence of new legal systems in the islands, from the problems of culture contact to the world-wide rivalries of the Great Powers at the close of the nineteenth century. My endeavour has been merely to illustrate the nature of the problems arising in each case and to relate them to British policy as I have seen it. My strong feeling is that the fields on which this book touches offer rich opportunities not only for all those interested generally in the history of the islands, but also for specialist students of public administration and of law in the making, for historians of international law and trade and commerce and for social anthropologists.

I put this book forward as a tentative appraisal of a very large subject. It is my hope that it may be of some use to others turning to the study of island history. Their work will probably amend my judgments and interpretations, which, indeed, are advanced only for the sake of suggesting the nature of the general picture. It is greatly to be hoped that further work on the social and economic history of the South Pacific will make it possible for the island background itself to be better understood than it is at present.

It is a pleasure to acknowledge the assistance that I have received in writing this book. My principal debt is to Professor S. H. Roberts, Vice-Chancellor of the University of Sydney. This book was written during Professor Roberts's tenure of the Challis Chair of History. It owes much to his continued interest. I am additionally indebted to Professor Roberts for the Foreword which he has contributed to this publication by one of his former students.

Several colleagues have aided me with criticism and advice. Professor A. H. McDonald, Mr. L. F. Fitzhardinge, and Miss M. G. Jacobs read through most of the book in manuscript and offered many suggestions. Mr. J. A. La Nauze gave me his assistance in clearing up several points at a time when I had little opportunity to solve problems for myself Dr. J. W. Davidson, of St. John's College, Cambridge, read some chapters during his visit to Australia in 1946 and made most valuable observations. Especially I wish to acknowledge the keen interest taken in this work by Professor Avery Craven, of the University of Chicago, while he was Visiting Professor of American History at Sydney University during 1947.

Of a different nature is my debt to Miss Mander Jones, of the Mitchell Library, Sydney, and Mr. K. Binns, of the National Library, Canberra, and their staffs. I owe much to those who drew my attention to sources that might otherwise have not been utilised.

Finally, I wish to thank the University of Sydney for assistance in the writing and publication of this book as research within the Faculty of Arts.

JOHN M. WARD.

Department of History,
University of Sydney,
November 19th, 1947.

CHAPTER I

THE ADJUNCT POLICY

BRITISH policy in the South Pacific began with the great voyages of exploration undertaken by Dampier in 1699 and by Byron, Wallis, Carteret and Cook in the eighteenth century. All of these voyages were officially sponsored and, except in Dampier's case, instructions were issued by the British Admiralty as to their routes and objectives.[1] Although the islands themselves were not the main objects of any of the explorations, discovery of the islands was in fact one of the main fruits of the expeditions sent out between 1764 and 1776 in search of the unknown Southern Continent, the mythical strait from the Pacific to Hudson's Bay, Juan Fernandez Land and other such *terrae nondum cognitae*.

By the time that Cook had demonstrated that there was no unknown continent in the South Seas, the nature of the island world was becoming known. Its picturesque qualities had captured the imagination of Europeans; its isolation and limited economic development were clearly understood. British interest in the South Pacific soon slackened perceptibly. No promising resources had been discovered and there really was no reason why the British Government should seize on its undoubted opportunity of making the greater part of the South Pacific lands British territory.

From the time of Cook's third voyage onwards the official British attitude towards the islands (and the whole South Pacific) was one of indifference. A limited and grudging departure in policy was made in 1786 when New South Wales was selected by the British Government as the site of a new penal settlement. In its plans for a colony at Botany Bay the Government gave a well-defined place to the islands of the South Pacific. The Home Office proposed that their resources should be used to supplement those of New South Wales. Captain Arthur Phillip, R.N., the first Governor, was ordered to obtain from them livestock, flax plants and women. Norfolk Island, as a place which might afterwards

---

[1] The details of Dampier's voyage were proposed by himself. As to the eighteenth century voyages, see J. C. Beaglehole: *The Exploration of the Pacific*; London, 1934; and J. M. Ward: "British Exploration Policy in the South Pacific during the Eighteenth Century"; *J.R.A.H.S.*, Vol. XXXIII, Part I, 1947.

become useful, was to be annexed immediately, lest it fall into the hands of a foreign power.[2]

In Phillip's instructions the resources of the islands were referred to in greater detail than were those of New South Wales. (The same difference appears in the three best known of the recorded unofficial plans for a British settlement in the South Pacific.)[3] The marked contrast between the references to the islands and the references to New South Wales in both the official and the unofficial plans reflected the state of knowledge then existing and the belief that the islands possessed resources of immediate usefulness to New South Wales, which was regarded as poor country.

It was only after prolonged enquiry into many possible places of settlement that the choice of New South Wales had been made. When the decision to found a colony at Botany Bay was announced, the Government was immediately castigated in the most violent terms. New South Wales, so the opposition declared, was too desert and distant a country to support even a penal colony. The eminent *Gentleman's Magazine* disposed of New South Wales in a single caustic sentence:

> "The eastern coast of New Holland is, perhaps, the most barren, least inhabited, and worst cultivated country in the southern hemisphere; and Botany Bay is at too great a distance from any European settlement to receive either succour or friendly assistance."[4]

A pamphlet, *Copious Remarks on the Discovery of New South Wales*,[5] justified the Government's plans on the rigorous ground that the poverty of the country would punish the offender in accordance with stern morality: "Offended justice in consigning him to the inhospitable shore of New Holland, does not mean thereby to seat him for his life on a bed of roses." Some of the soil around Botany Bay was admitted to be good, but the general summing up was in the stock phrase of condemnation, "it is upon the whole rather barren than fertile."

The somewhat savage criticisms of New South Wales made in 1786 were supported by the best first-hand evidence then available. When the Government decided to found a colony at Botany Bay, the only reports on New South Wales were those made as a result

---

[2] Phillip's Instructions, *H.R.A.*, I, i, p. 13.

[3] The plans of James Matra, Sir George Young and of the anonymous author of the undated plan found in the Home Office Records. All are referred to below.

[4] Oct., 1786; repr. in G. B. Barton: *History of N.S.W. from the Records*; Sydney, 1889; p. 467.

[5] See bibliography. There is a copy in the Petherick Collection, National Library, Canberra. References are to pp. iii, 18 and 47.

of the *Endeavour* voyage in 1770. These were slight and mostly unfavourable. Cook himself showed little enthusiasm for any part of the east coast.[6] Hawkesworth's *Voyages*, through which more than through any other source Cook's discoveries were made known to the public, gave a most unattractive picture of New South Wales. "It is upon the whole rather barren than fertile . . . the greater part is such as can admit of no cultivation." Even the unknown interior was condemned.[7] The outstanding impressions for the reader of Hawkesworth were those of a poor and desolate country. Barton, the author of *History of New South Wales from the Records,* was right in concluding that the *Voyages* would have given no one a high opinion of New South Wales, nor impressed anyone with the idea that it was destined to become a wealthy State.[8]

Sir Joseph Banks, who had accompanied Cook, wrote a famous and depressing description of New South Wales:

"In the whole length of coast which we sailed along, there was a very unusual sameness to be observed in the face of the country. Barren it may justly be called, and in a very high degree, so far at least as we saw . . . A soil so barren, and at the same time entirely void of the help derived from cultivation, could not be supposed to yield much to the support of man."[9]

In 1779, however, Banks somewhat modified conclusions drawn from his earlier descriptions of New South Wales. In evidence before the House of Commons Committee on Transportation, he stated that New South Wales could be regarded as a suitable place for a "colony of convicted felons." He went on to paint a rather glowing picture of a country well stocked with timber and with abundant water. When asked whether any benefit would accrue to Great Britain from the founding of a colony in New South Wales, Banks declared that:

"If the people formed among themselves a civil government, they would necessarily increase, and find occasion for many European commodities; and it was not to be doubted, that a large tract of land such as New Holland, which was larger than the whole of Europe, would furnish matter of advantageous return."[10]

[6] *Captain Cook's Journal, &c.* (ed. W. J. L. Wharton; London, 1893); pp. 317-325.

[7] Vol. III, pp. 218, 227.

[8] op. cit., p. lxviii.

[9] *Journal of the Rt. Hon. Sir Joseph Banks, &c.* (ed. J. D. Hooker; London, 1896); pp. 297-298.

[10] Qu. G. Mackaness: *Sir Joseph Banks;* Sydney, 1936; p. 19.

Here was powerful support for the school of thought which rejected Cook's findings and argued that, because of its great extent and geographical position, New South Wales must be richly endowed with resources. The succeeding years, when projects for a colony in the South Pacific were being continually debated, saw instance after instance of vague arguments based on generalities being opposed to the precise observations of Cook and Banks. Matra, for example, argued that New South Wales would produce an enormous variety of valuable produce because "part of it lies in a climate parallel to the Spice Islands."[11] Young wrote that so vast a continent would naturally have valuable resources. "The variety of climates included between the forty-fourth and tenth degrees of latitude give us an opportunity of uniting in one territory almost all the products of the known world."[12] "R.G." in a pamphlet, *Proposals for employing convicts within this kingdom; instead of sending them to Botany Bay,* went so far as to argue that New Holland was too good for convicts. "When I am informed that it is intended to sow some of the worst seeds in the world [the convicts] upon some of its best land, I cannot help thinking that there is an inconsistency in the conclusion."[13]

The Government's view, as embodied in the official "Heads of a Plan," assumed that New South Wales was capable of developing useful resources, rather than that it possessed such resources available for immediate consumption. It was thought that the country could sustain a penal colony, provided that a beginning were made by taking resources there for development. Phillip was instructed to obtain cattle and seeds at the Cape of Good Hope on his way to Botany Bay.[14]

The use of the islands as adjuncts to New South Wales was part of the same policy. In 1786 the islands were really better known

[11] *H.R.N.S.W.*, I (2), pp. 1 ff.

[12] *H.R.N.Z.*, I, pp. 45 ff.

[13] Publ. London, 1787. The pamphlet is very rare. There is a copy in the National Library, Canberra.

[14] Opinion in Great Britain regarding the resources of New South Wales has not yet been examined adequately. The conflict referred to above is, however, clearly attested. Sources for further research would include the following: A. Anderson: *Historical and Chronological Deduction of the Origin of Commerce;* Anon.: *Copious Remarks on the Discovery of N.S.W.;* Anon.: *History of New Holland from 1616;* R.G.: *Proposals for employing convicts within this kingdom;* T. Gilbert: *Voyage from N.S.W. to Canton in 1788;* A. Phillip: *The Voyage of Governor Phillip to Botany Bay;* and J. H. G. Forster: *Dissertatio Inauguralis Botanico-Medica de Plantis Esculentis Insularum Oceani Australis.* As to all of these, see bibliography. E. O'Brien (*The Foundation of Australia, 1786-1800;* London, 1937; p. 187 n.) refers also to *The Times,* the *Morning Post,* the *Public Advertiser,* the *Morning Herald* and the *Gentleman's Magazine.*

in Great Britain than was New South Wales. During the eighteenth century exploration of the Pacific had proceeded apace and the nature of the island world was pretty well known after the work of Cook. The explorers had remarked on the island resources and credited them with a picturesque character, which helped to attract public and official attention. The island peoples had been made to appear capable of trade and reasonably well disposed towards Europeans.

The Government itself used the resources of the islands quite independently of the New South Wales settlement. In 1787, at the request of a number of West Indies merchants in London, Lieutenant William Bligh was sent to Tahiti in H.M.S. *Bounty* with the object of obtaining breadfruit trees to be used as food for slaves in the West Indies.

Similarly, Phillip, as Governor of New South Wales, was instructed to obtain livestock from the islands—a procedure with the additional advantage of being cheap. Barter goods were provided for trading with the natives. When sending ships to the islands for supplies, Phillip was also to obtain women as companions for the convicts and soldiers. Flax plants were to be procured as the means of founding a useful industry. Partly in order to facilitate these transactions and to prevent the islands from becoming a refuge for escaped convicts, Phillip was given a vaguely defined jurisdiction over "adjacent" islands to the east of New South Wales. (See Chapter IV, below.)

In these minor and frequently trivial ways British policy towards the islands first took shape. The development of the adjunct policy is of little importance in its details. The record of how the island resources were used to assist New South Wales is a fascinating one, but its significance in British policy as a whole is slight. It is sufficient to note the origins of the various instructions laid on Phillip and the degree to which they were obeyed.

The plan to import native women into the colony arose from the disproportion of the sexes there. Lord Sydney, in writing to the Lords of the Treasury about the Botany Bay scheme, had recommended the importation of native women from the Friendly Islands, New Caledonia and other neighbouring islands.[15] Similar suggestions were made in the unofficial proposals of Matra and Young.[16] The Parliamentary Committee on Transportation had also enquired as to whether women could be brought from Tahiti.[17]

[15] Sydney to Treasury, Aug. 18, 1786; *H.R.N.S.W.*, I (2), p. 15.
[16] See nn. 11 and 12, above.
[17] *PP.*, 1785; xxxvii, No. 71.

In practice no women were brought from the islands to the colony by the authorities. In his Memorandum of 1787 on the proposed colony Phillip himself had suggested bringing women from the Friendly Islands and other islands as wives for the soldiers, who would be induced to settle on the land.[18] But experience in New South Wales changed his views. "To send for women from the Islands," he wrote to Lord Sydney in 1788, "would answer no other purpose than that of bringing them to pine away in misery."[19] No more was heard of the scheme. Instead, special efforts were made to send out to the colony female convicts, wives of convicts and "even women that cohabited with them."[20]

The instruction to develop flax from the islands was much better heeded, partly because of the great value of flax itself and partly because its cultivation and processing were deemed suitable work for convicts both on Norfolk Island and in New South Wales. Phillip's instructions were to cultivate flax plants from the islands in order to provide clothing and maritime supplies, some of which might be exported. During Phillip's term of office special attention was paid to the abundant flax resources (phormium tenax) of Norfolk Island. Flax was also grown in New South Wales, mainly along the River Hawkesbury. Governor King reported in 1804 that the growth and manufacture of flax were increasing "as well as can possibly be expected."[21] According to McNab, none of the early official attempts to cultivate flax achieved much success.[22]

The instruction to import livestock from the islands had apparently been inspired by the reports of multitudes of hogs on Norfolk Island and Tahiti.[23] The discovery of Lord Howe Island by the expedition sent to annex Norfolk Island in 1788 also attracted attention to food resources in the islands. For some years turtles from Lord Howe Island were in demand in Sydney as means of relieving the desperate food shortages of the new colony.[24]

The bringing of supplies from Tahiti began in 1792. The explorer, Captain George Vancouver, then instructed the com-

[18] H.R.N.Z., I, p. 69.
[19] H.R.N.S.W., I (2), p. 127.
[20] H.R.A., I, i, p. 132.
[21] King to Hobart, Aug. 14, 1804; H.R.A., I, v, p. 12.
[22] R. McNab: Murihiku; Wellington, 1909: p. 191. King also attempted to obtain flax direct from the Maoris of New Zealand. He suggested that whalers visiting the Bay of Islands should barter for flax and make it into rope on board.
[23] Goats, hogs, dogs and cattle had been left at Tahiti by the Spaniards between 1774 and 1776. Cook left cattle, sheep, horses and poultry in 1777. (See Cook to Stephens, Oct. 20, 1778; H.R.N.Z., I, p. 30.) According to the same source, Cook also left livestock at the Friendly Islands.
[24] D. Collins (ed. Maria Collins): An Account of the English Colony in N.S.W., 1804; ed. J. Collier, Christchurch, 1910; pp. 24, 28, 66 and 69.

mander of one of his storeships to call at Tahiti and other islands
(on his way from Nootka Sound in North America to Sydney) in
order to pick up castaways and to procure hogs, goats and fowls
for use in New South Wales.[25] Vancouver was acting in accordance
with arrangements made between the Home Office and the
Admiralty.

Systematic use of Tahitian supplies in New South Wales began
under Governor King, always noted for his interest in the industries of the colony. In 1801 King, wishing to reduce the cost of
food to the public exchequer, adopted a policy of obtaining salt
meat from Tahiti.[26] H.M.S. *Porpoise,* when despatched to Tahiti
for the purpose, returned with 30,000 lb. of salt meat. These
supplies were specially welcome in view of the colony's lack of
cattle and the high price of food imported from Great Britain or
purchased from visiting Americans.[27]

"With proper management and well-timed presents," King informed the Home authorities, the natives could be induced to
co-operate in the trade. Development would be hampered only
by the lack of a ship of war to send to Tahiti for supplies. King's
plans were officially approved in August, 1802.[28]

King carried his attempt to utilise island resources even to the
point of encouraging development by private investors—a policy
not altogether in accordance with the strictly penal character of
the early settlement. In 1803 he had to consider the application of
George Bass, the explorer, who had done good work in the Tahitian
meat supply, for monopoly fishing rights in the south of New
Zealand.[29] Bass intended to supply the public stores of New South
Wales with salt fish at a low price, the whole enterprise to be at
his own risk.[30] King apparently favoured the application, which
lapsed, however, when Bass was lost on a voyage to Chile (where
he had hoped to obtain provisions and livestock).[31]

It is doubtful whether King had authority to grant Bass the
concession he sought. New Zealand was not within the Governor's
jurisdiction.[32] Moreover, the granting of a concession in the islands
to a private trader would have raised problems in relation to the

[25] *H.R.N.Z.,* I, pp. 128-131.
[26] King to Banks, April, 1801; *H.R.N.S.W.,* IV, p. 357.
[27] Nov. 8, 1801; *H.R.N.S.W.,* IV, p. 614; Nov. 14, 1801; ibid, p. 620.
[28] Hobart to King, Aug. 29, 1802; *H.R.N.S.W.,* IV, p. 823.
[29] See R. McNab: *Murihiku,* cit. sup., pp. 128-130.
[30] Bass to Waterhouse, Feb. 2, 1803; *H.R.N.Z.,* I, pp. 244-245.
[31] As to allegations that Bass was privateering with the cognisance of King, see
H.R.A., I, v, p. 823 (n. 100).
[32] See Ch. IV, below.

monopoly rights of the East India Company, which within certain limits the Governors were strictly enjoined to preserve.[33]

Private trading ventures such' as those of Bass were probably not within the scope of the adjunct policy. In essentials the policy was one suggested by the desire to use the known resources of the islands as means of supplementing the temporary deficiencies of New South Wales. As such it was a policy for the early years only of the penal settlement and one which was not to be applied except by official agencies.

The total achievement of the adjunct policy was slight. The record of its details is often trifling. But the policy did have importance in later developments. Beginning in 1788, the use of island resources reinforced the interest of the free colonists of New South Wales in the island world. The way was opened for the type of trade development that later challenged the monopoly of the East India Company, helped to raise New South Wales from its penal colony status and produced all the problems of British contacts with native peoples of the Pacific.

[33] See next chapter.

CHAPTER II

JOHN COMPANY'S CITADEL

UNDER its Charter the East India Company possessed exclusive British rights of trade and navigation to countries lying between the Cape of Good Hope and the Straits of Magellan. Phillip was instructed to protect its interests:

> "And whereas it is our Royal intention that every sort of inter-course between the intended settlement at Botany Bay, or other place which may be hereafter established on the coast of New South Wales and its dependencies, and the settlements of our East India Company, as well as on the coast of China, and the islands situated in that part of the world to which any intercourse has been estab-lished by any European nation, should be prevented by every possible means: It is our Royal will and pleasure that you do not, on any account, allow craft of any sort to be built for the use of private individuals which might enable them to effect such intercourse, and that you do prevent any vessels which may at any time hereafter arrive at the said settlement from any of the ports before-mentioned from having communication with any of the inhabitants residing within your government without first receiving especial permission from you for that purpose."[1]

This elaborate paragraph reaffirmed the East India Company's monopoly rights by cutting off New South Wales from all hope of participating in the Company's trade. Taken in conjunction with the monopoly as a whole, Phillip's instructions made it clear that no British trade could be developed in the South Pacific apart from that between the islands and New South Wales (under the adjunct policy) and trade specially licensed by the Company. Legally, the commerce of the South Pacific could be developed only as the requirements of the penal colony in New South Wales necessitated and as the Company, whose main interest was the protection of its inner citadel, the Chinese market, chose to permit. British private traders in the South Pacific would probably have transgressed the monopoly rights of the Company, but, so long as their trade was between New South Wales and the islands, they did not come within the scope of the injunctions laid on the Governors.

Behind the insistence on the Company's rights lay a long story

[1] *H.R.N.S.W.*, I (2), p. 91

of bitter opposition to the foundation of any British settlement in the South Pacific. Apart from anti-colonialism and indifference, the greatest obstacle in the way of development of British interests in the Pacific had been the monopoly of the Company. It was generally conceded that, in view of the Company's rigid insistence on its rights, no settlement in the South Pacific could build up a trade of its own.[2]

The record of the Company's opposition to settlement within its monopoly area is well established. It is known that some time before March, 1782, the Company successfully objected to a proposal by Sir George Young for a settlement in Madagascar. Lord Sandwich, who had himself approved the scheme, pointed out that it was the Company's charter which precluded "every attempt of the kind."[3] Similarly in 1785 the Company rejected a plan for settlement on Norfolk Island. It may also be true that Sir George Young's plan for a settlement in New South Wales encountered the fatal hostility of the Company. In the Mitchell Library, Sydney, there is a copy of Young's pamphlet with a contemporary MS. note in ink on page 3 that:

> "This excellent Proposal was made by Sir George Young in 1785 & 6, but was objected to by the East India Company. . . ."

Mr. J. Shepherd, who investigated this comment at some length, concluded that it was not supported by precise corroborative evidence. But he was of the opinion that the MS. note was substantially correct. Shepherd also argued that the radical change in the plans for the New South Wales settlement between the original schemes of Matra and Young and the subsequent "Heads of a Plan" officially adopted in 1786 was to be attributed to fear of encroachment on the East India Company's monopoly.[4] Strong evidence to support this view is to be found in the complete absence from the scheme finally adopted for the Botany Bay settlement of any provision for encouraging trade between the colony and China, the most jealously guarded of the Company's monopoly markets.

The decision to plant a penal colony in New South Wales was followed immediately by further protests on behalf of the Company. On September 3rd, 1786, an anonymous pamphlet entitled *A Serious*

---

[2] Cf. the anonymous *History of New Holland from its first Discovery in 1616, to the Present Time*; London, 1787; p. viii. Also *Copious Remarks on the Discovery of New South Wales*, cit. sup., p. iii.

[3] Young to Davison, Feb. 3, 1793; *H.R.N.S.W.*, II, p. 9.

[4] J. Shepherd: "Austral-Asia"; *The Australian Geographer*; Vol. III, No. 4. Also J. Shepherd: *"Austral-Asia"* (unpublished M.A. thesis, Fisher Library, University of Sydney).

Admonition to the Publick on the Intended Thief Colony at Botany Bay[5] was published by John Sewell in London. The pamphlet declared that the scheme for a settlement in New South Wales infringed the Company's charter. It pointed out that the Court of Directors had already refused with "a positive negative" a request in 1785 for permission to settle at Norfolk Island. Because of this earlier decision against permitting a settlement in the South Pacific, the pamphlet bitterly condemned the Government for not consulting the Court of Directors before deciding to plant the "thief colony" at Botany Bay.

The principal part of the pamphlet consisted of a letter dated July 13, 1785, from the East India Company's hydrographer, Alexander Dalrymple, to the Court of Directors.[6] The letter was prompted by an enquiry from the Court as to Dalrymple's opinion of the scheme for a settlement on Norfolk Island. But its arguments were of general application and were used over and over again by the Company in later years when opposing relaxations of monopoly rights in the South Pacific. Dalrymple alleged that the proposed Norfolk Island settlement was intended to "carry on an *illicit Trade,* under pretext of a Colony." He predicted that the colony would soon secede from the Mother Country and, being thus freed from the legal restraints, would invade the chartered seas of the Company. Subsequent developments would be even more alarming:

> "The Establishment of a Colony in that quarter, wherever it may be first fixed, must have a View to New Holland and if an European Colony be established, on that extensive Country, it is obvious it must become very soon independant; and, I will add, very dangerous to England."[7]

The colony, Dalrymple did not hesitate to conclude, would become the base of piratical excursions against the islands and the coast of China, where the East India Company enjoyed a rich trade.

Fantastic as some of his allegations may seem, it must be remembered that most of them were justified by later developments. Moreover, the various plans of settlement in the South Pacific had stressed the trading potentialities of a colony there without so much as referring to the Company's Charter.[8]

[5] There are copies in the Dixson Collection, Sydney, the National Library, Canberra, and the Alex. Turnbull Library, Wellington. Dr. G. Mackaness has reprinted the pamphlet in his series, *Australian Historical Monographs*, as No. 7.

[6] See F. J. Bayldon: "Alexander Dalrymple"; *J.R.A.H.S.*; Vol. XIII, Pt. I.

[7] Pp. 14-15.

[8] For evidence that private merchants had been interested in plans for an Australian settlement, see Young to Davison, Feb. 3, 1793; *H.R.N.S.W.*, II, p. 10.

The official plans for a settlement at Botany Bay recognised the Company's rights. The strict injunctions just quoted were designed to limit the trade of the new settlement to the bare minimum essential for the existence of a penal colony. The fact that the Company itself was most unlikely to be interested in commercial development of the South Pacific assisted the restrictive policy. The complete absence of private enterprise made it easy to confine the new settlement within the limits of a penal colony. The Government's policy of treating New South Wales as a mere receptacle for convicts and the Company's desire to preserve its monopoly combined to produce the strictest prohibitions of private trade.

A less obvious reason for the accommodating attitude of the Government towards the Company's claims lay possibly in the reorganisation of the Company during the immediately preceding years. The rapid development of the political power and territorial responsibilities of the Company in India after 1757 had considerably alarmed the British Government. The prospect of a great empire being created and ruled by British subjects in India independently of the British Crown necessitated remedial action. After the failure of Lord North's Regulating Act (1773), the Select and Secret Parliamentary Committees of 1781 recommended the adoption by Parliament of a new system for both the home and the Indian management of the Company.[9] The matter proved to be highly contentious, the bills introduced by Fox and Burke in November, 1783, being met with strong opposition from the Court of Directors and the proprietors of the Company. Extensive parliamentary influence was brought to bear by the various interests connected with the Company. It was only after a major political struggle that Pitt's India Act in 1784 subordinated the political activities of the Company to the policy of the British Government.[10]

Opposition to the Act had been relaxed on the understanding that the Company's commercial privileges would remain intact. The protracted negotiations which made the 1784 Act possible also made it perfectly clear that the Government could not ask the Company to accept any restriction of its commercial rights for a long period to come. Accordingly the Company's monopoly rights in the South Pacific had a claim for the sympathetic protection of the Government. To have restricted the monopoly when founding

[9] C. H. Philips: *The East India Company, 1784-1834*; Manchester, 1940; p. 23.
[10] Philips, op. cit., discusses the ramifications of the Company's political influence in an Appendix.

the settlement in New South Wales would have raised again the complicated problem of the status and commercial privileges of the Company. It was easier and fully consistent with the major reasons for colonising New South Wales to preserve the monopoly and leave the question of future British trade in the South Pacific to be solved later, if ever the problem arose.

As a result the commercial development of New South Wales and the islands of the South Pacific was for long impeded by official restrictions. It has often been assumed that between 1788 and 1813 (when the back of the Company's monopoly was broken) New South Wales was too preoccupied with the struggle for survival to have any opportunity of building up trade and industry. In actual fact the contrary is the case. The maritime industries, based on the Australian coast and the islands, and the island industries such as sandalwood and trepang offered excellent prospects and were developed with considerable rapidity. But the best commercial prospects of the South Pacific at that time were seriously hindered by the rigid insistence that the rights of the East India Company had to be respected. It was only after years of struggle and agitation that the jealous protection of the Company's rights was modified sufficiently far to permit British subjects to develop the resources of the islands and the South Pacific seas.

CHAPTER III

THE END OF MONOPOLY

THE development of maritime and island industries soon raised problems of policy. Were the new industries to be restricted in order that New South Wales might remain a mere penal colony? If the Company's rights were to be invaded, who was to benefit, British traders or traders in the colony?

The whole basis of British policy towards the islands and even towards New South Wales was bound up in these questions. The trading future of the colony was involved and so was the future of the adjunct policy.

The Governors in general treated the new industries with favour, seeing in them useful means of employing the colony's labour and of reducing the financial burden of New South Wales on the Home country.[1] Their only doubts arose from the prospect of convicts escaping to the islands, from the invasion of John Company's monopoly and from the advent to the South Pacific of trading foreigners.

The whaling industry was the first to raise these policy problems. Whaling began in the South West Pacific soon after the establishment of the colony in New South Wales. Vessels, which had brought out convicts and had been intended to proceed to the whaling grounds in the North Pacific, were induced by the great number of spermaceti whales off the New South Wales coast to try for a cargo there.[2] As time went on the special advantages of these waters in contrast to those of the South East Pacific became increasingly recognised. In the Eastern Pacific, where British whalers had begun their Pacific operations, the lack of British bases had always been a drawback. The Spanish Government allowed British whalers to use its Pacific ports for repairs and refreshments, but clogged the indulgence with so many restrictions that it was of little value.[3] The Western Pacific in contrast possessed a

[1] But see King to Camden, Apr. 30, 1805; H.R.A., I, v, p. 323.
[2] J. Hunter: *Journal of the Transactions at Port Jackson and Norfolk Island*; London, 1793; p. 489.
[3] D. Macpherson: *Annals of Commerce, &c.*; London, 1805; Vol. IV, p. 329. The Pacific Fisheries were an extension from those of the South Atlantic.

splendid British base in Port Jackson with other harbours on the Australian coast and amongst the islands. These advantages were realised soon after the foundation of the settlement. They induced Sam Enderby and Sons, one of the pioneers of the Eastern Pacific fisheries, to experiment off the New South Wales coast. The experiments were a success, a favourable report being prepared by Captain Melville in 1791.[4]

The policy implications of these developments were soon perceived by Governor Phillip, who favoured the new industry but feared the difficulties which it would produce. In 1791 he wrote to Evan Nepean, the Under-Secretary, that whalers operating off the coast of New South Wales might tempt away valuable carpenters and seamen, especially convicts whose sentences had expired.[5] Phillip also foresaw that the new whaling industry would attract foreigners to the South Pacific, thus threatening the British ascendancy in these seas. "If the fishery draws an American vessel on the coast," he asked, "in what manner are they to be received?" Lastly, Phillip realised that the whaling industry based on New South Wales would cut through the monopoly rights of the East India Company and raise complicated questions of legal right. He requested the Colonial Office to send out the acts relative to the Southern Fishery (which had made certain concessions to whalers) and "such instructions as may be deemed necessary on that head."[6]

Phillip's despatches were not acknowledged.[7] The only official instructions sent to him at this stage were those of the Commissioners of the Navy in May, 1792, stating that the whaling industry would certainly develop and open up increasing communication with other colonies.[8] It was evident that the Commissioners regarded the new industry with favour but were not prepared to express any opinion on the desirability of allowing New South Wales to develop commercial contacts of its own. The importance of obtaining British sources of whale-oil to compensate for the loss of the American colonies was obvious. The prospect of whaling off the New South Wales coast came, however, as a surprise in Great Britain and policy was not formulated for some years.[9]

[4] J. Hunter, op. cit., pp. 490-496.
[5] Phillip to Nepean, Nov. 18, 1791; H.R.A., I, i, p. 307.
[6] Philip to Dundas, Oct. 4, 1792; H.R.A., I, i, p. 380.
[7] Synopsis of Despatches, H.R.A., I, i.
[8] May 15, 1792; H.R.A., I, i, p. 354.
[9] See G. B. Barton, op. cit., p. 373 n. Also A. Anderson: *Historical and Chronological Deduction of the Origins of Commerce;* London, 1787. There is a copy in the National Library, Canberra.

For several years after its early beginning whaling developed only slowly in the South West Pacific. The extensive developments sought by the Governors and hoped for by the British Government did not take place until after the outbreak of war with Spain. British whalers then lost the facilities which they had enjoyed in Spanish ports and promptly transferred to New South Wales.[10] Rapid development of the Western Pacific grounds followed the experimental voyage of the *Albion* (Captain Ebor Bunker) in 1799. Governor King reported in 1802 that the Australian whaling grounds were most popular and extended as far as the seas north-east of New Zealand. The New South Wales base was specially favoured because the passage via the Cape of Good Hope was easier than that via the Horn and because of the interest taken in the new industry by the Governors.[11]

Almost simultaneously with the development of whaling came the beginnings of the sealing industry. An unsuccessful expedition had sailed south of Sydney in quest of seals in 1791.[12] The following year saw the substantial beginning of sealing in the South Pacific when Captain William Raven of the *Britannia* (Sam Enderby and Sons), having a three years' trade licence from the East India Company, proceeded to Dusky Bay in New Zealand to procure seal skins for the China market.[13] Phillip favoured sealing and complained that the established fur trade on the north-west coast of America hindered sealing in the South Pacific. Development of sealing in New Zealand and Bass Strait became fairly rapid in the early years of the nineteenth century.

Originally the main market for South Pacific seal skins was China where a glut developed in the opening years of the nineteenth century. Later the fur seal of the southern hemisphere was specially prized in Great Britain as a result of a discovery by Thomas Chapman (an English trunkmaker), which permitted the use of its wool coat in the manufacture of hats.[14] Every species of seal and particularly the sea-elephant was sought for oil. Seals were obtained in large numbers off Tasmania, the south-west coast of the mainland of Australia and off the coasts of New Zealand.

[10] R. McNab: *From Tasman to Marsden*, cit. sup., p. 96.

[11] King to Portland, Mar. 29, 1802; *H.R.N.Z.*, I, p. 233. See also *H. of L., Committee on N.Z.*, 1838; p. 76; R. Jarman: *Journal of a Voyage to the South Seas in the "Japan"*; London, 1838; King to Hobart, May 9, 1803; *H.R.A.*, I, iv, p. 233; and Queries by Gov. King to Messrs. Turnbull, Quested and Gardiner, May 21, 1802; *H.R.N.Z.*, I, p. 234.

[12] Phillip to Nepean, Nov. 18, 1791; *H.R.A.*, I, i, pp. 307-308.

[13] R. McNab: *Murihiku*, cit. sup., p. 91.

[14] See "The Case of Thomas Chapman of Cropley . . . Southwark," a MS. record by Sir Joseph Banks in the *Brabourne Papers*, Vol. IV, pp. 233 ff.

The high authority of Sir Joseph Banks recommended the utmost encouragement of the colonists in the development of the sealing industry, which, declared Banks, had become "an object of speculation to every nation that has ships" and was thus in danger of passing out of British hands.[15]

More closely identified with the islands themselves than either of the maritime industries were the kauri and sandalwood trades. The kauri trade began in New Zealand in 1794. But the first ventures were financially unsuccessful and the trade lapsed for many years. The sandalwood trade, based mainly on the Friendly Islands (Tonga) and Fiji, was developed by both American and New South Wales interests, beginning in 1804.[16] The sandalwood was sent to China where it was burnt in temples as incense, used in making fans and other such objects and mixed in cosmetics.

The sandalwood trade, certainly the most curious of all the early links between China and the South Pacific, continued to be of importance up to about 1815, later coming into prominence again.[17] During the first ten years of its development, it had acquired a considerable importance. Europeans and some of the trading interests in New South Wales had come into contact with the natives over lengthy periods and in an intimate way. Important economic and administrative problems had been raised. (See Chapter IV, below.)

The same results flowed from the development of trade in such island products as bêche-de-mer (trepang) and pork. The maritime industries of whaling and sealing also raised the problem of future trade with the islands and in the seas around them and produced new associations with the natives.

The new industries soon called into question the East India Company's monopoly. Because trade based on New South Wales was no longer confined to East India Company ships and ships in official service, the problem of the Company's rights had become of immediate importance. It arose in three different aspects:

(1) Under its charter, as explained above, the Company had a monopoly of British trade and navigation in the Pacific. The

---

[15] "Some Remarks on the Present State of the Colony of Sidney, in New South Wales, and on the means most likely to render it a productive, instead of an expensive, settlement"; *Brabourne Papers*, Vol. IV, pp. 245-251. The remarks are in the handwriting of one of Banks's clerks. There are corrections in Banks's handwriting and the MS. is initialled by him.

[16] See introduction to W. Lockerby: *Journal of William Lockerby, Sandalwood Trader in Fiji, 1808-9;* ed. im Thurn and Wharton, (Hakluyt Society) London, 1925. Also King to Camden, Apr. 30, 1805; *H.R.N.S.W.*, V, p. 602.

[17] See *Report on State of Trade and Agriculture in N.S.W.; PP.*, 1823, No. 136; p. 60. Also Darling to Huskisson, Apr. 10, 1828; *H.R.A.*, I, xiv, p. 133.

operations of whalers, sealers and other British traders in Pacific waters were (save as legalised by licence or statute) in contravention of the charter. The British Government had to determine its policy towards the enterprising interests which were being obstructed by the Company's antiquated privileges. In doing so, it had also to determine how far the future development of New South Wales, the main centre of South Pacific trade, was to be restricted within the limits of a penal colony.

(2) The East India Company, by way of enforcing its rights, sought to prevent the exportation of Pacific whale oil, seal skins and other products to Great Britain and of Pacific sandalwood, trepang and seal skins to China in other than its own or neutral (i.e., foreign) ships. Similarly, it forbade the carrying of merchandise cargo to New South Wales and imposed rigid restrictions on trade between India and New South Wales. The shortage of supplies in the colony made the Company's policy specially irksome.

(3) Because of the repressive operation of the Company's charter British traders in the Pacific were at a disadvantage compared with foreigners. Early records contain instance after instance of warnings from New South Wales of the danger of allowing foreign countries to obtain a stranglehold on island trade. Were the trade and industry of the South Pacific to be lost to Great Britain for the sake of preserving the monopoly of a company which itself had no interest in their development?

The first conflict between the Company's rights and the new industries developed when British whalers entered the Eastern Pacific. The Company's interest in that region was slight. The British Government, on the other hand, was deeply concerned with developing the whale oil industry, especially as in the Atlantic fisheries British seamen were subject to much foreign competition and were at a disadvantage after the loss of the American colonies. Apparently there was little opposition from the Company when the Government proceeded to have Acts passed legalising British whaling within the monopoly area. By Imperial Statutes of 26 Geo. III, c. 50,[18] and 28 Geo. III, c. 20, British whaling ships entering the Pacific via Cape Horn were permitted to sail north to the equator and west as far as 180 degrees West. Bounties were offered to British whalers operating in these seas.

The admission to the South East Pacific proved to be the thin edge of the wedge so far as the East India Company's monopoly was concerned. Under 33 Geo. III, c. 52, by which the affairs of the Company were reorganised generally, the whole of the Pacific east of 180 degrees was opened up under a licensing system to the

18 Repealing 15 Geo. III, c. 31, and 16 Geo. III, c. 47.

whalers in the Southern Whale Fishery and the bounty system was extended to this enlarged area by 33 Geo. III, c. 58.

So far no concessions had been made west of 180 degrees, that is, in any area where the Company had an active interest.[19] In 1795, however, pressure from the whaling interests led to the enactment of 35 Geo. III, c. 92, permitting ships employed in the Southern Whale Fishery to sail east of the Cape of Good Hope under licence from the Company and to fish in the Indian Ocean south of the Equator as far as 51 degrees east. The effect of the Act was to admit the whalers to the Madagascar area, where previously the Company had opposed a settlement.[20] But the Company was compelled to license only ten ships annually.

Not long after their admission to the Indian Ocean, the whaling interests began to press for concessions in the South West Pacific, following the outbreak of the war with Spain. On December 26, 1797, a memorial was presented to the Board of Trade praying for the removal of restrictions on fishing farther north than the equator and farther east than 51 degrees east. The merchants asked that a Bill be brought before Parliament for this purpose, on the ground that the Spanish War was hindering activity in the Eastern Pacific and necessitating use of the Western Pacific.[21] Were the law amended, the petitioners argued, whale and seal fisheries might be carried on at Kerguelen Island in the Indian Ocean, off the Australian coast and from New Caledonia, New Zealand, the New Hebrides, the Philippines and Formosa.

The Board of Trade was inclined to view the application favourably. Because of the great importance of maintaining supplies of whale oil, the Board, in submitting the memorial to the Company, expressed the hope that "the Court of Directors will not be averse to a compliance with the prayer of the memorialists for the benefit of the southern whale-fishery (which is become an important branch of commerce), as far as they conceive may be done consistently with the security of their commercial rights."

In the event the merchants received much less than they had requested. Their memorial was answered by the enactment of 38 Geo. III, c. 57. Besides reorganising the bounty system, this Act opened the seas between 51 degrees east and 180 degrees as far north as 15 degrees south. Whaling was thus permitted to British

[19] Apparently early experiments in the South West Pacific were either illegal or specially licensed by the Company. For a case of licensing see Collins, op. cit., p. 157.

[20] The reference is to Sir George Young's proposal for a settlement in Madagascar. See Chapter II above.

[21] Minute of the Board of Trade, Dec. 26, 1797; H.R.N.Z., I, pp. 216-217.

ships throughout the whole of the Western Pacific almost as far north as Cape York and throughout the greater part of the Coral Sea.[22]

But the value of the concession had been greatly reduced by the strict northward limits imposed. Because of unfavourable conditions ("the weather was so rugged at all seasons"), effective whaling was difficult in the permitted area. The whalers sought permission to go farther north to the waters around New Guinea, where French and American interests were already active.[23] In 1802 the Act, 42 Geo. III, c. 18, s. 4, permitted the whalers to go as far north as the limits that they had requested, namely, 1 degree north between 123 degrees and 180 degrees east. A year later there was a still further concession under 43 Geo. III, c. 90, by which licensed ships sailing eastward from the Cape of Good Hope might proceed north to 10 degrees south between 51 degrees and 115 degrees east, after which they were permitted to sail north to 1 degree north until they reached 180 degrees east, beyond which the whole Pacific was free of restriction.[24]

These Acts broke the back of the Company's monopoly so far as the British whale fisheries were concerned, although whalers coming out to Australia via the Cape of Good Hope still needed a licence from the Company and, in strictness, no concessions had been made in favour of colonial whalers.

Nine years passed before there was any further legal change. Then in 1811 a request that the limits of the southern whale fishery eastward of the Cape of Good Hope be extended to 10 degrees north between 115 degrees and 180 degrees east was made by the British whalers and contested by the Company.[25] It was only after the whalers had agreed to restrict the desired privileges to a period of three years in the first instance[26] that a new Act, 51 Geo. III, c. 34, was passed in May, 1811. Under this Act the desired limits were established in favour of British vessels licensed under 38 Geo. III, c. 57.

[22] The Act preserved the licensing requirements of the earlier statutes. It applied to ships sailing both via South Africa and via South America. Contra 43 Geo. III, c. 90, mentioned below.

[23] See Memorial of Messrs. Enderby and Messrs. Champion to the Board of Trade, Nov. 27, 1801; Board of Trade 1/16. The memorial was referred to the E.I.C., which agreed to the request, partly on the ground that Great Britain was once again at peace.

[24] 42 Geo. III, c. 77, had already permitted British-built ships to fish in the Pacific east of 180 degrees without licence. The concession extended only to vessels sailing via South America.

[25] E.I.C. to Board of Trade, March 19, 1811; H.R.N.Z., I, p. 310.

[26] E.I.C. to Messrs. Enderby, April 10, 1811; H.R.N.Z., I, p. 312.

The long record of the steady encroachment on the Company's monopoly was completed in 1813. In that year, as part of a general reorganisation of its rights and functions, the Company by 53 Geo. III, c. 155, lost practically the whole of its monopoly rights save in the China trade and in tea (the main product of the China trade). The same Act, however, preserved some of the restrictions on the whaling industry and southern navigation. Section 32 provided that ships engaged in the southern whale fishery might sail between the Cape of Good Hope and the Straits of Magellan, but not north of 11 degrees south between 64 degrees and 150 degrees east without licence from the Board of Commissioners for the Affairs of India. Under the same section a licence was required for any British ship of less than 350 tons passing east of the Cape of Good Hope or west of the Straits of Magellan.[27] In effect whaling vessels of over 350 tons were permitted to enter the whole of the South Pacific without licence.

While British whaling interests were establishing their right to operate in the monopoly seas of the East India Company, two other issues affecting British policy in the South Pacific had arisen. First, there was the question of trade: was the East India Company to be permitted to preserve its monopoly rights over exports and imports in New South Wales and the islands? This question was important, not only to British whalers, but also to the growing class of independent traders and merchants in New South Wales. Second, there was the question of the mercantile policy of Gt. Britain towards its new colony: would colonial interests be conceded the right to share in the commerce and industry of the South Pacific, or would the British merchants and the East India Company be permitted to combine in suppressing any trade that they did not themselves control? The question touched the fundamentals of British policy towards the future of New South Wales, which, though still a penal colony, was giving signs of ability to develop into very much more.

British policy right from the first had been to protect the Company's trade rights with the utmost rigour. In 1792 it was decided that convicts and cargoes were to be sent out to New Holland in East India Company ships only.[28] This decision was intended to prevent breaches of the monopoly. In effect, it obstructed both exports and imports from and to New South Wales. The island industries also suffered because there was rarely

[27] The significance of the restrictions of size is discussed below.
[28] Dundas to Phillip, May 15, 1792; H.R.N.S.W., I (2), p. 623.

enough permitted shipping at Sydney for the exports to China and Great Britain which the local merchants wished to send.

In New South Wales the difficulty of importation was specially resented. Essential supplies were often low and the service of ships from England too infrequent. Governor King found a further reason for wishing to remove the import restrictions in the hope that whale-ships bringing out frequent and moderately priced cargoes might help to break down the trade monopoly established by the military officers in the colony.[29]

The case for relaxation of the restrictions on trade with New South Wales was strongly supported by the British interests in South Pacific whaling, which resented the necessity of sending their ships to New South Wales in ballast. In 1800 the firms of Enderby and Champion wrote to Lord Liverpool complaining of the restrictions and the favoured position in which their operation placed American whalers.[30] Governor King wrote in the same strain to Lord Liverpool several weeks later.[31] Although there is evidence of some official opinion in favour of the whalers' appeal,[32] it does not seem that any action was taken at that time to relieve the colony's importation problem, beyond the issue of licences.[33]

The export problem was made more serious every year with the rapid development of the island industries. Increasingly the restrictive effects of the adjunct policy came under fire, both in the colony and in England itself.

The general question of restrictions on exports was raised by Governor King in 1804. Perceiving that the virtual embargo on exports from New South Wales obstructed the growth of colonial interests in sealing, trepang and sandalwood and favoured foreigners, who were not bound by the East India Company's monopoly, King proposed that intercourse should be established between the colony and China.[34] Later in the same year he expanded his

[29] King to Portland, Sept. 28, 1800; H.R.A., I, ii, pp. 613 ff. Portland replied promising to submit to the Board of Trade "the suggested alterations of the Act for regulating the whale fishery." (Portland to King, June 19, 1801; H.R.A., I, iii, p. 99). It has not been possible to ascertain whether Portland did in fact do so.
[30] Messrs. Enderby and Messrs. Champion to Lord Liverpool, August 1, 1800; H.R.A., I, iii, p. 1.
[31] King to Portland, Sept. 28, 1800; H.R.A., I, ii, p. 613.
[32] Mr. King's Observations on the Whalers' Appeal to Lord Liverpool, H.R.A., I, iii, p. 3.
[33] Board of Trade papers are inconclusive. The matter was considered at a meeting on August 7, 1801. There is no further reference. (Board of Trade 1/16, No. 51, and 5/12.) But see Dakin, op. cit., p. 16, and G. Greenwood (Early American-Australian Relations to 1830; Melbourne, 1944; p. 70) stating that concessions were made.
[34] King to Hobart, Aug. 14, 1804; H.R.A., I, v, pp. 8-9.

suggestion by recommending that oil and other Pacific products should be exported to China or to England, the concession "not to extend at present beyond three vessels of not more than two hundred tons each and built within the limits of this territory and its dependencies."[35] It will be noted that King's recommendation applied only to what was known as colonial produce, that is, oil, sealskins, sandalwood, trepang and other commodities obtained by colonial merchants. British merchants already possessed all the liberties they needed in the whaling industry (save the right to bring out imports to New South Wales).[36]

King's recommendations were made at an unfortunate time. While they were still under consideration the British whalers and the Company were both engaged in an attack on colonial trade. The immediate provocation was the famous *Lady Barlow* case of 1805.[37] The *Lady Barlow* had left Sydney with the Governor's permission, carrying the first cargo (sea-elephant oil and fur seal skins) wholly caught by colonists.[38] On the arrival of the ship in London the Company promptly had the cargo declared contraband. It was only after a considerable delay, during which Sir Joseph Banks supported the claims of the Sydney merchants,[39] that the vessel was released, subject to a compulsory sale of its cargo. Seven thousand pounds were lost on the transaction. The British whalers began to complain that the value of whale oil would be endangered by such cargoes. Messrs. Enderby and other British firms expressed the fear that "a Fishery is establishing in New South Wales which threatens the destruction of the S. Whale Fishery carried on from Great Britain in British vessels."[40]

In view of these developments King's recommendations had little chance of success. Answering the suggestion that ships built in New South Wales should be permitted to export to China seal-skins, trepang and other island products and to bring Chinese goods into the colony, the Court of Directors stated that the main point at issue was the risk of the growth of a large European population in New Holland, which might come to dominate the "Indian Seas," presumably to the detriment of the Company.[41] The

[35] King to Hobart, Dec. 20, 1804; *H.R.A.*, I, v, pp. 202-203.

[36] As to sealing, see "Observations on Whaling and Sealing, 1805-6" by Sir Joseph Banks; *Brabourne Papers*, Vol. IV, p. 228.

[37] *H.R.A.*, I, v, p. 705.

[38] Wilson to Banks, June 27, 1806; *H.R.N.S.W.*, VI, p. 101.

[39] *Brabourne Papers*, Vol. IV, pp. 242-244.

[40] Banks's "Trade Questions, 1798-1805"; *Brabourne Papers*, Vol. IV, pp. 265-270.

[41] E.I.C. to Cottrell, July 6, 1805; *H.R.N.S.W.*, V, p. 645.

truth was that the Company continued to resent the existence of a British colony within its monopoly area and was anxious to keep British interests in the South Pacific within the narrow limits of a single penal settlement.

King himself admitted that the development of the sandalwood trade held a threat to the Company's monopoly.[42] In duty bound he penalised colonial trade for the sake of the Company. After the Aikin case in 1806, in which the Company's rights were most blatantly disregarded, King published a proclamation forbidding British subjects in New South Wales to enter into mercantile contracts with foreigners on pain of banishment.[43] Intercourse with China was specially forbidden. The expressed object of the proclamation was to protect the rights of the Company.

Although the Company succeeded in having King's appeals refused, the attack on its South Pacific monopoly was nearing success. For many years the monopoly had been under heavy fire from two different groups. These were the British merchants and whalers operating in the South Pacific and the colonial merchants and traders of New South Wales. Each group suffered from the monopoly. Despite their frequent conflicts,[44] each had an interest in the general onslaught then being made against the Company's rights in general.

In 1806 the colonists won powerful support for their side of the case when Sir Joseph Banks, the foremost English authority on Australia, recommended some relaxation of the Company's monopoly. Banks sought a complete change in commercial policy. Instead of being confined to a penal colony, New South Wales was to be allowed to grow commercially. The maritime industries, the wool trade and coalmining offered the colony a rich economic future, which, declared Banks, it was impossible either to ignore or to repress. Seeing the problem as one of high policy, Banks held that it would be an act of wisdom on the part of the Government and the Company to grant further concessions to the colony. Only by such means could its wealth be preserved to Great Britain.[45]

Banks suggested that those industries should be encouraged which held substantial promise of benefit to Great Britain. He frowned on the trepang trade with China, which would injure the Company without aiding the Mother Country, and advocated

[42] King to Camden, Apr. 30, 1805; H.R.N.S.W., V, p. 603.
[43] See H.R.N.S.W., VI, pp. 109 ff.
[44] For comment on the conflicts, see Wilson to Banks, n. 38 (above).
[45] See Banks's "Trade Questions, 1798-1805," cit. sup. (n. 40).

development of whaling, sealing, sandalwood (to be shipped to England, not China), woolgrowing and coalmining. To fit in with his ideas on policy, Banks also recommended some specific relaxation of the Company's monopoly. Colonial ships, he thought, should be allowed to navigate freely to the northernmost extremity of Australia. Rather dryly Banks added: "It must be remembered that the district now propos'd to be open'd to the investigation of British adventure is about as unknown to civilised nations as an equal portion of the moon."[46]

Proposals for further restrictions on the East India Company's monopoly were coming to a head at the time when these recommendations were made. The Company had had to borrow from the British Government and was compelled to accept·some modification of its restrictive policies. The Government itself, by now aware of the possibility of using South Pacific industries as a means of reducing the cost of the New South Wales colony, had determined to ease trade restrictions there.[47] Without going so far as did Banks in accepting the principle that New South Wales should be a commercial colony, the Government had perceived the profitable implications of permitting commercial development in the penal settlement.

In 1806 a Bill was drawn up "for the opening of the Trade of New South Wales, under licences from the East India Company and the South Sea Company."[48] The Bill provided for the export of goods from Great Britain to New South Wales and the importation into Great Britain of the products of the colony and the adjacent seas. The trade permitted under the Bill was to be confined to British built ships licensed by the East India and South Sea Companies. Otherwise it was to be subject only to the same restrictions as were imposed by the Navigation Act on the British colonies in America.

Finally, the Bill proposed to extend the trading limits of the colony, Banks himself going beyond his original recommendation of the northernmost point of Australia in order to argue in favour of 9 degrees south.[49] He also condemned the proposal to establish a statutory southward limit of 43° 39′ S. (corresponding to the southernmost point of the Governors' jurisdiction).

[46] "Some Remarks on . . . the Colony of Sidney," loc. cit. (n. 15).
[47] Board of Trade to E.I.C., June 30, 1806; *Brabourne Papers*, Vol. IV, p. 259. (Also *H.R.N.S.W.*, VI, p. 103.)
[48] For text of Bill, see *H.R.N.S.W.*, VI, pp. 241-246.
[49] "Some Observations on a Bill for admitting the produce of New South Wales to entry at the Customs-house of the United Kingdom," July 7, 1806; *Brabourne Papers*, Vol. IV, pp. 262-264. (Also *H.R.N.Z.*, I, pp. 277 ff.)

The Bill was submitted to the Board of Trade and then to the Company.[50] At a meeting of the Board, attended by representatives of the company, it was decided to place the New South Wales trade on the same footing as trade of other British colonies. The only limitations were that all New South Wales trade should be with the Port of London and that no trade would be permitted to and from New South Wales without licence from the Company or its agents. Regulations were to be drawn up for a period of five years from March 1, 1807.[51] The Company itself subsequently approved these proposals, requiring only some tightening up of the provisions inserted for its own protection.[52]

The Bill never became law, apparently being allowed to lapse after the change of Government in March, 1807. For the next five years there was little relief from the restrictive effects of the monopoly on trade in the South Pacific, although licences were granted by the Company from time to time for voyages between New South Wales and Great Britain.[53]

Throughout these years the Governors of New South Wales, prompted by constant agitation from within the colony, kept both the import and the export questions open. In 1807 Bligh complained that the "prohibition on the part of the Colony from trading to the East Indies" discouraged exports. The volume of shipping was so reduced by the trade restrictions as to cause great deprivation of necessary supplies.[54] Lieutenant-Governor Foveaux wrote to the British Government in 1809 that the ships which had gathered sandalwood in the islands were compelled to return to Sydney and store their cargoes pending a chance of "reshipping them in bottoms privileged to navigate beyond the extent of this territory."[55]

Matters came to a head in 1812. In that year the East India Company, which was about to be subjected to a thorough reorganisation by the Government, received from the British whaling interests a request for licences to ship goods from England to New South Wales in vessels proceeding to the Southern Whale Fishery. The Company requested the Government to define its attitude.[56]

[50] The Board foreshadowed its intentions in a letter of June 30, 1806; *H.R.N.S.W.*, VI, p. 103.

[51] The meeting was held on December 22, 1806. See *H.R.N.S.W.*, VI, pp. 222-223.

[52] E.I.C. to Tierney; *H.R.N.S.W.*, VII, pp. 240 ff.

[53] See E.I.C. to Holford (Sec. of India Board), Sept. 11, 1807; *H.R.N.S.W.*, VI, p. 285.

[54] Bligh to Windham, Oct. 31, 1807; *H.R.A.*, I, vi, p. 152.

[55] Foveaux to Castlereagh, Feb. 20, 1809; *H.R.A.*, I, vii, pp. 5-6.

[56] Chetwynd to Peel, Mar. 7, 1812; *H.R.A.*, I, vii, p. 457.

The Government already had under consideration a recommendation from Governor Macquarie, that spirits be imported into the colony free to check the use of illicit stills.[57] In considering both matters, the Government also examined the whole question of trade between New South Wales and the ports of the East India Company and between New South Wales and other settlements east of the Cape of Good Hope.[58]

The decision reached by the Board of Trade expressly permitted the importation of spirits, as sought by Macquarie, and added the general principle that:

> "the exportation of other Articles of Merchandise to Botany Bay should not be discouraged provided such Articles are confined to the Consumption of the Inhabitants of the said Colony."[59]

In effect the Board conceded not quite so much as had been granted in principle in 1806.

Meanwhile the Government had under review the status and organisation of the Company. Its declining hold on the Indian trade, the increasing protests against its trade monopoly in the South Seas, the diminishing need in England for Indian cloths and the political complications which the Company's vast powers were producing in the East lent support to the strong mercantile and colonial demand for reform. After prolonged negotiations between the Government and the various interests constituting the Company Lord Liverpool's Act (53 Geo. III, c. 155) was passed with the object of abolishing the exclusive commercial privileges of the Company save, as noted above, in China and in tea.[60]

The Act brought few benefits to island trade. The preservation of the monopoly in China meant that the trepang and sandalwood industries remained subject to the old restrictions until 1833 when the China monopoly was abrogated.[61] In consequence Americans were increasingly prominent in the island industries, carrying on a direct trade between the islands and China.[62] Moreover under the Act restrictions were imposed on the size of vessels to be employed in trade within the old monopoly area. Only ships of over 350 tons

[57] Macquarie to Castlereagh, Apr. 30, 1810; H.R.A., I, vii, p. 250.
[58] Liverpool to Macquarie, May 5, 1812; H.R.A., I, vii, p. 479.
[59] Chetwynd to Peel, Mar. 10, 1812; H.R.A., I, vii, p. 458.
[60] For other aspects of the act, see above, p. 21. The Act came into force on April 10, 1814. Its concessions were elaborated by 54 Geo. III, c. 34, permitting trade between the United Kingdom, places within the monopoly area and intervening ports.
[61] 57 Geo III, c. 1, did not apply to East India Company settlements.
[62] Report . . . on the State of Agriculture and Trade in the Colony of N.S.W., 1823, cit. sup., p. 60.

received the benefit of the Act. This provision bore with special severity on Sydney merchants, some of whom petitioned the Regent in 1819 for the complete lifting of the restrictions on small vessels.[63] They pointed out that few of the resident merchants of Sydney had the capital to employ ships of over 350 tons. The direct effect of the restrictions was to favour British as opposed to colonial merchants. So severe were the restrictions that there was inadequate shipping at the colony, which had had to depend on transport ships for much of its imports, until even that source was lost. The impediments to the import trade also injured exports as ships, which might have carried away exports, were discouraged completely from calling at New South Wales.

Some relief was granted in the same year as the petition by the enactment of 59 Geo. III, c. 122, providing that vessels without restriction of size might trade between any port in New South Wales and the United Kingdom. But the interests of the British merchants formerly protected by the restrictions on the size of vessels, were still protected in a different way. On July 2, 1819, only ten days before 59 Geo. III, c. 122, was passed, another Act, 59 Geo. III, c. 52, reimposed heavy duties on colonially caught black and sperm oil imported into the United Kingdom. Official policy still preferred to maintain existing British interests rather than to encourage colonial trade and commerce.[64]

Island and South Sea products were also subject to duty at the New South Wales end. The practice of imposing such duties by Government Orders and proclamations, commenced under King, had been continued by all his successors. In 1813 after a British query on colonial revenue[65] Macquarie introduced customs duties on sandalwood, pearl, shell, trepang, whale oil, sealskins and New Zealand timber and spars. The professed objective was to provide revenue.[66] Although at the time Macquarie considered that industry could "very easily bear the Small Duties I have fixed on them," four years' experience changed his views. In 1817 he protested against the "impolitic duties" imposed on the importation of these products into New South Wales and recommended substantial reductions when the goods were intended for re-export.[67] He added very significantly: "The subjecting them when brought hither to a weighty impost as at present renders it

---

[63] Encl. in Macquarie to Bathurst, Mar. 22, 1819; H.R.A., I, x, p. 61.
[64] Instructions to Mr. Commissioner Bigge; Return to an Address of the House of Commons for Earl Bathurst's Instructions to Mr. Bigge, 1823.
[65] Liverpool to Macquarie, May 5, 1812; H.R.A., I, vii, p. 480.
[66] Macquarie to Bathurst, June 28, 1813; H.R.A., I, vii, p. 721.
[67] Macquarie to Bathurst, May 15, 1817; H.R.N.Z., 1, p. 415.

impossible for our merchants to send them to England on such advantageous terms as to hold out sufficient encouragement for them to persevere in the trade." The merchants themselves drew attention to the burdensome customs duties in their petition of 1819 (already cited).

There were also legal difficulties in the way of continuing duties imposed merely by Government Order, for Mr. Justice Bent and Mr. Justice Field both doubted the validity of the duties.[68] Field's views were submitted to counsels' opinion by the British Government. As grave reasons to doubt the validity of the duties were revealed, a validating Act was passed.[69]

At the same time a major concession was granted to the Sydney traders in that all New South Wales duties applying to the re-export of articles the produce of the colony or of the South Seas were removed. Sandalwood, pearl shells, bêche-de-mer, sperm oil, black oil and kangaroo and seal skins were specially mentioned.[70] Duties in New South Wales were removed from these goods but they were still subject to heavy duties in Great Britain.

Opposition in Great Britain to the development of South Pacific trade otherwise than by British capital also played a part in the decision at the end of the Napoleonic Wars to apply the Navigation Laws to New South Wales. These laws operated against foreigners even more effectively than the British customs duties operated against the colonial merchants. By a despatch of December 11, 1815, soon after the war in Europe was ended, Bathurst reminded Macquarie that, although the trade of foreign vessels with New South Wales had been tolerated during the "war upon the plea of necessity," no such trade would be permitted in the future.[71] Attempts during 1816 to re-establish American trade with New South Wales led Bathurst to repeat his instructions.[72] Foreign intercourse with New South Wales declined immediately.[73]

In 1835, however, the Home Government acquiesced in the principle that the islands of the South Pacific were not foreign territories for the purposes of the Navigation Laws. As a result of the *Kaliopapa* Case, the New South Wales ordinance (11 Geo. IV, No. 6), placing island trade on the same footing as coastal trade, was tacitly approved by the British authorities.[74]

[68] *H.R.A.*, I, ix, pp. 24, 774.
[69] 59 Geo. III, c. 114.
[70] Bathurst to Macquarie, Aug. 4, 1819; *H.R.A.*, I, x, p. 196.
[71] Bathurst to Macquarie, Dec. 11, 1815; *H.R.A.*, I, viii, p. 648.
[72] Apr. 18, 1816; *H.R.A.*, I, ix, p. 109.
[73] See as to American interests G. Greenwood, op. cit., p. 141.
[74] Bourke to Stanley, June 30, 1834; Glenelg to Bourke, June 26, 1835; *H.R.A.*, I, xvii, pp. 459 and 750.

On the evidence it has to be concluded that the ending of the East India Company's monopoly was accompanied in the South Pacific by a policy designed to preserve trade and industry to British merchants. The colony in New South Wales might be a valuable base for South Pacific trade, but, being only a colony and a penal settlement, it was not encouraged to participate extensively in the development of island commerce.

CHAPTER IV

"SHAMEFUL DEPREDATIONS AND WANTON CRUELTIES"

"Of late Years there has been a great intercourse with Europeans with the Society and Sandwich Islands, which has not only furnished them with abundance of Firearms, but has also been the means of a number of Europeans continuing on those Islands, among whom are some of indifferent, not to say bad, Characters, mostly left from Ships going to the North-West Coast of America, Whalers, and several from this Colony, who have gained much influence with the Chiefs whom they have assisted in their Warfare."[1]

IN 1805 when Governor King summed up conditions in the islands in these words he thought the picture gloomy enough to warrant a prediction that the Pacific would become the "Seat of Buccaneering and Sea Robbers." His views were supported by those of Sir Joseph Banks. Attributing much of the mischief in the islands to the activities of convicts left there by Americans (who, he said, had stolen them from New South Wales), Banks in 1806 recommended action to control both the Americans and the convicts. His description of conditions at Tahiti is strikingly like King's comments on the islands as a whole.[2]

The fears of Banks and King were well founded. Conditions in the islands were coming to the point at which trade could be carried on only by fighting the natives and other traders. Early visitors had commenced a long tradition of outrages. In New Zealand, Fiji, Tonga, the Societies and the Marquesas dissolute traders, runaway convicts and castaways fought with one another and with the natives.

The root of the trouble was generally the wanton brutality and irresponsible greed of the traders and other whites in the islands. Lockerby's *Journal,* covering the early years of the sandalwood trade. teems with instances of insolent tyranny towards the natives,

---

[1] King to Camden, April 30, 1805; *H.R.A.,* I, v, p. 323.

[2] "Some Observations on a Bill for admitting the produce of New South Wales to entry at the Customs-house of the United Kingdom," July 7, 1806; *Brabourne Papers,* Vol. IV, pp. 262-264.

of quarrels between rival traders and of clashes between natives and whites.

Ignorance of native customs and the clash of moral standards produced much violence. Lockerby recounts how, on witnessing the customary ceremonial strangling of a Fijian widow, he unctuously engaged in a crude act of chastisement. Houses were destroyed, trees cut down and the bewildered natives driven into the woods.[3]

Nothing could demonstrate more clearly the conflict underlying such atrocities than Lockerby's own account a few lines below of how he played on the "superstitious fears" of the natives in order to obtain sandalwood from them.[4] The coarse brutality of the early clash between the practices of Europeans in the islands and the customs of the native peoples possessed few, if any, mitigating features. Bloodshed and disorder were the inevitable consequences.[5]

The traders did not hesitate to play politics with the natives for the sake of commercial gain. King in his despatch quoted at the head of this chapter had ample warrant for the statement that the traders had assisted the island chiefs in their warfare, especially by supplying firearms and teaching European modes of war.

The New South Wales Government received complaints not only of the violent crimes in which British subjects were involving themselves but also of the ill consequences to trade resulting from the incessant island disturbances. John Macarthur, the leader of the wealthy free settlers and traders, strongly urged the desirability of rescuing the island commerce "from the hands of foreigners, or from men, whose loose and immoral characters threaten to produce the most fatal effects upon the rising generation."[6] He also referred to the attempts of undesirable elements to capture the island trade through the instrumentality of American or other neutral flags, thus evading British control and the East India Company monopoly.[7] The problem for the Governors was one of providing sanctions for law and order. Legitimate trade had to be supported against illegitimate trade. British and colonial traders, adhering to the law, had to be protected against foreigners to whom the law did not apply.

The general condition of turmoil in the islands produced instance

---

[3] *Journal*, cit, sup., p. 64.

[4] ibid, pp. 66-67.

[5] For an interesting comment see *Gentleman's Magazine*, 1820; article by Joseph Arnold on Captain Siddons's experiences, reprinted in appendix to Lockerby's *Journal*. For later comment see *Edinburgh Review*, Vol. CVI, July, 1859; pp. 177-178.

[6] Macarthur to King, June 10, 1806; *H.R.N.S.W.*, VI, p. 93.

[7] ibid.

after instance in which the Governors were compelled to take action amongst the islands. Quite apart from any duties they may have possessed towards British subjects there, the Governors also had to deal with the problems of escaped convicts in the islands (some of them posing as representatives of King George III), of disputes between British nationals and foreigners, and even of direct appeals for their intervention.[8]

Until 1817 the Governors were left to their own devices in handling the island problem. The British Government, burdened by the Napoleonic Wars, and resenting the increase of responsibilities arising from the Australian colonies, remained almost indifferent to the mounting disorder in the South Pacific.

The whole burden of preserving law and order in the islands fell on the Governors of New South Wales. The British Government would not act. The native rulers were quite incapable of comprehending the nature of the problem or of coping with it in any effective way. The Governors were also the authorities most intimately concerned with the problem. It was convicts under their charge who were escaping to the islands. It was often traders from New South Wales who carried bloodshed and crime to the islands. It was in New South Wales that the loudest complaints were voiced by missionaries and traders against the unregulated condition of the islands.

Action by the Governors could not have been avoided. But what authority, legal and political, did the Governors possess in the distant and scattered islands? There is no clear answer to these questions and the former is of special difficulty.

The commissions of the early Governors gave them jurisdiction over *inter alia* "all the islands, adjacent in the Pacific Ocean, within the latitude . . . of 10 degrees 37 minutes south and 43 degrees 39 minutes south."[9] The same limits were set in defining the colony's "pirate" jurisdiction.[10] The precise extent of the jurisdiction thus conferred on the Governors has never been ascertained. From the standpoint of international law (even the international law of the eighteenth century), the reference to the adjacent islands certainly conferred no sovereignty on Great Britain and gave the Governors no right to exercise sovereign authority in the islands. Great Britain may have had an inchoate title to some of the islands by right of discovery or otherwise, but actual settlement and

---

[8] See the case of Pomare of Tahiti in 1809; Pomare to Paterson, Nov. 4, 1809; *H.R.A.*, I, vii, p. 300.
[9] See Phillip's Commission; *H.R.A.*, I, i, p. 2.
[10] *H.R.N.S.W.*, 1 (2). p. 81.

administration would have been necessary to perfect such titles.[11]

Further evidence against the view that there was any intention to claim sovereignty is to be found in the instructions given to Phillip regarding Norfolk Island. As already noted, Phillip was ordered to take possession of that island, lest it fall into the hands of some foreign Power. Norfolk Island was the nearest known island of any importance.[12] If it had to be made a special case in order to bring it under British sovereignty, obviously there was not even a claim to sovereignty over islands less "adjacent" to New South Wales.

In any case, the term "adjacent" is too elastic to have precise legal significance. Leaving the question of sovereignty aside, it is obviously impossible to determine from the commissions which, if any, of the islands were intended to be subject to the Governors' control. No eastward limit was ever fixed.

There is a considerable mass of evidence suggesting that some claim approximating to sovereignty was commonly regarded as having been made. For example, there are numerous instances of belief that the islands were part of New South Wales. In 1806, John Macarthur wrote to Governor King asking permission to send a vessel amongst the Fijis, Friendly Islands and "others within the limits of this territory."[13] Major Joseph Foveaux, the Lieutenant-Governor, in writing to Castlereagh in 1809, referred to the "Fejee Islands which lie within the limits of this colony."[14] Governor Bligh referred in 1807 to the sandalwood trade in "Islands within the limits of the territory."[15] An officer of the French expedition sent to the Pacific by the Consulate reported to the Governor of Mauritius that Great Britain was using New South Wales as a base for extending her rule throughout the South Pacific.[16]

All the claims made in New South Wales[17] attributed a greater degree of precision to British policy than an examination of the Governors' commissions and instructions can reveal. In actual

[11] Note the significant fact that Phillip, immediately on landing at Sydney Cove, took possession of New South Wales from 10° 37′ S. to 43° 39′ S., although Cook had taken possession as far as 38° S. in 1770. (*H.R.N.S.W.*, II, p. 543.) Phillip's action could not possibly have been construed as extending to the islands and it must be concluded that, so far as this action is indicative, no sovereignty was effectively claimed there.

[12] Lord Howe Island was discovered by the expedition sent to annex Norfolk Island.

[13] June 10, 1806; *H.R.N.S.W.*, VI, pp. 92-93.

[14] Feb. 20, 1809; *H.R.A.*, I, vii, p. 5.

[15] Bligh to Windham, Oct. 31, 1807; *H.R.A.*, I, vi, p. 152.

[16] E. Scott: *Terre Napoléon*; London, 1910; p. 144.

[17] See also *Brabourne Papers*, Vol. IV, p. 264.

fact the British Government itself never made any claim to exercise jurisdiction in the islands.

In the circumstances it is to be concluded that the jurisdiction conferred on the Governors was never intended to have precise legal significance. The intention was rather to mark out a sphere in which the Governors might represent the Crown. If the resources of the islands were to be used in New South Wales (in accordance with the adjunct policy) and if the East India Company's monopoly in the South Pacific were to be rigidly preserved, there was obviously need of some authority in the Governors of New South Wales to control British subjects in the islands. But just what authority was actually conferred remains doubtful, if only because there is no indication of the legal status accorded to the islands by Great Britain in the eighteenth century.[18]

Two main expedients were evolved for taking the law and order of New South Wales into the island world. Justices of the Peace were appointed in some of the islands; and good behaviour bonds were required from masters of ships clearing Port Jackson for the Southern Seas. No other methods than these, both of them probably illegal, were available to the Governors for extending their puny authority over islands as far distant as Tahiti (nearly 4,000 miles from Sydney) and as extensive as New Zealand.

The first Governor to tackle the problem of law and order in the islands was King. In 1801 he ordered Lieutenant Scott, who was proceeding to Tahiti in H.M.S. *Porpoise* for pork, to arrest and bring to Sydney the "Seamen on the Island . . . who have left different Ships and also several convicts who have made their escape from this Colony."[19] The following year King appointed the Rev. John Jefferson, one of the missionaries at Tahiti, as a Justice of the Peace for the island.[20] King's action was prompted by further reports of "noxious seamen" and others at Tahiti. Escaped convicts, deserting sailors and ne'er-do-wells had made the island a refuge. The presence of British missionaries[21] and the

18 As shown later in the Chapter, the Governors sometimes gave a colour of legal right to their actions in the islands by referring to them as "dependencies" of New South Wales. The word "dependencies" occurs three times in Phillip's commission and once in his instructions. In each case the reference is to New South Wales and its dependencies. The only legal significance to be attributed to the mention of "dependencies" is that Phillip and his successors were given jurisdiction over any territories specially acquired as dependencies of New South Wales, e.g., Norfolk Island. References to other islands as "dependencies" were without basis in law or in fact.

19 King to Scott, Aug. 21, 1801; H.R.A., I, iii, pp. 138-139.

20 H.R.A., I, iii, p. 727.

21 Cf. King to Scott, Aug. 21, 1801; H.R.A., I, iii, pp. 138-139.

value of Tahiti as a source of pork supplies completed the case for intervention.

When he measured them against the problem of law and order King was greatly dissatisfied with the results of Jefferson's appointment. The absence of force to support law in the islands led him to suggest in 1805 that two or three sloops of war should be stationed at Sydney to control the islands and "to prevent many abuses and irregularities on the part of the Americans as well as for the protection of these settlements generally."[22]

In the same year King resorted to the other expedient available for extending his authority over the islands, that is, the control in New South Wales of persons proceeding to and from the islands. A General Order to cope with the "perplexing and unwarrantable conduct of the Owners in the South Fishery and their Men" was issued in 1805. To prevent such lawlessness (and especially the ill-treatment of Maoris on whaling ships) it was provided that whalers, sealers and other traders setting out from Sydney were to enter into a bond containing the following article:

"(IV) Not to entice Seamen, or entertain Deserters from His Majesty's Ships, Merchant Vessels, or from any Colonial Vessel or Gangs engaged at this place or stationed under Agreement at any of the Islands within the Limits of the Territory, except in the case of their belonging to Colonial Vessels or Sealing Gangs who receive no Pay, Consideration or Maintenance from their Employers."[23]

The bond also required ships to keep within the "Limits of the Territory" defined as being within 10° 37' S. and 43° 39' S. and 135° E.

There is little direct evidence as to how the bonds worked. Atrocities certainly continued, but in the next few years New South Wales itself was in such a constant state of political trouble that it was not until 1813 that the attention of the Governors was given again to devising fresh means for controlling British subjects in the islands.

In that year Governor Macquarie was led by the continuance of outrages in New Zealand and elsewhere to review the whole problem. The Rev. Samuel Marsden had just founded a society in Sydney for the protection of South Sea Islanders.[24] There was the clearest possible responsibility resting on the Governor to use

[22] King to Camden. April 30, 1805; *H.R.A.*, I, v, p. 324.

[23] *H.R.A.*, I, v, p. 575.

[24] "The N.S.W. Society for affording Protection to the Natives of the South Sea Islands, and Promoting their Civilization." See Mitchell Library MSS., A. 857, p. 355. Also *Report . . . on the Judicial Establishments of N.S.W. and V.D.L. 1823*, cit. sup.; p. 27.

his authority to curb the depravities of the unscrupulous characters producing turmoil throughout the South Pacific.

A Government and General Order of December 1st stated that just complaints had been made against the ill-conduct of British subjects towards the natives of the islands. The Order declared that the natives had been provoked to acts of indiscriminate vengeance, endangering the lives, property and trade of both British subjects and foreigners. Holding that British subjects were themselves to blame for most of the attacks on Europeans, Macquarie took measures to restrain their excesses. A good behaviour bond of £1,000 was required of all ships trading in the South Seas from Port Jackson. The stipulations in the bond required protection of native property and the preservation of a peaceful demeanour towards the natives. No male natives were to be removed from their islands without their own consent and the consent of any persons to whom they were subject. Female natives were not to be removed without similar consents and also the prior consent in writing of the Governor of New South Wales.[25]

Macquarie's bond contained the statement that "natives of all the said islands are under the protection of His Majesty." It would be unreasonable to attribute exact legal precision to this statement, nor is it clear what Macquarie meant by "protection" of the natives. In 1814, however, Macquarie committed himself more specifically by issuing a proclamation to protect the natives of New Zealand and those of "every other dependency of the territory of New South Wales."[26] A Government and General Order of November 9th provided that no native of New Zealand was to be removed by a British subject "without first obtaining the permission of the chief or chiefs of the districts within which the natives . . . reside." The permission was to be certified under the hand of Mr. Thomas Kendall, a missionary, who was appointed a Justice of the Peace at the Bay of Islands under a commission of *dedimus potestatem* two days later. Macquarie made it clear beyond all doubt that he was exercising political authority within New Zealand when he ordered that no sailors or other persons were to be discharged there from any British ship without the written permission of certain of the chiefs (Ruatara, Hongi and Korokoro), certified in writing by Kendall. The three chiefs were to be obeyed by all persons to whom the Order referred.

Macquarie was attempting to cut through legal complications with a plan to take law and order to New Zealand. Kendall's

[25] *H.R.N.Z.*, I, p. 317.
[26] *H.R.N.Z.*, I, pp. 328-329.

appointment and the vesting of authority in the chiefs were both probably illegal. The Governor had to stretch the law to breaking point in order to discharge basic responsibilities towards British subjects in New Zealand.[27]

Macquarie's efforts to establish law and order in the islands and the South Pacific seas were mostly unsuccessful. The island justices had no means of enforcing their authority. The inadequacy of their resources is well attested in the documents.[28] In Tahiti, also, the value of the magistrates' work was greatly limited. Although Macquarie praised that of William Henry, whom he had appointed as a Justice at Tahiti in 1811, Henry in fact did little beyond pointing out undesirables to be removed from the island.[29]

The greatest difficulty of all was still the absence of clear authority in the courts of New South Wales to try offences committed in the islands. The Society established by Marsden had initiated several prosecutions in respect of violence against South Sea natives. These were unsuccessful, the magistrates holding that they had no jurisdiction.[30] All that the Courts could do was to report the facts to the Governor. The Vice-Admiralty Court itself could not try offences committed on the high seas.[31] Even if the Court had possessed jurisdiction, it would have been difficult to detect crimes in the distant islands, to capture offenders and to bring witnesses to Sydney.[32]

Macquarie himself pressed for action from the Home Government. His original request was for British action against "South Sea Whalers and other merchantmen frequenting these islands from England."[33] He was probably referring to ships which, having participated in crimes in the islands, sailed direct to England

[27] An even less secure legal foundation would have existed for the alleged action of Macquarie in authorising the masters of certain colonial vessels "to apprehend at sea, or wherever else they should meet with them, all persons whom they might know or get ascertained to them to be runaway Prisoners of the Crown, or persons escaping from the Colony to the injury of their Creditors." Evidence that such an authorisation was given exists in a paper signed by J. T. Campbell, who had been Secretary to the Government, in 1824, some years after the date of the supposed action. See McNab: *Murihiku*, cit. sup., p. 312.

[28] See the case of Captain Hammont; Hammont to Campbell, Oct. 4, 1816: *H.R.N.Z.*, I, pp. 408-409.

[29] Henry's appointment, *H.R.A.*, IV, i, p. 56. Macquarie's comment, Macquarie to Bathurst, Jan. 17, 1814; *H.R.A.*, I, viii, p. 97. As to success of Henry, see general evidence cited below on efforts to control British subjects in the islands.

[30] *Report . . . on the Judicial Establishments of N.S.W. and V.D.L., 1823*, cit. sup.; p. 27.

[31] Cf. the case of John Martin (the *Queen Charlotte*), Dec. 20, 1815; *H.R.N.Z.*, I, pp. 426-427.

[32] For an instance of a case where there was jurisdiction in N.S.W., see Collins, op. cit., p. 126.

[33] Macquarie to Bathurst, Jan. 17, 1814; *H.R.A.*, I, viii, p. 96.

without returning to Sydney. Macquarie also represented to the British Government that the massacres of English crews in such cases as the *Queen Charlotte* and the *Daphne* (news of which reached England) originated in the "shameful depredations and wanton cruelties" committed against the natives by masters and crews of ships frequenting the coast of New South Wales.

The problem was becoming one for the British authorities for many other reasons than those mentioned by Macquarie. With the opening of the islands to regular trade, their lawless state became a matter of high official concern. There was some prospect of a settlement being founded in New Zealand, Lord Bathurst in 1816 granting permission to five Sydney merchants to establish factories in New Zealand with the consent of the natives.[34] To have left British subjects in New Zealand subject only to the vague, probably illegal, supervision of the Governors of New South Wales would have been to invite further bloodshed and to risk conflict with foreign powers, whose subjects also resorted to the islands.

The case for legislative action was strengthened when the Church of England Missionary Society lent its powerful aid. The Society had settled in New Zealand in 1814, but found its work impeded by atrocities for which Europeans were generally to blame. In a memorial to Earl Bathurst, drawn up in 1817, the Society claimed that the missionary settlement in New Zealand was in peril so long as no effective check was exercised on whites resorting there. Was the British Government prepared to see missionary labour prevented by the shameful conduct of British subjects? Existing law, the memorial continued, provided no jurisdiction in New South Wales to try the offences being daily committed in New Zealand, the Marquesas and the other islands. The memorial concluded with a prayer for remedying the evils in such a way that offenders would be punished whether they proceeded to New South Wales or to Great Britain after committing their crimes.[35]

In due course the British Government, freed from the Napoleonic Wars, took action. In 1817 an Act of Parliament (57 Geo. III, c. 53) was passed to remedy the situation. The preamble recited that murders and manslaughters had been committed in the South Pacific both by sea and on land by British subjects, British seamen and deserters from British ships. Some of the offenders had settled in the islands. "Great violence" had been done and "a general

---

[34] Bathurst to Macquarie, Apr. 9, 1816; *H.R.N.Z.*, I, p. 407.

[35] *H.R.N.Z.*, I, pp. 417 ff. The memorial bears no date, but according to McNab, the editor of *H.R.N.Z.*, was made out in 1817. It was clearly drawn up before the enactment of 57 Geo. III, c. 53.

scandal and prejudice raised against the name of British and other European traders." It was to remedy these evils that the Act was expressed to be passed.

It provided that murders and manslaughters committed in New Zealand, Tahiti or other islands "not within His Majesty's dominions, nor subject to any European state or power, nor within the territory of the United States of America" should be cognizable "in any of His Majesty's islands, plantations, colonies," etc., as though they were offences committed on the high seas under 46 Geo. III, c. 54. This latter statute provided that offences committed at sea might be tried in any of His Majesty's islands or plantations or colonies by virtue of the King's Commission under the Great Seal. After the Act of 1817, therefore, certain crimes committed in the islands of the South Pacific by British subjects, or persons arriving in British ships, were assimilated as to matters of trial to offences committed on the high seas[36] and were made cognizable in British territories possessing a commission under 46 Geo. III, c. 54.

The Act marked the opening of a new era in British policy towards the islands of the South Pacific. The old vague claims to jurisdiction were explicitly abandoned by the reference to islands "not within His Majesty's dominions" and by the device of treating the islands as high seas. The Act really left the legal status of the islands undetermined beyond asserting that they were not British.

The main significance of the Act of 1817 was that it rested on recognition of the changes made in the South Pacific by the development of industry and trade. The adjunct policy had assumed that there would be little British activity in the islands. A mere general assertion of jurisdiction there was considered a sufficient definition of British political interests.

With the increasing entry of British subjects and other Europeans into the islands the vague, early policy came to involve the risk that the British Government might have to accept large responsibilities towards its nationals there. The only responsibility that the Government was prepared to accept was the punishment of the worst crimes committed by British subjects. Accordingly, the scope of official British action in the islands was redefined in narrow terms. The new policy, embodied in the Act of 1817, was one of minimum intervention. British authority would be exercised in the South Pacific only to the extent necessary to avoid a scandal to the British name and to preserve British trade from the worst consequences of extreme disorder.

[36] Compare on principle the later Act, 12 & 13 Vict., c. 96.

Chapter V

THE ORIGINS OF MINIMUM INTERVENTION

The Act of 1817 marked a diminution of British commitments in the South Pacific. By declaring that the islands to which it applied were not British possessions, it put an end to the vague claims that the Governors enjoyed jurisdiction there. The commissions of some of the Governors appointed after 1817, it is true, conferred upon them the usual vague jurisdiction over the "adjacent" islands,[1] but these commissions had to be read in light of the Statute. Legally, the Act was inconsistent with the exercise of any jurisdiction in the islands based on a British territorial title. The exercise of British jurisdiction in the islands would have been legally justifiable only by some arrangement of extra-territoriality or an arrangement like those made possible by the Foreign Jurisdiction Acts later in the century.[2]

The adjunct policy had become outmoded and was replaced by a policy of narrower interests—of indifference, tempered only by the necessity of providing protection and supervision for British subjects in the South Pacific. New South Wales continued to use the products of the islands to supplement its own resources,[3] but increasingly this was a matter of private trade, rather than of public policy.

The reasons for official British interest in the South Pacific had in fact diminished. So far as Great Britain was concerned, the South Pacific was given over more and more to private trade and to missionary labours. The only responsibilities of Great Britain were the defence of the Australian colonies and the control and protection of British subjects in the islands. As most of the traders showed little respect for law and as their ranks were not infrequently recruited from escaped convicts, the task of punishing

[1] See Darling's commission and instructions (H.R.A., I, xii, pp. 100 and 108) and Bourke's commission (H.R.A., I, xvi, p. 837).

[2] Nothing was done, however, about withdrawing Henry, the British Justice of the Peace at Tahiti, although his appointment was based on the pre-1817 conception. Henry resigned in 1821 (H.R.A., IV, i, p. 401).

[3] See Charlton to Canning, Oct. 18, 1825; Corr. rel to the Society Islands, Part I; No. 5.

crimes committed by British subjects in the South Pacific and of maintaining some supervision over their relations with the natives would have been considerable, had it ever been undertaken efficiently. The 1817 Act, of course, merely provided for the punishment of specially serious offences, thus averting a scandal to the British name and relieving the Governors of New South Wales of the burden of exercising a difficult and probably illegal form of magisterial control in the islands. For the rest, the Act left British subjects uncontrolled.

In effect Great Britain all but turned her back on the islands. There was no endeavour to follow up the tentative beginnings of island development made in the adjunct policy. Nor was there any substantial variation of the new principles for decades to come. Extensive intervention, to the point of annexation, proved inevitable in the case of New Zealand in 1839-1840. But New Zealand was a special case. For the greater part, the official attitude favoured keeping out of the islands as far as the growth of British trade and settlement and British missionary activity would permit.

The reasons for this attitude are clear. First, the South Pacific could not offer the type of investment opportunity which British merchants were seeking. Second, British trade and commerce in the South Pacific were of a type which not only did not need official protection, but flourished better without official supervision. Third, missionary activity in the South Pacific was strong and the missionaries opposed any regular system of colonisation (on humanitarian grounds). Fourth, the Colonial Office itself often shared the missionary viewpoint, was already over-burdened with administration, feared the expense of British intervention in the South Pacific and thought that the expanding settlements of Australia (and later New Zealand) constituted a sufficient British stake in that part of the world. Added together, these factors produced a prolonged inertia in British policy towards the South Pacific and, for that matter, towards many other possible areas of expansion also.

The commerce of the South Pacific offered little inducement to British merchants to establish permanent connections there. Whaling, the most important activity, was carried on over a wide area, but the only changes that it produced in the islands were the recognition of some harbours as regular places of rest and refreshment and the building up of familiar relations with the natives concerned. The sandalwood, bêche-de-mer and sealing industries were mainly in the hands of American and colonial merchants and were of little concern in Great Britain.

New Zealand flax and timber were almost the only South Pacific resources whose development might have led at that time to British settlement and rule. But, although use of these resources was discussed on several occasions, both officially and unofficially, no considerable settlement followed.[4]

The fact is that, up to the 'fifties "such trade as existed could be carried on without European settlement. Vessels visited the islands to collect sandalwood and bêche-de-mer for export to China and copra and tortoise-shell for the European market. A few white traders found comfortable nooks, and by honest dealing established safe and friendly relations with the natives."[5] Under these conditions there was no need for Great Britain to intervene in the islands for trade reasons.

Moreover, there was little prospect of intervention on more general grounds of colonial interest. The dominant commercial classes in Great Britain during the first half of the nineteenth century were not primarily colonisers. "They regarded the Empire from a profit and loss point of view. . . . Developed, populous, and civilised communities were the best markets; the resources of Africa and the Pacific Islands were little known."[6] It is true that some investors came to make an exception in the case of New Zealand, but the resources of timber and flax, the usefulness of its harbours for whaling and sealing and the extent of the territory made New Zealand an exceptional case. The prospect of land sales also attracted attention (especially after Wakefield's influence was felt in proposals for investment and colonisation in New Zealand). (See Chapter X, below.) For the greater part, however, the Pacific islands were too commercially backward to be of much interest to British merchants who were finding an ever expanding market in North America.

How far any sentiment, which could be described as "anti-colonialism," affected policy towards the South Pacific is most uncertain. The existence of strong feeling against colonial enterprise in Great Britain after the American War of Independence is accepted. The feeling was reinforced by those economic thinkers who followed the lead of Adam Smith in condemning the existing

---

[4] See *H.R.N.Z.*, I, pp. 36, 54, 71, 174, 180, 215, 250, 287, 298, 324, 352, 409, 410, 431-432, 513, 603, 606, 613, and 683.

[5] Benians, loc. cit., p. 345.

[6] P. Knaplund: "Colonial Problems and Colonial Policy" (*C.H.B.E.*, II, pp. 275 ff., at 277).

British colonial system.[7]   The depopulationist fallacy also contributed to anti-colonialism whenever the question of emigration was raised.[8]

Anti-colonial sentiment at the time when Great Britain swung from the adjunct policy to the policy of the 1817 Act was undoubtedly strong.   Whether the belief that colonies were dangerous and extravagant appendages could have had much influence in practical policy is, however, doubtful.   Anti-colonialism was not at all marked in the results of the Treaty of Paris and the Congress of Vienna.   After the Napoleonic Wars Great Britain retained Mauritius, Malta, the Ionian Islands, the Dutch settlement at the Cape of Good Hope, Demerara, St. Lucia and Tobago.   Admittedly the first four of these places were strategic points rather than developmental colonies.   But the Government which retained the other colonies, cannot be regarded as having been dominated by anti-colonial policies.[9]

Again, it is doubtful whether policy towards the South Pacific were discussed, in terms of colonialism and anti-colonialism at this stage.   Certainly there could have been no question in 1817 of founding a colony in the remote and scattered islands of the South Pacific which would have been in the same class as the American and West Indies settlements.   The great bulk of the anti-colonial arguments had no relation to prospects and possibilities in the South Pacific.   Nor is there any evidence that the Government even considered the possibility of official colonisation there.   Approval was given for an unofficial New South Wales commercial settlement in New Zealand in 1816 and in 1826 the first New Zealand Company sought promises of Government support for a proposed colony in New Zealand.[10]   Apart from

[7] Adam Smith: *Wealth of Nations* (2 vols.); Edinburgh, 1776; Book IV, Ch. VII, Part III.

[8] Depopulationism declined after the publication of the celebrated *Essay on Population* by Malthus in 1798.

[9] The influence of pro-colonial thinking has also to be taken into account. It was exemplified in Henry Brougham's *Enquiry into the Colonial Policy of the European Powers* (Edinburgh, 1803) and Robert Gourlay's *Statistical Account of Upper Canada, Compiled with a View to a Grand System of Emigration* (London, 1822).

[10] For earlier attempts to found settlements in New Zealand see as follows: 1810 Sydney plan in Macquarie to Castlereagh, Mar. 12, 1810; *H.R.N.Z.*, I, p. 297; 1814 Sydney plan in Memorial to Macquarie, Oct. 3, 1814; *H.R.N.Z.*, I, p. 324; and in Bathurst to Macquarie, Apr. 9, 1816; *H.R.N.Z.*, I, p. 407. For 1826 attempt, see J. S. Marais: *The Colonisation of New Zealand;* London, 1927; p. 25. According to a letter written by Lyall, one of the promoters, to Lord Glenelg in 1839, the Colonial Office, the Admiralty and the Board of Trade all approved the plan. (Lyall to Glenelg, Feb. 25, 1839; C.O. 209/4, qu. in Marais, loc. cit.) Stephen subsequently denied that there was any record of approval by the Colonial Office. (Memorandum, Feb. 27, 1839; C.O. 209/4; qu. ibid.)

these instances, however, there was no question of official interest in colonisation in the South Pacific until in the late 'thirties the movement for planting a settlement in New Zealand achieved importance. Indifference, founded on lack of inducement, was at this time a much more important factor in British policy towards the South Pacific than was anti-colonialism.

Conditions of trade in the South Pacific not only militated against development of British interest through their failure to provide any inducement to invest in the islands. They also led traders and planters in the islands to oppose any suggestion of British intervention. The greater part of the trade of the South Pacific was in the hands of men who preferred making their own terms with the natives and with one another to having law and order imposed upon them by the British Government. The whalers (and the traders who supplied them), the sealers and the bêche-de-mer traders had no wish for British supervision of their activities. The sandalwood traders, certainly the most violent and the most ill-famed of the Europeans then in the South Pacific, used methods in dealing with natives which the British Government, had it intervened, would have been bound to prevent and to punish by every means within its power. The traders and seamen were well enough content with conditions as they were. They profited by imposing their will on the natives, to the extent of joining in and promoting native struggles in order to suit their own ends. Even the jealous struggle with American interests did not make the British traders seek the protection of their government. Conditions in the islands, so far as the wishes of the traders and seamen were concerned, definitely favoured a British policy of non-intervention.

The same seems to be true, though for greatly different reasons, of the missionaries. Certainly the most influential and the most highly respected British subjects in the South Pacific, the missionaries eventually came to oppose any suggestion that British rule should be extended to the islands.

The prime factor in this attitude was the fear that British intervention would introduce the natives to western civilisation in a crude and sudden way. Humanitarianism had become a powerful factor in British policy and the growing missionary fear that colonisation was inimical to native welfare exercised a prolonged influence on the Colonial Office. The missionaries developed a solid and powerful phalanx of hostility to the traders who were threatening to debauch the South Pacific islands. With much African experience to prove their point, they claimed that colonisation would inflict lasting injury on native peoples and result in the despoiling of the whole of the islands.

The missionaries also had confidence in their own ability to exercise a growing and improving influence on the natives. Their wish to exclude colonisers and traders was not merely a matter of desiring to exclude potential evil influences. It was also an aspect of the missionary desire to provide the single means by which the native peoples would be introduced to Christianity and to the better elements of western civilisation. The success achieved by the missionaries in becoming the power behind the throne in Tahiti and the ascendancy with the chiefs that they were able to attain in New Zealand seemed to justify their pretensions.[11]

It would be wrong to hold that the missionaries in the South Pacific opposed official intervention right from the first. Actually, the anti-colonial aspects of their humanitarianism in the islands were not well established until the 'thirties. In the preceding period, little consideration seems to have been given to the problem, mainly because so few projects of colonisation came up for discussion.

Four instances revealing the missionary attitude to an extension of British rule in the South Pacific prior to 1830 may be noted here. Three of them concern New Zealand. In 1817 the Rev. Samuel Marsden, the father of missionary activity in New Zealand, wrote to the Church Missionary Society in England advocating a small, unofficial British settlement in New Zealand to "introduce the arts of civilisation."[12] Marsden's letter makes it plain that he regarded an official settlement as being, not undesirable, but so improbable as to be out of question. Similarly, in 1820 Marsden wrote to the Church Missionary Society referring to suggestions that the Government should be interested in the prospect of obtaining spars from New Zealand. Once again Marsden regarded an official settlement as out of question but he hoped for sufficient official action to relieve the Society of some of the expenses of establishing itself in New Zealand:

"If the spars are found to answer, New Zealand will be of great national importance, and there can be little doubt of this. The nation may derive all the advantages they may wish for from New

11 See Chapter IX, below.
12 Marsden wrote in conjunction with Cartwright and Youl, two other missionaries. The letter was dated Mar. 27, 1817, and is reprinted in J. R. Elder (ed.): *The Letters and Journals of Samuel Marsden, 1765-1838*; Dunedin, 1932; p. 226. As to Marsden's belief in commerce as paving the way for introduction of Christianity, see E. Stock: *History of the Church Missionary Society* (3 vols.); London, 1899; Vol. I, p. 206.

Zealand without the expenses of forming a colony, and what Government will do will relieve the Society of part of the expense, and at the same time forward your views."[13]

In 1824 Marsden stated his views on the proposed formation of a colony in New Zealand by Lieutenant-Colonel Nicholls. His view then was that, if there were no regular government, any unofficial colony would fail for lack of means of preserving law and order. Marsden even referred to the possibility that the Maori chiefs might accept British rule. He was far from opposing official colonisation; but in his opinion it was beyond the sphere of practical politics.

The attitude of the missionaries in other island groups towards British intervention is not well attested. There is one fairly clear case from the Societies. In 1826 the missionaries in the field and the London Missionary Society in England pressed for the establishment of a British protectorate over Tahiti for fear of French intervention. But the missionaries' intention was obviously to exclude the French (and French Catholic missionaries), rather than to procure an extension of British rule in the South Pacific. Their own influence in Tahiti was expanding rapidly and all that they required from Great Britain was protection from other Powers, whose nationals might introduce different religious teaching.[14]

It was not until late in the 'twenties that the missionary opposition to colonisation began to harden. Experience in other fields, especially Africa, led the London Missionary Society, the Church Missionary Society and the Wesleyan Missionary Society to adopt a common policy of hostility to colonisation and to the large-scale entry of British subjects into native territories. In the 'thirties the opinion that colonisation was inimical to the interests of native peoples was at its height and humanitarian opposition to colonisation became a powerful factor in sustaining the type of policy implicit in the Act of 1817—that is, of political non-intervention, coupled with control over British subjects entering native territories.

Finally, geography reinforced all the other factors militating against British intervention in the islands. Widely scattered and many of them surrounded by seas difficult of navigation, the islands

[13] Marsden to Pratt, Feb. 7, 1820; *H.R.N.Z.*, I, pp. 480-482.
[14] See Hankey (Treasurer, L.M.S.) to Canning, Nov. 23, 1826, and Hankey to Hay, Dec. 8, 1826; both F.O. 58/14. As to missionary objectives, see Hankey to Goderich, May 29, 1827; F.O. 58/14; also Missionaries at Tahiti to L.M.S., Dec. 15, 1826; ibid.

to this day present the problems of distance and poor communications to the investor and the administrator alike. While opportunities existed nearer at hand, there was little inducement for British action in the South Pacific.

The official British policy towards the South Pacific thus became one of non-intervention in the sense that no British Government had any wish or intention to establish a settled interest there or to become entangled in island affairs. But this policy (or, rather, this attitude) was politically impossible to sustain while British traders and missionaries were venturing into the islands in considerable numbers.

The troubles arising from the entry of British subjects into the islands presented constant problems to Great Britain. It was in answer to these problems that the Act of 1817 was passed. It was because of these problems that a policy of complete non-intervention was impossible. Some intervention there had to be, if only to protect and control British subjects mingling with the natives and associating with the nationals of other Powers.

British policy therefore became one of political non-intervention, coupled with action to discharge basic, inescapable responsibilities towards British subjects in the islands. The policy was really one of minimum intervention, rather than of non-intervention: the British Government would intervene in the islands but only to the extent that the protests of missionaries or of the Governors of New South Wales against crimes committed in the South Pacific, or fear of disputes between British subjects and foreigners, made unavoidable.

The policy of minimum intervention had three main constituents: (a) the absence of political interest or commercial ambition in the islands; (b) the recognition that Great Britain had a responsibility of control and protection towards British subjects in the islands; and (c) the desire to preserve the *status quo*, which made political non-intervention possible, despite the proximity of the Australian colonies.

Naturally minimum intervention was a policy with a changing content. What was legally, morally and politically unavoidable in 1875 differed vastly from what was similarly necessitated in 1817. The wish to preserve the political *status quo* in the islands led to considerable variations of policy later in the century. The growth of trade and commerce and especially the growth of planting industries (like copra and sugar) in the islands greatly increased the sphere of unavoidable responsibility towards British subjects.[15]

But the basic concept of policy remained the same—until almost the end of the century. Great Britain sought to avoid political responsibilities in the islands and to intervene only where circumstances forced her to recognise a duty towards British subjects there. The history of British policy in the islands for the greater part of the nineteenth century is, therefore, dominated by the changing degrees of control and protection needed by British subjects; by the legal and administrative problems of exercising such control in backward, often "uncivilised" states; and, finally, by attempts to preserve the political *status quo* in face of growing commercial and international interest in the islands.

[15] The degree to which the policy was defined, or even recognised as being a policy, also varied considerably. British policy towards the islands was rarely laid down with exactitude. It has to be extracted from a host of individual decisions, most of them clearly made *ad hoc*, whose significance becomes apparent only when they are compared with one another and viewed in the light of conditions in the islands and the decisions being made by other Powers facing the same problems.

CHAPTER VI

UNWORKABLE LAWS

THE Act of 1817 was the work of a Government far distant from the South Pacific. That Government's policy was limited to maintaining good relations with the powerful missionary societies, with preserving a measure of law and order for the sake of trade and with avoiding downright scandal to the British name. Passed as a concession to demands for reform, the Act satisfied those demands in the sense that certain serious crimes committed by British subjects in the South Pacific were made cognizable at law. Beyond this legal change, however, little was accomplished.

Legally and practically the Act was ill-designed for any purpose other than that of enabling the British Government to make some show of remedying the evils of which the Governors of New South Wales and the missionaries had complained. At almost every point the Act, which applied also to Honduras, bore the imprints of indifference, careless drafting and ignorance of the problems to be solved.[1]

Ostensibly it had been passed in order to take law and order to the South Pacific. But, so slight was the examination made of the legal problems involved that, for six years after its enactment, the nearest Courts competent to try the crimes of British subjects in the South Pacific were those of Ceylon.[2] Although the intention had been to relieve the Governors of New South Wales of legal difficulties in the South Pacific, no jurisdiction was conferred on the courts of New South Wales to try offences under the Act. The

---

[1] The inattention with which the Act was drafted had an interesting counterpart in the long-continued lack of proper administrative machinery in the British Government for handling island problems. For a time the Colonial Office and the Foreign Office each did its best to pass responsibility for the Pacific Islands to the other. "They can in no respect be considered in the light of colonies," stated the Colonial Office, "for we have no settlers amongst them recognised by the Government at home, nor ever have had, as far as I know; nor have we, I believe, any intention of making any of these islands our own by any summary or gradual process." The Foreign Office attempted to argue that, because the islands had been of interest to the Colonial Office in the early days of New South Wales, they should remain the responsibility of that Department. See *Corr. rel. to the Society Islands, Part I*; No. 11; and Hay to Planta, Dec. 8, 1826; Jan. 24, 1827; both F.O. 58/14.

[2] *Report of the Commsnr. of Enquiry on the Judicial Establishments of N.S.W. and Van Diemen's Land*, 1823; cit. sup.; p. 58.

Act provided that murders and manslaughters committed in New Zealand, Tahiti, or other islands "not within His Majesty's Dominions, nor subject to any European state or power, nor within the territory of the United States of America" by British subjects, or by persons arriving in British ships or by British subjects living in the islands, should be tried "in any of His Majesty's islands, plantations, colonies, etc.," as if they were offences on the high seas under 46 Geo. III, c. 54. The obvious effect of the 1817 Act was that only colonies to which a commission had been issued under 46 Geo. III, c. 54, had jurisdiction to try the offences to which the Act referred. Neither New South Wales nor Van Diemen's Land possessed such a commission. Hence the nearest colony whose courts were competent to try offences under the 1817 Act was distant Ceylon. As Bigge pointed out, this legal difficulty deprived the Act of almost all practical usefulness for several years.

Probably as a result of Bigge's Report, the New South Wales Act, 1823 (4 Geo. IV, c. 96, s. 3) and the Australian Courts Act, 1828 (9 Geo. IV, c. 83, ss. 3 and 4) conferred jurisdiction on the Supreme Courts of New South Wales and Van Diemen's Land to try serious crimes committed in New Zealand, Tahiti and other places by sea and by land in the Indian and Pacific Oceans not subject to His Majesty or to any European Power. Once again the jurisdiction was limited to the masters and crews of British ships, or British subjects sailing in or arriving in such ships, or living in such places.[3]

In 1828 also another obvious loophole in the Act of 1817 was closed with the enactment of 9 Geo. IV, c. 31. The new Act provided for the punishment of offenders who returned direct to Great Britain without calling at any colony. Section 7 authorised the trial of British subjects in England for murder or manslaughter committed abroad—a provision which the slightest foresight would have seen inserted in the Act of 1817.

The overwhelming evidence of the legal deficiencies of the 1817

---

[3] Section 3 of 4 Geo. IV, c. 96 reads thus: ". . . the said Supreme Courts of New South Wales and Van Diemen's Land respectively shall and may inquire of, hear, and determine all Treasons, Piracies, Felonies. Robberies, Murders, Conspiracies, and other Offences of what Nature or kind soever committed or that shall be committed upon the Sea, or in any Haven, River, Creek, or Place where the Admiral or Admirals have Power, Authority or Jurisdiction, or committed or that shall be committed in the Islands of New Zealand, Otaheite, or any Island, Country, or Place, situate in the Indian or Pacific Oceans, and not subject to His Majesty, or to any European State or Power, or by any British Ship or Vessel, or any of them or by any British Subject sailing in or belonging to, or that shall have sailed in or belonged to and have quitted any British Ship or Vessel to live in any part of the said Islands, countries or Places, or that shall be there living."

Act demonstrates the inadvertence and indifference with which it was passed. Ignorance of conditions in the South Pacific was another source of weakness. Goderich, the Secretary for War and the Colonies, himself stressed this point.[4] He admitted that much of the misconduct of British subjects in the islands was not cognizable at law because it had not been made illegal. The Acts of 1817, 1823 and 1828 had been based on English conditions and provided only for serious crimes of the types known in England. The legal complexities of the different environment of the South Pacific had not been understood. As examples of wrongs which could not be punished under the Acts, Goderich cited the "fomenting of Wars between barbarous tribes for selfish purposes" and the "extraordinary traffic in Human Heads, which prevailed between New Zealand and New South Wales."[5]

Similarly the Acts erred in not providing for the taking of oaths by native witnesses. In commenting on 4 Geo. IV, c. 96, Saxe Bannister, the Attorney-General of New South Wales, declared in 1824 that the practical exclusion of the evidence of natives would make the Act in many instances "perfectly inoperative."[6] The inadmissibility of native evidence seems to have ensured immunity for hundreds of white offenders.

Even after the Acts of 1823 and 1828 had brought justice nearer to the islands, there was still a substantial gap between offenders and the courts. No effort was made by the British Government to provide machinery for enforcing the law. The islands were thousands of miles away from Sydney, the nearest centre of British authority. Visits of men-of-war or officers of the Crown were irregular and infrequent. No provision existed for apprehending suspected persons nor even for detecting offences.

Perceiving these difficulties, Bigge recommended that the Governor of New South Wales should be empowered to appoint magistrates and constables in New Zealand, where disorder was rife and British subjects were settling in considerable numbers.[7] Because such appointments could only be made if New Zealand were British territory, Bigge went on to suggest that the Act of 1817 should be amended to declare that New Zealand was included within the British dominions. Such a declaration of course would have been nugatory even in the international law of the early nineteenth century. But Bigge's main point, that without the

---

[4] Goderich to Bourke, June 14, 1832; *H.R.A.*, I, xvi, p. 662.
[5] Goderich to Bourke, Jan. 31, 1832; *H.R.A.*, I, xvi, p. 513.
[6] *H.R.A.*, IV, i, p. 555.
[7] Bigge to Bathurst, Feb. 27, 1823; *H.R.N.Z.*, I, p. 594.

presence of British officials in the islands the Act of 1817 was of little use, could not be questioned. Within a few years the British authorities themselves had admitted that the Acts of 1817, 1823 and 1828 were practically unenforceable in the majority of cases.[8]

Although no apt legislative provision was made for the purpose until 1823, the British Government apparently intended the Government of New South Wales to enforce the new legislation right from the first. Apart from the problem mentioned by Bigge (that New South Wales jurisdiction could be exercised effectively in the islands only if they were brought under British rule)[9] there were serious obstacles in New South Wales itself to the efficient enforcement of the law.

Lack of information as to events in the islands and legal difficulties arising from the absence of witnesses probably accounted for the general failure in New South Wales to apply the laws against island offences. Articles in the *Sydney Gazette* during May, 1831, suggest that there were very few prosecutions under the Acts of 1817, 1823 and 1828. It seems that even the existence of the 1817 Act had been forgotten by most people.[10]

One of the few cases heard under the Acts, *R. v. McDowell,* resulted in the discharge of the accused, after he had been found guilty, because of an unexpected legal difficulty. McDowell was charged in 1827 under Lord Ellenborough's Act (43 Geo. III, c. 58) with stabbing a seaman on board the brig *Rosanna* in New Zealand waters and was convicted in the Supreme Court of New South Wales. A motion in arrest of judgment[11] succeeded on the ground that, although Lord Ellenborough's Act was in force in England and New South Wales, it was not extended to British subjects in New Zealand waters by the New South Wales Act, 1823, which did not create new offences, but merely provided for trial and punishment of acts committed in the specified places against English law operative in such places.[12]

Apart from legal difficulties and the obstacles in the way of detecting offences and providing evidence, it has to be admitted

[8] Goderich to Bourke, June 14, 1832; H.R.A.. I, xvi, p. 662.

[9] The same difficulty led the Government to drop Lord Howick's Bill of 1832, designed to give the Governor and Legislative Council of N.S.W. power to make laws for the punishment of crimes committed by British subjects in South Pacific islands, "not being H.M. dominions." It is not clear whether the alternative of some such remedy as the later Foreign Jurisdiction Acts were considered at that time.

[10] May 5, 14, 17, 19, of 1831.

[11] *Sydney Gazette,* Mar. 24, Apr. 6, 1827, and May 14, 1831. The first report gives the accused's name as McDougal.

[12] As Lord Ellenborough's Act was extended to offences committed at sea by 1 Geo. IV, c. 90, it is not clear that the decision of the Court was correct.

E

that the New South Wales authorities proved incapable or unwilling of making any determined effort to enforce the law. The test case was that of the *Elizabeth* in 1831, when the Governor did his utmost to enforce the law but was defeated by his own subordinates and, probably, by some hostility in public opinion itself. The case is also of special interest in that the legal aspects were thoroughly examined by the Crown Solicitor of the colony and the legal advisers of the British Government and judgment pronounced on the Acts of 1823 and 1828.[13]

The facts in the case of the *Elizabeth* were simple. The *Elizabeth*, a brig, had been sailed to New Zealand by Captain John Stewart in search of flax. In order to obtain a cargo the master and crew joined sides in a Maori conflict and lent their aid to a particularly atrocious massacre. When the matter was reported to him Governor Darling of New South Wales ordered an immediate prosecution. He had been urging the British Government to intervene in New Zealand at least to the extent of stationing a man-of-war there or of appointing a British Resident,[14] and he felt it politic to enforce the law in this case with the utmost rigour. But his good intentions were frustrated by Moore, the Crown Solicitor, who raised legal difficulties. As Stewart and his men had participated in a native war and the whole of the killing had been *in bello*, could they be guilty of murder or accessories to murder? What admissible evidence was there? Did the admissible evidence establish a case of felony against the accused? Wearied of such technicalities, Darling ordered the prosecution to continue. In order to strengthen his case for British intervention in New Zealand, he desired to prove that every effort was being made to enforce the existing law.

His orders were not obeyed. It is an extraordinary commentary on the legal institutions of the time that witnesses and others implicated were permitted to escape from the colony. According to Darling, the fault lay with the negligence—or worse—of Moore. Stewart himself, who had been granted bail in circumstances of doubtful legality, escaped later.

It is difficult to avoid suggesting that Moore's conduct was rendered possible by the lack of public support for Darling's attempt to enforce the law. Darling was at the time engaged in a savage controversy with the press. He was firmly opposed by

13 For the *Elizabeth* case, see *H.R.A.*, I, xvi, pp. 237, 405, 513 and 650. Also *Sydney Gazette*, May 5, 14, 17 and 19 of 1831.
14 Darling to Murray, Aug. 12, 1830; *H.R.A.*, I, xv, p. 702. See Chapters VII and IX, below.

powerful sections of public opinion. The *Sydney Gazette* had indicated its opinion that "His Excellency is one of the weakest and wickedest men that ever held office under a British King."[15]

The principal press comments on the Stewart case were those of the *Sydney Gazette* and *The Australian.* The *Gazette,* which deplored the crime, nevertheless regarded the case as experimental and on repeated occasions found it necessary to protest its anxiety and the anxiety of the leading citizens of Sydney that Stewart should be punished. Twice it referred to charges that powerful interests were attempting to free Stewart from the charges.[16] *The Australian* openly condemned the principle of treating the massacre of natives in war as murder. It could not "divine the justice of denouncing the master of a British vessel, as a British subject, as amenable to laws, which, however strict and necessary, under certain circumstances, were not applicable to savage broils and unintentional acts of homicide to which he must have been an unwilling party, and over which he could not probably exercise the slightest control."[17]

The shocking irregularities in the case and the serious doubts raised as to the sincerity of the New South Wales attempts to enforce the law led the Home authorities to treat the matter as one of prime importance. The missionaries also strongly represented that such atrocities would embitter relationships between Maoris and white men everywhere.

Goderich referred Moore's legal points to the King's Advocate, the Attorney-General and the Solicitor-General. In their opinion King and his mate, Clements, were both guilty as accessories before the fact of murder. The legal advisers of the Crown added that the courts of New South Wales and Van Diemen's Land both possessed jurisdiction to try the cases under 9 Geo. IV, c. 83, ss. 3 and 4. It was recommended that Stewart and the mate be arrested and charged immediately.[18]

Summing up the case, Goderich condemned the conduct of the proceedings in New South Wales as "inefficient" and "discreditable." The new Governor, Bourke, was instructed to seek out the blameworthy in New South Wales and censure their misconduct.[19]

[15] Apr. 30, 1831.

[16] Apr. 2 and May, 19, 1831.

[17] June 3, 1831, p. 3, Col. 3.

[18] Neither was apprehended. According to G. W. Rusden (*History of New Zealand,* 1882; 2 ed., 3 vols.; Melbourne, 1895; Vol. 1, p. 163, n. 7) Stewart was drowned on a trip round Cape Horn.

[19] Moore was later suspended by Governor Bourke on the grounds of negligence and impertinence to superior officers. (Bourke to Stanley, Jan. 24, 1834; *Despatches from the Governor,* 1834; pp. 137 ff.)

During the decade and more in which the inadequacies of the British legislation and the difficulties of enforcing the law in New South Wales deprived the Acts of 1817, 1823 and 1828 of most of their usefulness, a heavy burden was placed on native rulers. There were no native governments competent to deal with the types of social and commercial activity in which the white men were engaging. In New Zealand, where conditions were particularly bad, there was a complete lack of centralised authority and settled systems of law. The very presence of white men tended to disrupt native society and to remove what law and order did exist by undermining the foundations of native authority.

Reports from British officials themselves soon illustrated the degree to which conditions in the islands were deteriorating. Writing to Canning at the Foreign Office in 1825, Charlton, the British Consul in the Pacific, complained that masters of vessels visiting the islands (except the Sandwich and Society Islands) had to be constantly on guard against the "treachery of the natives."[20] Thomas Elley, Acting Vice-Consul in the Society Islands, reported to Canning in 1827 that there were serious disturbances on Tahiti.[21] Elley himself had fled to Huahine, where he awaited assistance and protection from some British warship. He argued that the importance of missionary work as an agency in accustoming the natives to European intercourse had been much exaggerated in Great Britain. "Two-thirds of the population of this island," he commented in disgust, "are lawless, unprincipled ruffians."

Conditions were worst in New Zealand. Here European intercourse, attracted by the wealth of the country, had developed rapidly. Both missionary and official observers constantly deplored the chaotic state of affairs in New Zealand and united in urging extensive remedial measures.

By the close of the 'twenties the consequences of the first form of the minimum intervention policy were fully revealed. The attempt of a distant Government to control its subjects in the South Pacific had been proved to be legally inadequate, incapable of practical enforcement and productive of the most serious ill-consequences to the natives. Viewing South Pacific affairs, not as a problem which Great Britain was bound to solve but merely as a problem of satisfying the missionaries and the New South Wales authorities that British subjects would not be left totally without supervision, the British Government had done virtually nothing to improve the conditions in the islands that had led to the original

20 Charlton to Canning, Oct. 18, 1825; F.O. 58/14.
21 Elley to Canning, Mar. 29, 1827; F.O. 58/14.

passage of the 1817 Act. Such action as had been taken had been left over much to the heavily burdened authorities in New South Wales, who could not even rely on the support of public opinion in suppressing outrages against the natives and were themselves not always in sympathy with the task assigned to them.

By 1830 the demand for British intervention was again strong. The missionaries and the New South Wales authorities were urging that the narrow limitations imposed on British action by the minimum intervention policy should be abandoned. As a result of this renewed pressure Great Britain was constrained to vary the minimum intervention policy by adopting a system of naval policing visits to the islands, supplemented in some cases by the appointments of consuls and representatives, who might supervise the conduct of British subjects and assist them in their relations with the natives.

CHAPTER VII

POLICING THE PACIFIC: THE ROLE OF THE ROYAL NAVY 1805-1844

THE importance of "commodore justice" after the growth of the Pacific labour trade has been generally recognised. But insufficient attention has been paid to the work of the Royal Navy under the adjunct and minimum intervention policies. In the first half of the nineteenth century, even more than in the second half, it was the Royal Navy which discharged the basic responsibilities of the British Government towards British subjects in the islands of the South Pacific. Particularly under the minimum intervention policy, when such makeshifts as the appointment of justices of the peace in the islands were no longer possible, the Royal Navy provided the only effective British justice, law and administration available in the island world.

The original recommendation that naval patrols be established to police the islands was made by Governor King in 1805.[1] The Admiralty does not seem to have agreed to the suggestion, although a ship (detached from the East Indies squadron) was subsequently stationed off the New South Wales coast.[2] This ship was intended to protect the new settlement rather than to keep British subjects in the islands under surveillance. Occasional visits were, however, made to most of the important islands when the requirements of the service permitted. On these visits naval commanders assisted the justices of the peace by removing offenders and maintaining the prestige of the law. Sometimes they undertook expeditions at the express request of the Governors of New South Wales.[3]

The growing commercial contacts between New South Wales and New Zealand led to the British Government's Commissioner of Enquiry, Bigge, to suggest in 1823 that visits by a British man-of-war to New Zealand would have a most beneficial effect.[4] The

---

[1] King to Camden, Apr. 30, 1805; *H.R.A.*, I, v, p. 324.

[2] Cf. Bathurst to Brisbane, May 8, 1821; *H.R.A.*, I, x, p. 498.

[3] See Maihara to Darling, 1829; *H.R.A.*, I, xiv, p. 738; Laws to Admiralty, Mar. 11, 1829; F.O. 58/14; and Jefferson to King; *H.R.A.*, I, iii, p. 336.

[4] *H.R.N.Z.*, I, p. 594; Barrow to Gage, June 15, 1826, encl. in Hay to Bourke, Mar. 26, 1832; *H.R.A.*, I, xvi, p. 574.

Admiralty ordered such visits in 1826 and it was reported by the East India station in 1830 that the instructions were in force and that visits were still being made.[5] The mounting turbulence of Europeans in New Zealand led Governor Darling of New South Wales and the Rev. Samuel Marsden, who played so notable a part in early missionary work in New Zealand, to recommend that a British ship of war be stationed regularly on the New Zealand coast.[6] The recommendation was not accepted, the Admiralty merely informing the Colonial Office that the ship off the New South Wales coast was under orders to obey the Governor of New South Wales as to making visits to New Zealand.[7]

The first regular naval visits to the islands were begun in 1829 when, acting on a report from Captain Laws,[8] the Foreign Office induced the Admiralty[9] to arrange annual visits by the ship of war on the New South Wales coast to the Society and Friendly Islands. An order was also given to Pacific commanders generally that they were to visit the islands when possible without inconvenience to the public service

The circumstances which prompted Laws's recommendation for regular visits to the islands were graphically set out in his despatch to the Admiralty.[10] Laws explained that he had sailed to Tahiti in 1829 at the request of Governor Darling of New South Wales in order to·apprehend sixteen escaped convicts who had settled in the Societies and were "committing the most violent acts of robbery and even murder amongst the inhabitants." The Tahitians had complained bitterly of desperadoes escaping from ships and arriving in a clandestine fashion. Although strict laws had been passed at the instigation of the missionaries in order to deal with the problem,[11] there was no authority in the islands strong enough to control these dissolute whites. The missionaries themselves had been driven to recommend annual visits by British men-of-war and Laws perceived a further reason for such visits in the growing commercial contacts between New South Wales and the islands.

A recommendation similar to that made by Laws was sent in to the Admiralty in 1832 by Captain J. C. Hill, who suggested that

[5] Owen to Croker, July 20, 1830; ibid.

[6] Darling to Murray, Aug. 12, 1830, enclosing Marsden to Darling; *H.R.A.*, I, xv, p. 702.

[7] Barrow to Hay, Mar. 24, 1832, encl. in Hay to Bourke, Mar. 26, 1832; *H.R.A.*, I, xvi, p. 573.

[8] Laws to Croker, encl. in Croker to Dunglas; *Corr. rel. to the Society Islands*, *Part 1*; No. 26.

[9] Backhouse to Croker, Sept. 12, 1829; ibid, No. 27.

[10] Laws to Croker, loc. cit. (n. 8).

[11] F.O. 58/14; pp. 153-154.

the officer commanding the South America squadron should be given a blanket authority to send out ships to all the islands, when convenient, as a supplement to the visits from New South Wales.[12] Visits were made as recommended by Hill. As the South America command extended to 170° W., these visits included the Societies.

The visits of men-of-war to the islands were of two classes. There were expeditions sent out specially to deal with some reported outrage or known abuse, such as the crimes of a group of escaped convicts or an attack on British subjects by natives. There were also routine visits of inspection, on which some tasks specified in advance might have to be performed, but on which the work of the expedition was mainly determined by the commanding officer as he moved from place to place.

An example of the former type of voyage is the second H.M.S. *Alligator* expedition to New Zealand in 1834, which is extensively recorded both in official documents[13] and in the personal narrative of William Barrett Marshall, the ship's surgeon.[14] The expedition was sent out as a result of the decision of Governor Bourke and the Legislative Council of New South Wales to rescue British subjects detained by the Maoris after the wreck of the barque *Harriet* in April, 1834.

The official instructions to Captain Lambert of the *Alligator* forbade the use of force lest the Maoris be provoked to retaliate by attacking British subjects after the vessel had departed.[15] But force was used and the despatch and conduct of the expedition were adversely criticised both in Great Britain and in New South Wales. The attacks reflected considerable dissatisfaction with the use of the Navy for such a purpose and in such circumstances.

The main criticism was that there had never been any proper investigation of the charges made against the Maoris. A naval vessel had been sent out on what was very like an errand of retribution on the mere complaint of some of the survivors. C. D. Riddell, the Colonial Treasurer of New South Wales, wrote to Governor Bourke, after the Legislative Council had resolved to send out the expedition, expressing his strong objection. Riddell argued that the whole trouble arose only from the ill-advised con-

12 Hill to Palmerston, May 12, 1832; F.O. 58/14.

13 C.O., N.Z., Sept. 1835; *Communications received at the C.O. rel. to an Expedition sent from N.S.W. to N.Z. in August or September last, for the Recovery of British Subjects, who had been detained by the Natives.*

14 See appendix to J. Beecham: *Remarks upon the Latest Official Documents rel. to N.Z.*; London, 1838. Also W. B. Marshall: *A Personal Narrative of Two Visits to New Zealand, in H.M.S. "Alligator"*; London, 1836.

15 Bourke to Lambert, Aug. 23, 1834; Official Correspondence, cit. sup.

duct of those who had been wrecked. The principal complainant, he added, was Guard, a former convict, whose "dealings with New Zealanders have, in some instances, been marked with cruelty." Riddell thought that the prisoners should be ransomed, because an isolated act of force would merely exasperate the Maoris.[16] A similar complaint against the failure to enquire into the justice of the case against the Maoris was made by Marshall, the ship's surgeon. Marshall pointed out in his journal that the only interpreter sent with the expedition was incompetent and, being a former spirits retailer and billiard-marker, might be presumed to be not well fitted for his office. There was and there could have been no proper investigation in New Zealand of the crimes alleged to have been committed.

Marshall also perceived the serious political consequences of permitting such an arbitrary act of force. The British Government, he pointed out, had already appointed a Resident in New Zealand, who was supposed by his example and prestige to show the natives the meaning of government by law and order. Was it consistent with such an appointment, Marshall demanded, to send out what amounted to a punitive expedition without even consulting the Resident?. Repetition of such incidents, he concluded, would destroy completely the usefulness of the Resident's position.

The brutality of the expedition and the consequent injury to relationships between white men and Maoris also provoked unfavourable comment. The Rev. John Beecham, a prominent humanitarian writer on colonial questions, attacked the expedition as an act of violent and unnecessary chastisement.[17] A similar objection, made with special reference to the prospect of retaliatory action by the Maoris, was sent from Sydney to the Foreign Office by Fowell Buxton, the humanitarian Member of Parliament.[18]

The tone of these criticisms may justify the conjecture that there was dissatisfaction in both Great Britain and New South Wales with expeditions like that of the *Alligator* and with the conditions responsible for such punitive voyages. The critics were certainly more alarmed at the clumsy brutality of the expeditions than they were aware of the true nature of the island problem. They did not perceive that only a systematic extension of the governing responsibilities of European Powers could restore order to the islands. What they did realise was that the Navy was being

[16] Riddell to Bourke, Aug. 25, 1834; Official Correspondence, cit. sup.

[17] J. Beecham, loc. cit. (n. 14 above); p. 42.

[18] F.O. 58/14; p. 192. For contemporary comment on the tendency of naval action to stir up native revenge, see *Edinburgh Review*, Vol. CVI, July, 1859, p. 178.

employed in tasks for which its methods and resources were unsuited. Moreover, existing British policy clearly involved a contradiction: naval officers were permitted to perform acts of war against native peoples with whom Great Britain was supposedly at peace.

Official opinion in New South Wales regarded the *Alligator* expedition as a regrettable necessity.' Without considering the possibility of any more thorough-going measure, the Legislative Council, in deciding to send out the *Alligator*, also resolved that a ship of war ought to be stationed permanently in New Zealand waters. Governor Bourke made the same point in his despatch to the Home Government, reporting the results of the expedition.[19] Routine naval visits of the type for which Bourke and the Council pressed were, as noted above, already established in the South Pacific. It was merely an extension of the existing system that was sought.

The uses to which such naval visits were put had proved to be as varied as conditions in the islands themselves. The naval officers were often the only representatives of the British Government to visit the islands and a wide range of duties, judicial, administrative and political devolved upon them. Native rulers regarded naval officers as representatives of the Great Powers, able to counsel, to protect and to punish. There are even cases of proposed laws, affecting whites, being referred to naval officers for approval.[20] Where there were British representatives stationed permanently in the islands (for example, at Tahiti from 1836) the naval officers supported law and order, consulted with and reported upon the representatives and impressed upon native rulers the wisdom of dealing justly and liberally with British subjects.

One of the best recorded of these voyages is that of Captain Bruce in H.M.S. *Imogen* during 1837 and 1838. According to his report to the Admiralty, of which a copy exists amongst the Foreign Office papers,[21] Bruce sailed from Valparaiso with instructions to visit the Marquesas, the Sandwich Islands, the Societies and Pitcairn.

At the Marquesas his principal task was to ascertain that all was well with the missionaries. Reporting on the group generally,

[19] Leg. Council Decision and Bourke to Spring Rice, Dec. 6, 1834; both in Official Correspondence, cit, sup.

[20] E.g., the Port Regulations of the Samoan Islands; *Tahiti British Consulate Papers*; Misc., 1827-1842; Captain Bethune's note, Dec. 27, 1837.

[21] Bruce's Report to the Admiralty, encl. in Bruce to Backhouse, Dec. 17, 1839; F.O. 58/15. Cf. Captain Lord Edward Russell's voyage in H.M.S. *Actæon* in Russell to Hamond, Feb. 3, 1837; *Corr. rel. to the Society Islands, Part I*; Encl. 2 in No. 58.

Bruce declared that the natives were a "dissolute and depraved Race," not very amenable to missionary teaching. Though the missionaries had been well treated, Bruce thought that their work would be attended with greater success, if the islands were visited more often by British men-of-war.

At the Societies, where trade and navigation were fairly abundant by 1837, Bruce's duties were of a different character. He handed Pritchard his commission as consul and, with him, adjudicated in various disputes involving complaints against the native government. Bruce does not appear to have attached much significance to this type of work, although, as will be shown below, it was a matter in which some commanders had to be very active.

Bruce's visit to Pitcairn in December, 1837, was merely one of inspection. He found the Pitcairners themselves to be decent, well-behaved people, although English settlers amongst them had been guilty of *"deep, bad and disgraceful profligacy."* He recommended the removal of the Pitcairners to Toubouai (Tubuai in the Austral Group).[22]

Bruce was entrusted with a somewhat miscellaneous group of tasks and endowed with a wide range of discretion. While some of his work of inspection may have been of a purely routine character, his adjudication between British subjects and native rulers obviously raised complicated questions of policy.

What those questions of policy were may be readily explained by considering some specific instances of naval adjudication between British subject and native ruler. The best recorded instances of this type of work all occurred in Tahiti. British interests had been substantial in that island for years before the minimum intervention policy was adopted. Traders, missionaries and planters all frequented Tahiti and several other islands in the Societies.

Two examples of the work of naval commanders at Tahiti are those of the indemnity claimed by Lieutenant G. W. Cole and of the misappropriation of a wreck, the property of a Mr. Ebril (also given as Ebrill and Avril). Both complainants were British subjects and their cases are set out in detail in the official documents.[23]

The Cole case arose in 1832 from the plundering of Lieutenant Cole's schooner, the *Truro,* at Buckerow (Puka Ruha), one of the islands in the Dangerous Archipelago (the Tuamotus), by natives of the Chain Island (Anaa). Cole alleged that Pomare, the ruler of Tahiti, was to blame. Pomare had given out, declared Cole,

[22] Removal of the Pitcairners. See Chapter XV, below.
[23] *Corr. rel. to the Society Islands, Part I;* Nos. 30-35. Also F.O. 58/14.

that she would cut off all vessels visiting the Dangerous Archipelago without her permission, for which she proposed to demand 2,000 dollars. Cole sought restitution of his property (in the first instance) in the sum of 2,853 dollars, although the claim was re-stated subsequently to include further amounts.

The case was dealt with at the first stage by Charlton, the British Consul in the Pacific, and by Captain Seymour (H.M.S. *Challenger*), who brought Charlton from Hawaii to Tahiti and then assisted in the handling of the claim. Seymour and Charlton supported Cole and required Pomare to make the desired compensation and also to deliver up the offending natives for trial, if Great Britain should so wish. They justified their intervention, not only on the ground that justice had to be done by Cole, but also on the more general ground that Pomare had no right to restrict the intercourse of British vessels with the Dangerous Archipelago. The second ground was evidently thought to be of some special value in justifying British intervention in respect of the *Truro,* which was registered in the Sandwich Islands. Charlton particularly represented to the Home Government that action was necessary in the interests of all trade in the Societies. Unless a firm line were taken, he argued, unreasonable restrictions would continue to be imposed by the natives.

The Ebril case (also in 1832) arose from the purchase by the complainant of a wreck on the shore of one of Pomare's islands. The property was denied to Ebril by the natives who, he claimed, were under Pomare's jurisdiction. Once again coercive action against Pomare was justified on the ground that the natives had to be taught to respect European (especially British) property and trade. Ebril claimed that he acted, not only in order to recover his own property, but "for the better protection of any British or American property that may happen to be wrecked at this or any of the neighbouring islands." The case was handled first by Captain Fremantle (H.M.S. *Challenger*), who wrote to Pomare, stating the facts as alleged by Ebril and avowing his intention of protecting "British subjects and property, whenever it appears that such are improperly and illegally treated." The matter was adjusted for the time being through Fremantle's intervention.

The underlying policy in these cases was made clear in the memorandum left by Fremantle in 1832 for the commander of the next British ship of war to visit Tahiti. After recounting the various cases in which Pomare still had obligations to discharge, Fremantle wrote that:

"I am of the opinion that, if the Queen does not do her utmost to prevent the piracies that have lately taken place amongst the Low Islands that a man-of-war should visit them and apprehend the offenders, as I should fear that, if this last act of murder is not noticed, that every European vessel visiting the islands for the purposes of trade or otherwise would be seized and plundered as the natives are, I understand, of a very bad disposition."

What Fremantle and his fellow-officers really meant when they complained of the "very bad" disposition of the natives was simply that natives had little interest and less concern in European trade and European ideas of property. The task of inducing them to respect trade and property was discharged only partly by missionary teaching. For the rest, it fell mainly upon what influence the traders themselves could attain and on the work of men-of-war.

To naval officers visiting an island and investigating a complaint against the natives these wider issues did not appear. Having to obtain restitution or to inflict punishment in accordance with their own ideas of law and justice, the important problem for them was how to apportion responsibility for what had happened. With whom should they deal?[24]

Each of these questions received a delusively simple answer. The usual practice was to attach the legal blame and lay the responsibility for obtaining redress on the nearest considerable native ruler. Naval officers even went so far as to attribute to native rulers all the rights, powers and duties of a foreign sovereign in international law.

The conception was that a native authority could and should perform the same functions and adopt the same general codes of conduct as would a European Government, at least so far as British lives and property were concerned. The complexities arising from the clash of moral standards, the probability that native rulers did not have the powers ascribed to them, the fact that the principles of property and trade adopted by Europeans differed from those prevailing amongst the natives, were not taken into account. All the emphasis was laid on what naval commanders regarded as the only practicable course—requiring native rulers to accept responsibility in the European fashion for what happened around them. When they failed to do so, men-of-war would bring them to reason.

The *Truro* case, already cited, may have involved the mistake of attaching responsibility to the nearest considerable ruler, without enquiring whether that ruler had any power to prevent the crime

[24] See the case of Capt. Moreshead at Raiatea in 1856 when these questions were asked; *Tahiti British Consulate Papers* (Misc. 1843-1874).

complained of or to procure redress. According to a letter in the Foreign Office papers for 1835, marked as "Forwarded to Lord Palmerston by Mr. Fowell Buxton,"[25] Pomare could not possibly have known of the offence of which Cole complained. The island on which the offence was committed, stated the letter, was merely tributary to Pomare and was not part of her territory. Finally, British subjects were to blame for the whole incident, as they had offered the provocation. The plain implication of the despatch, that the *Truro* case was handled in ignorance throughout, is not discussed in the available Foreign Office papers.

Whether Pomare really had any authority in the Dangerous Archipelago was doubted.[26] It is important to note, however, that the attempt to sheet home responsibility to her for the *Truro* affair was not attended with immediate success. Whether from lack of authority, or lack of will, the Queen was slow in discharging the obligations laid upon her by the British Navy. The principal difficulty in the Cole (and also the Ebril) case was not in inducing the Queen to acknowledge her responsibilities in the presence of a man-of-war, but in ensuring that her promises were fulfilled after the man-of-war had departed. Thus in 1832 both Captain McMurdo (H.M.S. *Zebra*) and Captain Fremantle had occasion to draw the Queen's attention to promises unkept. McMurdo, like Fremantle, over-estimated the Queen's ability to implement her promises and attributed to unwillingness or bad faith what may have been in some cases the result of lack of authority. He had written to Pomare on leaving Tahiti in April, 1832, that:

"When another British ship of war calls here, the captain will enquire particularly of you, that he may know what you have done in this business."

Pomare had repeated her promises and very significantly requested British assistance in implementing them. When Fremantle arrived at Tahiti in December of the same year he found that the promises had not been kept and wrote to the Queen threatening to report the whole incident to the King of England.[27]

25 Jan. 31, 1835; F.O. 58/14. Available documents shed no light on this despatch.

26 That the islands were within her jurisdiction is implied in the letter, Pomare to the Captain of the Ship-of-War, Nov. 22, 1834; F.O. 58/14. It is so stated in Charlton to Canning, May 12, 1826; *Corr. rel. to the Society Islands, Part I.*

27 See also the comment of the missionaries, forwarded to Governor Gipps through the Rev. Dr. Ross in October, 1842, that the rulers of Tahiti had "been in the habit of promising everything to the Captains of Ships of War, and, as soon as they have left the Port, of performing nothing or as little as they could." (Gipps to Stanley, Dec. 8, 1842; *H.R.A.,* I, xxii, p. 398.)

From one point of view the excessive readiness of naval commanders to lay responsibility on native rulers was an aspect of another basic problem—the lack of information as to conditions in the islands. It can readily be understood that an officer paying a short visit to an island might be misled very easily concerning local conditions. Even where there were official British representatives on the island, these were usually too few in number and too isolated in position to be able to give adequate information to visiting naval commanders. There is a contemporary admission of this fact in the evidence given before the House of Lords Select Committee on New Zealand (1838) by Captain Fitzroy, R.N. In discussing the usefulness of naval visits to the islands, Fitzroy drew attention to obstacles arising from commanders' ignorance of local conditions.[28] Detailed investigation of cases, or even an attempt to lay blame exactly where it was due, was usually out of the question.

Naval commanders did sometimes enquire thoroughly into the cases laid before them—especially when the facts were contested, a condition which presupposed that the natives concerned were given a hearing. An interesting example of thorough enquiry, leading to the rejection of a complaint by a British resident, is afforded in the case of King, a British trader in the Bay of Islands. King alleged that a Maori chief, Pomare, had seized his schooner in execution of a debt, although the vessel had previously been sold to a third party. Busby, the British Resident, requested Captain Lambert (H.M.S. *Alligator*) to rescue the schooner. On the intervention of the missionaries, however, and on hearing Pomare's version of the facts, Lambert decided that the Maori had been completely justified in his action. The Rev. William Yate, who described the case in his evidence before the Aborigines Committee in 1836, summed the matter up this way:

"We found that Pomare was perfectly right, and the Englishmen had been altogether wrong; Pomare had been cheated out of the whole of his property; and so convinced was the captain of the *Alligator* that the New Zealander was right, that he gave him the full payment for the property which he had been cheated out of, and Pomare then restored the vessel which he had taken possession of as payment for it."[29]

The justice of the final decision in the King case is irrelevant here. What matters is the revelation of constant danger in naval

[28] *H. of L., Committee on N.Z., 1838;* p. 165.
[29] *Report from the S.C. on Aborigines (British Settlements), 1836;* Evidence, questions 1603-1607.

police work that British subjects would be able to present their side of the case unfairly to an officer, who himself would find it easier to act against natives than against his own countrymen and would possess few facilities for independent enquiry.

Sometimes ignorance of island conditions produced disaster to the Navy as well as injustice to the natives. A well-known instance is the case of Captain Croker's visit to Tongatabu in H.M.S. *Favorite*. Croker was induced by the Wesleyan missionaries to take up arms in order to reconcile warring native factions and to assist the missionary cause. Much bloodshed resulted. Croker himself was killed, the first lieutenant and a mate wounded, and twenty seamen were either killed or wounded.[30]

The Foreign Office itself perceived the danger that naval action, being so often directed against native rulers, might undermine the native authority, which, for the sake of minimum intervention, the British Government wished to sustain. If native rulers were continually being coerced by the Navy and if their affairs with Europeans were continually being taken out of their hands, their independence and prestige would be destroyed. In that case, the demand for British intervention in the islands would be strengthened considerably.[31]

Enlightened naval officers fully recognised the dangers of using naval patrols purely for the detection and punishment of offences. Erskine, one of the wisest of the officers stationed in the South Pacific during the nineteenth century, condemned much of the Navy's work in the islands and praised men like Captain Bethune, Captain Sir Everard Home and Captain Maxwell, who tried to perform constructive work and do more than visit offending natives with "peremptory menace or a show of force."[32]

So long as minimum intervention continued to be the main feature of British policy in the South Pacific, the chief responsibility for controlling British subjects clearly rested on the native chiefs, whose authority the British Government had strong reason to support, and whose sovereignty the British Government in some cases recognised. (See Chapter VIII, below.)

Naval commanders were able to exercise no effective control over British subjects. Except where warrants had been taken out in New South Wales or Van Diemen's Land against suspected

[30] Gipps to Russell, July 25, 1840; *H.R.A.*, I, xx, pp. 722-723.
[31] See F.O. to Admiralty, Oct. 4, 1842; *Extracts from PP. concerning the Society Islands, 1843*; No. 10.
[32] Erskine, op. cit., pp. 3-4.

offenders, the only sanction available to officers dealing with British subjects was to remove them from the islands they were harassing. This procedure was of doubtful legality, but, just as later in the century, was probably some inducement to good behaviour.

In evidence before the Lords Committee on New Zealand in 1838, Captain Fitzroy gave important evidence of the difficulties in the way of naval police work amongst British subjects. Asked how Pritchard, the British Consul in the Societies, maintained his authority, Fitzroy answered, "By making Complaints or Reports to British Ships of War when they come there from Time to Time." The evidence then reads thus:

Q. Do the Captains of Ships of War punish the Offenders when they they are pointed out?

A. No; there have been no urgent Occasions as yet; neither could they, I apprehend. It is only by the Influence of Office, by giving Advice, and by consulting with the Captain of a Ship of War, that the Consul can affect a person who has misconducted himself. The Consul or Captain might lecture him, but nothing further could be done except in the Case of a British Subject committing a Crime, or an Aggression against the Natives; and then the Captain of a Ship would be authorised to take him on board as a Prisoner (with the Consent of the Natives, if on shore, supposing they gave him up as a Prisoner) and carrying him to Sydney or Van Diemen's Land.

Q. Have Powers such as those been found sufficient to maintain Order with the Ships, Crews and Settlers?

A. Yes, tolerably.[33]

Despite all the difficulties in the way of naval action against British subjects, the visits of men-of-war were regarded as powerful agencies in sustaining the prestige of British representatives in the South Pacific. The British Resident stationed in New Zealand after 1833 was instructed to rely on the visits of men-of-war for the removal of convicts.[34] Pritchard in the Societies relied on men-of-war as the final arbiters in preserving law and order in the island, even in questions not within his jurisdiction at all. Thus after a murderous attack by foreigners on the United States Consul and his wife, Pritchard requested that a ship of war be sent to Tahiti, although the matter was not properly one for British intervention.[35] Pomare appealed to the Navy at the same time in an attempt to

[33] H. of L., Committee on N.Z., 1838; p. 344.
[34] Bourke to Busby, Apr. 13, 1833; encl. in Stephen to Backhouse, Dec. 12, 1838; Corr. rel. to N.Z., 1840; No. 1.
[35] Pritchard to Sullivan, June 23, 1838; F.O. 58/15.

have the disorderly foreigners removed and runaway sailors sent back to their own countries.[36]

The Navy also co-operated with British Consuls and Residents by providing almost their only reliable means of communication. Most despatches were sent by the Navy, which also did much to help consuls move around the various islands in their jurisdictions.[37] In these ways the Navy contributed to the solution of what is even to-day one of the most serious problems of administration in the South Pacific—that of distances, poor communications and inadequate means of travelling.

Intervention to assist British representatives in the islands became increasingly difficult with the entry of foreign Powers into the South Pacific. The Tahitian affair of 1842-1843 proved that the actions of isolated men-of-war were likely to produce serious diplomatic friction where other European Powers were concerned. Thus Captain Toup Nicolas of H.M.S. *Vindictive,* who proceeded to Tahiti early in 1843 contrary to orders so as to convey there the returning British Consul, behaved in a fashion highly embarrassing to the Foreign Office. So ignorant was Toup Nicolas of the official policy of his country towards the French intervention in Tahiti that he wrote to the Admiralty in September, 1843, after leaving Tahiti, in terms which clearly revealed his confident belief that Great Britain would protect Pomare and restrain France.[38] Toup Nicolas had adopted the Consul's views and supported him fully. The embarrassment in which his ignorance and good intentions involved the Foreign Office were referred to in a remonstrative despatch to the Admiralty in April, 1844:

". . . His Lordship directs me to request that you will convey to the Lords Commissioners of the Admiralty his sense of the inexpediency of the Commander of a British man-of-war taking upon himself, without express orders from his government, to prejudge the course which they may see fit to pursue, and in so doing to act in such a manner towards a Foreign Power as might induce or involve the two nations in hostilities."[39]

Fortunately, some other officers were more circumspect than Toup Nicolas and a few even earned the commendation of the Foreign Office for their diplomatic behaviour in circumstances of

[36] Pomare to the English Commodore, June 22, 1838; F.O. 58/15.
[37] After the appointment of William Miller as Consul-General for the Pacific in 1844, the Navy at the request of the Foreign Office placed a ship at his disposal. (F.O. to Miller, Sept. 29, 1843; F.O. 58/17. Wyllie to F.O., Nov. 5, 1844, F.O. 58/29, states that the ship was unseaworthy.)
[38] Toup Nicolas to Admiralty, Sept. 15, 1843; F.O. 58/23.
[39] Addington to Admiralty, Aug. 19, 1843; F.O. 58/23.

great difficulty. A notable case was that of Sir Thomas Thompson (H.M.S. *Talbot*) at Tahiti in 1843.[40]

It is obvious that the advent of foreigners supported by their own navies and officials also raised difficulties in the way of the police work of the Royal Navy. Where foreigners were involved, it was difficult to act with the sweeping disregard of the niceties of international law that might be displayed in cases where only natives or British subjects were concerned.[41] The coming of foreigners, by raising problems which men-of-war were not able to solve with any satisfaction to the British Government, hastened the next step in the breakdown of minimum intervention, that is, the appointment of British representatives in the islands. Naval support was necessary for these representatives, as has already been noted. But naval work alone could not have discharged the functions which the representatives were appointed to perform.

[40] Cf. Aberdeen to Rohan—Chabot, Aug. 18, 1843; *Corr. rel. to the Society Islands, Part I.*

[41] See Barrow to Hay, Mar. 24, 1832; encl. in Hay to Bourke, Mar. 26, 1832; *H.R.A.*, I, xvi, p. 573.

Chapter VIII

NATIVE SOVEREIGN STATES (1817-1844)

THE naval commanders who treated native rulers as foreign sovereigns did so as a matter of expediency, rather than of principle. Simultaneously the British Foreign Office was gradually evolving recognition of native sovereignty as a prime principle of policy in some of the islands. In answering appeals for British intervention in these islands, the Foreign Office declared that all such action was impossible because the islands were politically independent communities, or because they were sovereign states, in whose affairs Great Britain was not legally competent to intervene.

The foundation of this reliance on recognition of native sovereignty was the desire to avoid intervention. Native rulers, whose authority had been undermined by the advent of Europeans unamenable to native law and disruptive of native society, found that naval visits did little to solve their new problems. They appealed to Great Britain for intervention. In New Zealand appeals also emanated from Europeans, who were aghast at the growth of disorder and crime to proportions which made trade a perilous business. These appeals constituted an unwelcome and frequent challenge to the minimum intervention policy. The British Government itself had no wish to intervene in island affairs on behalf of hard-pressed native rulers. Still less did it wish to accept colonial responsibilities there. Missionary influence and all the vehemence of the humanitarian school of anti-colonialists weighed heavily against any ready response to requests for intervention in the distant and unpromising islands of the South Pacific. The readiest solution to the problem was found in the formula of recognition of native independence and even sovereignty.

The Acts of 1817, 1823 and 1828 had left the British recognition of native sovereignty an open question. Though it was made clear that Great Britain claimed no title to the islands, nothing was stated as to the degree of recognition accorded to their rulers.

The first unambiguous recognition of native sovereignty, as

distinct from recognition of the independence of island territory, came in 1827. In that year the Foreign Office, replying to an unwelcome request for British protection of Tahiti and for permission to use the British flag, corresponded with Pomare of Tahiti in terms which implied that Tahiti was recognised as a foreign sovereign state under the rule of Pomare.[1]

In succeeding years there were several acts amounting in the aggregate to recognition of Tahitian sovereignty. The acts referred to occurred in dealings between Great Britain and Tahiti, and in communications between Great Britain and France.[2] There were also significant communications between British Departments of State.

In 1837 the British Government accredited its first Consul in Tahiti to Pomare.[3] As the Consul's functions were diplomatic as much as consular in the ordinary sense of the term, the act of accreditation probably provided some evidence of recognition of sovereignty. Two years later the Colonial Office advised the Foreign Office that no "offer of sovereignty" should be accepted from Tahiti which was seeking British assistance in government.[4] No question was raised as to the capacity of the Queen of Tahiti to make an offer of sovereignty. In 1843, when Great Britain was being urged to intervene in Tahiti to restrain the aggression of France, the British Foreign Secretary informed the French Ambassador in London that the British Government approved the act of Sir Thomas Thompson, R.N., in saluting the independent flag of Tahiti and declining to salute the new French flag of the Tahitian protectorate.[5] The British Ambassador in Paris reported to the Foreign Office in 1844 that the French Cabinet had declined to deprive Pomare of her sovereignty.[6] Despatches written from the Foreign Office in 1843 clearly imply that Pomare was deemed capable of ceding sovereignty to France.[7] Throughout the period of French aggression in Tahiti, the British Government emphasised its recognition of Tahitian sovereignty, partly to justify its own non-intervention, partly to put a brake on French activity.[8]

[1] Canning to Pomare, Mar. 3, 1827; F.O. 58/14.
[2] Not all the acts of recognition relied on are cited here. They are numerous, most occurring at the time of the French aggression in Tahiti. See *Corr. rel. to t'e Society Islands, Part 1.*
[3] Palmerston to Pomare, Feb. 14, 1837; F.O. 58/15.
[4] Stephen to Fox Strangways, Aug. 1, 1839; *Corr. rel. to the Society Islands, Part 1*; No. 70.
[5] Aberdeen to Rohan-Chabot, Aug. 18, 1843; ibid, No. 121.
[6] Cowley to Aberdeen, Feb. 26, 1844; ibid No. 154.
[7] E.g., Aberdeen to Pritchard, Sept. 25, 1843; *Extracts from PP. concerning the Society Islands, 1843*; No. 130.
[8] See Chapter XII, below.

Evidence concerning the recognition of native sovereignty in Tahiti is specially important as an indication of general policy. Tahiti was one of the islands to which Great Britain might be held to have established some legal claim. The explorer, Wallis, had hoisted the British flag there in 1767. Governors King and Macquarie had established administration of a kind there by appointing Justices of the Peace. Even admitting that these acts constituted no valid claim in international law and were none of them confirmed by the British Government, it is perhaps arguable that in the conditions of the time and place, the acts might have been avowed and been made the basis of a territorial claim.

Recognition of native sovereignty was also forthcoming in the case of New Zealand. Here, too, Great Britain had established claims in the eighteenth century. Acting under his Additional Secret Instructions, Cook had taken possession at Mercury Bay in November, 1769, and at Queen Charlotte Sound in January, 1770. It is doubtful just what possession Cook intended to take. It seems clear that he had no intention of taking possession of New Zealand as a whole. Comparison of his reports with his instructions lends weight to the view that he intended to take possession of no more than "convenient situations."[9]

Governor Macquarie, if he considered the legal aspect at all, must have held the view that British sovereignty had been established in New Zealand, because he declared New Zealand to be a dependency of New South Wales and appointed a magistrate there in 1814.[10] But his view, which was based on a liberal interpretation of his own commission rather than on fine points of law concerning sovereignty, was never supported by the British Government. Official British policy recognised that any claims arising from Cook's actions had become obsolete through failure to establish administration in New Zealand.[11]

Macquarie's view was adopted by Bigge (or shared by him). Bigge recommended the appointment of further British magistrates in New Zealand.[12] The recommendation was not implemented and both in 1831 and 1838 the legal authorities of New South Wales ruled that the Governor had no power to appoint magistrates

9 Cf. T. L. Buick: *Sovereignty in New Zealand* (typescript in Mitchell Library, Sydney); pp. 9 ff.

10 See above, Ch. IV.

11 Later, however, Hobson, in proclaiming British sovereignty over New Zealand took possession of South Island by right of discovery. See below, Ch. X.

12 Bigge to Bathurst, Feb. 27, 1823; *H.R.N.Z.*, I, p. 594.

in New Zealand, which was in no sense a dependency of New South Wales.[13]

The development of British policy towards sovereignty in New Zealand was discussed systematically in a Colonial Office memorandum of 1839, which, however, treated some inconclusive acts as evidence of recognition.[14] The memorandum, which was addressed to the Foreign Office and drawn up by Sir James Stephen, an advocate of the native sovereignty doctrine, pointed out that the Acts of 1817, 1823 and 1828 had all treated New Zealand as independent of Great Britain. The additional step of recognising New Zealand as "a substantive, independent state," whose sovereignty was vested in the Maori chiefs, was taken, argued Stephen, in 1832 when William IV in replying to a petition from thirteen of the chiefs referred to their "friendship and alliance with Great Britain." The petition had requested British protection and intervention. In answer the Colonial Office expressed regrets for injuries suffered by the natives and made it clear that official British intervention in New Zealand would be confined to the appointment of a Resident. When a Resident was sent out his instructions treated the chiefs as foreign sovereigns and he was accredited to them.[15] A little later Lord Howick's Bill for the prevention of crimes committed by British subjects "in New Zealand and in other islands in the Pacific, not being within His Majesty's Dominions," was rejected on the ground that Parliament could not legislate for foreign states.

In New Zealand itself there had been formal recognition of sovereignty. Owing to the growth of unregistered shipping based on New Zealand, the British Resident, Busby, induced the chiefs to adopt a flag under which such ships could sail. On a flag being chosen, it was hoisted alongside the English flag and saluted with 21 guns by H.M.S. *Alligator*. Stephen regarded this act, which had been approved by the Foreign Office, as legally conclusive.

In 1835 the British Resident again took steps to have the native chiefs assert their own sovereignty in New Zealand. Having been advised that the French adventurer, the Baron de Thierry, was coming to New Zealand to establish a "sovereign government," Busby assembled thirty-five of the principal chiefs of the North

[13] A.G. to Col. Sec., encl. in Bourke to Goderich, Dec. 23, 1831; *H.R.A.*, I, xvi, p. 486.

[14] Encl. in No. 38; *Corr. rel. to N.Z. 1840*. It is difficult to avoid the conclusion that some of the acts mentioned by Stephen were not conclusive recognition of sovereignty. But Stephen's Memorandum was accepted and the recognition of native sovereignty in New Zealand became a key point in British policy.

[15] *Corr. rel. to N.Z., 1840*; Encls. in No. 1.

Island and had them declare New Zealand an independent state, under the designation of the United Tribes of New Zealand:

> "All Sovereign power and authority within the territories of the United Tribes of New Zealand is hereby declared to reside entirely and exclusively in the Hereditary Chiefs and Heads of Tribes in their collective capacity."[16]

Although the declaration was later derided in New South Wales as a mere "paper pellet fired off at the Baron de Thierry," the British Government supported Busby's action.[17] Governor Bourke also gave it his commendation as a desirable "approach" to a regular form of government.[18] Stephen accepted the Declaration at face value and interpreted "sovereign power" as a precise legal phrase.

Throughout the succeeding years when projects of colonisation in New Zealand were being actively debated and there was constant demand for British intervention, the British Government never swerved from the fullest recognition of the sovereignty of the native chiefs. Intervention without a specific request from the chiefs was officially regarded as legally impossible. "Great Britain," wrote Lord Glenelg at the Colonial Office to Lord Durham of the New Zealand Association, "has no legal or moral right to establish a colony in New Zealand without the free consent of the natives, deliberately given without compulsion and without fraud."[19] The same principle appears over and over again in the official papers.

Doubts as to the means by which sovereignty could be transferred to Great Britain appeared again when the British Government finally resolved to seek the cession of New Zealand. Sovereignty in New Zealand, it was then pointed out, resided in a "people composed of numerous, dispersed and petty tribes, who possess few political relations to each other, and are incompetent to act, or even to deliberate in concert."[20] Subsequently, when Hobson, who had been sent out as Consul to obtain the cession and later became Lieutenant-Governor, suggested that the natives of the South Island were too backward to sign a treaty with understanding, he was instructed to consult with the Governor of New South Wales and to use his own discretion.[21]

16 Bourke to Glenelg, Mar. 10, 1836; *H.R.A.*, I, xviii, pp. 352 ff.
17 Glenelg to Bourke, Aug. 26, 1836; *H.R.A.*, I, xviii, p. 506.
18 Cf. E. Ramsden: *Busby of Waitangi*; Wellington, 1942; p. 98.
19 Harrop, op. cit., p. 26.
20 Normanby to Hobson, Aug. 14, 1839; *Corr. rel to N.Z., 1840.*
21 Hobson to C.O., Aug., 1839, and Normanby to Hobson, Aug. 15, 1839; ibid. Nos. 17 and 18.

Hobson arrived at the Bay of Islands in February, 1840. Within nine days he had signed the desired treaty (the Treaty of Waitangi) with the chiefs living round Hokianga in the north-west of North Island. Sovereignty was ceded by the first Article of the treaty:

"The chiefs of the Confederation of the United Tribes of New Zealand, and the separate and independent chiefs who have not become members of the Confederation, cede to Her Majesty the Queen of England absolutely and without reservation all the rights and powers of sovereignty which the said Confederation or individual chiefs respectively exercise or possess, or may be supposed to exercise or possess over their territories as sole sovereigns thereof."[22]

After the signatures of other chiefs in North Island had been obtained, British sovereignty over that island was proclaimed by right of cession on May 21st, 1840.

In the North Island Hobson's proceedings had been based on the principle that sovereignty resided in the native chiefs and could be transferred by them. In the case of South Island and Stewart's Island, however, British sovereignty was proclaimed on May 21st by right of discovery, although a mission had been sent under Major Bunbury to obtain signatures from the chiefs. The reason for this action was that the independent settlers under the New Zealand Company at Port Nicholson had already attempted to establish a government of their own. Hobson considered the situation urgent enough to warrant his making a proclamation of sovereignty without waiting for the return of Bunbury.

From a legal point of view declaration of sovereignty by right of discovery over seventy years earlier was a mere nullity. Moreover, as British recognition of New Zealand sovereignty had never been confined by express words to North Island,[23] the claim of title by right of discovery to South Island was completely inconsistent with previous British decisions. Finally, the argument by which Hobson attempted to justify his action, that the natives of South and Stewart's Islands were too barbarous to be parties to a treaty, was severely shaken by Bunbury's report, not received till June 28th, that their intelligence had been greatly underrated.[24]

The plain fact is that Hobson's actions in connection with the acquisition of South Island and Stewart's Island were contrary to

[22] *Despatches from the Governor of N.S.W., rel to N.Z., 1840*; Encl. 3 in No. 4.

[23] But the 1835 Declaration of Independence had been confined to "the Northern Parts of N.Z." See *H. of L. Cttee. on N.Z., 1838*; p. 179.

[24] Gipps to Russell, Oct. 18, 1840; qu. Marais, op. cit., p. 99 (n. 2) from C.O. 209/6.

established British policy (though impliedly sanctioned by the Colonial Office), of doubtful validity in international law and inconsistent with his own policy in North Island. In the circumstances Stephen's comment on a despatch from Hobson reporting the signature of the Treaty of Waitangi has a certain irony:

"It seems to me to prove, if proof were wanting, how much wiser was the course taken of negotiating for a cession of the sovereignty than would have been the course of relying on the proceedings of Captain Cook or the language of Vattel in opposition to our own statute book."[25]

The true conclusion to draw in respect of the acquisition of New Zealand is that the British authorities were prepared to abandon the recognition of native sovereignty in very much the same spirit as that in which they had taken the principle up. Native sovereignty was originally recognised, not because of belief in native right, still less because the native governments were thought to be capable of performing the functions of sovereign states in international law, but rather, because the doctrine of native sovereignty helped to make the policy of minimum intervention workable. So soon as native sovereignty impeded the main objectives of British policy, it was promptly shelved. The *Monthly Chronicle* summed the matter up aptly when it declared that:

"In the case of New Zealand it would be a very ridiculous piece of international etiquette, which would make our government hesitate about appropriating a remote island for the national advantage, while they suffer a company of gentlemen to appropriate it for themselves."[26]

To that there seems nothing to add.[27]

[25] Qu. Harrop, op. cit., p. 142. For the contrary view, see *The Australian,* Aug. 13, 1840.

[26] August, 1839; Vol. IV, No. xviii.

[27] There was never any general recognition of island sovereignty. Only Tahiti, New Zealand and Fiji provide clear instances of recognition before the period of the treaties commencing in the late 'seventies. As to recognition of sovereignty in Tonga and Samoa, see below, Chapters XX, XXIV et seq.

Chapter IX

CONSULS AND REPRESENTATIVES

Even in the early years of the minimum intervention policy some problems arose in the islands which Great Britain could not leave in the hands of naval officers and native rulers. In islands where British subjects and other white men settled in large numbers naval justice was clearly inappropriate. Nor could the native rulers alone handle the social and political problems arising from the presence of hundreds of Europeans in the native societies.

The British Government had either to intervene in the government of these islands or to find some means (short of political intervention) by which the burden on the native rulers might be relieved. The latter course, in the form of the appointment of British consuls and representatives, was adopted without exception up to the acquisition of New Zealand in 1840. The appointment of British consuls and representatives in the islands was, of course, fully consistent with recognition of native sovereignty and fitted in well with the work of the Navy.

The conditions in which naval visits alone sufficed to represent Great Britain disappeared first in Hawaii. On the recommendation of the Admiralty and of the Board of Trade, Canning in 1824 appointed Captain Charlton to be British Consul for the Sandwich Islands. The Society Islands and the Friendly Islands were also included in his commission.[1] Charlton's main work was to be in the Sandwich Islands and he was empowered to appoint Vice-Consuls or consular agents in the other groups, should actual representation there ever become necessary.[2] Charlton exercised his jurisdiction outside the Sandwich Islands only rarely. In practice his work was not an instance of British representation in the South Pacific.[3]

Up to 1844 only three British officials were appointed to reside in the South Pacific islands. James Busby was appointed in 1832

[1] F.O. Memorandum, Nov. 31, 1829; F.O. 58/14.
[2] ibid.
[3] For missionary criticisms of Charlton, see Missionaries at Tahiti to L.M.S., Dec. 15, 1826; *Corr. rel. to Society Islands, Part I*; encl. in No. 22.

as British Resident in New Zealand,[4] and established himself at the Bay of Islands. Thomas McDonnell was appointed two years later as additional British Resident in New Zealand with head-quarters at Hokianga.[5] The Rev. George Pritchard, a missionary, was appointed British Consul to the Society Islands,[6] the Friendly Islands and the Navigators (Samoa) in 1837.[7]

There was an earlier appointment in 1827 of a Vice-Consul, Thomas Elley, to the Society Islands. This appointment was made by Charlton under the powers granted to him in his commission.[8] Elley's appointment, however, was not confirmed by the Foreign Office[9] and lapsed when he himself was compelled by disorders on Tahiti to flee to Huahine.[10] Like Charlton's own appointment that of Elley was not in any important sense an instance of British representation in the South Pacific.

The same conclusion is to be reached concerning Captain Hobson's appointment as Consul in New Zealand. By its nature, Hobson's appointment as Consul was merged in his appointment as first Lieutenant-Governor of New Zealand and cannot be regarded as an instance of representation policy.[11]

The only relevant appointments of the early period are those of Busby, McDonnell and Pritchard.

REPRESENTATION IN NEW ZEALAND

The appointment of a British Resident in New Zealand was first mooted in New South Wales. Traders from the colony resented the wild disorder prevailing in the most frequented commercial regions of New Zealand. The missionaries, certainly the most reliable observers of conditions in New Zealand, had their complaints voiced for them in New South Wales by the Rev. Samuel Marsden. Continual reports of atrocities and of outrageous conduct by irresponsible whites were received in New South Wales.

Even apart from the problem of disorder, the growth of trade between New South Wales and New Zealand necessitated some regulation. In 1830 twenty-eight different vessels, averaging about

[4] See page 82, below.
[5] H.R.A., I, xvii, pp. 472-473; and see page 89, below.
[6] Including the Georgian Islands.
[7] See pp. 92 ff, below.
[8] Charlton to Byng, Dec. 30, 1829; Elley to Palmerston, Aug. 13, 1831; F.O. 58/14.
[9] ibid.
[10] Charlton to Canning, March 1, 1827; Elley to Canning, Mar. 29, 1827; Corr. rel. to the Society Islands, Part I; Nos. 15 and 24.
[11] See Chapter X, below.

110 tons each, made the voyage across the Tasman. Of 78 vessels clearing from Sydney for "Foreign States, South Sea Islands and Fisheries" in the same year, 56 were for New Zealand; of 64 vessels reported as arrived from the same places 46 were from New Zealand.[12] Australian merchants strongly favoured the establishment of some British authority in New Zealand by which trade, commerce and property might be protected.[13]

Taken together with the mounting record of violence, the increase of New Zealand commerce based on New South Wales provided a strong argument for British intervention. In 1830 Governor Darling of New South Wales forwarded to the Colonial Office a letter from Rev. Samuel Marsden in which the deplorable condition of New Zealand affairs was described. Darling recommended that a man-of-war be stationed in New Zealand waters.[14] In this despatch he also mentioned the possibility of the appointment of a British Resident in New Zealand. After examining the terrible record of the *Elizabeth* at Banks Peninsula, Darling advised the Colonial Office that it would be necessary to have a British Resident in New Zealand in addition to stationing a man-of-war off the coast.[15]

Before any action was taken to remedy the dreadful state of affairs in New Zealand Governor Darling was succeeded by Governor Bourke. The new Governor fully agreed with his predecessor, both as to the need for action and as to the desirability of action emanating from New South Wales.

"Finding upon my arrival," he wrote to the Colonial Office in 1831, "that Considerable anxiety was expressed by the Merchants of this place that the intercourse with New Zealand should be placed upon a better footing, I brought the matter under the Notice of the Executive Council on the 22d instant, proposing to place a Resident in New Zealand, with one of the Colonial Vessels under his orders for the purpose of protecting and promoting Commerce and effecting the apprehension of fugitive Convicts, of whom many are said to be lurking in New Zealand, and taking a principal Share in the atrocities Committed there."[16]

Bourke emphasised that existing naval visits to New Zealand were quite inadequate to maintain order. "I should state," he

[12] J. Busby: *Authentic Information rel. to N.S.W. and N.Z.*; London, 1832; p. 59.

[13] *The Australian*, July 1, 1834; p. 2.

[14] Darling to Murray, Aug. 12, 1830; H.R.A., I, xv, p. 702.

[15] Darling to Goderich, Apr. 13, 1831; H.R.A., I, xvi, p. 240. For *Elizabeth* case, see above, Chapter VI.

[16] Bourke to Goderich, Dec. 23, 1831; H.R.A., I, xvi, pp. 482-483.

reported, "that the annual visit of a British Cruiser for a few days does not add in any perceptible degree to the Security of the Trade or the prevention of Crime."

Three months later Goderich sanctioned the appointment of a Resident and nominated James Busby for the post.[17] The objects of the appointment, which closely resembled the work usually performed by the Navy, were described by the Colonial Office as the protection of British trade, the prevention of outrages involving British subjects and the apprehension of escaped convicts.[18] Like the work of the Navy, the work of the Resident was expected to protect and control British subjects without necessitating political intervention by the British Government.

Busby was appointed as British Resident in New Zealand under the orders of the Governor of New South Wales, and not as Consul or Vice-Consul under the orders of the Foreign Office. The reason for placing him under New South Wales authority seems to have been that the main British interest in New Zealand flowed, not from Great Britain, but from New South Wales. The escaped convicts and the traders from the Australian colonies had made British action in New Zealand necessary The suggestion for the appointment of a Resident had emanated from New South Wales. The New South Wales authorities had an interest in New Zealand and a knowledge of conditions there much greater than those possessed by the Foreign Office. As a result of these factors, the Resident was placed under the immediate supervision of the Governor of New South Wales. Even his instructions were drawn up by the Governor and his salary of £500 per annum was ordered by Goderich to be paid from New South Wales funds.[19]

Busby's appointment was made on a basis fully consistent with the legal aspects of the existing form of minimum intervention. Accordingly he could not be granted magisterial powers. A magistrate's jurisdiction is territorial merely. Hence it was impossible to appoint Busby a Justice of the Peace in New Zealand, the sovereignty of whose chiefs was fully recognised. (The remark in *The Australian* that "Mr. Borer Busby Junior" had been made a justice of the peace in New Zealand for "some fresh humbug or other" was as inaccurate as it was spiteful.)[20]

17 Goderich to Bourke. Mar. 18, 1832; H.R.A., I, xvi, pp. 562-3. For reasons for choice of Busby see A. B. Chappell: *James Busby, &c.* (Austrln & N.Z. Assocn. for Adv. of Science, Auckland, 1937), p. 11; also E. Ramsden: *Busby of Waitangi*; Wellington, 1942; Ch. I.

18 Cf. Hay to Bourke, Jan. 21, 1832; H.R.A., I, xvi, p. 505.

19 Goderich to Bourke, Mar. 18, 1832; H.R.A., I, xvi, p. 563.

20 *The Australian* constantly opposed Busby's appointment, although later it supported the Resident principle.

The impossibility of investing the Resident with legal powers had been realised even in 1831 when the Resident system was being discussed in New South Wales. In commenting on the Governor's plan to send a Resident to New Zealand, the Attorney-General of New South Wales then pointed out that, as New Zealand was not a "dependency of this colony," no magistrate could be appointed there. The Attorney-General declared that the Act, 9 Geo. IV, c. 83, which conferred on New South Wales courts jurisdiction to try offences committed by British subjects in New Zealand, gave no power to establish administrative or judicial process in New Zealand.[21] The Attorney-General's opinion went on to state, however, that the Resident could arrest British subjects in New Zealand for crimes committed there by them, provided that information had been sworn against them in New South Wales. The Resident could also arrest escaped convicts. (It is submitted that the Attorney-General's opinion as to the Resident's power of arrest was mistaken and inconsistent with recognition of the sovereignty of the chiefs.)

The Colonial Office had also noticed the impossibility of granting the Resident adequate powers so long as the existing form of minimum intervention continued. In a despatch of January, 1832, Goderich mentioned that because of the lack of adequate legal institutions in New Zealand, many of the Resident's acts might have to exceed what would normally be regarded as legal and therefore need to be justified on grounds of necessity rather than of law. He considered that an indemnity provision might be needed to cover acts done "with upright intention and becoming circumspection."[22]

Because of the legal difficulties, Busby's instructions included these extraordinary words:

> "You are aware that you cannot be clothed with any legal power or jurisdiction, by virtue of which you might be enabled to arrest British subjects offending against British or Colonial law in New Zealand."[23]

Busby was instructed to resort to New South Wales for bench warrants against offenders. Bourke frankly added that:

[21] A.G. of N.S.W. to the Col. Sec. (N.S.W.), encl. in Bourke to Goderich, Dec. 23, 1831; *H.R.A.*, I, xvi, p. 486.

[22] Goderich to Bourke, Jan. 31, 1832; *H.R.A.*, I, xvi, p. 512.

[23] Busby's Instructions (Bourke to Busby, Apr. 13, 1833); encl. in Stephen to Backhouse, Dec. 12, 1838; *Corr. rel. to N.Z., 1840*; No. 1. See also Goderich to Bourke, June 14, 1832; *H.R.A.*, I, xvi, p. 662.

"This process, which is at best a prolix and inconvenient operation and may incur some considerable expense, will be totally useless unless you should have some well founded expectation of securing the offender upon or after arrival of the warrant, and of being able to effect his conveyance here for trial, and that you have provided the necessary evidence to secure his conviction."[24]

The position of the Resident was worsened by the fact that no troops could be provided for his protection. The New Zealand chiefs, being regarded as sovereigns, were not asked to receive a Resident backed by troops. There is some evidence that troops might have been sent, had the chiefs been favourable, but no attempt to consult them seems to have been made.[25] As Bourke wrote to Spring Rice in 1835, the Resident was to rely "on the influence he could obtain over the Native Chiefs."[26]

A more fantastic situation than that which ultimately developed could hardly be imagined. The chiefs who had petitioned Great Britain for protection and had been informed that the proposed British Resident would guard their interests[27] were asked by Busby on his arrival for their assistance and support. His request was in accordance with his instructions.[28] Any lingering doubts that the chiefs might have entertained as to Busby's powers should have been removed by the extraordinary language of a letter to them from Goderich, in which the Secretary of State referred in only conditional terms to the prospect of preserving law and order. British offenders in New Zealand were to be punished "whenever they can be apprehended and brought to trial." The chiefs were also informed that Busby would "endeavour to prevent" the arrival of convicts.[29]

The British thought it sufficient that Busby should be sent to New Zealand without either legal authority or armed support (beyond a promise of visits by men-of-war). But the practical needs of the situation required that he should be entrusted with a wide and varied range of responsibility. In the instructions drawn up by Bourke and approved by the Colonial Office eight main duties were laid down:

(1) To investigate all complaints involving British subjects.
(2) To prevent the arrival of convicts.

24 Busby's Instructions, loc. cit.
25 Goderich to Bourke, Mar. 18, 1832; *H.R.A.*, I, xvi, p. 563.
26 Bourke to Spring Rice, Feb. 1, 1835; *H.R.A.*, I, xvii, p. 645.
27 Goderich to Chiefs, June 14, 1832; *Corr. rel. to N.Z., 1840*; Encl. 4 in No. 1.
28 loc. cit. (n. 23 above).
29 Goderich to Chiefs, cit. sup.

(3) To apprehend escaped convicts and send them back for trial and punishment, taking care that no free men were apprehended in error, as an action for damages would probably follow.
(4) To give reputable settlers general assistance.
(5) To encourage trade.
(6) To supply the Government of New South Wales with statistics as to crops and shipping.
(7) To obtain the goodwill of the native chiefs, using the natural ascendancy of "an educated man over wild or half-civilised savages"; to secure the authority of the chiefs on the side of law and order.
(8) To keep on good terms with the missionaries, who in turn were requested to give the Resident their support.

The inadequacy of the Resident's powers to accomplish even one of these duties was obvious right from the first. Busby appears to have accepted office in the belief that an Act of Parliament would increase his authority.[30] There was no legal reason why such an Act could not have been passed, as is shown by the history of the Foreign Jurisdiction Acts later in the century. Busby could have been given power over British subjects in New Zealand without any breach of international law. If questions over the sovereignty of the chiefs had arisen, treaties of extra-territoriality could have been signed, just as they were with Tonga and Samoa in 1879. What militated against the passage of an Act giving Busby large powers was the minimum intervention policy, not any difficulty in international law. Rather than pass an Act giving the Resident extra-territorial jurisdiction in New Zealand, the British Government preferred to leave him nearly powerless and to justify inaction on such grounds as the necessity of not invading the sovereignty of the chiefs and the impossibility of legislating for a foreign sovereign territory.

Busby was left to rely on the assistance of the missionaries (who were powerful), on the goodwill of the chiefs (if it could be maintained) and on the visits of men-of-war (which were infrequent).[31] The main facts are clear; jealous adherence to minimum intervention led to the appointment of a Resident with inadequate powers; moreover, the failure of the Resident was recognised very early.

Busby went to New Zealand in April, 1833. In September, 1834,

[30] See Bourke to Spring Rice, Feb. 1, 1835; *H.R.A.*, I, xvii, p. 645.
[31] As to Busby's views on the powers required see his *Brief Memoir Relative to the Islands of New Zealand* (suggesting that the Resident be a magistrate) and his *Authentic Information rel. to N.S.W. and N.Z.* (suggesting effective British administration in New Zealand). His opinions in the lecture *Colonies and Colonisation* show some modification of these views. (See bibliography on all these works.)

Governor Bourke sent a strongly worded despatch to Lord Stanley, intimating that, unless a ship of war could be "permanently stationed in these Seas," the Resident should be withdrawn and "British nationals in New Zealand informed that they were without protection."[32] In February, 1835, the official New South Wales view was again made clear when Bourke declared in a despatch to the Colonial office that "the Resident had failed to obtain any considerable degree of respect among the New Zealanders."[33] Bourke attributed the Resident's failure to the lack of military forces, inadequate legal powers and the infrequency of naval visits.

White residents in New Zealand also took the view that the Resident had failed. Nine British residents there wrote to Busby in 1834 after an attack on his home, calling upon him to sustain the character of his office, relying, if necessary, on the assistance of respectable Europeans.[34] *The Australian* published in July, 1834, the comments of "A Looker On" who declared that Busby was both unwilling and unable to control the crews of vessels touching at New Zealand, and that he regarded his duty as the protection of natives against whites rather than the safeguarding of European interests from native depredations.[35]

Busby himself was disappointed with his position and in May, 1836, wrote to Bourke stating that he considered his office to be in abeyance and requesting permission to proceed to Great Britain to lay the case of New Zealand before Parliament. Bourke regarded this letter as presumptuous. In a memorandum of August 21st, 1836, he sternly rebuked the Resident (with whom his personal relations were not good) and instructed him to remain at his post.[36]

The Colonial Office itself had to recognise in 1835 the failure of the Resident system (although some aspects of Busby's work were subsequently praised).[37] Glenelg wrote to Bourke in October, 1835, stating that Busby had not succeeded in the task to which he had been assigned. "The consequence," declared Glenelg, "is that the lives and properties of British Subjects, including even the Resident himself, are in a state of the utmost insecurity."

Despite the repeated evidence of failure and the aspersions cast on the capacity of the Resident, the British Government was slow to remedy the position. The year after he recognised the failure

32 Bourke to Stanley, Sept. 23, 1834; H.R.A., I, xvii, p. 545.
33 Bourke to Spring Rice, Feb. 1, 1835; H.R.A., I, xvii, p. 645.
34 *The Australian*, July 1, 1834. (Letter dated May 6, 1834.)
35 ibid.
36 E. Ramsden, op. cit., pp. 151-2.
37 Glenelg to Bourke, Oct. 28, 1835; H.R.A., I, xviii, p. 171. For praise of Busby see Ch. VIII, above.

of the appointment, Glenelg was still toying with the possibility of remedial legislation to patch up the representation policy sufficiently to escape the necessity of British intervention.[38]

The reason for governmental inaction was officially alleged to be that, legally speaking, the possibilities of British action in New Zealand had already been exhausted unless the whole policy of minimum intervention were sacrificed. No Resident sent out under the minimum intervention policy could have been given greater powers than those which Busby had in fact received.[39] To have remedied the position of the Resident, Great Britain would have had to change fundamental policy. Political responsibility might have had to be accepted. The recognition of native sovereignty would have had to be abandoned, or at least invaded; for example, an Act on the lines of the later Foreign Jurisdiction Acts might have been passed.

These facts were made plain in the recommendation of the Select Committee on Aborigines (British Settlements), which suggested the establishment of British extra-territoriality in New Zealand. The Committee's view was that the only practicable course lay in the appointment of several consuls endowed with the same judicial and executive authority as that possessed by British Consuls in the Barbary States (i.e., with "a judicial authority to arrest, commit for trial, and try all British subjects committing offences within the limits of the consul's commission").[40] Such appointments would have necessitated the conclusion of treaties with native rulers whose sovereignty Great Britain had recognised.

The various suggestions made by the missionaries, who strongly opposed British intervention, to establish a government in New Zealand and sought some improvement in the Resident's position, all involved the idea of some form of extra-territoriality. The missionaries wished that the natives should continue to be ruled by their own chiefs (under missionary influence sometimes) and that the British Resident, with native assistance, should control British subjects. The missionary attitude was compounded of desire to preserve their own influence on the chiefs, of genuine fear of the evil results of colonisation and of alarm at the turbulent state of affairs in New Zealand.

[38] Glenelg to Bourke, Aug. 26, 1836; H.R.A., I, xviii, p. 506.

[39] Cf. Goderich's comment in 1832, that "H.M. Government will be acquitted of the reproach of an acquiescence in crime, which they will have done the utmost in their power to prevent." (Goderich to Bourke, June 14, 1832; H.R.A., I, xvi, p. 663.)

[40] *Report of the Parlt. S.C. on Aboriginal Tribes (British Settlements)*, 1837; repr. with comments by the Aborigines Protection Society; London, 1837; pp. 129-130.

In evidence before the Select Committee on the Aborigines the missionaries advocated an increase in Busby's powers and authority. The Rev. W. Yate, for example, considered that, even with defective powers, the principle of Busby's appointment had been vindicated. Yate testified that one British Resident in New Zealand was enough and added that, although the natives would resist any attempt to take possession of their country, they would co-operate with a British representative endowed with the authority of a "consul or minister" or "something of the kind."[41]

Mr. Trapp, who coined the famous phrase describing Busby as a "man-of-war without guns," wished the Resident to have the assistance of a small naval force and military detachment. Only with such forces, considered Trapp, could the Resident be expected to control Europeans.[42]

The most intelligent of the missionary evidence given to the Committee was that of Dandeson Coates, the vigorous Lay Secretary of the Church Missionary Society. Coates approved the principle of appointing a British representative in New Zealand, but pressed for the conferring of greater powers on the Resident and for the more frequent visits of men-of-war. "Without some further legislative authority given to the governor of New South Wales to deal with parties committing crimes in New Zealand and elsewhere in the islands of the Southern Sea," Coates concluded, "crimes by British Subjects will not be effectively punished."[43]

The evidence of the Rev. John Beecham, who like Coates referred to the problem of law and order in the islands, also suggested extra-territoriality. He advocated an extension of the representation policy through the appointment of "suitable persons" to "the principal islands of the South Sea, who shall be invested with sufficient powers to bring to justice British subjects offending against the natives."[44]

Not one of the missionary suggestions was practicable unless minimum intervention and recognition of native sovereignty (with its attendant legal complications) were abandoned. So long as fundamental policy continued unchanged, the only possible steps for improving the Resident's position were the appointment of additional Residents (to which some of the missionaries were opposed), the replacement of Busby by a more vigorous administrator and the increase of naval visits.

41 PP., 1836, vol. vii, pp. 193-198.
42 ibid, p. 460.
43 ibid, pp. 504-505.
44 ibid, p. 507.

The only additional Resident ever appointed was Lieutenant Thomas McDonnell, who in 1834 on his own motion was made Additional Resident with his seat at Hokianga. McDonnell's appointment was made without the knowledge of Busby and without consulting the Governor of New South Wales. He himself had applied for the position to be created on the ground that "Mr. Busby's authority is necessarily confined to that portion of the island which from distance and other physical causes is entirely separated from the north-western shores of New Zealand, and it becomes otherwise the more necessary to have a British Consul or Agent at Hokianga, because the chiefs whose confidence I possess there . . . are the most powerful, civilised and influential in the island."[45]

Not one of these claims was justified, but the Colonial Office seems to have appointed McDonnell (who asked no salary) without much enquiry. Busby strongly opposed the appointment on both official and personal grounds. In practice McDonnell's work, which was complicated by his commercial dealings and his bad relations with some of the missionaries, embarrassed Busby very much and widened the gulf between Busby and Governor Bourke. By 1836 when McDonnell resigned, his personal unsuitability and the undesirability of having two Residents working so close to one another had been sufficiently demonstrated. The whole record of McDonnell's appointment indicates that his selection was badly judged and that the decision to establish a second Resident was certainly not based on consideration of Busby's needs.

The second means by which the position of the Resident might have been strengthened (consistently with minimum intervention) was the replacement of Busby by some more active administrator. No suggestion of this kind appears to have been considered.[46]

The third mode of improving the Resident's position, that is, the increase of naval visits, was never tried thoroughly. The failure to maintain adequate naval visits to New Zealand was officially admitted to be on account of the high expense involved.[47] Both Bourke and Busby complained that the assistance of men-of-war was too infrequent. In 1835 Bourke wrote to the Colonial Office that "no additional ships of war have been sent to these seas" and indicated his disappointment at the British attitude.[48] He

[45] McDonnell to Auckland, May 27, 1834; C.O. 201/244; quoted in E. Ramsden: *Busby of Waitangi* (cit. sup.); p. 103. For discussion of McDonnell's work see Ramsden, pp. 103-113 and 115-140.

[46] Until, of course, Hobson's appointment as Consul in 1839.

[47] Glenelg to Bourke, Oct. 28, 1835; H.R.A., I, xviii, p. 173.

[48] Bourke to Spring Rice, Feb. 1, 1835; H.R.A., I, xvii, p. 645.

made a request in 1834 for more naval visits[49] and repeated the request in 1836.[50] It is clear that the men on the spot believed that naval visits would help the Resident materially. It is equally clear that the British Government failed to order such visits, not only because it was unwilling to remove the legal difficulties raised by naval action in New Zealand, but also because it believed that New Zealand affairs did not warrant the expense.

This parsimony was typical of the British attitude towards the Resident right from the first. The British Government even involved itself in disputes with the colonies over contributions towards Busby's salary, on the ground that the appointment was of colonial rather than home interest.[51] When enclosing a copy of the King's reply to the chiefs, which Busby read to them on his arrival in New Zealand, Goderich stated that expenditure was not to be incurred so far as the chiefs were concerned.[52] Any gifts were to be few and of inconsiderable value. When in 1835 Glenelg authorised the expenditure of £300 per annum on measures to increase the Resident's influence with the natives, he stipulated that the greater part should be prudently laid out in the employment of native constables and the education of sons of chiefs.[53]

Parsimony and fear of involvement in the problems of troubled New Zealand restrained the British Government from taking even such action in aid of the Resident as was consistent with minimum intervention. The range of such action was limited, but its possible usefulness was attested by the missionaries, by Governor Bourke and by Busby himself.

Judgment on the record of Busby's experiences up to 1837 must be that Great Britain was more concerned with maintaining the policy of minimum intervention than with discharging the unwelcome responsibilities produced by the advent of British subjects in New Zealand. The slight action that was taken was mainly at the instigation of the missionaries and the New South Wales authorities. The British Government was prepared to leave the New Zealand problem to the civilising labours of the missionaries, who claimed almost a proprietary interest in the New Zealand field and deprecated any substantial departure from minimum intervention, and to the administrative supervision of New South Wales, which was subject to the Home Government on all matters of policy.

49 Bourke to Stanley, Sept. 23, 1834; H.R.A., I, xvii, p. 545.
50 Bourke to Glenelg, Jan. 6, 1836; H.R.A., I, xviii, p. 259.
51 Bourke to Glenelg, Sept. 8, 1837; H.R.A., I, xix, pp. 82 ff.
52 cf. T. L. Buick, op. cit. p. 12.
53 Glenelg to Bourke, Oct. 28, 1835; H.R.A., I, xviii, p. 173.

As a result Great Britain adhered to the principle of representation in New Zealand long after the inadequacies of any such appointment as Busby's had been demonstrated beyond a doubt. The period of Busby's office is to be regarded as one of makeshift compromise, engendered by the Government's firm determination to keep out of island affairs.

REPRESENTATION IN THE SOCIETIES

Conditions in the Society Islands up to the late thirties were greatly different from those in New Zealand. Essentially the difference lay in two factors: (a) the existence in the Societies of some measure of central government (at least in Tahiti), with which negotiations could be conducted and on which responsibility for internal conditions could be laid; and (b) the existence of powerful British missionary influence on Tahiti and the other islands of the group.

The background of British representation in the Societies has to be sought in the history of these two factors. Missionaries from the London Missionary Society had arrived in Tahiti in 1797. At the time of their coming there was a struggle in progress in the islands, directed partly against the nominal sovereignty of the principal ruler of Tahiti, Pomare I.

There were three autonomous political divisions in Tahiti— Teva in the south, which had the highest ranking chief, Oropaa in the west, and Aharoa in the north. Pomare was the ruler of Aharoa and his ascendancy really resulted from the fact that most of the Europeans visiting Tahiti came to Matavai in his territory. Pomare was shrewd enough to treat the Europeans well and in consequence received considerable support from them. Most Europeans, indeed, commencing from the very earliest visitors to Tahiti, had regarded the ruler of Aharoa as the King of Tahiti.

The missionaries eventually sided with Pomare in his struggle for supremacy and, as Russier remarked, "demandèrent à la politique le secours que la persuasion seule ne pouvait leur donner."[54] Pomare confided to them the education of his son, and when the latter succeeded his father in 1803, the missionaries helped him to overcome the rival chiefs. The final victory of Pomare II in 1815 at once brought a semblance of unified government to the islands and assured the political position of the missionaries. Pomare's triumph is to be regarded as one of the first instances of

[54] H. Russier: *Le Partage de l'Océanie*; Paris, 1905; p. 129

European influence underlying the emergence of a new island government. (See Chapter XX, below.)

For at least twenty years thereafter the missionaries enjoyed a considerable pre-eminence in Tahitian affairs. They were regarded as counsellors of the Crown. Under their inspiration a legal code, largely on English lines, was adopted first in Tahiti and later in Tahaa, Borabora, Maupiti and Huahine. After securing the succession of the son of Pomare II in 1821, the missionaries instituted a form of representative government.

In the Societies after about 1820, despite frequent instances of disorder (as in 1827), affairs were never so disorganised as in New Zealand, where the missionary influence was slighter and where there was no attempt to centralise government. The forces working on the side of law and order in the Societies were always clearly visible. Captain Fitzroy stated in his evidence before the Lords Committee of 1838 that a regular system of government had been established in Tahiti through the moral influence of the missionaries.[55]

In practice these circumstances made it easy for the British Government to abstain from active intervention in the Societies. Although active British interest in the Societies dated from the arrival of the missionaries in 1797, Great Britain did not have to establish representation there until 1837. The Societies were placed within the general charge of the first British Consul at Hawaii, but his authority was rarely exercised in the group. The British Government and British naval officers were able (when necessary) to negotiate fairly successfully with the rulers of Tahiti and other islands, sometimes in association with the missionaries.

So satisfied was the British Government with the success attending naval visits that several suggestions for the establishment of British representation in the Societies were rejected. In 1832 two such suggestions were made. The Queen and Chiefs of Tahiti requested in January that the missionary, the Rev. George Pritchard (or else Captain Hill) should be appointed to represent Great Britain at Tahiti.[56] Nothing came of the request. In October John Harrison, a sugar planter, wrote to Lord Palmerston offering to perform the duties of British Vice-Consul at Tahiti without fee.[57] Harrison pointed out that the Consul at Hawaii was too far distant

55 Qu. in L.M.S.: *Brief Statement of the Aggression of the French on the Island of Tahiti*: London, 1843; pp. 10-11. For contrast with New Zealand see J. Busby: *Colonies and Colonisation*; Auckland, 1857; p. 7.

56 Queen and Chiefs of Tahiti to Gt. Britain, Jan. 6, 1832; *Corr. rel. to the Society Islands, 1822-1837*; Encl. 1 in No. 29.

57 Harrison to Palmerston, Oct. 6, 1832; F.O. 58/14.

to exercise effective control at Tahiti and added that the island was much visited by ships, whose masters and crews fought both with the natives and with one another. Harrison's offer, according to the available Foreign Office papers, was summarily rejected, on the ground that no sufficient cause for the appointment had been shown.[58] So far as the Foreign Office was concerned British interests at Tahiti could continue to be protected by naval visits alone.

The whole position was changed when an American Consul was appointed at the Society Islands in 1834 and the French began to take an active interest in the Pacific again. These two new factors clearly threatened to increase necessary intervention. A man-of-war might be able to reduce Pomare to obedience, but against Great Powers it was a much less potent, indeed a very dangerous, weapon. Missionary influence on the native rulers had been capable of easing the relationships of British subjects and natives in the past, but could it be relied upon to do so in the future when foreigners would come to the islands in increasing numbers? The problem of international relations was changing the very basis of the situation.

The American role in the South Pacific was becoming specially important. American whalers, sealers and traders had been active there almost from the establishment of the colony of New South Wales. In 1836 the American Government was suspected by observers in the Pacific of harbouring plans for annexation. Rear-Admiral Hamond reported that an increase in the American Pacific squadron implied a design on Hawaii. Shortly afterwards he feared that other preparations in the United States fleet were leading towards the annexation of Tahiti.[59]

With the appointment of the American Consul, British residents in the Societies became alarmed at their isolated position. At the instance of the Rev. George Pritchard, Pomare IV and her principal chiefs wrote to Great Britain in February, 1836, requesting the appointment of a British Consul.[60] The letter, which nominated Pritchard for the post, mentioned that the Consul at Hawaii, who was supposed to serve in the Societies also, was too far distant to be of any use. At the same time over twenty British residents wrote to their Government stressing the fact that an American

[58] F.O. to Harrison, June 11, 1833; F.O. 58/14.
[59] Brookes, op. cit., p. 64. See also Bidwell to Pritchard, Feb. 20, 1837; *Corr. rel. to the Society Islands, Part I; No. 52.*
[60] Pomare to F.O., Feb. 23, 1836; F.O. 58/14.

Consul had been appointed and recommending that Pritchard, who had long performed some consular functions gratuitously, should be appointed to that office.[61] "The lives and property of British subjects now partly protected by the good feeling of the natives," stated the letter, "may from one moment to another be endangered by runaway seamen and other bad characters; and it is our opinion that British ships are forsaking these islands in consequence of the want of efficient protection and consular assistance."

The case for an appointment was also taken up by the naval officers, on whom fell the main burden of protecting British subjects in the Societies. Rear-Admiral Hamond, in forwarding to the Foreign Office a letter from Pritchard (in which Pritchard had strongly advocated his own claims to be Consul) stated that there were nearly 800 leagues of sea between Hawaii and the Society Islands. "The few opportunities for communication between them," Hamond thought, "render a separate appointment for each group very desirable."[62] Captain Fitzroy of H.M.S. *Beagle* reported to the Foreign Office in similar terms. He added that there was a growing trade between Tahiti and Australia and between Tahiti and South America. Moreover, British subjects had acquired assets in the islands, mainly in the form of sugar plantations, which stood in need of protection.[63]

The official recommendations, together with the pressure from Pritchard, the most active of the British missionaries at Tahiti, and the complaints of the British residents there, left the Foreign Office no choice. The time had come at which the British Government could not have remained unrepresented in the Societies without failing in its most obvious duties towards British interests and involving itself in dispute with the powerful London Missionary Society, which distrusted any increase of foreign authority in the islands (for example, the appointment of an American Consul) as likely to diminish its own influence.

The choice of the Foreign Office fell on Pritchard, whose claims had been pressed by Pomare, by some of the British residents and, most strongly of all, by himself.[64] The character of the office was sufficiently unusual to make an appointment difficult. Even in acceding to the local demand for the selection of Pritchard the

61 Feb. 25, 1836; ibid.
62 Hamond to Wood, Oct. 13, 1836; *Corr. rel. to the Society Islands, Part I*; Encl. 1 in No. 41.
63 Fitzroy to Backhouse; ibid, No. 42.
64 See especially Pritchard to Melbourne, Mar. 3, 1836; *Corr. rel to the Society Islands, Part I*; No. 40.

Foreign Office had to face complications arising from his long established position in the Tahitian community.

The recorded opposition to Pritchard's selection proceeded partly from John Robson, a sugar planter in Tahiti, and partly from the difficulty of investing a missionary with the commercial, administrative and diplomatic duties of a Consul.

Robson stated his views in a somewhat angry despatch to Palmerston in which Pritchard was accused of having instigated the demand for a British Consul in Tahiti in order to suit his own ends.[65] Those who had signed the petition for Pritchard's appointment, declared Robson, belonged to "the extreme low class of Society." The reputable sugar-planting class (of which he himself claimed to be a member) was opposed to Pritchard almost to a man.

Robson's protests were probably unimportant. The appointment of a British Consul, who could report misconduct to the British Government, was certain to be resented in some quarters. Pritchard, who had been performing the duties of that office in an unofficial way for some years[66] and had several times written to the British Government on matters properly within the sphere of Pomare,[67] had probably acquired a position unacceptable to some of the British settlers at Tahiti. The Foreign Office itself attached no particular significance to Robson's protests.

The second difficulty in the way of Pritchard's appointment, that is, his missionary character, was more serious. After correspondence with the London Missionary Society, it was arranged between the Society and the Foreign Office that Pritchard's services should be made available as Consul and that his resignation as missionary should be accepted. The Society's view was that Pritchard might be replaced as a missionary, but that no better man could be found for appointment as Consul. The two offices were regarded as inconsistent.[68] Pritchard's letter of appointment (February, 1837) included an express instruction to resign his missionary office, "the duties and character of which will be incompatible with those of Consul."[69]

There is not much evidence as to the work accomplished by Pritchard apart from his episodes with the French.[70] He performed important work as an unofficial counsellor and interpreter

[65] Robson to Palmerston, Mar. 31, 1836; F.O. 58/14.
[66] Cf. Petition of the British Residents, cit. sup. (n.61).
[67] E.g., Pritchard to F.O., June 18, 1835; F.O. 58/14.
[68] Ellis (Foreign Sec., L.M.S.) to F.O., Jan. 11, 1837; *Corr. rel. to the Society Islands, 1822-1847*; No. 44.
[69] F.O. to Pritchard, Feb. 14, 1837; F.O. 58/15.
[70] See Ch. XII, below.

to Pomare, some of which was inconsistent with his accreditation to her as Consul. He adjudicated in cases of dispute between masters and crews of British vessels and represented British interests in dealings with the native authorities.[71] The official papers suggest that his work was performed efficiently and to the satisfaction of the Foreign Office, which in 1842 increased his salary in order to permit his visiting all the main islands within his jurisdiction at least once a year.[72] Whatever the disadvantages of his long association in Tahiti, Pritchard was a well-known resident, high in the confidence of the ruling natives and thoroughly well acquainted with local problems. In almost every particular his position differed to the greatest degree from that of Busby. Giving evidence before the Lords Committee on New Zealand in 1838, Captain Fitzroy, R.N., declared that Pritchard was able to exercise control over British subjects "by virtue of his Office and having the Influence still which he acquired as missionary."[73]

The problems arising from his position as part missionary, part consul were not easily solved. Pritchard continued to perform many of his missionary functions and the difficulties in which he involved himself provide an interesting commentary on the problems facing a diplomatic representative selected on the ground of his first-hand knowledge of the state to which he is accredited.

Commander Elliot of H.M.S. *Fly* reported in 1838 that Pritchard had acquitted himself well, though he still "naturally had much to learn in the principles and details of his consular duties."[74] Elliott, who had been sent to Tahiti to report on Pritchard's work, referred specially to the highly contentious matter of the Consul's continuing to perform his missionary duties. Perceiving the difficulties under which the missionaries laboured, Elliott reported that:

"I do not think Mr. Pritchard's scruples of conscience would have deserved much respect, had he allowed his new appointment to deprive a large congregation of a pastor."

The British Government appears to have accepted tacitly Pritchard's anomalous position. It is not clear whether in doing so the Government realised the degree of Pritchard's influence on Pomare and her chiefs. In his character as their pastor Pritchard

[71] For details of his work see *Tahiti British Consulate Papers* (Misc., 1843-1874) in the Mitchell Library, Sydney.

[72] Pritchard to Aberdeen, June 29, 1842; F.O. to Pritchard, July 30, 1842; F.O. 58/16.

[73] *H. of L. Committee on N.Z., 1838*; p. 344.

[74] Elliot to Ross, Nov. 13, 1838; *Corr. rel. to the Society Islands*, Part I; No. 72 (encl.).

had come to occupy a unique place in the counsels of the native rulers of Tahiti. He acted as interpreter to the Queen on state occasions even after his appointment as Consul.

The French missionaries and naval officers in the Pacific bitterly resented the ubiquitous character with which circumstances allowed him to invest his office. In 1837 the French Bishop of Oceania wrote to Walpole, the British Consul-General in Chile, complaining that the evil and improper influence exercised by Pritchard was responsible for the expulsion of the two priests MM. PP. Laval and Caret from Tahiti the previous year.[75] The commander of the French ship *Pylade,* which visited Tahiti in 1840, considered that British rule there would be more favourable to French interests than what he called Pritchard's anti-French, anti-Catholic influence with Pomare.[76] Jore, probably the most recent French writer on the subject, openly blamed Pritchard's combination of functions and his anti-Catholic feeling for most of the trouble in Tahiti.[77]

The French condemnation of Pritchard was personal to him. It reflected adversely on the selection of Pritchard, not on the decision to establish representation in Tahiti. The minimum intervention policy, varied by the appointment of a Consul, worked well in Tahiti up to 1838.

The record of British representation in Tahiti differs completely from that of representation in New Zealand. Conditions in Tahiti were settled enough to make the appointment of a Consul a reasonable and workable proceeding. Until France began a policy of intervention, the main difficulties confronting Pritchard were personal to himself. In contrast conditions in New Zealand were too disorderly and the country too lacking in central authority to make a representation policy successful.

[75] Bishop of Oceania to Walpole, Jan. 12, 1837; encl. in Walpole to Palmerston, July 21, 1837; F.O. 16/32; qu. in Brookes, op. cit., p. 83.
[76] Vincendon-Dumoulin et Desgraz: *Les Iles Taïti;* Paris, 1844; Vol. II, p. 935.
[77] Jore, op. cit, pp. 28-29.

Chapter X

INTERVENTION IN NEW ZEALAND

The developments after 1837 which culminated in the establishment of British rule in New Zealand are too well known to need recapitulation here.[1] Some reassessment of the record is, however, necessary, if only because of the number of controversial issues affecting the interpretation of the British policy. The period also has a special interest in that the British acquisition of New Zealand marked the first and the best recorded account of the breakdown of the original concept of minimum intervention.

The British Government failed in 1837 to improve the position of the Resident. Dissuaded from action by its own distrust of colonisation, by fear of the probable expense, by the protests of the powerful missionary societies and by the recent experiences of the Kaffir War, the Colonial Office declined to intervene in New Zealand. The protests of the authorities in New South Wales and of the missionaries in the New Zealand field could not overcome the long established resistance to intervention.

Pressure on the British Government was greatly intensified after the formation in October, 1837, of the New Zealand Association. The most forceful personality in the Association was Edward Gibbon Wakefield, who was anxious to see his theories of colonisation applied in a new territory.[2] Before the House of Commons Committee on Colonial Lands in 1836 Wakefield had recommended New Zealand as a suitable place for colonisation under his system.[3] Partly as a result of Wakefield's evidence before the Committee, partly because his exertions were favoured by the growing desire to invest outside England, the Association was formed with a strong committee. Predominantly Whig in opinion, the Committee included the Earl of Durham, Lord Petre, W. B. Baring, M.P., Rev. Dr. Hinds, W. Hutt, M.P., Sir William Molesworth, M.P., and

[1] See especially J. S. Marais: *The Colonisation of New Zealand*; London, 1927; A. J. Harrop: *England and New Zealand*; London, 1926.

[2] Although he did not publicly condemn the South Australian experiment until 1841, Wakefield was by this time dissatisfied.

[3] PP., 1836, xi, p. 614.

H. G. Ward, M.P. All of these men were prominent in colonial matters.

The new Association had to challenge the jealous anti-colonialism of the Colonial Office, the long-established policy of minimum intervention and the fervid· hostility of the humanitarian movement in England.[4] Its objectives counted on a complete reversal of British policy in the South Pacific. The Government which had appointed an ineffectual Resident and done nothing to improve his position was being asked to sanction a large-scale project of colonisation.

The Association's objectives were first brought under the official notice of the Government at the end of 1837 when it solicited a Charter which would have conceded an exclusive right to found and govern a colony in New Zealand. The sovereign independence of the chiefs was to be recognised, but the Association was to receive the right to establish Courts administering British law, to make regulations having the force of law within its settlements, to raise defence forces and to appoint and remove officers.[5]

Although the Government was at first frigid and later hostile in its attitude to the application, an important admission was made by Glenelg. In an interesting exchange of letters with Lord Durham of the Association, Glenelg admitted that the establishment of some settled form of government in New Zealand had become absolutely necessary.[6] As the country was already being colonised, he wrote, "the only question . . . is between a colonisation desultory, without law and fatal to the natives, and a colonisation organised and salutary."

In substance this was the same view as that taken more and more by missionaries at work in the New Zealand field. Unlike the dignitaries of the missionary societies at home, the men in the field had learnt that British intervention was indispensable for the sake of peace, order and good government. "A native government cannot be formed by natives," reported a sub-committee of the New Zealand missionaries, adding that in the Bay of Islands

---

[4] Both the C.M.S. and the W.M.S. passed resolutions condemning the Association's plans. For C.M.S. resolution see *H. of L. Committee on N.Z.*, 1838; p. 243. For W.M.S. resolution see D. Coates: *Notes for the Information of the Deputation to Lord Glenelg*; London, 1837, p. 5.

[5] E. G. Wakefield: *The British Colonisation of New Zealand*; London, 1837; pp. 65-66. After consultation with Lord Melbourne and Lord Howick the Association's proposals were embodied in a Bill. A copy of the Bill is to be found in the Mitchell Library, Sydney. ("Bill for the Provisional Government of the Settlement in New Zealand, 1838.")

[6] Glenelg to Durham, Dec. 29, 1837; *Corr. rel. to N.Z.*, 1840.

district, effective political authority already belonged to the white settlers.[7]

It was useless for the missionary societies to advance humanitarian arguments, whatever their intrinsic merit, against colonisation in New Zealand when colonisation had already begun. Such was the conclusion to be drawn from the evidence before the Colonial Office and from the statements of missionaries in the field. "If," wrote the Rev. Dr. S. Hinds, one of the clerical advocates of colonisation and a committee member of the Association, "during one year 151 vessels (many of them of considerable size) anchor in the Bay of Islands, is it not too late to talk of averting from the New Zealanders the risks of civilized society? . . . Regular Colonization has now become indispensable as a remedy to the evils of irregular Colonization."[8]

Hinds might have added that a powerful pro-colonial movement, of which the New Zealand Association was a product, had already developed in Great Britain. The movement had its origins in the social and economic consequences of the Industrial Revolution. Between 1750 and 1830 the population of England and Wales doubled itself. Industrial production increased in a degree out of proportion to capacity to consume. As a result unemployment became common and social conditions deteriorated. Amongst the classes with capital the demand was for new markets and new chances of investment. The unemployed, it was believed, should be permitted to emigrate so as to establish new markets and free their own country from the burden of their support.

Hinds himself thought in terms of economic expansionism. In evidence before the House of Lords Committee on New Zealand in 1838, he said:

"There is an Abundance of Capital and an Abundance of Labour in Gt. Britain, and the Abundance of Capital the Capitalists can hardly employ so as sufficiently to remunerate them by any Investment in this Country; at the same Time there is a great Mass of the labouring Population who can no longer obtain sufficient Wages to keep up what have become the necessaries of life to them. The proposed Colony would, therefore, be a Measure of Relief both to Capitalists and to Labourers."[9]

[7] Report of a Sub-Committee of N.Z. missionaries on Coates to Glenelg, July 23, 1838; C.M.S. N.Z. Papers, qu. Marais, op. cit., p. 36. See also the views of William Yate, N.Z. Secretary of the C.M.S., in Scottish Colonial Investment Company: *Notices of New Zealand*; n.p., 1839?; p. 22. (There is a copy in the Petherick Collection, National Library, Canberra.)

[8] S. Hinds: *The Latest Official Documents rel. N.Z.; with Introductory Observations*; London, 1838; p. 8.

[9] *H. of L. Committee on N.Z., 1838*; pp. 124-125.

The Colonial Office did not espouse these views. But it did—through Glenelg—recognise by the end of 1837 the case for intervention in New Zealand.

The missionary societies in London, however, could not be induced to abandon their stand in favour of the Resident system. Dandeson Coates, the energetic Lay Secretary of the Church Missionary Society, strongly attacked the argument of the New Zealand Association, that regular colonisation would benefit the natives. Coates, backed up by the Wesleyan Missionary Society, brought to bear the whole of his considerable influence with the Colonial Office in an effort to have the views of the Association rejected. Glenelg himself, like Sir George Grey and James Stephen (the Under-Secretaries), was an ardent evangelical. He continually consulted Coates on New Zealand affairs and was soon informed of the missionary opposition to his declaration of December, 1837, and to the claims of the New Zealand Association generally.

A month before Glenelg's admission was made Coates had attacked the Association's plans in a pamphlet, *The Principles, Objects and Plan of the New Zealand Association Examined,* striking at the weak links in the Association's armour—its lack of a consistent and realistic native policy, the over-simplification of the land problem and its facile assumption that colonisation would solve all native problems.[10] Early in 1838 Coates arranged a deputation to Glenelg and in his *Notes for the Information of the Deputation to Lord Glenelg* he declared that Glenelg's decision of December, 1837, which had been officially described as justified on the ground of necessity, was really unjustified because no necessity existed for colonisation until all alternative measures had been tried.[11]

Glenelg himself failed to act on his admission that regular colonisation would be a benefit to New Zealand. Even in making the admission, he had not explicitly agreed that the British Government should undertake the responsibility for instituting effective government in New Zealand. He had merely stated that the British Government, acting in the best interests of New Zealand, would be prepared to incorporate a Company by Royal Charter to plant a colony in New Zealand.[12] The Government would reserve

[10] pp. 12 ff.

[11] p. 9. The *Notes* were written in December, 1837, and were signed by Coates a day before Glenelg sent his formal letter to Durham (cit. sup.).

[12] Glenelg to Durham, Dec. 29, 1837; cit. sup. Cf. Grey to Coates, Jan. 25, 1838; qu. Coates: *The Present State of the New Zealand Question Considered;* London, 1838; pp. 6-7.

to itself the right of veto as to the persons forming the governing body of the company and the persons appointed as officials in the colony. Laws and regulations promulgated for the government of the colony might be disallowed by the Queen. Protection of the natives was specially required and any settlement effected was to be made only with the consent of the natives.

Glenelg's cautious concession of principle, weighted at every point with stipulations for the benefit of the natives, was of little use to the Association. The grant of the proposed Charter had been made conditional on the formation of a Joint Stock Company. The Association, whose committee consisted entirely of men with no direct pecuniary interest in the venture,[13] found the condition completely unacceptable. Despite considerable protest, Glenelg declined to remove the condition, holding that it would give additional security for the proper execution of the Charter.[14]

Whether or not his original intention in stipulating that the Association should become a joint stock company was to choke off colonisation plans in New Zealand, Glenelg probably adhered to the stipulation with the object of discouraging and dissuading the Association. His position was that, while colonisation was necessary, it would have to be colonisation on the terms laid down by the Colonial Office. As his stand was tantamount to refusal of the Association's request for a Charter,[15] the missionary societies had every reason to be satisfied.

Glenelg was supported in the House of Commons, when a no-confidence motion moved by Sir William Molesworth was rejected despite convincing evidence that the Government's delay was certain to produce evil consequences.[16]

The combined forces of the "Saints," of anti-colonialism, of laissez-faire and of the great mass of opinion and tradition opposed to intervention in the South Pacific won the day for the somnolent Glenelg. Even stronger support was forthcoming when the House of Lords Select Committee appointed to enquire into "the present state of the Islands of New Zealand and the expediency of regulating the settlement of British Subjects therein" resolved that the best hope for New Zealand lay in extension of missionary work.[17]

13 See E. G. Wakefield: *The British Colonisation of New Zealand*; London, 1837; pp. ix-x, for account of the two classes of members of the Association, viz. (a) heads of families and others willing to emigrate; (b) public men politically interested in the project.

14 Glenelg to Durham, Feb. 5, 1838; *PP*., 1840, vii, p. 611.

15 The Government had been asked to grant a Charter in 1837.

16 *Parlty. Debates*, 1838, XLI, 495.

17 *PP*.. 1837-8, xxi, 327-710.

By the time that the Association's Bill was introduced in the House of Commons (June, 1838) the opposition to its enactment had been well marshalled. The Government, though constrained to admit that remedial action was necessary, denied that the Association's measure was suitable. The powerful missionary societies, carrying with them a great · mass of public opinion, vehemently opposed any suggestion of organised colonisation. The Association itself came in for a great deal of hostile criticism, notably in *The Times,* which repeatedly condemned the Association and all its works.[18] In favour of the measure were the commercial interests in sympathy with the Association and all those who looked for an opportunity of emigrating to New Zealand. To this rather scanty band should be added the missionaries in the New Zealand field and the authorities and traders of New South Wales, who, although they might not have favoured the Association's plans, certainly wished for some regularisation of the position in New Zealand.

The widespread hostility to the Association's measure led to its being introduced into Parliament by Francis Baring without the support of the Government. The Bill was rejected at the second reading, Gladstone and Howick leading the opposition to its passage.[19] In putting the case for the Bill, Baring, Hawes, Ward and others stressed that colonisation in New Zealand had already begun. Of all the schemes which might be adopted to regularise the position, they argued, the Association's plans involved the least public expense, the least risk and the greatest potential benefit both to Great Britain and to the natives. In opposition to these claims, Gladstone reiterated the humanitarian case against colonisation and declared that no satisfactory policy towards New Zealand could be devised at that stage of the Session. Howick declared that the Bill did not meet the two essential conditions necessary to obtain the Government's approval, viz.: (i) security against the inveiglement of British subjects; and (ii) security for the just treatment of the aborigines. Sir George Grey summed up the Government's case against the Bill when he declared that the Association's plans contained every objectionable feature which it was intended to exclude from the charter proposed to be granted by H.M. Government.

At no stage in the 1838 debates did the Government itself deny that some form of intervention in New Zealand was necessary. But the Government did not indicate what alternatives it proposed

18 See especially June 20, 1838, June 21, 1838, and Oct. 19, 1838.
19 *Parlly. Debates,* 1838, XLIII, 871 ff.

to the measures of the Association. The bitter opposition of the missionary societies to any fundamental change of policy and the strength of the Government's own attachment to minimum intervention prevented any formulation of official policy.

Evidence reaching Great Britain, however, continued to demonstrate that some policy would have to be decided upon swiftly. The Association (and later the Company)[20] kept the problem of New Zealand before the public eye. In 1838 the Lords Committee received evidence of the lawlessness of Europeans in New Zealand. Francis Baring declared that one-third of the European population of the Bay of Islands district disappeared as soon as a British man-of-war appeared. Captain Robert Fitzroy stated that, apart from eight or ten families, the whites at the Bay of Islands were "ragamuffins."[21]

So bad had the position at the Bay of Islands become that some of the settlers there were driven in May, 1838, to form the Kororareka Association as an instrument of mutual self-protection.[22] The Association was intended to provide common defence against attack on persons or property by the natives. It also laid down a code of conduct as to tenancy, robbery, harbouring deserters from ships and the like. Every member was to be armed with "a good musket and bayonet, a brace of pistols, a cutlass and at least 30 rounds of ball-cartridges." The rough form of self-help envisaged by the Association was justly described by the missionaries as "opposing force to force," with an aggravation of existing evils as the probable consequence.

The case for British intervention was stronger than ever. But between the needs of the situation in New Zealand and the capacity and willingness of the Colonial Office to act there was a great gulf fixed. The Colonial Office had strong reasons for accepting missionary arguments as grounds for delay, quite apart from the powerful missionary influence on the heads of the administration. In common with general opinion at the time, the Colonial Office had serious doubts as to the utility of colonisation in general. New Zealand, in particular, was regarded with little enthusiasm. The Office already had more work to undertake than it could con-

---

[20] The New Zealand Colonisation Co. was formed on Aug. 29, 1838, after the dissolution of the Association. On May 2, 1839, the New Zealand Colonisation Co. ceased to exist and was replaced by the New Zealand Land Co., later known as the New Zealand Co. (Durham to Normanby, May 22, 1839; *Corr. rel. to N.Z., 1840;* No. 8.)

[21] *H. of L. Committee on N.Z.,* 1838; pp. 146 ff., 161 ff.

[22] *Documents Exhibiting the View of the Committee of the C.M.S. on the N.Z. Question;* London, 1839; pp. 50-54.

veniently handle. In comparison with the affairs of Canada, South Africa and the West Indies, the troubles of New Zealand ranked insignificantly. Though the Colonial Office admitted that something should be done, New Zealand affairs had, so to speak, a low priority and almost up to the end of 1838 the Government produced no plan.

The New South Wales authorities, the missionaries and the New Zealand Company, on the contrary, produced a whole battery of plans, all competing for the support of the Colonial Office.

The Colonial Office itself was most impressed with the plan drawn up by Captain Hobson (H.M.S. *Rattlesnake*) and forwarded to England by Governor Bourke.[23] Hobson proposed the introduction of commercial establishments in New Zealand on the model of the early trading factories in India. Within prescribed areas British subjects would be placed under their own laws, "premising as an inflexible condition, that nothing whatever be established on the part of the British Government which is not cheerfully conceded on terms of clear mutual interest by the natives." A Colonial Office memorandum to Glenelg described this plan as "all that is essential for the present."[24] Bourke himself warmly supported Hobson's plan and made it clear that any future policy in New Zealand would have to be financed at the expense of Great Britain, not of New South Wales.[25] Bourke also sent to England a plan drawn up by Busby, which, however, he condemned as likely to lead to abuses and misinterpretation. Busby suggested that New Zealand should be governed by the Confederate and other Chiefs under the protection of Great Britain, with provision for British extra-territoriality.[26]

The missionaries condemned the plans of Hobson and Busby, although not in like degree nor with complete unanimity. Rev. John Beecham admitted that there was merit in Busby's plan, which would obviously have worked to preserve missionary ascendancy.[27] But the general attitude of the missionaries was that, because both plans involved some contraction of New Zealand sovereignty, both were to be condemned.[28]

The missionaries themselves produced a series of plans designed to preserve native sovereignty (with its concomitant of strong

[23] *Copy of a Despatch from . . . Bourke to . . . Glenelg, rel. to the affairs of N.Z., 1838.* Hobson's plan is Enclosure A. (Hobson to Bourke, Aug. 8, 1837.)
[24] May 4, 1838; C.O. 209/3; qu. in T. Williams: "James Stephen and New Zealand, 1838-40"; *Journal of Modern History*, Vol. XIII, No. 1, p. 21.
[25] Bourke to Glenelg, Sept. 9, 1837; *Official Corr.* (cit. sup., n. 23).
[26] Encl. C. (Busby to Colonial Secretary, N.S.W., June 16, 1837); *ibid.*
[27] J. Beecham: *Colonization, &c.*; London, 1838; pp. 27 ff.
[28] See Evidence of Coates before Lords Committee on N.Z.; *loc. cit.*, p. 269.

missionary influence), while at the same time permitting some exercise of British authority in New Zealand.

Coates's plan, put forward in *The Principles, Objects and Plan of the New Zealand Association Examined*,[29] had six main points:

(i) Continued recognition of native sovereignty.

(ii) Continuance of the "consular agent" (i.e., Resident) system and extension of the Resident's powers.

(iii) Organisation of a native police force under the chiefs, the force to be at the disposal of the Resident.

(iv) The stationing of a small ship of war off New Zealand.

(v) Judicial powers to be conferred on the Resident, on the Commander of the ship of war and possibly on some other individuals; but in deference to native sovereignty, "no individual should be arrested in New Zealand, nor any act of authority exercised in the island, except with the concurrence of the Native Authorities, given either upon some general system, or, in each particular case, *pro re nata.*"[30]

(vi) A Code of Laws to be introduced by the Chiefs.

The main characteristics of this plan might fairly be said to be an elaborate and clumsy attempt to preserve native sovereignty, coupled with the obvious intention of maintaining missionary ascendancy.

Wakefield had little difficulty in exposing the administrative weaknesses of the Coates plan:

". . . who can believe that a plan of British authority, for the administration of British law, so disguised and so feeble as that of Mr. Coates, and of which the operation, too, would be confined to one corner of a country nine hundred miles long, would accomplish the objects in view?"[31]

Another elaborate missionary attempt to combine the reality of British law and order with the shadow of native sovereignty was that proposed by Beecham in his book, *Colonization . . . with an Examination of the Proposals of the Association . . . for Colonizing New Zealand.*[32] To overcome the obstacle that the exercise of British jurisdiction in New Zealand would be contrary to the recognition of native sovereignty, Beecham proposed that Great Britain should take possession of an islet in the Bay of Islands and establish a court there. This would obviate legal complications as to sovereignty and also remove the necessity of

[29] London, 1838 (with signature dated 1837).

[30] pp. 33 ff.

[31] E. G. Wakefield: *Mr. Dandeson Coates and the N.Z. Assocn.*; London, 1838; p. 11.

[32] cit. sup. (n. 27).

conveying witnesses and accused persons to the distant courts of New South Wales.[33] What Beecham overlooked was that offences committed in New Zealand would still have been committed within the sphere of native sovereignty. Hence, as Coates saw, special arrangements would have been necessary in order to make such offences subject to British jurisdiction.

The recommendation for the establishment of a "judicial station" on an islet had already appeared in a letter from the Church Missionary Society to Glenelg on January 3, 1838,[34] so that it may have originated with Coates. In his pamphlet, *The Present State of the New Zealand Question Considered,* Coates repeated the suggestion and added that another "Judicial Station" might need to be established farther South, perhaps on Entry Island (Kapiti), in Cook Strait.[35]

In considering the plans and in attempting to formulate a plan of its own, the Colonial Office sought not only to steer a course between the fears of the missionaries and the ambitions of the Company but also to guard against unnecessary increase of the responsibilities of the Crown and to preserve due caution lest British action in New Zealand arouse recrimination and possible rivalry in France.

The first step taken by the Colonial Office in formulating a new policy towards New Zealand was in December, 1838, when Stephen proposed to the Foreign Office that a British Consul be appointed in New Zealand in view of the failure of the Resident system.[36] The Consul was to communicate directly with the Colonial Office, not the Foreign Office, apparently because even at this stage it was intended that Great Britain should accept some political responsibility in New Zealand. There does not seem, however, to have been any definite scheme in view beyond the replacing of Busby by an official under the direct supervision of the Colonial Office, not (like Busby) under the Governor of New South Wales. Only twelve days after the Foreign Office had been informed of the new plan, Gairdner, one of the Colonial Office clerks, prepared a minute to Glenelg referring to "the necessity of establishing some more competent authority in the Islands."[37] When Hobson, who was chosen as Consul, asked whether the Government contemplated

[33] op. cit., 4th ed., London, 1838; p. 64.
[34] Qu. in Coates: *The Present State of the New Zealand Question Considered;* London, 1838; p. 12.
[35] p. 13.
[36] Stephen to Backhouse, Dec. 12, 1838; *Corr. rel. to N.Z., 1840;* No. 1.
[37] Gairdner to Glenelg, Dec. 24, 1838; C.O. 209/3. Qu. in T. Williams, cit. sup., p. 23.

"any change in our present relations with the Natives of New Zealand," he was informed that he would receive verbal instructions on his arrival in London.[38]

The difficulties faced by the Colonial Office in its attempt to formulate a policy clearly appeared in even the very limited plan of intervention drawn up by Stephen as Hobson's draft instructions in January, 1839.[39] The greatest difficulty of all arose from unwillingness to accept responsibility for the government of New Zealand. The January plan therefore extended only to areas where British subjects were already settled. As the sovereignty of the chiefs had been recognised by Great Britain, any part of New Zealand to be brought under British law would have to be ceded by the chiefs—a transaction whose difficulties were fully conceded in advance. In order to reduce the financial and administrative burden of the proposed colony on the British Government, it was proposed that a charter be granted to the "persons now applying for it" as a joint stock company to act as broker in the land sales which would provide the colonial revenue.[40]

The limitations of this plan were many. Though it avoided legal difficulties, it would still have left British subjects outside the proposed colony quite unamenable to English law. Moreover, foreign states could have established neighbouring colonies with consequent possibilities of friction. The January plan represented the minimum concession to the obvious need for intervention.

The plan was included by Glenelg in a memorandum for Cabinet drawn up by him immediately prior to his retirement in February, 1839.[41] Glenelg made it clear that he sought, not "an extended system of colonisation," but rather the most limited form of intervention consistent with obvious necessity, that is, the "establishment of a regular form of government" in "certain portions of land . . . where the British are already settled."

The February scheme did not come to fruition. In March the provisional committee of the New Zealand Colonisation Company applied to the Government for a charter in New Zealand.[42] The Company declared that the conditions as to joint stock constitution laid down by Glenelg in December, 1837, when considering the

38 C.O. 209/4; qu. ibid.
39 January 21, 1839; C.O. 209/4; qu. ibid., p. 24.
40 For account of the influence of the Wakefield system, see Marais, op. cit., passim.
41 No copy of this minute has been found in papers locally available. It is discussed at length in Marais, op. cit., p. 38, and Harrop, op. cit., p. 64. Cf. Williams, op. cit., p. 25.
42 Motte to Normanby. Mar. 4, 1839; *Corr. rel. to N.Z., 1840*; No. 4.

Association's request for governmental support, had been fulfilled and that a charter should be granted accordingly as a matter of course. The Colonial Office replied almost immediately that, as Glenelg's offer had been rejected by the Association (to which alone it had been made), it had become a nullity. Moreover, it was added, the 1839 list of directors differed from that presented in 1837.[43]

In view of the January and February plans, it is difficult to accept the reasons given by the Colonial Office as the true explanations of its attitude. The fact appears to be that the Colonial Office refused to treat with the Company because of Stephen's objection to the strong Catholic representation on the provisional committee. In his view the grant of a Charter to a company so constituted would have given grave offence to the New Zealand missionaries.[44] It is certain that the Colonial Office, whose plan for intervention in New Zealand went beyond what the "Saints" desired, would have been gravely embarrassed if a cry of "No Popery" had been raised at that stage.

So far was Stephen from having rejected the plan for encharter-ing a company that only a day after an unfavourable answer had been sent to the New Zealand Colonisation Company, he drafted a new minute, suggesting that New Zealand should be governed by a Joint Stock Company "on the model of the old New England constitutions—that is as a body corporate with a joint stock" and with a board of Directors, "which would disarm the opposition of the great missionary societies."[45]

The whole conception of government through a joint stock company went by the board when on May 2nd, 1839, the New Zealand Company[46] was incorporated with a nominal capital of £400,000 and three days later a land-purchasing and survey party sailed for New Zealand on the *Tory*. The Company's actions proceeded from conviction that no help was to be expected from the Colonial Office.[47] Moreover, rival companies were forming in England and the land grab in New Zealand, where the Company itself had purchased large holdings,[48] was developing rapidly.

The immediate response of the Colonial Office to the news that

---

[43] Labouchere to Motte, Mar. 11, 1839; ibid, No. 5.
[44] Stephen's Minute, Mar. 6, 1839; C.O. 209/4; qu. Marais, op. cit., p. 39.
[45] C.O. 209/4; qu. Harrop, op. cit., p. 65.
[46] The new Company at first known as the New Zealand Land Co. was formed from a union of the companies of 1825 and 1838.
[47] See Hutt to Normanby, Apr. 29, 1839; PP., 1840, xxxiii, p. 608.
[48] Motte to Normanby, Mar. 4, 1839; cit. sup. (n. 42).

the expedition was projected[49] was not, as might have been expected, an attempt to forbid the sailing on the ground that British subjects could not set up a government independent of the Government of Great Britain, but a mere threat of non-co-operation. The Company was warned that titles to land in New Zealand which it might acquire would not necessarily be recognised by the British Government. "Her Majesty's Government," it was added, "cannot recognise the authority of the agents whom the Company may employ" in its attempt "to establish a system of government independent of the authority of the British Crown."[50]

The sailing of the *Tory* at least simplified some of the problems as to the form of British intervention in New Zealand. Rather than acquiesce in the plans of the Company, Stephen dropped the idea of rule through a joint stock company and concentrated his attention on plans for establishing British sovereignty in places where British subjects had acquired land from the chiefs. The views of the Colonial Office, when confronted with the choice of either rule through the Company or intervention followed by full cession of sovereignty, were set out in the instructions issued to Hobson, who received an appointment as Lieutenant-Governor:

"It is impossible to confide to an indiscriminate body of persons, who have voluntarily settled themselves in the immediate vicinity of the numerous population of New Zealand, those large and irresponsible powers which belong to the representative system of Colonial Government. Nor is that system adapted to a colony struggling with the first difficulties of their new situation. Whatever may be the ultimate form of government to which the British settlers in New Zealand are to be subject, it is essential to their own welfare, not less than to that of the aborigines, that they should at first be placed under a rule which is at once effective and, to a considerable degree, external."[51]

The Colonial Office stood committed at last to decisive intervention in New Zealand. British rule was to be established there. At the end of May Stephen enquired of the law officers whether it would be lawful to accept a cession in sovereignty of the "Territories which have been, or may be, acquired by Her Majesty's

[49] Hutt to Normanby, Apr. 29, 1839; cit. sup (n. 47).

[50] Labouchere to Hutt, May 1, 1839; *Corr. rel. to N.Z., 1840;* No. 7.

[51] Normanby to Hobson, Aug. 14, 1839; ibid; No. 16. Between September and November, 1839, a long correspondence ensued between the Company and the Colonial Office on this point. British sovereignty was not established until the Treaty of Waitangi. In the interim period the Company attempted to establish its own law in New Zealand through voluntary agreements signed by each emigrant. The Colonial Office, in accordance with the law, treated these agreements as illegal and compelled their abandonment.

Subjects by proprietory Titles derived from the grants of the different Chiefs" and to add the colony so formed to New South Wales as a dependency. The law officers agreed.[52]

The form by which it was decided to establish British sovereignty in New Zealand reflected the combined influences of the long recognition of native sovereignty[53] and the political expediency of securing native agreement to British rule. Although it was doubtful whether the natives really had any sovereignty to cede, the British Government determined to proceed by negotiating for a cession of sovereignty. In this way consistency was to be maintained with previous policy in the vital matter of securing British sovereignty against possible competition. Moreover, the solemn treaty between the British Government and the Maori chiefs was to include such recognition of the rights of the natives as would ensure them just compensation for sale of their lands and proper privileges under British rule. In this latter respect the Treaty marked a new departure in British colonial policy. It was one of the first attempts made to protect a native people against the pressure of the incoming civilisation and showed the continued influence of humanitarianism in the attitude of the Colonial Office towards New Zealand.

The record of the negotiations for the Treaty of Waitangi is not relevant here.[54] The importance of the Treaty in a study of

[52] C.O. 209/4, qu. T. Williams, loc. cit., pp. 29-30.
[53] See Ch. VIII, above.
[54] For discussion of sovereignty in relation to the Treaty, see Ch. VIII, above. The three Articles of the Treaty were as follows:

ARTICLE THE FIRST:
The chiefs of the Confederation of the United Tribes of New Zealand, and the separate and independent chiefs who have not become members of the Confederation, cede to Her Majesty the Queen of England, absolutely and without reservation, all the rights and powers of sovereignty which the said Confederation or individual chiefs respectively exercise or possess, or may be supposed to exercise or possess over their territories as the sole sovereigns thereof.

ARTICLE THE SECOND:
H.M. the Queen of England confirms and guarantees to the chiefs and tribes of New Zealand, and to the respective families and individuals thereof, the full exclusive and undisputed possession of their lands and estates, forests, fisheries, and other properties which they may collectively or individually possess, so long as it is their wish and desire to retain the same in their possession; but the chiefs of the United Tribes and the individual chiefs yield to H.M. the exclusive right of pre-emption over such lands as the proprietors thereof may be disposed to alienate, at such prices as may be agreed upon between the respective proprietors and persons appointed by H.M. to treat with them in that behalf.

ARTICLE THE THIRD:
In consideration thereof, H.M. the Queen of England extends to the natives of New Zealand her royal protection, and imparts to them all the rights and privileges of British subjects.

general British policy towards the unannexed islands lies in the conditions on which sovereignty was obtained and the reasons for the final reversal of the minimum intervention policy. Measured against the long record of British failure to intervene in New Zealand, it is obvious that the Treaty and the decisions on which it was based were not satisfactory to the Colonial Office, the missionaries nor the New Zealand Company.

The Colonial Office had never wished to intervene in New Zealand. Even after intervention had been recognised as necessary, the British Government had proceeded only with the utmost reluctance. A year after the first admission of the need for intervention, a vague plan of appointing a consul had been produced. "The projected appointment of a consul had grown into the plan of finding him land, so much land in the long run that the plan had swollen into that of full annexation. Another colony meant for the Colonial Office more overwork, more squabbling with its mentor, the Treasury, and more attacks upon its position in the government of the Empire from prejudiced outsiders or sentimental negrophilists. The Colonial Office found no peace in the Treaty for which James Stephen had coached Hobson so patiently."[55]

Nor were the missionary societies satisfied. British rule in New Zealand meant the end of any hope of missionary dominance there. While Busby had been Resident, British authority in New Zealand had frequently relied on missionary prestige. But the arrival of Hobson and the establishment of British rule signified the end of the missionaries' political power. It signified, too, the disappointment of the cherished missionary hopes that "civilisation" would be introduced in New Zealand through their work and guidance alone. Missionaries in the field, of course, had sometimes favoured British intervention and they gave Hobson active support in concluding the Treaty. They had recognised at least three or four years previously the folly of Coates's dreams.

The New Zealand Company also regretted the Treaty of Waitangi and the conditions of the advent of British rule. The Company had been the most vehement advocate of British intervention in New Zealand. Its motive had been desire to guarantee order and good government. The self-assertion of the Kororareka set and the crumbling institutions of supposed Maori rule had alike become anathema to regular settlers and investors. British sovereignty, so it was hoped, would bring discipline, security for property and the rule of law. To their surprise, the settlers and

[55] T. Williams: "The Treaty of Waitangi"; *History*, Vol. XXV, No. 99, p. 241.

the Company found that the British Government proposed to act retrospectively and to examine all titles to land acquired before British rule was established. Moreover, the strictest control was to be exercised over land purchases in the future. The Company had purchased extensive areas and could regard the Treaty only as a direct threat to its investments and profits.

The common disappointment of the Colonial Office, the missionary societies and the Company with the form of British intervention in New Zealand reflected their own competing interests. The Colonial Office was still much in the grip of laissez-faire and anti-colonialism. The missionary societies, which through adventitious personal factors, enjoyed a specially strong influence at the Colonial Office, opposed any extension of British government amongst the natives. Relying mainly upon experience in South Africa, the "Saints" opposed political intervention amongst native peoples and particularly condemned the signing of incomprehensible treaties with native races. The New Zealand Company, representing the economic expansionism of England, was reviving imperialist sentiment and asking the protection of British government for its investments and the benefits of British rule for its settlers.

The Company saw its main point achieved when Great Britain intervened. But the intervention was on the terms of the Colonial Office, still much subject to the humanitarian influence which had for so long bolstered up the policy of minimum intervention. And it is even doubtful whether the Company's influence had been of much importance in procuring the intervention. The initiative in seeking British action in New Zealand seems all along to have been taken by the authorities in New South Wales. Darling and Bourke established the Resident principle. Bourke sent home to England Hobson's plan of intervention which the Colonial Office so strongly favoured. Bourke made it clear that the time had come for Great Britain to accept a larger degree of direct responsibility in New Zealand than had been accepted during Busby's office. The decision to make New Zealand a dependency of New South Wales, though not necessarily indicative of New South Wales influence, shows how the New Zealand problem was regarded in Great Britain. It is true that the Association secured the 1837 admission from Glenelg, that intervention was necessary, but Glenelg laid down conditions which prevented the Association from establishing itself in New Zealand. The sailing of the *Tory*, so long described as the final inducement for intervention, was preceded by the New South Wales recommendations and by clear decisions of the

Colonial Office itself in favour of establishing British rule in parts of New Zealand.

At most the Association and the Company influenced the form of British intervention and, partly through Wakefield's work on land policy, played some part in shaping the various plans considered by the Colonial Office. The Association and the Company fought the open battle with the great missionary societies and with the Colonial Office itself. But all the evidence goes to show that the Colonial Office, though for so long dissuaded from action in New Zealand by doctrinaire influences (amongst others), finally decided to intervene because of the evidence from New South Wales and New Zealand that, without British intervention, New Zealand, its missionaries, its natives and its trade would be drawn into a single cataclysm of disaster.

It is perhaps still necessary to justify specifically the view that the British annexation of New Zealand was in no sense a consequence of French rivalry. There is no evidence in Foreign Office or Colonial Office papers to suggest that fear of French action played any part in inducing the British decision to establish a government in New Zealand.

It is true that on several occasions Great Britain was warned that if she did not assert her own sovereignty in New Zealand, the islands (or at least the South Island) would become French. In 1831 Acting Governor Lindesay of New South Wales informed the Colonial Office of reports that a French ship, alleged to have been *La Favorite* (Captain La Place), had taken possession of New Zealand. But within a month Governor Bourke had reported that no possession had been taken, "nor does it appear to have been contemplated."[56] In 1837 the Frenchman, the Baron de Thierry, who claimed to have purchased 40,000 acres of land in New Zealand, arrived there with a grandiloquent offer of liberal government. But the British Resident, Busby, had prepared for his arrival and the Baron's claim to be "Sovereign Chief of New Zealand and King of Nukuhava" was not taken seriously by either whites or natives.[57] A year later Busby himself expressed fears that France

[56] Lindesay to Goderich, Nov. 4, 1831; and Bourke to Goderich, Dec. 23, 1831; *H.R.A.,* I, xvi, pp. 442 and 483.

[57] Cf. *H. of L. Cttee. on N.Z., 1838*; p. 301. Thierry's importance lay in the French disposition to take him seriously. For some years France had been taking a growing interest in New Zealand. From about 1835 one or two French men-of-war had been frequently in New Zealand waters to protect French whaling ships. (Marais, *op. cit.*, p. 92, n. 5.) The French Minister of Marine, in 1838 seriously considered entering into negotiations with Thierry, who was thought to be "possesseur en chef d'un établissement naissant sur cette grande île." (See Marais, *op. cit.*, pp. 92-93.)

was meditating the formation of a settlement in New Zealand. His anxiety, which proved to have been without foundation, was not unconnected with the arrival of the French missionaries in 1838 under Bishop Pompallier.[58]

The only other reference in the documents is to a letter from G. F. Angas to Glenelg (December 20, 1838) suggesting that the Baron de Thierry was likely to be appointed as French Consul in New Zealand. Glenelg wrote to Palmerston concerning this report, not with any intention of countering the French action, but simply to enquire whether it would be possible to remonstrate with the French Government against the selection of the Baron as French Consul.[59]

Fears of French activity in New Zealand thus proved uniformly groundless up to 1838. France was interested in the trade and commerce of New Zealand, but not to the point of establishing a colony there. While it is true that France did endeavour to plant a colony in New Zealand in the same year as Great Britain acquired sovereignty there, no evidence exists to prove that the British Government ever regarded seriously the possibility of a French settlement or feared possible repercussions on her Australian settlements. Even when the French Government agreed in December, 1839, to co-operate with the Nanto-Bordelaise Company in sending out a colonising expedition to the South Island, Stephen's official memorandum merely observed that "it was now clear, first that the French Government are seriously engaged in making a settlement in New Zealand, secondly that they are doing this in a very feeble manner."[60] The Foreign Office was kept informed by its own agents about the preparations for the expedition but remained indifferent, if only because British plans were too far advanced to run any risk of anticipation by France.

The importance of the French expedition lay in the action which it precipitated in New Zealand. The expedition, organised by the Nanto-Bordelaise Company and using a French ship of war, was intended to found a French settlement at Banks Peninsula in the South Island. But Hobson, hearing of the risk of French action, took steps to assert British sovereignty in the South Island. Captain Stanley (H.M.S. *Britomart*) was sent to Akaroa in order that prior British occupancy might be established in addition to the proclama-

[58] Gipps to Glenelg, Nov. 2, 1838; *H.R.A.*, I, xix, p. 642. Also Same to Same, Dec. 17, 1838; ibid, p. 700.

[59] Glenelg to Palmerston, Dec. 29, 1838; qu. Harrop, op. cit., pp. 63-64.

[60] Memorandum, Apr. 29, 1840; C.O. 209/7; qu. Marais, p. 195. The French expedition was viewed much more seriously in New South Wales. Cf. *The Australian*, Aug. 13 and 18, 1840.

tion of British sovereignty on May 21st. Stanley raised the British flag at Akaroa and left a magistrate there, to show that sovereignty was being exercised.[61] The French captain accepted the inevitable and his Government eventually approved his conduct. But the French recognition of British sovereignty was not made until 1844, by which time it was long overdue and had been rendered politically necessary by French action in Tahiti. (See Ch. XII, below.)

French influence on British policy towards the annexation of New Zealand was at most confined to the Akaroa incident and to strengthening the general determination of the Colonial Office that British sovereignty should be established beyond doubt. How far French ambitions conduced to the decision to establish sovereignty throughout the whole of New Zealand cannot be assessed. Plainly the Government's determination to bring the land position in New Zealand thoroughly under control also worked to this end.

The main reasons for the reversal of minimum intervention in New Zealand were undoubtedly the growth of British interests there, especially those based on New South Wales, and the peculiar difficulties with which the Colonial Office was faced when beset on the one side by the humanitarians and on the other by the New Zealand Company and the settlers and traders from New South Wales demanding order and good government.

From the wider standpoint of general British policy in the islands the annexation of New Zealand is to be regarded as the first case in the South Pacific of a group in which the advent of Europeans raised problems that the local rulers could not solve and resulted in the growth of a substantial body of settlers and traders subject to no effective law and rapidly disturbing the fabric of native law and custom. The various expedients adopted in New Zealand to solve the problem of government, including British representation, the development of rudimentary attempts amongst the whites to maintain order (e.g., the Kororareka Association) and Busby's recommendation of a Maori Government under British protection, all had counterparts in other islands later in the century. New Zealand was merely the first (and the best known) instance of the new problem of government in the South Pacific islands. It was a problem that Great Britain could not solve without abandoning her minimum intervention policy. In each case where the policy was abandoned a long and difficult struggle, comparable in nature, if not in degree, to that over New Zealand, ensued and the final reversal of policy was accomplished only with the greatest reluctance.

[61] Cf. J. C. Andersen: "The Mission of the *Britomart* at Akaroa . . . in 1840"; *Transactions of the N.Z. Inst.*, Vol. LII, pp. 78-79.

CHAPTER XI

THE AMBITIONS OF FRANCE

ONE of the embarrassments faced by the Colonial Office in handling the New Zealand problem during 1839-40 was the increasing probability of French intervention. But, as the Colonial Office was able to establish British rule before the French could take decisive action, the full implications of the presence of foreign Powers in the South Pacific islands had not become apparent. In the succeeding years, however, the minimum intervention policy was frequently subjected to strain by foreign activity in the islands. French action, which had been too late in New Zealand, was undertaken effectively in Tahiti, New Caledonia and in other islands where British interests were well-established.

Amongst the factors originally underlying the adoption of the minimum intervention policy had been the political and naval dominance of Great Britain in the South Pacific. Secure in the power of the Royal Navy and with the Australian colonies as a base, Great Britain had been able to leave her subjects in the islands to fend for themselves. British traders and missionaries, having no stronger authority than that of native rulers to contend with, and no more powerful competition than that of American and other traders, had been able to establish themselves strongly. Minimum intervention suited British subjects in the islands almost as well as it suited the British Government.

These easy conditions were disturbed by the development of the political activity of foreign Powers. When France and the United States of America appeared on the scene and entered into political relations with the natives, the whole balance of conditions in the islands was upset. When France adopted a policy of territorial acquisition and took advantage of the presence of French missionaries in the islands,[1] the ascendancy of British missionaries and their political influence were abruptly challenged.

The first foreign Power to indulge political ambitions in the South Pacific was the United States of America. In 1826, at the prompting of trading and whaling interests, which had been alarmed by the growth of British interests in the islands, the

---

[1] See R. P. Perbal: *Les missionaires français et le nationalisme*; Paris, 1939.

United States sent out Captain ap Catesby Jones (U.S.S. *Peacock*) to impress native rulers with American might and, where possible, to enter into agreements with them. Jones arranged treaties at Hawaii, Tahiti and Raiatea, but in the last case the interference of British subjects prevented his achieving as much as he had desired.[2]

The agreements, which were to be construed as part of the consistent American drive in Pacific commerce at that time, apparently attracted little attention at the Foreign Office, although they excited alarm in New South Wales. The *Sydney Gazette* in a leading article entitled "The Society Islands—The Americans and the French" expressed the fear that the American wish to obtain bases in the Pacific was not unconnected with an intention of attacking the Australian settlements. The United States was also accused of encroaching on the "innumerable isles that bespeck that Ocean of which Australia is destined to hold the imperial sway." The *Gazette* recommended prompt action to maintain British predominance in the Pacific against possible American and French threats.[3]

The *Gazette's* reference to French activity bore out the long-continued complaints of the British missionaries at Tahiti against French ambitions. The Tahitian missionaries had been warning the Foreign Office of French interest in the Sandwich and Society Islands for over a year. Hankey, the Treasurer of the London Missionary Society, had supported the 1825 request from Tahiti for British protection. His ground was the imminence of French action to introduce the Catholic faith and French government into Tahiti. In December, 1826, Hankey wrote to the Colonial Office referring to a "reported expedition from France" to the Pacific.[4] No French expedition was sent to the Societies at that time, but the alarm of the missionaries, anxious to preserve Tahiti for their thirty-years old Protestant labours, was communicated to the Government in the most forceful terms. At that stage, however, the Foreign Office was not obliged to make any choice between sup-

[2] Elley to Canning, encl. agreement, Dec. 12, 1826; F.O. 58/14. Also F.O. *Memorandum on Society and Georgian Islands, 1846*; Encl. in Papers, No. 23.

[3] G. Greenwood: *Early American-Australian Relations*; Melbourne, 1944; pp. 115-6. Other U.S. expeditions soon followed. In 1829 the U.S.S. *Vincennes* visited the Marquesas, the Society Islands and Hawaii. (C. S. Stewart: *A Visit to the South Seas in the U.S.S. "Vincennes"*; 2 vols., N.Y., 1832). In 1838 the U.S.A. sent out the famous Wilkes expedition, which was equipped for scientific exploration. (C. Wilkes: *Narrative of the United States Exploring Expeditions*; 5 vols. Philadelphia, 1845; ed. 1852.)

[4] Hankey to Canning, Nov. 23, 1826; F.O. 58/14; and Hankey to Hay, Dec. 8, 1826; F.O. 58/14.

porting the missionaries at the risk of offending the French Government and acquiescing in French designs at the cost of stirring up missionary objections and seeing the British position in the South Pacific threatened.

When foreign Powers took the step of seeking territories in the South Pacific the whole policy of minimum intervention was brought to stake. The passing of a single island into the hands of a foreign Power was capable of raising the problem for Great Britain of deciding whether she would contest the issue in the interests of her missionaries and traders and in the interests of the strategic and commercial position of her Australian colonies, or whether she would adhere to minimum intervention, even at the cost of seeing the interests of her subjects pass under the control of foreign governments in the islands.

Humanitarianism did not enter into the question of foreign rivalry at all. If the islands were to be annexed or protected, the annexing or protecting Power, so the British humanitarians thought, might more reasonably be Great Britain, which had pioneered Protestant missionary work in the South Pacific, than France, a Catholic country, whose missionaries disturbed the labours of their Protestant predecessors.

A territorial challenge from a foreign Power was first felt in the Marquesas and the Societies, which the French resolved to bring under their rule. In the late 'thirties the French Government began to work out a policy of seeking Pacific bases, as part of a general drive to expand French commerce. In the Eastern Pacific, the Minister of Marine and the Colonies specially directed his attention to acquiring keypoints for the expansion and protection of French commerce.[5] The attraction of the region was the prospective construction of a Panama Canal, not Colonisation.

In 1838 the Colombian Government gave France the right to cut a canal through the isthmus and a party of French engineers was sent out to investigate Limon Bay a few years later. French policy was officially explained in 1843 by the Minister of Marine and Colonies in presenting a *projet de loi* for an extraordinary credit for the French establishments in the Pacific. The Minister then said that France needed naval establishments in the Pacific in order to protect French commerce there. Foreseeing the cutting of the canal, he envisaged an increasing importance for the East Pacific islands.[6]

[5] As to French policy in the Western Pacific, see Ch. X, above.
[6] *Moniteur* report of speech by Minister of Marine and Colonies, encl. in Cowley to Aberdeen, Apr. 25, 1843; *Corr. rel. to . . . French at Tahiti, 1825-43*; No. 14.

By the 'fifties French commercial ambitions in the Southern Pacific had taken definite shape. An interesting example of how the new French acquisitions amongst the islands were viewed in France is provided in Arnaudtizon's *Exploration Commerciale dans les Mers du Sud et de la Chine* (1854).[7] A chapter on the Societies visualised the development of a trade triangle consisting of Chile, the Sandwich Islands and the Society Islands, with headquarters at Valparaiso.

There can be little doubt that political jealousy of Great Britain, which had acquired so much of the lost fruits of the first French colonial Empire, also accounted for some of the French ambition to be established in the South Pacific. In 1841 the French Government received the report of Bruat, later the first French Governor at Tahiti, on the prospects of French policy in the Pacific:

"... la France ne peut pas rester sans points de protections pour la marine, sans asiles pour ses navires et sans avoir un centre d'action Sur ces mers qui, elles aussi s'éveillent et dont les populations sortent de leurs langes. Doit-on laisser toujours la même puissance exercer seule son influence, s'étendre, se créer des débouchés, donner le goût des produits, des ces moeurs, de sa religion? nous priver, enfin, de rayonner dans ces mers sans un passe-port anglais?"[8]

Several French naval officers reported to their government that the British predominated in the South Pacific and that the British position was founded on missionary enterprise. Bérard reported in his *Campagne de la corvette l'Alcmène* that:

"Ce n'est pas seulement comme puissance commerciale que l'Angleterre règne sans conteste sur l'Océanie; c'est surtout comme puissance religieuse que son action est grande, et, sous son patronage, le protestantisme succède à l'idolâtrie."[9]

Bérard, like La Place (*Compagne . ... de la frégate l'Artémise*), argued that France should adopt the same policy as (according to him) Great Britain had adopted, in order to undermine the British hold by extension of French missionary labours:

"Sans doute, nous aussi, nous avons des missionaries, et ceux-là n'ont qu'uin but détaché de toute pensée terrestre: la gloire de Dieu —mais quelle différence entre leurs moyens d'action et ceux des ministres du culte réformé."[10]

---

[7] Publ. by Chambre de Commerce de Rouen.

[8] M. Besson: "L'Annexion des Iles Marquises." (*Revue de l'Histoire des Colonies Françaises*, Vol. XVII, 1924.)

[9] A. Bérard: *Campagne de la Corvette l'Alcmène; in Nouvelles Annales de la Marine et des Colonies.* (See bibliography.)

[10] Ibid.

Bérard concluded with a plea for the establishment of a French missionary, political and trading centre in New Caledonia.[11]

That British missionaries did in fact constitute outposts of British influence and civilisation is obvious. It is also obvious, from their own admissions, that they regarded themselves as emissaries of Britain. The famous John Williams, in dedicating his *Narrative of Missionary Enterprise* to the King, declared that:

> "In prosecuting the one great object to which their lives are consecrated . . . [the missionaries] will keep in view whatever may promote the Commerce and Science, as well as the Religious Glory of their beloved Country."[12]

Although the British Government itself had no ambitions in the South Pacific, the degree to which missionaries had established British influence not unnaturally led French observers to assume that the missionaries were serving the political and commercial ambitions of their country. How far any French Government ever regarded French missionary labours as preparing the way for French rule is not clear. But it is certain that from the 'thirties to the 'fifties the French flag followed French missionaries and the needs of the missionaries were regarded as justifying major acts of political intervention in the islands. Brookes states that, after the Bachelot episode in Hawaii,[13] France "gave its officers definite instructions specifying that the question of the right of French citizens to reside and proselytize be carried to a finish, both at Hawaii and Tahiti."[14]

From the first the British missionaries were most suspicious about the activities of the French. Never was the fear disguised that the Catholic emissaries of France would be supported by the French Government. The activities of the early French missionaries in trade, though apparently no more extensive than those of some of the early English missionaries, were regarded as yet further proof of the French intention to use missionary labours as the spearhead of their infiltration of the islands. In 1846 the *Samoan Reporter* accused the French missionaries of winning over the natives with cheap merchandise and of opposing British interests in the islands.[15]

[11] See also M. Wilks: *Tahiti, &c.*; London, 1844; p. 22.
[12] J. Williams: *A Narrative of Missionary Enterprise*; London, 1837, p.v.
[13] Alexis Bachelot, a French priest, had been ordered by the chiefs to leave Hawaii.
[14] Brookes, op. cit., p. 82.
[15] Cf. S. Masterman: *The Origins of International Rivalry in Samoa*; London, 1934; pp. 50 ff.

Even the preliminary steps of establishing French missionaries in the island raised problems of policy for Great Britain. The French in several instances chose to commence their Catholic missionary work on islands where British Protestant missionaries were already in the field.

The commencement of French missionary work in the Gambiers involved no immediate threat to British missionary interests, but the coming of the French to Tahiti, where the London Missionary Society had pioneered Protestant missions in the Pacific in 1797, raised strong objections. The first French attempt on Tahiti was made when Murphy, from the Catholic mission in the Gambiers, attempted to land there in 1835. He was turned back under the Tahitian law requiring express permission for foreigners to land and settle on the island.[16] The British missionary, Pritchard, who reported the occurrence to the Foreign Office, admitted that the law had been applied against Murphy because he almost certainly intended to commence Catholic missionary work in Tahiti. "It appears to us unreasonable, ungentlemanly and un-Christian for a body of Roman Catholics to come to these shores and enter into other men's labours."[17]

Pritchard's despatch, which was rather significantly omitted from the printed documents on the proceedings of the French at Tahiti published in 1843,[18] established two important points. By implication Pritchard admitted that it was British missionary influence which had secured the application of a law, originally intended for escaped convicts and deserting seamen, to Murphy. By implication also the British missionaries requested the Foreign Office to lend them support, although no mention of French objectives beyond proselytization was made in the despatch.

No action was taken by the Foreign Office on receipt of the despatch. Indeed, it is difficult to see what could have been done without requesting the French Government to induce Catholic missionaries to avoid fields where Protestants were already established, or alternatively of encouraging Pritchard and his associates to persist in using Tahitian law to further their own opposition to French missionary labour on Tahiti. Either course would have involved the risk of unfavourable reaction in France and there really was no reason why the intolerance of the British missionaries should have been allowed to embroil the British and French Governments.

16 Pritchard to F.O., June 18, 1835; F.O. 58/14.
17 ibid.
18 Corr. rel. to the proceedings of the French at Tahiti, 1825-1843; 1843.

A year later, however, the problem was raised again, this time by Pomare herself[19] and also by Pritchard.[20] The latter complained of "several Frenchmen who are determined to land and reside on this island as Roman Catholic missionaries." He asked whether, as Tahiti was recognised as "independent nation" by Great Britain, she might not enact for her own government laws consistent with international law. More particularly, did not Pomare have power to refuse foreigners permission to settle in her dominions? Pomare herself wrote in similar strain:

"The Roman Catholic missionaries belong to France; we conceive they have nothing to do with our island and hence we are determined not to receive them."

These attempts to win Foreign Office support for the missionary attitude by means of raising general issues won support from Palmerston. Pritchard's request on the face of it raised no new problems. Great Britain had already recognised the sovereignty of Tahiti. Hence Palmerston's curt minute on Pomare's despatch: "Of Course She has a Right to request these R.C. miss. to go."[21] Palmerston evidently treated the matter at this stage as a simple request from a British missionary and a friendly native ruler for advice as to the legal competence of a native state.

In the despatch which was sent out to Pritchard from the Foreign Office, in July, 1837,[22] the issues underlying the correspondence had, however, been taken into account. Some attention was paid to the likely French reactions to any attempts by the Tahitian Government, notoriously dominated by the British missionaries, to exclude the Catholic French. A state might refuse to accept foreigners, Palmerston wrote to Pritchard in July, but it was contrary to usage to force them to leave once they had been admitted, "provided they do not infringe the laws of the land."[23] The qualification was a clear warning to the missionaries and to Pomare that they should not expect the British Government to support them in any extreme measures taken against the French Catholic missionaries. The despatch could be construed only as advice to admit the French missionaries and to allow them to pursue their labours uninterruptedly.

Several months before Palmerston sent this despatch, two French

[19] Pomare to Palmerston, Nov. 18, 1836; F.O. 58/14.
[20] Pritchard to Palmerston, Nov. 19, 1836; F.O. 58/14.
[21] Palmerston's note (June 15, 1837) on Pomare to Palmerston, Nov. 11, 1836; F.O. 58/14.
[22] Palmerston to Pritchard, July 19, 1837; F.O. 58/14.
[23] Palmerston to Pritchard, July 19, 1837; F.O. 58/14.

priests, MM. PP. Laval and Caret, had been expelled from Tahiti in circumstances raising clear political issues. The expulsion, which Palmerston later described as an "unjustifiable act of violence,"[24] was complicated by the conduct of the United States Consul, Moerenhout, who received the Frenchmen into his own home and protested at an insult to the American flag when he was not permitted to retain them.[25] Moreover, it was beyond doubt that the Catholics had been expelled in consequence of the representations of the English missionaries.[26]

The incident, which was speedily magnified by the French, gave the French Government all the pretext that it needed for introducing political and (later) naval force to back the French missionaries. The Bishop of Oceania wrote to Walpole, the British Consul-General in Chile, complaining that it was the "pitiless fanaticism" of Pritchard which had led to the expulsion of Laval and Caret.[27]

The Foreign Office refused to express an opinion on the merits of the incident but was moved at last to take action in defence of the *status quo*. With the prospect of intervention in Tahiti coming near, the Foreign Office took some steps to avert such an unwelcome necessity. Walpole was instructed to enquire of the Bishop whether:

> "Seeing there are so many Islands in the Pacific and South Sea, the inhabitants of which are still ignorant of the Doctrines of Christianity, would it not be better and more useful that the French Missionaries should endeavour to diffuse the Light of the Gospel amongst Populations to whom its Truths are as yet wholly unknown, rather than to embark in a struggle of Rivalship with Protestant Missionaries, in Islands where Christianity has already made some degree of progress."[28]

No change in the policy of the French missionaries followed.

The importance of the correspondence arising from the expulsion of Laval and Caret was that the Foreign Office had at last been induced to intervene in an attempt to preserve the *status quo*. The British Government had no wish to adopt an active policy in the South Pacific. It would have been well content to allow

[24] Palmerston's note (July 16, 1839) on Pritchard to Palmerston, Nov. 9, 1838; F.O. 58/15.
[25] Pritchard to the U.S. Sec. of State, Dec. 31, 1836; F.O. 58/15.
[26] Gipps to Glenelg, Dec. 24, 1838; *H.R.A.*, I, xix, p. 709.
[27] Bishop of Oceania to Walpole, Jan. 12, 1837; encl. in Walpole to Palmerston, July 21, 1837; F.O. 16/32; qu. Brookes, op. cit.; p. 83.
[28] Fox Strangways to Walpole, Dec 14, 1837; F.O. 16/30; qu. ibid.

the existing state of things to continue. But French action threatened British interests in a powerful (and highly vocal) quarter.

In the middle of the nineteenth century missionary labours commanded a high degree of political support in England and were esteemed as one of the noblest aspects of English civilisation. The London Missionary Society was certain of being able to enlist a substantial force of public opinion behind any attempts it might make to induce the Government to remonstrate with France.

Actually the degree of missionary pressure exerted on the Government was considerable. Ellis, the Secretary of the London Missionary Society, endeavoured to convince Palmerston that the natives themselves, and not merely the English missionaries, earnestly wished the French to be excluded. Missionary meetings in England revealed a most deep-rooted distrust of the French. Speaking at the valedictory service of the Rev. John Williams prior to his departure from England in 1838, the Rev. William Ellis condemned the Catholic activities in angry and resentful terms.

The Foreign Office was actuated by unwillingness to embroil Great Britain with France over the trivial affairs of a South Pacific island. It wished to preserve the minimum intervention policy. But the strength of missionary influence was such that some action had to be taken. Accordingly the Foreign Office acted in the mildest possible manner. It did not remonstrate with the French Government. It merely asked a Consul-General to enquire of a Catholic Bishop whether it really were necessary for Catholics and Protestants to labour in the same missionary field. A blind eye was turned to the possible political implications of French activity in Tahiti and the matter was treated as one of missionary, not international, rivalry.

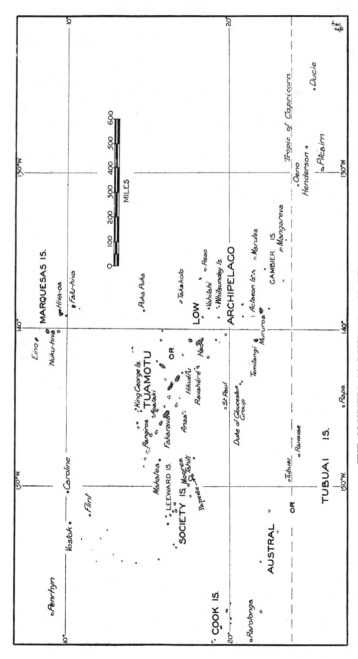

THE SOCIETIES, MARQUESAS AND TUAMOTUS.

Chapter XII

THE TAHITIAN AFFAIR

The weakness of British action following the Laval and Caret affair left the way open for French aggrandisement in a region where British influence was strong, British interests had been established for forty years and strategic needs indicated the advisability of preserving British dominance. The actions of Commodore Dupetit-Thouars of the French frigate *Venus* in 1838 indicated that his government was fully prepared to make political capital out of the missionary cause in the islands. First, the Commodore landed two missionaries, Desvault and Borgella, both of the Society of Piçpus, at the Marquesas, where British Protestant missionaries were already at work.[1] Leaving the Marquesas, where he had planted the seeds of future political dissension, Dupetit-Thouars sailed to Tahiti and demanded from Pomare an apology for the expulsion of Laval and Caret in 1836.[2] A letter from Dupetit-Thouars complained of ill-treatment of French subjects in the island and required an indemnity of 2,000 Spanish dollars in respect of the expulsion of the missionaries. All demands had to be met within twenty-four hours or acts of war would follow.[3] "The frigate immediately assumed a very hostile appearance. . . . The only alternative to prevent devastation and death was to comply with the requisitions," wrote Pritchard.[4] Subsequently a convention was proposed by Dupetit-Thouars, providing for perpetual peace between France and Tahiti and exchanging promises of most favoured nation treatment.[5]

The actions of Dupetit-Thouars compelled the Foreign Office to assess French policy in the Pacific at its true worth, that is, as a calculated attempt to acquire political influence and territory. Great Britain had to face the fact that the easy British ascendancy in the South Pacific, on which the minimum intervention policy had been partly founded, was being threatened in a vital quarter.

[1] L. Rollin: *Les Iles Marquises*; Paris, 1929; p. 237.
[2] Pritchard to Palmerston, Nov. 9, 1838; *Corr. rel. to the . . . French at Tahiti, 1825-1843*; No. 6.
[3] Encl. in No. 6, ibid.
[4] No. 6, ibid.
[5] Encl. 2 in No. 6, ibid.

The question was whether the British Government should intervene in an attempt to preserve the *status quo,* that had been so favourable to British interests, or whether it should permit France to proceed uninterruptedly with consequent disadvantages to British subjects and with consequent new difficulties for British policy.

The problem presented itself in the form of a petition from Pomare and the chiefs of Tahiti to Queen Victoria. Having recited their great faith in the British Crown, the petitioners went on to state:

"That the commerce and industry which civilization attracts to our islands puts us daily into relations with the white people, superior to us in mind and body, and to whom our institutions appear foolish, and our Government feeble. . . . Let your flag cover us and your Lion defend us—determine the form through which we could shelter ourselves lawfully under your wing."[6]

This petition was received at the same time as Pritchard's despatch, quoted above, relating the conduct of Dupetit-Thouars. The Government had already received strong representations from the London Missionary Society.[7] A memorandum presented to Palmerston by representatives of the Society on April 15, 1839, had requested British mediation with the Government of France so that French men-of-war might have orders "to respect the independence of all those Islands in the Pacific Ocean and elsewhere, in which, with the consent of the Natives, English and other Protestant Missionaries are found to be settled."[8]

Thus primed with the missionary point of view and not unaware of the probable consequences to British policy of further French action at Tahiti, Palmerston was induced to give serious consideration to Pomare's request for protection. To provide some brake on French action, the Admiralty was requested to send a ship of war to Tahiti "to look after British interests, and, in conformity with the spirit of Mr. Secretary Canning's letter of the 3rd March, 1827, to afford the Queen such moral support as she may appear justly entitled to in any negotiation she may be engaged in with any foreign Power."[9]

Having anticipated the charge that the Government had allowed foreign men-of-war to dispossess British missionaries of their influence and position without affording even elementary protection,

[6] Pomare and Chiefs to Gt. Britain, Nov. 8, 1838; encl. 3 in No. 6, ibid.

[7] Cf. L.M.S. to Palmerston, Apr. 9, 1839; F.O. 58/15.

[8] Memorandum presented by the L.M.S. at the F.O., Apr. 15, 1839; F.O. 58/15.

[9] Fox Strangways to Barrow, July 19, 1839; *Corr. rel. to the Society Islands, Part I;* No. 68.

the Foreign Office turned to consider the Tahitian petition. The task was complicated by the fact that on the same day as Pomare wrote to Queen Victoria, the Tahitian Parliament passed a law declaring Protestantism as taught by the London Missionary Society to be the only lawful religion in Tahiti. Deportation was prescribed as the punishment for coming to Tahiti with intent to disturb the established faith. Having thus played into French hands, the Tahitian Government relied on the assistance of Great Britain.

The Foreign Office, which had been induced only with difficulty to suggest in 1837 that Catholic missionaries should not be sent to disturb the work of Protestants, was certainly not so anxious to intervene as to take advantage of the proffered opportunity of defending the laws of Tahiti. Palmerston referred the Tahitian despatch to the Colonial Office with a very strong expression of his own views:

> "Send this to Lord Normanby and ask his opinion as to the Expediency of Entering into any Engagement with the Queen of Taheite by which Gt. Britain would undertake to afford to the People of Taheite Protection or good offices in case of need—Stating at the same time that the Law prohibiting any Person from teaching any Religious Doctrines different from those of the English Missionaries appears to be an intolerant and indefensible Edict; and that although perhaps the Proceeding of the French Frigate was somewhat harsh and peremptory, it must nevertheless be acknowledged that the expulsion of the French Missionaries was an unjustifiable act of violence." (July 16, 1839.)[10]

In reply Stephen wrote that, because of the great extent of the existing British dominions in the Pacific and of the recent decision to acquire New Zealand, no obligation should be incurred towards Tahiti and no offer of sovereignty there should be accepted.[11] This decision was communicated by Palmerston to Pritchard in September, 1839.[12]

The decision of 1839 really involved very little advance from that of 1837. Intervention had proceeded to the point of sending a warship to Tahiti to watch events, but beyond that the British Government declined to go. Moreover, the Foreign Office had made up its mind that no protection would be given to British

[10] Palmerston's note, July 16, 1839, on Pritchard to Palmerston, Nov. 9, 1838; F.O. 58/15.

[11] Stephen to Fox Strangways, Aug. 1, 1839; Corr. rel. to the Society Islands, Part I; No. 70.

[12] Palmerston to Pritchard, Sept. 9, 1839; ibid, No. 71.

missionaries in Tahiti if they attempted to exclude their Catholic rivals. The Foreign Office still regretted that the French should attempt to commence missionary work in Tahiti, but did not deny their right to do so.

How far the real balance of factors involved in these decisions was ever considered is not disclosed in the documents. Palmerston's minute showed that he had not even considered the possibility of granting more than a promise of protection (not a protectorate) and good offices to Tahiti. The form in which the Tahitian Government might have been permitted to shelter under the wing of the British lion (to use Pomare's phrases) would have been merely a repetition of the promises of good neighbourliness made by Canning in 1827 with some undertaking to intervene in defence of Tahitian independence. The Colonial Office objected to even the limited prospect of intervention envisaged in this undertaking.

The Tahitian problem arose just after Great Britain had resolved to acquire sovereignty in New Zealand, a decision to which there had been an unfavourable reaction in France. (See Chapter X, above.) Was Great Britain to give to Tahiti guarantees which could only be construed as an attempt to hinder French ambitions? Again, of what value was it to Great Britain to keep France out of Tahiti? Admittedly, the island possessed strategic importance, but it was almost 4,000 miles away from Sydney. Its trade was of little interest to Great Britain. In fact the only British interest in Tahiti capable of exercising significant pressure on the British Government was that of the missionaries, who sought the maintenance of the *status quo* dominated by themselves, to the exclusion of the French.[13]

There was no sufficient reason for dispensing with the accepted policy of minimum intervention. Accordingly the British Government adhered to its policy of 1837 but took slightly stronger action. An agreement was made with the French Government in February, 1840, under which British and French missionaries were supposed for the future to work in separate fields.[14]

The British unwillingness to intervene in the South Pacific and the policy of treating French action there as purely a matter of missionary rivalry continued up to the establishment of the French protectorate over Tahiti in 1843. The British Government ignored

[13] Memorandum presented by the L.M.S. at the F.O., Apr. 15, 1839; F.O. 58/15. As to trade at Tahiti, see Salmon to Palmerston, July 29, 1841; *Corr. rel. to Society Islands, Part I*; encl. in No. 81.
[14] Palmerston to Granville, Feb. 14, 1840; Granville to Palmerston, Feb. 17, 1840; *Corr. rel. to the Society Islands, Part I*; Nos. 78a and 78c.

warning after warning that France intended to acquire Tahiti and that British interests would suffer, if she succeeded in doing so. The visit of Captain La Place in *L'Artémise* to Tahiti in 1839 and the pressure put on Pomare to repeal the anti-Catholic law were officially unnoticed. France was left free to extend her influence in Tahiti, where her missionaries gained through the frequent visits of French men-of-war and through the friendship of Moerenhout, who became Consul for France in September, 1838. In 1840 Pritchard warned that, "it is the opinion of the Tahitians and also of many foreigners that the French want to get the islands in their own hands."[15] He appealed for more frequent visits of British men-of-war and his request was passed on to the Admiralty, but with what result is not disclosed.[16] The appeal of Pomare to Queen Victoria in January, 1841, for British protection went unanswered.[17] In 1842 Pritchard wrote to Aberdeen commenting on the growth of French commercial interests in the Societies and suggesting that the French Government might be informed that the British Government could not contemplate any interference with the independence of the islands. Stressing the potential economic value of Tahiti to Great Britain, Pritchard again asked for more frequent naval visits.[18] Still no action was forthcoming. In 1843 Pritchard, writing from Sydney, expressed most bluntly his fear that the French would soon have in their possession all the important groups in the South Pacific with resulting strategic disadvantage to the Australasian colonies.[19] Though his arguments were supported by sentiment in New South Wales and by a despatch from Captain Toup Nicolas, R.N., to the Foreign Office, in which Papeete Harbour was highly praised and the strategic advantages of Tahiti dilated upon,[20] the British Government took no action.

The decisive aspect of the record is the unwillingness of the British Government to do anything that might involve re-opening the Tahitian question. For the sake of minimum intervention and good relations with France, the difficulties of Tahiti continued to be regarded officially as a mere matter of missionary rivalry. Requests for decisions on policy were shelved. Serious charges of

[15] Pritchard to Palmerston, Feb. 18, 1840; *Corr. rel. to the Society Islands, Part I*; No. 78.
[16] Leveson to Barrow, Aug. 14, 1840; ibid, No. 79.
[17] Pomare's Secretary to Queen Victoria, Jan. 20, 1841; F.O. 58/16.
[18] Pritchard to Aberdeen, Mar. 11, 1842; *Corr. rel. to the Society Islands, Part I*; No. 82.
[19] Pritchard to Bidwell, Jan. 3, 1843; ibid, No. 103.
[20] Toup Nicolas to Aberdeen, Mar. 15, 1843; ibid, No. 116.

political bad faith made against the French were later ignored. When Pritchard himself visited London in July, 1841, he had to wait until March, 1842, before receiving an audience with the Foreign Secretary. When he was received, Lord Aberdeen gave him evasive replies and left policy unchanged,[21] although he did approve Pritchard's plan for sending presents to Pomare.[22] As Jore drily remarked:

"Malgré toutes ses démarches, George Pritchard n'avait pas obtenu pendant les douze mois qu'il avait passé en Angleterre que le Foreign Office s'intéressât à Tahiti."[23]

The instructions sent by the Foreign Office to British representatives at Tahiti during this period of ignoring their warnings were in purely general terms. Aberdeen forwarded to Pritchard in December, 1842, a copy of a letter addressed by the Foreign Office to the Admiralty with reference to the policy to be followed by naval officers towards the "Chiefs and Governors of the Islands of the Pacific, and especially in the Sandwich and Society Islands."[24] The instructions were to treat native rulers "with great forbearance and courtesy" and to increase their authority by giving them a sense of their own independence.[25]

While the British Government was laying down a policy of recognising native sovereignty, the French Government planned a final coup in the Marquesas and the Societies. In the Marquesas, concerning which British opinion was never much agitated, the French missionaries had acquired a dominant position. "La France," wrote Simeon Delmas, "s'implantait avec eux car ils introduisaient aux Marquises sa langue, ses usages, la faisaient connaître, et disposaient à l'aimer."[26] In 1841 the French Government, seeking "un point d'escale pour les longues croisières qui avaient doublé le cap Horn," had its attention drawn to the Marquesas through Dumont d'Urville's reports. Confidential instructions were sent to Dupetit-Thouars to take possession of the Marquesas, which he did in May, 1842. No protest appears to have been made to the British Government, probably because the British missionaries had already departed in December, 1841.[27] After

21 Pritchard to Bidwell, Mar. 30, 1842; ibid, No. 83.
22 The plan was approved by Capt. Bruce, R.N. See Bruce's Memorandum to Palmerston and also Pritchard to Aberdeen, June 29, 1842; F.O. 58/16.
23 Jore, op. cit., p. 47.
24 Aberdeen to Pritchard, Dec. 1, 1842; *Extracts from PP. concerning the Society Islands, 1843.*
25 Canning to Admiralty, Oct. 4, 1842; ibid.
26 Qu. Rollin, op. cit., p. 237.
27 Paulet to Thomas, Oct. 17, 1842; F.O. 58/22.

over eight years of work amongst the natives, who were of an undeveloped type, the Protestants, according to M. Francois of the Catholic mission, had made no converts. The Catholics themselves claimed only fifteen converts (including 12 or 13 children and two or three women) after four years' labour.[28] British trade had no substantial interests in the Marquesas, so that French action there, apart from its strategic implications, had little significance for Great Britain.

Matters at Tahiti came to a head in September, 1842, when Dupetit-Thouars returned in *La Reine Blanche*. The British Government was informed by the Acting Consul, Wilson, that Dupetit-Thouars had complained of the "iniquitous" and "rigorous" conduct of the Tahitian Government towards Frenchmen. Tahiti's treaties with France, declared Dupetit-Thouars, had been violated "in the most outrageous manner." He demanded either an indemnity of 10,000 Spanish dollars to be paid within 48 hours, partly in respect of past injuries, partly as an assurance of good conduct in the future, or in default thereof, the occupation of certain parts of the island by French troops as a "pledge for the due execution of treaties, until satisfaction shall be given . . . for the wrongs of which we complain." Failure to comply with his demands would be followed by "more rigorous measures."[29]

Faced with these demands, the Tahitian Government, feeling sure that no assistance could be expected from Great Britain in time to save the situation, made complete submission. Pomare sought the protection of the French Government, subject to guarantees as to freedom of worship, ownership of land and the continuity of the royal and chiefly successions.[30] To this request Dupetit-Thouars gave a conditional acquiescence,[31] and forthwith established a provisional government. His arrangements were ratified by the French Government in April, 1843.

These circumstances are important in their details—partly because the French use of force helps to explain the vehemence of the popular reaction in Great Britain and New South Wales and partly because the events show the type of high-handed French methods, working to the probable detriment of British interests in the South Pacific, in which the British Government was prepared to acquiesce.

[28] ibid. It was also asserted that the Catholics had driven the Protestant missionaries out of the Marquesan field.
[29] Dupetit-Thouars to Pomare, Sept. 8, 1842; *Corr. rel. to the . . . French at Tahiti, 1825-43*; Encl. in No. 8.
[30] Pomare and Chiefs to Dupetit-Thouars, Sept. 9, 1842; encl. 2 in No. 8, ibid.
[31] Dupetit-Thouars to Pomare and Chiefs, Sept. 1842; encl. 3 in No. 8, ibid.

News of the French action in Tahiti appears to have occasioned surprise in Great Britain. Some venture in the Pacific by France had been expected, but Tahiti, where France seemed to enjoy all reasonable advantages already, had not been regarded as the probable destination of the long-reported expedition.[32] So little was further French action in Tahiti expected that Pritchard had been allowed to proceed home on sick leave and Rear-Admiral Thomas, commanding officer of the British South America squadron, regarded the French actions as "extraordinary and unexpected," while Walpole, the British Minister to Chile, had anticipated that the French expedition would proceed to the Marquesas or to North California.[33]

In the circumstances it was not to be expected that the British Government would be able to consider its attitude towards the Tahiti affair in the light of the general British position in the South Pacific. Relations with France were in question rather than British interests in the South Pacific. French action had precipitated the need for a prompt decision and France was obviously determined to push her Tahitian claims. Guizot himself warned that there was danger of disturbance in the Pacific "on account of the differences of the religious tenets of the Catholic and Protestant missionaries."[34]

Having impressed upon the British Government that French ambitions in the Pacific were dearly regarded, Guizot went on to relieve the worst embarrassment in relation to Tahiti—the fear of the missionaries that they would be dispossessed. Answering a question in the Chamber of Peers, Guizot promised that, "equal protection would be given to Protestant and Catholic missionaries."[35] With this promise and with the stipulation in the treaty between France and Tahiti for the protection of missionaries, the British Government agreed to be content. Pursuing his tactics for easing the way for British acquiescence, Guizot also sent orders to the French admiral in the Pacific to ensure "equal treat-

[32] Stanley to Gipps, Sept. 23, 1842; *H.R.A.*, I, xxii, p. 297. The expedition had been reported from Rio de Janeiro (Canning to Stephen, May 3, 1842, encl. Hamilton to Aberdeen) and from Santiago (Walpole to Aberdeen, Mar. 20, 1842); *H.R.A.*, I, xxii, pp. 298-300. Foreign Office enquiries in Paris as to whether New Zealand were the objective of the expedition received the answer that no expedition to New Zealand was contemplated. (Ibid, p. 299.)

[33] Thomas to F.O., Apr. 15, 1842; F.O. 58/15. Walpole to Aberdeen, Mar. 3, 1842; *H.R.A.*, I, xxii, p. 300.

[34] Cowley to Aberdeen, Mar. 20, 1842. *Corr. rel. to the . . . French at Tahiti, 1825-43*; No. 9.

[35] Cowley to Aberdeen, Mar. 24, 1843; ibid, No. 10.

ment" for the British missionaries at Tahiti. He embodied his promises in a written note handed to the British ambassador.

Guizot's efforts to prevent the missionary question from forcing the British Foreign Office into unfavourable action were maintained to the end. When Dupetit-Thouars proceeded in 1844 to deprive Pomare of her sovereignty, a matter on which the British missionaries were adamant in their views, the French Government refused to confirm his action. Instead France adhered to the treaty of 1842[36] and later agreed to pay Consul Pritchard an indemnity for his arrest and imprisonment by the French authorities in Tahiti.[37]

The astute discretion of Guizot was matched in England by the determination of Peel and Aberdeen to avert friction with France over Tahiti. Relationships were somewhat eased by the personal friendship of Guizot and Aberdeen and by the fact that Guizot himself was a Protestant. Though public feeling in both countries was inflamed, both over Tahiti and in 1844 over the Moroccan affair, and though there had been fears of a clash over New Zealand as late as 1842,[38] the British Ministers were determined that Anglo-French relations should stand the strain. They welcomed Guizot's assurances concerning the treatment of British missionaries and announced in Parliament that they were perfectly satisfied with Guizot's good faith.[39] (Nevertheless, Pritchard was advised to report to the Foreign Office on the French attitude towards British Protestants in Tahiti.[40])

The vehemence of the missionary reaction in Great Britain to the news from Tahiti was such that the slightest expression of ministerial dissatisfaction with the French assurances would probably have been followed by instant demands for breaking off diplomatic relations. The Foreign Office was flooded with memorials,[41] protesting against the French action and demanding, in the names of Protestantism and fair dealing, that France should be forced to undo that which she had done. The London Missionary Society and the Wesleyan Missionary Society joined in

[36] Cowley to Aberdeen, Feb. 26, 1844; *Corr. rel. to the Society Islands, Part I*; No. 154.

[37] Aberdeen to Cowley, Sept. 6, 1844; *Corr. rel. to . . . Mr. Pritchard*; 1845. W. T. Pritchard (*Polynesian Reminiscences*; London, 1866; p. 48) states that the indemnity was never paid.

[38] Cf. n. 32 above.

[39] *The Times*; Mar. 28 and 29, 1843; Aberdeen in answer to Marquis of Lansdowne; Peel in answer to Sir George Grey.

[40] Aberdeen to Pritchard, July 12, 1843; F.O. 58/22.

[41] See F.O. 58/22.

deputations and recommendations to the Foreign Office.[42] The London Missionary Society took the very reasonable course of requesting only that Great Britain withhold recognition of the French protectorate until the methods by which it had been obtained became known.[43] In a pamphlet produced to set out the Society's views, the Directors stated their hope "that the Government, sustained by the voice of the British Nation, will interpose its powerful influence, by remonstrance and every other just and appropriate measure, on behalf of an old and faithful, though feeble, Ally."[44]

Apart from the missionary reaction, there was considerable protest in the press, together with many recommendations to the Foreign Office of solutions for the Tahitian problem. The best supported of the recommendations was that of eleven prominent public men, including Sir George Grey, C. Cholmondeley, the Bishop of Chester and Lord Bexley, who joined in suggesting to Aberdeen that Tahiti be placed under the joint control of Great Britain, France and the United States in the interests of religious equality and commercial security.[45]

In response to all demands the British Government stood firm on three points: (1) that the only substantial British interest in Tahiti was that of the missionaries, whose protection had been assured by Guizot's promises; (2) that the French actions, even though founded at some stages on bad dealing and threats of force, were perfectly legal; and (3) that the French action had been freely acceded to by Pomare and the chiefs of Tahiti.[46]

In effect, Great Britain adhered to her previous policies towards Tahiti. Recognising the sovereignty of Pomare, the British Government saw no reason for intervening when Pomare requested (even under duress) a French protectorate. Holding that the missionaries constituted the only reason for British interest in Tahiti (just as had been held in 1837 and 1839), the Government claimed that Guizot's promises removed the slightest pretext for British action.

The policy laid down for the British representatives at Tahiti was one of non-intervention. In reply to Pritchard's letter of March 13, 1843, explaining that he and Captain Toup Nicolas had "endeavoured to act in accordance with the repeated promises of

[42] L.M.S. on Mar. 20, 1843; L.M.S. and W.M.S. on Apr. 1, 1843; F.O. 58/22.
[43] L.M.S. to Aberdeen, Mar. 27, 1843; F.O. 58/22.
[44] Brief Statement of the Aggression of the French on the Island of Tahiti and the Unjust Assumption of French Dominion in that Island; London, 1843; p. iv.
[45] Apr. 15, 1843; F.O. 58/22.
[46] Peel's speech, cit. sup. (n. 39).

assistance and protection made by the British Government to Queen Pomare," Aberdeen curtly set forth the pure milk of the minimum intervention policy:

> "You appear to have altogether misinterpreted those passages in the letters of Mr. Canning and Lord Palmerston, which you cite in support of the principle of active interference on the part of Gt. Britain, in behalf of Queen Pomare, against France. . . . From the whole tenor of those letters it is obvious that H.M. Government of that day were not prepared to interpose actively in support of the Sovereign of the 'Society Islands, although they willingly proffered her such protection and good offices as, without active interference, they could properly afford."[47]

Pritchard was instructed to recommend a prudent line of conduct to the Queen and to assure her of British sympathy, "although H.M. Government are precluded from authoritatively interfering on her behalf." He himself was to avoid giving offence to the French at Tahiti and to consider himself for the future under the orders of the British Consul-General for the Pacific Islands, stationed at Hawaii.[48]

In the same despatch the mainsprings of British policy in the final decisions on the Tahitian affair were laid bare:

> "It is not to be supposed that, at the very moment when they were declining to take the Society Islands under the protection of the British Crown, H.M. Government could have intended to engage themselves to interpose their good offices in behalf of the Sovereign in such a manner as to incur the almost certainty of collision with a foreign Power."

The British fear of a war in the Channel over an island in the Pacific and the deep-rooted desire of the Foreign and Colonial Offices to avoid political entanglements in the South Pacific were the main factors underlying British policy towards French action in Tahiti.[49]

[47] Aberdeen to Pritchard, Sept. 25, 1843; F.O. 58/22.

[48] This was a new appointment. See Chapter XIII, below.

[49] As to the possibility that the British Government believed that French rule was not unacceptable to British residents in Tahiti, see Aberdeen to Pritchard, Sept. 29, 1843, referring to addresses presented by British residents and missionaries to Dupetit-Thouars. (F.O. 58/22.) For comment from Tahiti on the addresses, see Hunt to Aberdeen, Mar. 24, 1844 (F.O. 58/30) and "Extracts from Missionaries' Correspondence at Tahiti," Oct. 18 and Nov. 25, 1842 (F.O. 58/32).

CHAPTER XIII

PRESERVING THE *STATUS QUO*

"It is unnecessary to add that Her Majesty's Government will not view with indifference the assumption by another Power, of a Protectorate, which they, with a regard for the true interests of those islands, have refused." (Aberdeen to Pritchard, Jan. 15, 1845; F.O. 58/38.)

Though provision was made in 1844 for the protection of British interests in Tahiti, the British missionaries, who felt themselves dispossessed, and the people of New South Wales, who for strategic and commercial reasons wished for a British Oceania, remained hostile to the establishment of French rule. In 1844 four thousand residents of New South Wales petitioned Great Britain for the reinstatement of Pomare and the preservation of the independence of Tahiti.[1] French visitors to Sydney commented on the perceptible frigidity of their reception after events in Tahiti had become known in New South Wales.[2] In June, 1844, the citizens of Sydney held a public meeting of protest.[3] Whipped up by fiery speeches from John Dunmore Lang and others, they passed a resolution declaring that the French usurpation of Tahiti touched British national honour. Lang himself, with all his wonted force of language, proclaimed that nothing since the loss of Calais had been so dishonourable to the British name as the French action in Tahiti. A member of the Legislative Council espoused a policy of colonial imperialism:

"The young lion of Sydney would arouse the old lion of Britain from its present apathetic feeling upon the matter; and he doubted not that, by its roar it would speedily disarm the aggressive intentions of the Gallic cock."

What the missionaries and the colonists perceived was that the

[1] Encl. in Gipps to Stanley, July 28, 1844; *H.R.A.*, I, xxiii, p. 709. The petition referred to the former practice of exercising N.S.W. jurisdiction in Tahiti. (See Chapter IV, above.) The C.O. replied that developments in Tahiti, though regrettable, were Pomare's own will and act and within her competence. (Stanley to Gipps, Mar. 20, 1845; ibid, xxiv, p. 301.)

[2] La Place: *Campagne . . . de la frégate L'Artémise*; 6 vols., Paris, 1841-1854; Vol. V, p. 333.

[3] *S.M.H.*, June 8, 1844.

basis of British policy had changed. Minimum intervention no longer necessarily implied that the islands were to continue under native rule (a condition which suited both unofficial and official British interests very well). Its implication could also be that Great Britain would have to permit further islands to pass under the control of foreign Powers.´ The advantage of the previous British policies had been that they permitted British subjects to follow their pursuits in the South Pacific without imposing any extensive responsibilities on Great Britain for their protection and government. The entry of other Powers into the South Pacific, however, placed obvious complications in the way of adhering to minimum intervention.

If other Powers proposed to seize territories, then sooner or later Great Britain also would be compelled to accept responsibilities of government in the South Pacific. If she failed to do so, her subjects would be at a disadvantage in comparison with foreigners while the British hold on Australasia might be threatened by the establishment of foreign colonies in the neighbouring islands.

These points were made in a memorial to the Foreign Office, dated August 14, 1843, from the Rev. Thomas Heath of the London Missionary Society.[4] Heath declared that France intended to establish a line of naval stations from the Gambiers and the Marquesas to Australasia and the Indian Archipelago. The French, he declared, had long been active in surveying the islands and were ready to carry their plans to completion. Would not Great Britain intervene to preserve in British hands the wealth of island groups like Samoa which might become to Australia and New Zealand what the West Indies had become to Great Britain?

Whether or not the Foreign Office really believed in a threat to the Australasian colonies, a decision was made to strengthen British representation in the Pacific. Shortly after Heath's memorial was received, the Foreign Office decided to appoint a Consul-General for all the Pacific Islands. On September 23, 1843, Major-General William Miller was appointed as H.M. Consul-General "in the Sandwich, Society, Friendly and other islands in the Pacific."[5] Miller was given a general supervision over all other British consuls in the islands, Pritchard being specially instructed to consider himself under Miller's orders.[6]

[4] F.O. 58/23.
[5] Aberdeen to Miller, Sept. 23, 1843; F.O. 58/27. Distinguish the G. C. Miller, who became Consul at Tahiti on the nomination of Consul-General W. Miller. (Miller to Aberdeen, Jan., 1845; *Corr. rel. to the Society Islands, Part II*; No. 295.)
[6] F.O. to Miller, Sept. 29, 1843; F.O. 58/27; and Aberdeen to Pritchard, Sept. 25, 1843; F.O. 58/20.

The objects of Miller's appointment were, first, to clear up the tangled strain of British affairs in the Sandwich Islands, which were to be his headquarters, and, second, to supervise and co-ordinate the administration of British policy in the other islands with special reference to relations with France and the United States of America. The instructions sent to him on September 29, 1843,[7] made his duties regarding the South Pacific perfectly clear. He was to report on the activities of France and the United States, without, however, making any "parade of vigilance." It was not required of him that he extend his personal jurisdiction beyond a few of the island groups, a reserve power being given to him to appoint Vice-Consuls in the Navigators, the Friendly Islands and other groups where British interests might require protection. Finally, a ship of war was to be placed at his disposal, to permit his visiting the islands within his jurisdiction.[8]

It is obvious that, so far as the South Pacific was concerned, Miller's main work was to be an extended version of that entrusted to Pritchard and Busby. He was to perform ordinary consular duties and he was also to watch with special vigilance French and American activities. His appointment represented a tightening up of the British system of representation with a view to avoiding any recurrence of the way in which the British Government's hand had been forced over Tahiti. As a further precaution and as part of the same policy as that involved in Miller's appointment, regular naval visits to all the main island groups were initiated soon after the establishment of the new Australian naval station.[9]

Events soon demonstrated the wisdom of the new appointment. Miller acted as a restraining influence in Tahiti early in 1844, when Pritchard in a clash with the French authorities was imprisoned and deported.[10] He represented the true state of affairs there to Aberdeen and recommended that "there should be some person of temper, prudence and judgment, to act as Consul at Otaheite."[11] Although some of the French officials in Tahiti made complaints against Miller himself, both the British and French Governments professed themselves satisfied with his conduct.[12]

Miller was also able to assess more accurately than any of his

7 F.O. 58/27.
8 As to the ship made available, see Ch. VII, above.
9 J. E. Erskine: *Journal of a Cruise . . . H.M.S. "Havannah"*; London, 1853; pp. 2-3.
10 See Miller to Pritchard, Feb. 7, 1844; same to same, Feb. 26, 1844; and Miller's despatches from Tahiti; all F.O. 58/26.
11 Miller to Aberdeen, Feb. 27, 1844; F.O. 58/26.
12 *Corr. rel. to the Society Islands, Part II.*

predecessors amongst British officers in the Pacific the exact scope and importance of French activities. In 1844 he reported the establishment of a French protectorate over the Gambiers.[13] These he described as "small and surrounded by dangerous coral reefs." Their only European occupants for about six years, added Miller, had been French missionaries. As, however, the French Government did not confirm the establishment of a protectorate, which had been merely granted by a naval officer pending advice from his Government, the question of British recognition did not arise.[14] Miller made similar reports about French action in Wallis and Futuna in 1844.[15]

The policy that Miller had to apply was basically one of preserving the *status quo*. The British Government sought no changes in the South Pacific. Least of all did it seek to precipitate rivalry with France by acquiring an increased territorial stake in the islands. So when the Foreign Office received during the 'forties and 'fifties a series of petitions from island rulers, fearful of French aggression, and anxious for a British protectorate, or annexation, every one of them was rejected. In considering the appeals for British intervention, the Foreign Office had in mind the clearest possible warnings that France would probably procure a cession to herself. Nevertheless, each petition was answered in the negative.

The minimum intervention policy was unmistakably reaffirmed by the Colonial Office in 1848 in dealing with the recommendation of Sir George Grey, the Governor of New Zealand, that Great Britain accede to the Tongan and Fijian desire for British alliance and protection.[16] Grey, like Selwyn, the missionary bishop, wished for a British Oceania.[17] He had written to the Colonial Office in March, 1848, arguing that the proposed new colonies would be no burden and would provide a valuable protection for the Australian settlements. Moreover, he added, if Great Britain did not act, France would. Lord Grey, who then presided at the Colonial Office, proved averse to any extension of British rule save on the most serious consideration. He opposed the inclusion of Tonga

---

[13] Miller to Aberdeen, May 21, 1844; F.O. 58/25.

[14] Miller himself, however, informed Governor Bruat at Papeete that Captain Beechy had hoisted the British flag over the Gambiers eight or nine years previously. (Miller to Aberdeen, Aug. 23, 1844; F.O. 58/26.) Miller's action was a mere insurance against any further British decision in relation to the Gambiers. Beechy's action, not having been confirmed, had no weight in law.

[15] Miller to Aberdeen, July 13, 1844; F.O. 58/26.

[16] Benians, loc. cit., p. 336.

[17] The influence of Grey and Selwyn needs further examination in British and New Zealand sources.

and Fiji within the Empire, on the general grounds of the minimum intervention policy, on the ground that British action would provoke France to further aggression and on the ground that British interests in the groups were slight.

When Sir George Grey's recommendation was referred to the Foreign Office, Lord Palmerston suggested a compromise. Partly with a view to avoiding further clashes with France, Palmerston recommended to the Colonial Office that treaties should be negotiated with those chiefs who would pledge themselves to protect British interests and commerce, to accept such officials as Queen Victoria might send to them and, in the event of international dispute, to turn to Great Britain for advice. The treaties, he considered, would hinder the aggressive designs of France, would not entail much expense and would provide for the extension of commerce amongst the islands.[18]

The Colonial Office declined to accept Palmerston's suggested combination of intervention and non-intervention. For fear of attaching an "inconvenient responsibility" to Great Britain, the Colonial Office argued that the giving of advice to native rulers was the utmost obligation that should be accepted. When the Treasury, with its usual strong hand in colonial matters, requested that all expense on the project be deferred for at least a year, it was allowed to drop. Sir George Grey was advised that his plans could not be accepted because of the expense and risk of foreign complications. The offers from Fiji and Tonga were to be declined in a manner "as conciliatory as possible."[19]

The same fate had attended an appeal from the chiefs of Tutuila in 1844 when they were induced by the missionaries and by the British Consul, George Pritchard, to ask for British protection in view of possible French aggression.[20] In 1845 Pritchard was advised that the offer would not be accepted. Great Britain hoped to preserve the independence of all the island groups and expected her non-intervention to be emulated by foreign Powers.[21]

Similarly, George Pritchard's suggestion in 1852 that the Samoan Group be colonised was rejected on the grounds that no good would come of such a venture and that the United States and France would resent British action there. Lord Malmesbury observed in a minute on Pritchard's despatch that, "I have heard

18 Cf. Brookes, op. cit., p. 183. See also Masterman, op. cit., p. 86.
19 Benians, loc. cit., p. 336.
20 Chiefs to Victoria I, Apr. 23, 1844, encl. in Barrow to Canning, Nov. 12, 1844; F.O. 58/33.
21 Aberdeen to Pritchard, Jan. 15, 1845 (No. 2); F.O. 58/27.

of him as a busy, active, meddling man and he will be doing something on his own account, if you do not stop him."[22]

The persistent refusals on the part of Great Britain to go outside the orbit of minimum intervention in adjusting policy to the new conditions created in the Pacific by French action were the measure of the British determination to avoid commitments there. But the British policy was not wholly passive. The suggestion of some modification of minimum intervention that emanated from Palmerston in 1848 was not the only indication that the British Government had more in mind than mere non-intervention as the means of preserving the *status quo*. When further French acquisition was threatened in islands where British interests were relatively strong, both Miller and the Foreign Office acted readily enough. The British Government showed that it would intervene in defence of the *status quo*, provided that intervention would not cost the acceptance of a permanent governing responsibility.

The main case of British action to defend the conditions on which minimum intervention was founded was that of the French attempt to include the whole of the Society and Georgian Groups in the Tahiti Protectorate.[23] Miller, having noted the importance of the good harbour at Borabora[24] and mindful of the British chagrin at the establishment of the Tahiti protectorate, took an early opportunity of challenging the French attempt to control the islands of Raiatea, Huahine and Borabora. These islands had not been part of Pomare's dominions, although they acknowledged a certain suzerainty in the ruler of Tahiti.[25]

When Bruat, the French Governor of Tahiti, claimed that the Protectorate extended to the whole of both groups and imposed restrictions on English vessels calling at Raiatea, Huahine and Borabora, Miller promptly challenged the legality of the assumed jurisdiction:

"These islands are, and have been from time immemorial, governed by Independent Sovereign Chiefs, never having formed part of Queen Pomare's Dominions, beyond which, it does not appear, the French Protectorate was ever intended to extend."[26]

Bruat and Miller agreed that the matter should be submitted to

[22] Qu. Masterman, op. cit., p. 51.
[23] On the British insistence that the French had acquired only a protectorate in Tahiti, see the *Ann* case; *H.R.A.*, I, xxiv, pp. 671 ff.
[24] Miller to Aberdeen, Nov. 4, 1844; F.O. 58/26.
[25] See Bruce's Report to the Admiralty; F.O. 58/15.
[26] Miller to Bruat, Dec. 7, 1844; Miller to Aberdeen, Dec. 11, 1844; F.O. 58/26.

their respective governments for decision and the restrictions were withdrawn.[27]

But in January, 1845, Bruat had the French flag hoisted on Huahine, Raiatea and Borabora.[28] His action was protested by the natives, who on Huahine and Raiatea pulled down the French flag and appealed to Great Britain.[29] The London Missionary Society acted immediately and lodged a strong protest with the Foreign Office.[30]

In this way Great Britain was once again called upon to negotiate a Pacific settlement with France. British policy had not changed. The British Government still wished to preserve the minimum intervention policy. The example of Tahiti had proved that minimum intervention was consistent with the well-being of British interests only so long as foreign Powers did not set up governments in the islands.

The British attitude towards the new Society Islands question was thus clear right from the first. Having been brought into the matter by the fact that British interests, including missionary interests, were involved, Great Britain wished only to see independent native government continue. Moreover, as the British Government had declined in 1845 an offer of the cession of their territories from the Kings of Raiatea and Borabora and from the Queen of Huahine,[31] there was a strong case for applying the principle that, if Great Britain did not intervene, other Powers should refrain from intervention also.

The legal position as to the French claims was thoroughly examined and the British lawyers reported unfavourably on Bruat's actions.[32] A justification of decisive British intervention was found in the position of those Tahitians who refused to accept French rule. Many of these sought to withdraw to the neighbouring islands where British Protestant missionaries held the field.[33] The

[27] Bruat to Miller, Dec. 7, 1844; Miller to Bruat, Dec. 10, 1844; F.O. 58/26.

[28] Miller to Aberdeen, July 28, 1845; *Corr. rel. to the Society Islands, Part II.*

[29] Memorial from Queen of Huahine to Queen Victoria, Feb. 15, 1845; Miller to Aberdeen, Apr. 8, 1845; ibid, Encl. in Nos. 348 and 350.

[30] L.M.S. to Aberdeen, July 29, 1845; ibid, No. 332.

[31] Kings of Raiatea and Borabora and Queen of Huahine to Paulet, July 23, 1844; F.O.: *Memorandum on the Society Islands as distinct from the Georgian, 1846;* Papers, No. 6. Also Aberdeen to Cowley, Mar. 14, 1845; *Corr. rel. to the Society Islands, Part II;* No. 262.

[32] Compare and contrast the F.O. *Memorandum on the Society Islands as distinct from the Georgian, 1846,* with the French *Memorandum rel. to the Independence of Raiatea, Huahine and Borabora, 1846.*

[33] The L.M.S. had been established at Huahine and Eimeo since 1808 and Borabora and Eitutaki since 1820.

missionaries themselves pressed for recognition of the independence of the Leeward Group.[34]

British policy was defined in March, 1845. Only the protectorate over Pomare's dominions would be recognised and the independence of the other islands would be regarded as unaffected by the French treaties with Pomare.[35] But the problem lingered on for two more years. In January, 1847, a request was made by Palmerston to the French authorities that no obstacles be placed in the way of natives leaving Tahiti for the neighbouring islands.[36] Palmerston's letter was courteously acknowledged by the French with an intimation that instructions to the desired effect had already been sent to the Governor of the French Establishments in Oceania.[37]

Four months later Great Britain and France settled the whole problem in the Declaration of London, June 19, 1847. (The Reciprocal Independence Agreement.) The two Powers agreed to acknowledge the independence of Huahine, Raiatea, Borabora and other small islands adjacent thereto. They contracted:

> "Never to take possession of the said islands, nor of any one or more of them, either absolutely, or under the title of a Protectorate, or in any other form whatever."[38]

The Declaration remained in force until May, 1888, when the Anglo-French Convention relative to the New Hebrides (1887) took effect.

How far Great Britain was actuated in seeking the Declaration by conscious desire to preserve the basis of the minimum intervention policy, how far she was acting on the mere prompting of missionary interests and British Protestantism generally, are not revealed in the documents. But it is clear that, by checking further French developments at this point, the British Government did strengthen, or at least preserve, the basis of its chosen policy. The Declaration represented a change in British policy only in so far as intervention was undertaken in defence of the *status quo* on which the policy of minimum intervention rested.

The Declaration of London represented the culminating point in the policy of tightening up British representation in the Pacific.

[34] See especially the communication from Mr Threlkeld, formerly L.M.S. representative in the South Seas, which was forwarded to the C.O. by Governor Gipps. (Gipps to Stanley, Mar. 7, 1846; *H.R.A.*, I, xxiv, p. 809.)

[35] Aberdeen to Miller, Mar. 7, 1845; *Corr. rel. to the Society Islands, Part II*; No. 260.

[36] Palmerston to Aulaire, Jan. 20, 1847; *Papers rel. to Tahiti, &c., 1847*; No. 1.

[37] Aulaire to Palmerston, Jan. 21, 1847; ibid, No. 2.

[38] Declaration of London, June 19, 1847; ibid.

which the British Government adopted after the Tahitian affair. The years from 1843 to 1847 had been marked by a significant increase in the degree of official representation in the islands. In addition to the major appointment of William Miller as Consul-General and the increase of naval patrol work, there were minor consular appointments. Pritchard was appointed as Consul in the Navigators (Samoa) in 1844,[39] partly because it would have been politically unthinkable to drop him from the service merely because he had proved unacceptable to the French at Tahiti,[40] partly because the Foreign Office had accepted Pritchard's own recommendation for the appointment of a full-time Consul in the Group. (Previously the Navigators had been included in the jurisdiction of the Consul in the Societies.[41])

In 1844 also Miller appointed Henry Sea as Vice-Consul for the Navigators, the Friendly Islands and Fiji.[42] Miller made this appointment without knowledge of Pritchard's selection for the Navigators post. He had previously recommended to the Foreign Office the appointment of a British Consul in Fiji and had taken steps to exercise his own authority there,[43] in the familiar form of holding the chiefs to blame for any violence suffered by British subjects.

After 1847 British interest in the South Pacific again died down, largely because of the slackening in French aggrandisement, which in the next few years was confined to the claim (conceded by Great Britain) to include the Paumotu Group (the Tuamotus) in the Societies.[44]. Traditional policy again pursued its regular course. The admonitions of Pritchard regarding French ambitions were dismissed as biased reports, coloured by his own experiences in Tahiti.[45] There were even cases of Anglo-French co-operation in dealing with native rulers, one of which, at Huahine in 1851, earned the special commendation of Palmerston.[46] Then in 1853 Pritchard was suddenly justified when France seized New Caledonia and took the British Government by surprise.

[39] Aberdeen to Pritchard, Apr. 10, 1844, and F.O. to Pritchard, Apr. 30, 1844; F.O. 58/27.

[40] The French Government declined to permit Pritchard to act as Consul. (Miller to Aberdeen, Feb. 27, 1844; F.O. 58/25.)

[41] Pritchard had nominated William Cunningham for this post. (Pritchard to F.O., May 14, 1839; F.O. 58/15.) For full discussion of Pritchard's position, see also correspondence between the L.M.S. and the F.O.; F.O. 58/32.

[42] Miller to Aberdeen, Nov. 4, 1844; F.O. 58/26.

[43] Same to same, Oct. 4, 1844; F.O. 58/26.

[44] Addington to Hamilton, May 19, 1848; *Tahiti British Consulate Papers*; Vol. 3.

[45] As to suspicions of naval officers, see Hornsby to G. C. Miller, July 10, 1848; ibid.

[46] Palmerston to G. C. Miller, Jan. 31, 1851; ibid, Vol. 4.

CHAPTER XIV

THE FRENCH IN NEW CALEDONIA

FRANCE acquired New Caledonia in 1853 without serious opposition from Great Britain. In contrast to the careful attempts of 1845-47 to restrict the French protectorate in the Societies, little was done to prevent France from establishing herself in New Caledonia, a group nearly 3,000 miles closer to Sydney, and well within the range of British interests extending from Australia and New Zealand.

The contrast is the more surprising in view of early British interests in New Caledonia and the previous British refusal to countenance French claims there. British interest dated from the discovery of the group by Captain Cook and his taking possession. The statement of Scholefield, that "New Caledonia had been taken possession of by Captain Cook by right of discovery,"[1] implies too much. Even if a title founded on mere discovery were good in the case of New Caledonia, which is improbable, no title stemmed from Cook's actions because no efforts were made to assert British sovereignty in the group by establishing administration there. By a clerical error New Caledonia was included within the boundaries originally assigned to the colony of New Zealand (which were made to include the New Hebrides also), but no importance appears to have been attached to this fact by the British Government.

More active British interests were, however, in evidence. In 1842 Governor Gipps of New South Wales forwarded to the Colonial Office a plan drawn up by Major Benjamin Sullivan for forming a Sydney company to colonise New Caledonia.[2] Sullivan's prospectus stated that:

"It may be said that England does not yet possess the Sovereignty of the islands . . . ; nevertheless, it cannot be denied that she does possess the same right of sovereignty over them as she possessed over New Zealand and that consequently, it is both her duty and her interest to have them colonised as soon as possible."[3]

[1] Op. cit., p. 245.
[2] Gipps to Stanley, Sept. 15, 1842; *Despatches from the Governor, 1842*; Vol. 40, No. 168.
[3] *Prospectus for forming a British Colony on the Island of New Caledonia . . . by Company under Royal Charter, without Causing Expense to the British Government*, p. xii. (There is a copy in the Mitchell Library, Sydney.)

Nothing came of the proposal which is interesting, however, in that it was made at about the same time as the French were sending their first missionaries to New Caledonia and received sympathetic support from Gipps, who advocated greater British interest in the group.

When the French missionaries were sent to New Caledonia in 1843, Captain Laferrière, the commander of the *Bucéphale* (in which they sailed), negotiated a cession of the group to France. But Great Britain was already protesting against French activity in the Pacific islands and Laferrière's action seems to have been disregarded by the French Government.[4] Of course, at that time the great mineral wealth of New Caledonia was quite unknown.

From this time on until the annexation in 1853 British interest in New Caledonia was repeatedly reaffirmed by officials in the South Pacific, though not, apparently, by the British Government itself. Pritchard warned the Foreign Office of French ambitions in New Caledonia again and again.[5] Partly as a counter to prospective French action, John Dunmore Lang, the great advocate of Australian nationalism, recommended to the Frankfort Parliament in 1848 that a German colony should be established in New Caledonia.[6] (There was no fear of German ambitions in the South Pacific until much later in the century). In 1849 Captain Erskine, the senior naval officer on the Australian station, recommended that New Caledonia, the Loyalties and the New Hebrides be annexed "because of their proximity to Australia and because of the lawless character of the trade carried on there."[7] His recommendation was the more significant in that it was made as the result of the first cruise in the new series of regular naval visits to all important islands within the limits of the Australian station.[8] No action followed the recommendation.

While British officials and colonists were exhorting the Foreign Office to annex New Caledonia, French interests were active in the group. The French missionaries kept the group under official notice. After the visit of Bishop Douarre to Paris in 1846-47, the corvette *L'Alcmène* was sent out to report on New Caledonia as a

---

4 See de Salinis: *Marins et Missionaires; Conquête de la Nouvelle-Calédonie 1843-1853*; Paris, 1892; p. 17. Also Bernard: *L'Archipel de la Nouvelle-Calédonie*; Paris, 1895; p. 320; and Scholefield, op. cit., p. 244.

5 Cf. Pritchard to Palmerston, July 30, 1847; F.O. 58/57.

6 F.O., Historical Section, Handbook No. 145, 1920: *French Possessions in Oceania*; p. 18.

7 Erskine, op. cit., p. 198.

8 See Ch. XIII, above.

place for colonisation.[9] In 1853 the French Government decided to annex. The strategic value of the group was obvious, as was also its importance in Pacific sea-lanes. Its possibilities as a penal colony had been recognised. Catholic interests hoped to make it the centre of the Church's work in Western Oceania.[10] Secret instructions were sent in May, 1853, to the commanding officers of the La Plata, Pacific and Indian squadrons. The first to act was Rear-Admiral Febvrier-Despointes. His sealed orders were to proceed to New Caledonia, to obtain assurances that the group had not been claimed by the British and to take possession for France. This he did on September 24.

The details are important, because it appears that the British Government had no idea of what was going on in New Caledonia. The French had preserved the utmost secrecy for fear of being forestalled as they had been in New Zealand. A British ship, H.M.S. *Herald*,[11] commanded by Lieutenant Denham, arrived at the Isle of Pines either about the same time as, or very shortly after, Febvrier-Despointes took possession in New Caledonia.[12] The exact purpose of Denham's visit is obscure. Salinis, followed by Bernard, states that the senior naval officer on the Australian station had had orders for over a year to take possession of New Caledonia and the Isle of Pines on behalf of Great Britain.[13] But the authority of the statement is difficult to assess. As against the view that the British Government had given orders to annex, it is to be noted that the researches of Brookes in Foreign Office, Colonial Office and Admiralty Papers, undertaken to clear up this point, revealed no evidence to suggest that either Denham or his commanding officer (Everard Home) had had orders to annex.[14] The Foreign Office Handbook, *French Possessions in Oceania,* states on undis-

[9] Bernard, op. cit., p. 325. Also Scholefield, op. cit., p. 244.

[10] Bernard, op. cit., pp. 325-6; Russier, op. cit., p. 163. The *Moniteur* report of February 14, 1854, cited the following motives: "to assure to France in the Pacific the position demanded by her naval interests, military and commercial, and to afford the opportunity of putting into force the Government's views with regard to its treatment of criminals." As to allegations that the French had designs on Australia, see Scott: *Terre Napoléon,* cit. sup., p. 279.

[11] Note the contrary account of Jules Parquet: *La Nouvelle-Calédonie*; Alger, 1872; p. 17.

[12] According to S.M.H. (Nov. 1, 1853) the *Herald* reached the Isle of Pines after Febvrier-Despointes had taken possession of New Caledonia. The ship's log states that the *Herald* arrived in the afternoon of Sept. 24. (*Log Book of H.M.S. "Herald,"* 1852-59, in M.L., Sydney.)

[13] Bernard, op. cit., p. 326; Salinis, op. cit., p. 320. Salinis discusses his sources on pp. 1, ff. He shows strong anti-British bias.

[14] op. cit., p. 202.

closed authority that "the French in 1853 narrowly anticipated a British occupation."[15]

Sources locally available are inconclusive. The *Herald's* log book, certainly poor evidence in a case such as this, treats the visit to the Isle of Pines as made for surveying purposes only.[16] (A survey could have been a prelude to the establishment of a coaling station, as alleged by the French.) The *Sydney Morning Herald,* though it featured the news of the French action, mentioned nothing about British ambitions in New Caledonia, and, indeed, violently castigated the indifference of the British Government to so valuable a group.[17]

Febvrier-Despointes himself appears to have assumed that Denham's intention was to establish a coaling station at the Isle of Pines, which would ultimately be used as a base for the British infiltration of New Caledonia. He hastily proceeded to the Isle of Pines and, with the aid of the French missionaries, obtained its cession to France. One account claims that Denham had already taken possession of the island and that he had to withdraw the British flag when the natives sided with the French.[18] Evidence against this view exists in a despatch from Denham to Grey, dated January 13, 1854,[19] in which, states Brookes, it is made clear that, on the occasion of his second visit to the Isle of Pines in December, 1853, Denham was still unaware that possession of the island had been taken by the French.[20]

The evidence is by no means conclusive, but the balance of probability seems to lie with the view that Great Britain in 1853 had no intention of annexing New Caledonia. It is quite certain that the British Government was surprised by the French action. Whether or not Denham or Home had orders to annex, whether or not Denham had taken possession of the Isle of Pines, it seems clear that Great Britain was quite ignorant of the French plan. France had stolen a march and taken the initiative all along the line. Bernard states the French plans were prepared with special secrecy so that Great Britain could not again forestall France as she had succeeded in doing in the case of New Zealand.[21]

[15] cit. sup. (n. 6).
[16] cit. sup. (n. 12)
[17] S.M.H., Nov. 1, 2, 3 and 5, 1853.
[18] See *"Notice sur la Nouvelle-Calédonie et ses Dépendances"* (*Extrait de la Revue maritime et coloniale*); Paris, 1866; p. 3.
[19] Denham to Grey, Jan. 13, 1854, encl. in Wynyard to Newcastle, Feb. 2, 1854. C.O. 209/122; qu. Brookes, op. cit., p. 202.
[20] See Scholefield, op. cit., p. 244.
[21] Bernard, op. cit., p. 326.

The first reference to the affair published in Great Britain was in *The Times* on February 4, 1854. Quoting a Sydney letter, *The Times* stated that:

> "The French have taken possession of New Caledonia. There is plenty of gold there; at least so it has always been believed from the large granite regions among the group. If such be the case, Gt. Britain ought to have been beforehand . . . as it lies so near New South Wales."

No editorial comment was made in *The Times,* nor was the matter discussed in Parliament. Few British interests, apart from the sandalwood traders, were affected and the matter passed over with little public attention.

Both the Foreign Office and the Colonial Office appear to have been ill-informed regarding New Caledonia. After investigation, the Colonial Office reported that Great Britain had never taken any steps towards taking possession of the group. (The erroneous inclusion of New Caledonia within the boundaries originally defined for New Zealand was disregarded.[22]) The Foreign Office considered that no case could be made out against the French action. After so long a period of British indifference, the Foreign Office pointed out, it would be "difficult now to sustain that they (New Caledonia and the Isle of Pines) are so important to Her Majesty's Colonies and to British Commerce in those Seas that their occupation by the French cannot be allowed."[23]

The Foreign Office was no doubt influenced by the fact that Great Britain and France were already allied against Russia and by the well-established British opinion that Pacific affairs must necessarily be subordinated to European diplomacy. It is significant that on the day on which *The Times* so briefly reported the French annexation of New Caledonia, it featured continental reports of the Anglo-French coalition against Russia.[24]

Although the British Government was prepared to have its hand forced over New Caledonia in this way, when wider diplomatic issues were at stake, the Australasian colonies were deeply resentful. The *Sydney Morning Herald* protested from November, 1853, until early in 1854. The "laxity of the British Government, notwithstanding the repeated and earnest representations which have been made to it," was bitterly condemned in a leading article of November 2, 1853. The next day a further leading article attacked the "cowardly policy" of Great Britain and claimed that France

[22] Brookes, op. cit., p. 204.
[23] ibid; Hammond to Merivale, Apr. 27, 1854.
[24] *The Times*, Feb. 4, 1854.

was getting everything in the South Pacific by the simple expedient of seizing one group at a time. The old fear of a recrudescence of convictism in the Pacific through the planting of a French penal settlement in the islands added virulence to the *Herald's* complaints.

Governor Grey of New Zealand urged the senior naval officer at Sydney to warn the French that New Caledonia was within the boundaries of New Zealand. This attempt on the part of one who made no secret of his wish for a British Oceania to capitalise the clerical error referred to above was prevented when Sir Charles Fitzroy, the Governor-General at Sydney, opposed taking any such action without instructions from London.[25] Eventually in Australasia, as in Great Britain, the British case for New Caledonia had to go by default.

For the lack of clear views and adequate information in high places, Great Britain paid the price of seeing France acquire a rich colony not ten days' sail from Australia. The truth appears to be that the future of New Caledonia was never adequately considered in Great Britain before the French action and could not be adequately considered thereafter.

British acquiescence in the French acquisition of New Caledonia was thus devoid of any great significance so far as her South Pacific policy was concerned. It reflected the natural consequences of the continued British refusal to accept political responsibilities in the islands, or to intervene in any way which might necessitate decisive action. Great Britain was taken by surprise and, since her policy of minimum intervention had not allowed her to establish claims over New Caledonia, she had to choose between acquiescence in the French action or rupture of a valuable European alliance in the prospective interests of her subjects in the South Seas.

Like the Tahitian affair, the French annexation of New Caledonia produced a tightening up of British representation in the islands. The complete lack of British representation in New Caledonia had been one of the most embarrassing factors confronting the British Government when it considered the possibility of objecting to the French action. Within a few years steps had been taken to increase the number of British Consuls in the islands.

In 1854 Merivale, the Permanent Under-Secretary for Colonies, acting on the plea of a resident Wesleyan missionary, revived the question of appointing a higher official to superintend British

---

[25] See Grey to Newcastle, Dec. 15, 1853; C.O., N.Z., 209/118; qu. Brookes, op. cit., p. 203. Also W.L. and L. Rees: *The Life and Times of Sir George Grey, K.C.B.*; London, 1892; 3 ed., p. 131.

policy in Oceania.[26] The scheme came to nothing, though it contained the seeds of the High Commission principle, adopted in 1875-78. The question of extending British representation was raised again in 1855 when a memorandum by Charles St. Julian, Hawaiian Commissioner and Commercial Agent in New South Wales, was forwarded to the Colonial Office by Governor Denison. St. Julian recommended British intervention in the islands on six grounds:

(a) The natives were unable to provide stable government and were in fact being reduced in numbers by tribal warfare.

(b) That the safety of trade could be preserved only through British action.

(c) That Great Britain would gain in prestige by acquiring a political stake in the islands.

(d) That many of the islands occupied strategic positions on important trade routes and had an obvious commercial and political interest to Australia.

(e) That the islands were rich enough to become a paying proposition under British rule.

(f) That Oceania was certain to pass under the control of one of the Powers and that, as a matter of safeguarding her interests, Great Britain ought to intervene.

St. Julian wished for British annexation of the leading groups. But as an alternative, he suggested that several additional consuls might be appointed—at Fiji, Tonga, Bonabe (Ascension Is.), the Carolines and the New Hebrides.[27] A scheme for annexation of Fiji, Tonga and Samoa was put forward about the same time as St. Julian's plans by Captain Fremantle, R.N., as a result of his voyage amongst the islands in 1856.

With the recommendations of Fremantle and St. Julian before them, the Foreign Office, the Colonial Office, the Admiralty and the Board of Trade determined to extend British consular representation in the Pacific. The objectives were to bolster up minimum intervention by putting a check on foreign activities in the islands and by providing some alleviation of the position under which British subjects would otherwise have been left under weak, unstable native rule without official protection in commerce and subject to the continual menace of the acquisition by some foreign Power of the islands in which they traded. The 1857 decision is

[26] ibid, p. 229.

[27] C. St. Julian: *Official Report on Central Polynesia*; Sydney, 1857; *Latent Resources of Polynesia*; London, 1851. The reference in the text is to St. Julian's *Suggestions to the British Government*, originally published in *S.M.H.*, later included in the *Official Report*, cit. sup.

comparable with that made in 1843 when Miller was appointed as Consul-General in the Pacific Islands.

Under the new decision W. T. Pritchard, son of George Pritchard, was made consul in Fiji and John C. Williams, son of the missionary, became consul in Samoa. Both appointments were made in 1857. In April, 1858, it was decided to appoint a consul to Tonga partly as a counter to French activity there. Though it is doubtful whether any appointment were made at the time,[28] the decision to send out a consul was used as a justification for refusing a Tongan petition for alliance with Great Britain and British recognition and protection of Tongan independence. A Wesleyan deputation in support of the petition was informed that Her Majesty's Government could not guarantee Tongan independence, nor enter into a formal alliance, but that recognition of Tongan independence was implied in the decision to appoint a consul.[29]

The consular appointments made at this time were due to increasing international interest in the islands rather than to problems arising from the presence of British subjects. In Fiji, for example, there were only thirty or forty Europeans of all nationalities when Pritchard was appointed.[30] In Samoa in 1856 there were only two British residents.[31] The decision to appoint a British Consul at Tonga was avowedly made because of French activity there. France had concluded a convention with Tonga on January 9, 1855, under which religious toleration was guaranteed in Tonga and the French were allowed to settle there freely, reciprocal privileges being extended to any Tongans visiting France.[32]

The extent to which the British Government was prepared to intervene, even by the appointment of Consuls, was still limited by its determination to avoid entanglements in the islands. Where intervention could reasonably be expected to lead to political complications, intervention did not take place. This limitation was specially important when the complications that were feared concerned France. For example, in 1859-60 the Foreign Office rejected official advice from New South Wales to appoint a Consul in New Caledonia, then under French rule. The Governor of New South Wales, following the execution by the French authorities of some British subjects in New Caledonia, had recommended the appoint-

---

28 Subsequently consuls were appointed to Fiji and Tonga as a joint post.
29 Brookes, op. cit., p. 242.
30 Derrick, op. cit., I, p. 138.
31 *Corr. resp. Samoa, 1889* (No. 1).
32 C. St. Julian: *Official Report on Central Polynesia*, cit. sup., pp. 12 ff.

ment of a British Consul in the group. The Foreign Office declined to do so, lest the presence of a British Consul encourage the fostering of "Imaginary grievances."[33]

The decision made clear that the process of extending consular representation was to be kept within the ambit of the minimum intervention policy. Consuls would not be appointed where their presence might embarrass Great Britain (whatever the justice of any cases they might take up) but only where their presence could be expected to serve the cause of the *status quo*. Similarly the British Government continued to decline all requests for annexation or protectorate. Most of the requests originated in fear of French aggression. In 1854-55 the Foreign Office declined to accept the suggestion of Nicolas, the Consul at Tahiti, that it should co-operate with the French in measures to secure political stability in Huahine, Borabora and Raiatea, three of the islands whose independence had been guaranteed by the Declaration of London. The British Government refused to take the step recommended by Nicolas of guaranteeing the crown of each island to a particular dynasty, pledged to reside in that island. Nicolas's representation that this action was the only means of preserving peace in the islands was disregarded. The British refusal was justified on the ground that the recommendation envisaged active intervention in the islands with the prospect of use of naval force.

Likewise in July, 1857, when a deputation of members of Parliament submitted to the Colonial Office a memorial from the Chiefs of Aneityum in the New Hebrides praying for British protection, the Foreign Office advised that the protection of a single island in a group was inexpedient. When British missionaries at Aneityum revived the request a year later and stressed the fear of the chiefs concerning possible French aggression from New Caledonia, they were staved off with the information that a Consul would probably be appointed at Aneityum.[34]

In the case of Samoa three opportunities of intervention were refused within six years. An offer of cession was declined in 1859 on grounds of general policy.[35] In 1862 the officers of H.M.S. *Fawn* reported that French missionaries were attempting to procure an offer of cession to France.[36] The French move failed, but it did lead to the Foreign Office being asked by the British Consul in

[33] Hammond to Merivale, Dec. 29, 1859, and Newcastle to Denison, Jan. 6, 1860; *Despatches to the Governor of N.S.W., 1860.*

[34] Brookes, op. cit., pp. 239-240.

[35] C.O. to Admiralty, June, 1859; C.O. 201/510; qu. Brookes, op. cit., p. 247.

[36] T. H. Hood: *Notes of a Cruise in H.M.S. "Fawn"*; Edinburgh, 1863; pp. 106-109.

Samoa for further instructions. He was told to watch and wait. In 1865, under missionary influence, the chiefs of Tutuila applied for a British protectorate. The Foreign Office, on the advice of the Colonial Office, rejected the offer[37] and thus lost an easy opportunity of acquiring Pago Pago, whose strategic importance was by then realised.

British policy in the decade following the annexation of New Caledonia was clear. The major objective was the preservation of the *status quo* as the means of maintaining the policy of minimum intervention. Where limited intervention was useful for that purpose, intervention took place. But acceptance of governing responsibilities, or any act that might lead to active commitments in the South Pacific, was quite beyond the scope of British policy. Great Britain wished to be as little concerned with political events there as possible. Given continuance of existing conditions, her missionaries, planters and traders could pursue their respective avocations with reasonable security. Intervention on the other hand would only bring a crop of troubles—all the tasks of colonial administration, all the problems of international rivalry and all the expense of new establishments.

[37] Chiefs to Williams, June 28, 1865, encl. in Williams to F.O., July 14, 1865; F.O. 58/105. Also F.O. to Williams, May 1, 1866; F.O. 58/109. Cf. Brookes, op. cit., p. 288.

Chapter XV

THE CHANGING PACIFIC

The impact of the West on the Pacific Islands was both increased and radically changed during the second half of the nineteenth century. Beginning about the middle of the century the whole basis of European activity in the South Pacific was transformed by important economic changes. Technological discoveries enhanced the usefulness of island products. Planters began to use the islands for new crops. Economic developments on both sides of the Pacific (including the gold discoveries) led to the establishment of new trade routes and gave many of the islands importance as coaling stations and naval depots. The Great Powers, whose subjects and citizens settled rapidly in the islands, were compelled by force of changing circumstances to intervene more and more in the South Pacific.

One of the most striking of the new changes was effected through improvements in means of transport. The growth of world trade and the development of steam power combined to speed up oceanic communications. In 1852 the Australian Mail Steam Packet began a monthly service to Australia via Panama.[1] Though for some years coaling difficulties delayed the development of Pacific steamship routes, commercial and political interest in the acquisition of Pacific bases was substantially increased.

The same result followed from the improvement of communications between the Pacific and the Atlantic through Central America. Schemes for a Panama Canal had been discussed in the eighteenth century, but it was not until 1851 that the first regular survey took place—under the auspices of the United States of America.[2] One of the French motives for intervention in the Eastern Pacific had been the realisation that the commercial importance of the islands there would be increased whenever the projected canal was completed.[3]

Although the canal was not open for traffic until the present

[1] H. J. Habakkuk: "Free Trade and Commercial Expansion, 1853-1870"; (*C.H.B.E.*, II, pp. 751 ff. at 760).

[2] J. C. Rodrigues: *The Panama Canal, its History, its Political Aspect and its Financial Difficulties*; London, 1885; p. 233.

[3] See Chapter XI, above.

century, construction of the Panama railway (completed in 1855) helped to attract attention to Pacific sea-routes.[4] It is true that the significance of the Pacific line of communications between Europe and Australia was reduced by the completion of the Suez Canal in 1869. But growing trade and commerce in the Pacific itself had by then established the importance of Pacific sea-ways. In 1871 fast steamer services were commenced across the Pacific between Sydney and San Francisco, connecting with the New York-San Francisco railway.

The improvement in transport and communications is to be attributed partly to the rapid economic development on both sides of the Pacific. The discovery of gold in Australia, New Zealand and California stepped up the economic vitality of the entire South Pacific region and opened up Pacific trade routes with prospectors pouring from one continent to another. Whereas in the 'forties island trade had consisted mainly of the supply of provisions to whalers and the acquisition of sandalwood, the growth of trade based on Australia, New Zealand and North and South America during and after the 'fifties made the Pacific a commercial highway in which island bases were sought as coaling stations and ports of refreshment.

In 1867 a protectorate was acquired over Rapa (Aparo) by France while the United States annexed Midway Island. Great Britain was repeatedly urged to annex or protect Pacific islands of strategic advantage or which might be of use in the new Pacific trade routes. Arguments of this kind were used especially in the cases of Fiji[5] and Samoa.[6] Like the United States and Germany, Great Britain acquired rights to a naval base in Samoa late in the 'seventies.[7] In the same period Germany also acquired treaty rights to naval or coaling stations at Neiafu (1876) and at Jaluit in the Marshalls (1878).

A new use for small isolated islands was found in connection with the proposal for a trans-Pacific cable. As a result of the voyage of Commander Oldham (H.M.S. *Egeria*) in 1889, Great Britain acquired several islands for possible use as cable stations. Oldham visited mainly the Phoenix Group, lying just south of the Equator in longitude about 170 degrees west. He took possession of Phoenix Island; Birnie was placed under British protection and Sydney and Hull were formally placed under British protection. All of these islands were mere dots to which the cable proposal

[4] Benians, loc. cit., p. 343.
[5] See Chapters XVIII and XXII, below.
[6] See Chapter XX and XXIV, below.
[7] See Chapter XXIV, below.

gave importance.[8] The Tokelau Group was also officially declared by Oldham to be a British protectorate.

In the islands themselves new industrial processes increased the value of the staple product of the South Pacific—the cocoanut. Raw cocoanuts had long been exported from the islands in large quantities.

Technological advances, however, transformed the whole cocoanut trade. In 1829 a British patent had been taken out for separating cocoanut oil into solid and liquid constituents. In 1840 the use of cocoanut oil in the manufacture of soap became a commercially recognised process. Before 1850 cocoanut oil was being used in the manufacture of candles. Within twenty years the price of the oil rose to a point at which plantation development became profitable and export problems were being eased by the practice of shipping copra instead of oil.[9]

The outbreak of the American Civil War and the consequent falling off in American cotton supplies turned attention to the cotton possibilities of the South Pacific. Great Britain had already shown some interest in Pacific cotton when in 1857 the Colonial Office sent a despatch to the Governor of New South Wales relating to cotton produced in the South Pacific islands. The despatch suggested that New South Wales should undertake the cultivation of the cotton tree, as grown in the islands. Tree culture, it was argued, was easier and less expensive than the methods used in the United States. The despatch went on to add that "a supply of good Cotton can be drawn from the Islands in the Pacific Ocean within the Tropics, if the natives can be induced to be industrious."[10] These opinions were put to the test during the American Civil War when cotton planting in Fiji and Samoa, especially, was greatly stimulated.

Cotton prospects became one of the strongest arguments in favour of British intervention in Fiji. The growth of a cotton planting class, including many British subjects, in Fiji was one of the reasons for the British acceptance of the cession of that group in 1874.[11]

The development of copra and cotton (and also of sugar) involved the emergence of a new class of planters and settlers, whose contacts with the islands were of a more stable and intimate

---

[8] A declaration of British protection was made over the adjacent Gardner Island in 1892 by Captain Gibson (H.M.S. *Curacoa*). Gardner did not come within Oldham's purview, as he was concerned only with possible cable stations.

[9] The facts cited here are taken from Masterman, op. cit., pp. 57-58.

[10] N.S.W., Leg. Council: C.O. to Governor, Aug. 6, 1857.

[11] See Chapter XXII, below.

character than those of the old traders. Previously what trade did exist had been carried on in the main without European settlement. In Fiji, for example, one of the first groups to be settled, there were only 30 or 40 settlers in 1858,[12] whereas by 1867 there were 830[13] and in 1873 the number was estimated at 2,000.[14]

Up to the 'sixties and 'seventies missionaries had represented a more stable connection with the islands than had the traders, many of whom had merely visited the islands in transient vessels, sometimes calling for rest and refreshment, sometimes collecting articles for export. The development of the plantation system with its white settlers more or less permanently resident in the islands effected an important change in the mode of contact between Europeans and natives. It also opened the way for increasing native participation in European trade, commerce and industrial activity.

There was an important difference between the cotton planter of Fiji in the 'sixties and the sandalwood trader of the New Hebrides in the 'forties and 'fifties. The planter needed stability and had to live on reasonably good terms with the natives. The traders, even where, as on Aneityum and Eromanga, they established regular stations, were often noted for their brutal violence and dishonest methods. Their excesses sometimes drove the natives to desperate and bloody acts of retaliation.

A different type of development flowed from the exploitation of Pacific phosphate resources. It was in the 'thirties and 'forties that experiments were made in Europe in the soil revitalising powers of guano from the islands off the coast of South America. Once the value of guano was established, the inadequacy and high price of supplies from the Peruvian Islands became apparent. Rocky islets in the Pacific, which had little other recommendation than their phosphate deposits, became the objects of commercial interest.

American interests were first in the field. Guano islets were worked through the American Guano Company and its subsidiary, the Phoenix Guano Company. In 1856 an Act of Congress empowered the President of the United States to establish American sovereignty over unoccupied islands on which phosphate (or "American guano") was discovered by American citizens.[15] Altogether 48 islands were claimed under the Act of 1856.[16]

12 Derrick, op. cit., I, p. 138.
13 Corr. rel. Fiji, 1871; Appendix No. 2 (Thurston's Report, 1867).
14 Robinson to Kimberley, Jan. 27, 1873; repr. in Henderson, op. cit., p. 59.
15 E. H. Bryan: American Polynesia; Honolulu, 1941; p. 33.
16 ibid.

Apparently in order to protect the commercial interests of British subjects, Great Britain also claimed title to some of the guano islands. In 1857 the British occupant of Fanning Island was given permission to hoist the British flag because of the activity of guano-hunting vessels in the vicinity.[17] The intention was to forestall any American action in the island. In 1865 a lease was granted over Christmas Island[18] to the Anglo-Australian Guano Company, but was cancelled in 1869. A further lease was granted by Great Britain to Alfred Houlder in 1871.[19] Christmas Island, however, had previously been worked by the United States Guano Company, and when Houlder's representative arrived at the island he found that Commander Meade of the U.S.S. *Narragansett* had just taken formal possession. Houlder's lease was then cancelled at his own request. Possession was taken of another guano island, Starbuck (in the Southern Line Islands) in 1866 by Commodore Swinburn (H.M.S. *Mutine*). The deposits on Malden (in the same group) were being utilised by a Sydney company when possession was claimed by Americans under the 1856 Act. The American claim, however, collapsed in view of the presence of the Sydney firm. Caroline Island (also in the Southern Line Islands) was annexed for Great Britain in 1868 by Captain Nares (H.M.S. *Reindeer,* some accounts stating H.M.S. *Encounter*). It had previously been occupied by an English cocoanut planter for over twenty years. Caroline, Starbuck, Flint and Vostock were all worked under British occupation licences in the early 'seventies. (No phosphate appears to have been obtained at Vostock, although a settlement was established there).

British action in the phosphate islands involved only a slight degree of intervention. As the islands mostly had no native populations there was no problem of conflict between natives and whites to arise. The prospect of international conflict was specially guarded against. The occupant of Fanning was informed that he would not be protected internationally in the event of disputed title or other interference with his possession. The island was not formally annexed until 1888. The leases over Christmas Island, which also was not annexed until 1888, were for a limited period of years. They provided that, in the event of international complications, British protection might be withdrawn.

[17] Brookes, op. cit., p. 226; Bryan, op. cit , p. 164, gives the date as 1855, i.e., prior to the U.S. Act. The permission was not equivalent to British annexation. Fanning did not become British until 1888.
[18] As to legal aspects, see M. F. Lindley: *The Acquisition and Government of Backward Territory in International Law*; London, 1926, p. 7.
[19] Bryan, op. cit., p. 165.

The precise legal position in case of most of the islands concerned in the guano trade cannot be determined from the available documents. It would seem that, in the majority of instances all that was intended was to give recognition and legality to the occupation by a device of "partial sovereignty"[20] capable of protecting British interests against dispossession.

The guano industry was a special case. The islands involved were of slight importance apart from their phosphate deposits. Having in almost every case bad anchorages and poor water supplies, they were not even of use as coaling stations or naval depots. It was possible to use such a device as occupation licences without involving any substantial risk of more extensive intervention becoming necessary. When the cable project did increase the value of some of the islands later, they were then annexed (as in the cases of Fanning and Christmas Islands in 1888).

For the greater part the new industrial and trade developments in the South Pacific produced no immediate change in British policy. There were new challenges to that policy arising from the promise of industrial wealth like the cotton of Fiji. And there were new difficulties confronting the policy, especially the problems arising from large-scale European settlement in the islands and the increasing activity of Germany, the United States and France. But the adjustment of policy to the new conditions was made only slowly.

In the 'fifties when economic conditions in the South Pacific began to change so rapidly, British policy was still dominated by the desire to avoid political responsibilities in the islands. An exception had been forced on the British Government in the case of New Zealand. Another exception had been made in the case of Pitcairn Island. Occupied by the descendants of the *Bounty* mutineers, Pitcairn had attracted British attention and sympathy. In 1831, because of the diminishing resources of the island and the increasing population,[21] the islanders were removed by the British Government to Tahiti.[22] The Pitcairners, however, disliked Tahiti, where the health of many of them suffered, and the missionaries arranged for their return to their own island in September, 1831.[23] Pitcairn was annexed on behalf of the British

20 Lindley, op. cit., p. 7.
21 Barrow to Hay, Nov. 29, 1826; F.O. 58/14; Goderich to Bourke, Dec. 23, 1831; *H.R.A.*, I, xvi, p. 482.
22 Hay to Planta, Feb, 28, 1827; ibid; Goderich to Bourke, Dec. 23, 1831; cit. sup.
23 Bourke to Goderich, Aug. 3, 1832; *H.R.A.*, I, xvi, p. 688.

Government in November, 1838, by Captain Russel Elliot (H.M.S. *Fly*) in order that the islanders might elect a magistrate responsible to Great Britain.[24]

Apart from the dependencies of Australia, the only island acquisitions made by Great Britain during the seventy or eighty years of her unrivalled opportunity of seizing as many groups as she pleased were New Zealand[25] and Pitcairn. For the rest, British responsibilities in the islands had been discharged through the work of the Royal Navy, of consuls and of the Government of New South Wales. Great Britain herself had intervened occasionally in defence of the *status quo*, but the general tenor of British policy had clearly been against any more intervention than was absolutely necessitated by the presence of British subjects in the islands. This was the policy which was being challenged by the growth of large-scale British settlements, by increasing British investment and by the growth of foreign interest in the island world.

In the early years of the new developments there was little question of foreign rivalry. None of the Great Powers showed much inclination to annex South Pacific islands. The general tendency was rather to concentrate on economic and commercial development and on the problems of settlement and government thereby produced. The grab for island territories did not begin in any substantial way until growing commercial contacts and increasing white populations had marked out spheres of influence, until the presence of several Powers in the South Pacific (with their treaty rights and naval establishments) had made it necessary to establish clear political claims, and until the general process of sharing out colonial territories was extended to the South Pacific.

The immediate problems produced by the economic changes during the second half of the nineteenth century were those of trade, settlement and island government. The presence of planters in the islands, the growing participation of natives in white modes of commerce and the need for white men's law in communities dominated by white men's institutions were the outstanding factors in the new island situation.

[24] See C.O.: *Pitcairn Island, General Administrn. Report, 1938.* The Pitcairners were removed to Norfolk Island in 1856 in consequence of reports that the island resources were becoming exhausted. (C.O.: *Corr. rel. the removal of the Inhabitants of Pitcairn Island to Norfolk Island, 1857.*) Some of the families returned to Pitcairn in 1859 and 1864. An earlier offer of removal to a larger island had been declined in 1846. (Quintal to W. Miller, Feb. 12, 1846; *Corr. rel. to the Society Islands, Part III; Encl. in No. 5.*)

[25] And dependencies of New Zealand.

Chapter XVI

SETTLEMENT AND GOVERNMENT

THE emergence of the new planter class and the increase of the European and American populations of the islands greatly complicated the problem of preserving internal order. Native rulers, who according to British policy were to be left to maintain their own governments in the islands, found their duties becoming intolerably heavy. The considerable white populations settling in the South Seas required forms of government and systems of law that native societies could not supply. Their very presence tended to disrupt the foundations of native society.

The disorders which resulted from the heavy burdens thrown on native societies led to appeals by natives and Europeans alike for the intervention of the western Powers in the islands. In Fiji and Samoa the whites even attempted to set up their own governments on European models, or to put a native on the throne who would maintain conditions stable enough to suit foreign interests. In Tonga the missionaries helped in building up a native kingdom— an achievement made possible by the relative absence of traders and planters.

Whereas in the previous period British traders and missionaries had generally preferred that the Powers should maintain a policy of minimum intervention, they were now frequently constrained to seek the intervention of their Government. The economic and political basis of the old order had passed away. Planters could not profit from the disintegration of native society in the same way as had the traders. They required a greater degree of stability even if only to use a system of law as the means of securing their own interests. They also sought protection against the nationals of other Powers. Traders who would not have hesitated to fight their way against natives were naturally wary of resorting to the use of arms against Europeans and Americans. Similarly, the missionaries often found themselves faced with an influx of whites who either had little interest in missionary efforts to preserve native rule, or who, representing a different church and a foreign state, commenced proselytization on their own account.

That the presence of missionaries greatly complicated the problem of government in many islands is certain. In Fiji they alternatively opposed and favoured cession to the British Crown. In Samoa the opposition of the missionaries was one of the final causes of the downfall of the Steinberger Government in the late 'seventies. In Rotuma the jealousy of rival missionaries so convulsed the government of the island, that British intervention became unavoidable.[1] Although in many instances the missionaries sincerely worked for law and order, it has to be admitted that their disputes with one another and their claims of a special right to interfere with native governments were prime factors in complicating the major problem of island government.[2]

The disorder which appeared in Fiji, Samoa and other island groups during the 'fifties, 'sixties and later decades was different in both kind and degree from that which had existed earlier, save, perhaps, in New Zealand during the 'thirties. The full consequences of the clash of cultures and civilisations became unmistakably apparent.

The tottering of native systems of rule under the pressure of increasing European penetration was bound to prove fatal to the British policy of minimum intervention in its original conception. A fundamental point of that policy had come to be the recognition of native sovereignty and the belief that matters of island government should be left in the hands of the natives, judiciously aided and guided by British consuls, and effectively coerced, where necessary, by British men-of-war. Great Britain had intervened in the South Pacific to mitigate the external challenge of France to the minimum intervention policy. But, never save in the case of New Zealand, had she made any considerable attempt to preserve minimum intervention from the internal challenge of disintegration of native systems of rule.

When it became apparent that native rulers could no longer make even a show of performing the functions with which British policy credited them and when it became clear that not all the stiffening provided by consular advice and the pressure of men-of-war could make native rulers perform the functions of civilised

[1] Rotuma was annexed by Great Britain in 1881 as a result of disorder produced by disputes of Catholic and Protestant missionaries. (C.3905, 1884, para. 39.) In August, 1872, the chiefs of Rotuma had requested Great Britain to annex their island because of fear that an unjust fine levied by the French would prove to be the prelude to loss of political and religious liberty. This was before Great Britain acquired Fiji and the appeal was ignored. Cf. Brookes, op. cit., p. 418.

[2] Only France made political capital out of the labours of missionaries in the South Pacific.

governments, then it was obvious, as the case of New Zealand had proved, that the British policy of supervising British subjects through minimum intervention was doomed. Even if the form of minimum intervention might have been preserved, the substance of the policy would have disappeared.

It is to be noted that minimum intervention, even before native societies and institutions had begun to crumble under European penetration, had done little to increase the effectiveness of government in the islands. The difficulties which had been apparent in the minimum intervention policy during the 'twenties and 'thirties remained unabated in the 'forties and 'fifties. Captain Erskine (H.M.S. *Havannah*) after his island cruise of 1849-50 wrote a *Journal* containing good contemporary evidence of the ineffectiveness of minimum intervention during the middle years of the century. Three excerpts from the journal will indicate how the early difficulties encountered by the minimum intervention policy continued even thirty and forty years after its adoption:

(1) "The subjection under which British subjects . . . are placed by act of parliament to the courts of New South Wales becomes nearly a dead letter when a lengthened and almost impracticable process is required to bring an accused person to trial, but might be most advantageously enforced in many cases, were naval officers furnished with the necessary authority for carrying out the law, and which might be so regulated as scarcely to admit of abuse."[3]

(2) "I was not sorry to have an opportunity of proving to the white men that attempts on the part of the natives to establish and enforce just laws would meet with no opposition, but rather with encouragement from British officers."[4]

(3) "I was desirous of showing the vagrant English [in the New Hebrides], who, when amongst these islands, fancy themselves above all restraint, that offences wantonly committed here were punishable by our own laws; and although in this case it was not probable that any evidence could be procured which would weigh with a Sydney jury, even in the doubtful case of their considering the murder of a savage a blameable action, yet the inconvenience the culprit would be put to by his removal might operate in some degree as a check upon others, if it were understood that our domiciliary visits were to be annually repeated."[5]

Evidence as to the success of the consular appointments made at this time is meagre, but what there is indicates the continued failure of the representation system to secure order amongst British sub-

[3] J. E. Erskine: *Journal of . . . H.M.S. "Havannah"*; London, 1853; p. 199.
[4] ibid, p. 117.
[5] ibid, p. 139.

jects under the aegis of the minimum intervention policy. The *Vulture* episode in Fiji is a striking instance of the powerlessness of the British Consul in that group. The mates of the *Vulture* refused to proceed to sea and the master appealed to Pritchard for aid. But Pritchard's authority to intervene was doubtful and his resources for doing so were nil. Had not the commander of a United States man-of-war lent him a boat's crew, the dispute would have remained unsettled so far as the British authorities were concerned.[6]

The elder Pritchard, who was consul in Samoa from 1844, also felt the powerlessness of his position. Destitute of executive authority, his only sanction was threats of reprisals from visiting men-of-war. His pleas for more frequent naval visits provoked the wearied Foreign Office to inform him in 1851 that:

> "The Navigator Islands have lately been more frequently visited by H.M. ships of war than any other of the groups in the Pacific, and I have to observe that the naval establishment of the British Empire is not sufficiently large to enable the Admiralty to place a ship at the disposal of each of H.M. consuls in distant stations. . . . The intervention of a ship of war must be reserved as a last and extreme remedy."[7]

Throughout the 'fifties the power at the disposal of British representatives in the Pacific fell far short of the vague commitments in which even the minimum intervention policy involved them. The insolence of white men far removed from their own courts, the powerlessness of native rulers threatened at once by the disruption from internal forces of their own kingdoms and by the turbulence of white men within their territories, the inability of whites and natives alike to understand one another's law and ethics—these factors dominated the South Pacific during the 'fifties and made the position of a British consul invidious indeed. Until experiments were made in the development of extra-consular jurisdiction,[8] the contribution of the consuls to effective government in the islands was subject to the gravest limitations.

A similar conclusion has to be reached concerning the role of naval visits to the island in relation to the problem of government. As established in Chapter VII above, naval visits had for long tended to undermine native authority. Frequent acts of coercion in the interests of white residents naturally impeded any attempt

6 W. T. Pritchard, op. cit., p. 213.
7 Qu. Masterman, op. cit., p. 46.
8 See below, Chapter XVII.

THE GROUPS AROUND FIJI

that might have been made to subject white men to native rule. Most of the naval work of the 'fifties and 'sixties was indistinguishable from that of previous decades. Even the enlightened Erskine performed the familiar police work at New Caledonia, the New Hebrides and the Loyalties. In Samoa his work was more closely concerned with the problem of government, as here he composed warring factions.[9] The cruise of H.M.S. *Fawn* in 1862 produced a case of coercive judgment against a native ruler[10] fit to rank with any of the examples of the 'thirties. In Fiji there were several instances of naval intervention on behalf of individual British subjects, such as that of the Englishman, Davis, in 1861, an attack on whom was punished by Sir Malcolm MacGregor (H.M.S. *Harrier*).[11] In the same year, however, Commodore Seymour (H.M.S. *Pelorus*) reconciled warring natives.[12]

Even where their work was specially directed towards preserving the peace, there was little in any of these visits, or in the training and resources of the commanders, to help solve the basic problems of government in islands frequented by Europeans. In so far as the tendency was to intervene to protect Europeans, rather than to punish crimes committed by them, the naval visits probably increased the difficulties of native rulers.

The record of naval visits and consular representation into the 'sixties proved that existing British policy had no significant contribution to make to the problem of island government. The same may be concluded of the policies of the United States and France in the unannexed islands.[13]

Left virtually to their own resources so far as the problem of government was concerned, the Europeans and natives in the islands evolved at various times three main solutions to their problem. Every one of these solutions affected the existing institutions of British policy (consuls and naval visits) and demanded new decisions on policy towards the islands. The three solutions to the problem of government, all of which suffered complications from the interference of the Great Powers on behalf of their subjects, were:

[9] Erskine, op. cit., pp. 233, 235-6.
[10] T. H. Hood: *Notes of a Cruise in H.M.S. "Fawn"*; Edinburgh, 1863; pp. 146, 158.
[11] W. T. Pritchard, op. cit., p. 277. MacGregor acted at Pritchard's request. For an earlier similar case, see record of H.M.S. *Calypso* at Unduvau in *N.Z. Journal*, Vol. IX, No. 244, p. 78.
[12] Pritchard, op. cit., p. 338.
[13] See Brookes, op. cit., on U.S. and French policies.

(1) The investing of British and other consuls with judicial and administrative powers; this extension of consular powers was generally effected, either by informal agreement with the native rulers, or by express act of the native rulers, who, according to the British Government, had the sole right to permit or forbid the exercise of such powers in their territories.

(2) Appeals by native rulers (sometimes supported or instigated by whites) for annexation or protection by the Great Powers. These appeals, when made to Great Britain, were usually favoured by the Australasian colonies and were distinguished from earlier offers of cession and the like in that they stemmed from the problem of internal government as much as from fear of foreign aggression.

(3) Attempts to establish independent governments in the islands organised on European lines. The attempts were generally made by whites with native concurrence, or by natives under white guidance.

Each one of these developments compelled the British Government to reconsider the policy of minimum intervention. It was no longer possible, as in the days of French aggression, to compromise by intervention to preserve the *status quo*. Pacific conditions were changing too rapidly to make any such policy possible. The matter was beyond the possibility that action external to the islands might be sufficient to meet the demands on the British Government. Internal action, in the form of direct assistance in the task of island government, had become the only alternative to maintaining minimum intervention at the cost of seeing British subjects and their interests swallowed up in the mounting lawlessness of the islands. International rivalries complicated the situation, so that Great Britain, which regarded annexation of the islands as no alternative at all to other possible policies, was faced simultaneously with the problem of government (as encountered in New Zealand) and the problem of foreign aggrandizement (as encountered in Tahiti, the Societies and New Caledonia).

Chapter XVII

EXTRA-CONSULAR JURISDICTION

THE inability of the natives either to put their own house in order or to induce some European Power to do so for them led to several attempts being made in the islands to strengthen local administration. One of these attempts was the vesting of judicial and administrative powers in the consuls of the Great Powers. This step was taken both in Fiji and in Samoa.

Even before formal arrangements were made by native rulers to transfer to the consuls jurisdiction over foreigners in the islands and over the relations of foreigners and natives, the position of the consuls as representatives of the Great Powers had led to their exercising unofficially a wide range of extra-consular functions. Though Great Britain officially frowned on participation by her consuls in judicial and administrative duties beyond the scope of their office—on the grounds that native sovereignty was thereby infringed, the British Government involved in internal island problems and complications with foreign Powers made likely—there was not a British Consul in the islands during the 'fifties and 'sixties who did not develop a very considerable extra-consular jurisdiction.

The British Consuls were, indeed, in an invidious position. The true reasons for their appointments were threefold: (a) that a watch might be kept on the attempts of any other Powers to annex the islands or to obtain unreasonable advantages there; (b) that British subjects might have the ordinary benefits and restraints of an official representative of their government living amongst them; and (c) that through the work of the consuls amongst British subjects the strain on native rulers might be alleviated. The powers confided to the island consuls, however, were the same as those accorded to consuls, who had been accredited to civilised states which were capable of maintaining order in their territories.

The British Consuls could have been given limited administrative and judicial functions in the islands by special arrangement with the chiefs, ratified by British Act of Parliament—a procedure adopted in the case of consuls serving in some other backward countries.[1] But Great Britain made no attempt to secure such powers for her consuls, although serious attention was given to the question of doing so in 1870-72 when the demand for British action to control the labour trade was rising fast.[2] In practice a gap was allowed to develop between her consuls' powers and supposed functions on the one hand and the duties which circumstances imposed upon them on the other hand. W. T. Pritchard complained that the difficulties of the consuls' position were still further increased by the failure of the Foreign Office to issue instructions to guide the consuls in their anomalous position.

The fact was that the consuls were looked upon by natives and whites alike as the representatives of the "Great Governments." Inevitably, they found themselves adjudicating in disputes, even assisting in the administration of the native kingdoms. Under the energetic W. T. Pritchard, Fiji provided a most conspicuous example of this tendency. Always eager for the development of the group as a British colony, Pritchard—with the acquiescence of the native rulers and of a majority of the whites—exercised extraordinarily wide powers. The necessity for his exercising extra-consular jurisdiction was explained by Pritchard in simple terms of elementary law and order:

> "I had to deal with men of every conceivable disposition. To pass their complaints unheeded was simply to foster their angry feelings, which in a country like Fiji, without government or law, would surely result in violence."[3]

According to Pritchard himself, his verdicts were generally well received and whites of diverse nationalities, glad to have some European authority in the islands, freely laid claim to British nationality in order to bring their cases under his notice.[4] "Where the parties to a complaint were of different nationalities," wrote Pritchard, ". . . the U.S. Consul and I together endeavoured to settle their disputes for them."[5]

In its early stages Pritchard's extra-consular jurisdiction was completely unofficial. It was sanctioned only by general opinion amongst the whites, the acquiescence of the chiefs and the general respect for the official representative of Great Britain. In 1859,

[1] Cf. Appendix No. 1; Memo. by Mr. Hertslet; F.O.: *Confidential Memorandum respecting Mr. Liardet's Recent Proceedings at Samoa, 1878.*
[2] Cf. Kimberley to Canterbury, Mar. 16, 1871; *Corr. rel. to Fiji, 1871.*
[3] W. T. Pritchard, op. cit., p. 261.
[4] ibid, pp. 255 ff.
[5] ibid, p. 257.

however, Pritchard, concerned to remove any British fears of lawlessness in Fiji, which might stand in the way of acceptance of the offered cession, accepted legal powers from the native rulers of Fiji. On December 15th, 1859, in the same month as Smythe[6] received his instructions from Newcastle, Pritchard and Thakombau, together with other chiefs representing the various districts of Fiji, met at the British Consulate, Levuka, and reached decisions fundamental to the government of Fiji.[7] "In the absence of native courts competent to hear causes wherein British subjects are litigants," wrote Pritchard to the Foreign Office, "I applied to the chiefs of Fiji, when assembled in council on the 15th inst., for a commission authorising the constitution of a court in this consulate for that purpose."[8]

Pritchard received his commission and established a court forthwith. Only a little over a fortnight later he received still wider powers, clearly designed to pave the way for British rule in Fiji. On December 16 the Fijian chiefs in council unanimously agreed:

"That we hereby delegate, cede and make over to and vest in the said William Thomas Pritchard the full unreserved, entire and supreme right, authority and power to govern Fiji, according to the broad and plain principles of justice and morality.

"That this enactment and agreement shall be in force and valid until the final answer of the Queen of Great Britain to the cession of Fiji made on the 12th day of October, 1858, and duly ratified and renewed by us in council assembled on the 14th day of December, 1859."[9]

Pritchard admitted that this delegation of powers was made to him at his own instigation.

The only comment on this agreement to come from Great Britain was a despatch from Lord John Russell to Pritchard.[10] The consul was informed that in accepting the powers of government entrusted to him by the agreement he had exceeded his authority. Pritchard was in fact sharply rebuked, the Imperial Government being concerned with the objective of not getting entangled in Fiji rather than with the problem of good government there. Lord John Russell based part of his objection to Pritchard's extra-consular activities on a suspected lack of authority in the chiefs themselves to confer the power:

[6] Smythe was sent to Fiji as Special Commissioner to investigate the offer of cession made in 1858. See Ch. XVIII below.

[7] Cf. Henderson, op. cit., pp. 5-7.

[8] Pritchard to F.O., Dec. 31, 1859; Encl. 3 in No. 8; *Corr. rel. to Fiji, 1862.*

[9] Sub-encl. in Encl. 4 in No. 8; ibid.

[10] Russell to Pritchard, Aug. 20, 1860; *Corr. rel. to Fiji. 1871*; No. 38.

"It appears that you have likewise procured the enactment of a law giving yourself full, unreserved, entire and supreme authority to govern Fiji, and to make what laws you please. . . . Whether the persons making this law are competent to bind the other natives, or whether they understood themselves the real import of what they were doing, are questions on which it is impossible for Her Majesty's Government to form any opinion, but on which the future peace of the Fiji Islands may in no slight measure depend."[11]

This raising of legal issues was apparently the product, less of any real doubt as to the competence of the chiefs to confer the powers, than of fears that Pritchard would embroil himself with the subjects of other European states. The Government which permitted its naval officers to undertake acts of war against native tribes with which it was nominally at peace cannot be held to have had an over-nice conscience as to the legality of its policies in the South Pacific. Moreover, if the British Government were prepared to consider an offer of cession from the chiefs, thus recognising their sovereignty, it could not query with conscience their competence to vest authority in Pritchard.

Despite the erroneous character of his report on the facts which he had been instructed to investigate, Smythe, the Special Commissioner sent to Fiji in 1859-60, at least perceived the difficulties of the consul's position. However much the British Government might rely on the doctrine of native sovereignty, when convenient, the fact remained that white residents looked to the consul to maintain order and settle their disputes. Each task was beyond consular powers, although, as Pritchard had received authority from the native chiefs, that is, from the sovereigns of Fiji, to hold consular courts, no objection could be raised in law to the grant of the powers, save by doubting the competence of the chiefs to confer them. This was certainly an extension of the native sovereignty doctrine with which Great Britain had never reckoned.

Smythe suggested that, in order to remove the embarrassments of the consul's position, the British Government itself should invest him with magisterial powers and provide him with means of enforcing his authority. Smythe also recommended that the British Consulate be removed to Suva in order that a fresh start might be made with the white settlement. So long as Great Britain adhered to the policy of recognising native sovereignty, Smythe's main suggestion could be adopted only through establishing British extra-territoriality in Fiji—a complicated and troublesome procedure, which might have raised more problems (for example, in

11 ibid.

determining where sovereignty resided in Fiji) than it could solve.[12]

More attention was paid to Smythe's charges that Pritchard had wantonly interfered in native affairs. At the request of the Duke of Newcastle the Governor of New South Wales appointed three commissioners to enquire into Pritchard's administration. Several weighty charges were set down for their investigation. In addition to fraud, the extortion of unauthorised fees and misrepresentation at the time of the Smythe Report, Pritchard was charged with attempting to dictate to the chiefs and with having established an unlawful consular court. The commissioners were also required to report on Pritchard's personal qualifications for office and (rather surprisingly) on whether it were really necessary for Great Britain to maintain a consul in Fiji.[13] The commissioners reported against Pritchard and recommended his removal from office. In January, 1863, Pritchard handed over to Captain Jones.

Whatever his personal failings, Pritchard had understood the situation which developed in Fiji as a result of the crumbling of native society and the lack of efficient control over either natives or foreigners. In endeavouring to remedy this situation he inevitably exceeded his consular powers and made enemies through his attempts to impose law and order on a mixed and rather turbulent population. Realising that sooner or later Fiji would pass under the control of one of the Great Powers, Pritchard did his best to prod the British Government into taking action. But Great Britain, already vexed with an empire larger than she had ever contemplated, would not add a single square mile to her territories unless she would clearly be the gainer. Even Pritchard's attempt to solve the problem by himself accepting responsibility for government was opposed by the British authorities as likely to prove a fruitful source of international complications.[14]

Although partly owing to the more active interest of other foreign states, the British Consuls at Samoa never received such powers as were bestowed on Pritchard in Fiji, they did have extra-consular powers conferred upon them. Mr. Consul John C. Williams reported in 1864 that the foreign residents of Apia had formed themselves into an association for the mutual protection of

[12] An Order-in-Council was drafted but not adopted because of legal difficulties. (F.O. 58/124 and 58/2314.)

[13] Encl. in Layard to Rogers, Mar. 15, 1862; *Despatches from the Secretary of State to the Governor of N.S.W., 1862.*

[14] Evidence as to the state of affairs which necessitated Pritchard's actions is afforded by the fact that, when his powers lapsed in July, 1862, the white residents of Fiji (or some of them) promptly formed the Foreign Residents' Self-Protection Society. (Derrick, op. cit., I, p. 154.)

life and property and that a Consular Court had been established with the approval of the chiefs. Williams declared that he himself had been appointed to the Presidency of the Court and asked the Foreign Office to advise him as to his position.

At the request of Lord John Russell the case was considered by the Law Officers of the Crown. On September 28, 1864, Williams was informed that:

> "However desirable it may be that order should be preserved and that justice should be fairly administered wherever British subjects reside, a British officer must be especially careful not to involve either his Government or himself in difficulties by pursuing a course not sanctioned by his own national law or by international usage.

> "In no foreign country has a British officer power to exercise authority over foreigners.

> "You say in your despatch that the arrangement made by the foreign residents in Apia has met with the approval of the Chiefs. If, therefore, it rests on any sanction, it is upon that of the local authority, and if it should prove to have been established by the authority of the Chiefs who are recognised as exercising the powers of Government at Apia, it may not be necessary for Her Majesty's Government to object to it; but it will, even in that case be necessary that you should make it clearly to be understood that this arrangement is one with which Her Majesty's Government has no concern."[15]

Finally, Williams was instructed to resign his judgeship. Though he had not incurred official disapproval in the same manner as had Pritchard, who had obviously angled for power, the Foreign Office clearly opposed Williams's attempt to engage in extra-consular activities. British policy, as laid down in Williams's case, was practically the same as that enunciated when dealing with Pritchard's extra-consular activities in Fiji. Once again legal difficulties were used as arguments to bolster up an objection to extension of consular powers, although the real grounds of the objection were —and in Williams's case were admitted to be—the fear of incurring entangling responsibilities in the islands.

These fears were realised in 1877 when Mr. Consul Liardet at Samoa ordered the arrest of, amongst others, Martin, a British subject in official United States employ. There was an immediate protest from the United States Consul. Liardet had also involved himself in a dispute with the German Consul, Weber, when he

[15] Memo. by Mr. Hertslet on British Consular Jurisdiction in the Navigators, April 28, 1877; *Confidential Memorandum resp. Mr Liardet's Recent Proceedings at Samoa, 1878.*

declared to the Samoans that he held the whole group as security for fines of 60,000 dollars which he himself had imposed upon them. Weber promptly protested against the fines and against the "sequestration of the islands being held to include German property in any way."

The Foreign Office strongly condemned the actions of Liardet, whose personal unfitness for his position seems to have been proved beyond a doubt. A confidential Foreign Office memorandum commented that:

> "He must have been at the aware that, beyond the use of moral influence, he had no judicial power over British subjects. This was explained to him in a despatch dated May 12, 1877."[16]

The despatch referred to had cited Williams's case and had indicated that the policy laid down in respect of that case still applied.[17]

Liardet's defence of his actions was that the internal position of Samoa made extra-consular jurisdiction the only effective form of government over Europeans there. Before his own arrival in Samoa, Liardet pointed out, the British, American and German consuls had together framed laws and carried out sentences on subjects of all nations.[18] The Foreign Office declined to accept this reasoning. Instead it relied on the letter of the law and the usual policy of non-intervention in the problems of island government. The Foreign Office made it perfectly clear that British Consuls would not be allowed to incur risks by exercising jurisdiction other than that sanctioned by national law and international usage.

In 1869, however, there was a break away from this narrow adherence to minimum intervention in relation to consular powers. Great Britain then admitted—in one case and with explicit reservations—that, subject to all legal doubts being removed as to the capacity of native chiefs to delegate powers to the consuls, there would be no objection to the British Consul concerned acting in extra-consular matters, where foreign consuls were admitted to act in the same way.

The case from which this new principle arose was that of Mr. Consul March at Fiji. In December, 1869, March suggested that he should be invested with magisterial powers over British sub-

[16] ibid, p. 3.

[17] In 1877 the case of Acting-Consul J. F. Williams, who had imposed a fine on S. Dean, a British subject, for breach of quarantine regulations, was discussed in a despatch to Liardet with the intimation that Williams had exceeded his powers. (F.O. to Liardet, May 12, 1877; ibid.)

[18] Liardet to Derby, Aug. 14, 1877; Appendix No. 3; ibid.

jects in the group.[19] The same recommendation had been made earlier in the Smythe report and was repeated by March in view of the growing abuses of the labour trade:

"At present Her Majesty's consulate is permitted to exercise some authority over this traffic, but, until steps be taken to regulate it by law, it cannot prevent all irregularities. In many instances the office has intervened with success in preventing abuses, but as the movement increases, it will become more difficult to do so."[20]

Clarendon himself had already written to March in August, 1869, praising *ex post facto* the work done by Thurston, while Acting British Consul, in controlling the trade. Clarendon had added, however, that opposition to this form of extra-consular jurisdiction was growing and that, being itself beyond the consul's legal powers, it would "soon be openly defied."[21]

March suggested the adoption of detailed regulations to be administered by the British Consul. He claimed that he was already exercising a semi-official control over the trade. British subjects engaged in the labour traffic, he considered, generally adhered to his wishes. On the other hand, it had to be admitted that "some of the men have at times cajoled natives on board, and carried them away against their wishes.[22]

The Foreign Office was deeply concerned with the evils of the labour trade and was therefore disposed to view more tolerantly than in the past extensions of consular functions in the islands. In fact Spring Rice of the Foreign Office had written to the Colonial Office in December, 1869, enquiring whether any means existed by which the British Consul at Fiji or other consular officers in the Pacific might be given extended powers to deal with labour trade offences.[23] When the Governor of New South Wales, Lord Belmore, felt constrained to advise that the British Consul in Fiji should be invested with certain magisterial powers because "the present state of things cannot long continue,"[24] the Foreign Office decided that something ought to be done. Lord Clarendon wrote to March only three months after the date of March's despatch to point out that:

"Her Majesty's Government are fully aware of the difficulties which you must experience from the limits of the jurisdiction entrusted to

19 March to Clarendon, Dec. 17, 1869; *Corr. rel. to Fiji, 1871.*
20 ibid.
21 Clarendon to March, Aug. 3, 1869; C. 399, 1871.
22 Cf. C. 496, 1872, Encl. 1 in No. 1 and Encl. in No. 2 (F.O. and C.O.).
23 Spring Rice to C.O., Dec. 14, 1869; ibid, No. 2 (F.O. and C.O.).
24 Belmore to Granville, Nov. 5, 1869; ibid, No. 4 (N.S.W.).

Her Majesty's Consuls. It is satisfactory, however, to find that those difficulties have been diminished by the disposition shown by the settlers to recognise your authority, and to co-operate with you in measures to place the position of the labourers on a satisfactory footing."[25]

Clarendon then referred to "local laws . . . which are said to disclaim all rights of jurisdiction over the persons and property of foreigners." He added that, if the chiefs were willing to confer power on the consuls subject to Her Majesty's approval, then no objections would be raised by Great Britain, provided the chiefs had authority to exercise the powers which they purported to delegate.

Subsequently regulations were drawn up by March and approved by Earl Granville.[26] Narrow and guarded as was the admission of March's right as consul to exercise jurisdiction beyond the scope of his authority, it definitely constituted a departure in policy. The sorry spectacle of the uncontrolled labour trade, which by 1869 was being represented to Great Britain as an abuse crying out for remedy, naturally inclined the Foreign Office to strengthen any authority in the islands which could regulate the traffic and by mitigating its evils prevent any necessity for official intervention on a large scale. The departure from minimum intervention was a grudging one, but unmistakable nevertheless. This was the first time that Great Britain allowed her non-naval representatives in the Pacific to acquire or receive powers adequate to the duties which circumstances imposed upon them. An endeavour had been made in the same direction in 1832 when Lord Howick's Bill was presented and when subsequent attempts were made to bring down a Bill conferring ampler legal powers on Busby. All these efforts having proved nugatory, it was left to Granville and Clarendon to usher in an officially recognised departure in policy.

It will be noticed that no change was made in British law. March was merely permitted to acquire powers from the native chiefs on the understanding that consuls of other states were permitted to acquire similar powers. The 1869 decision, therefore, was of political, rather than of legal, significance. The position in British law remained as described by Clarendon in a despatch to the British Embassy in Washington:

"Her Majesty's Government have found that legal difficulties interfere with their powers of extending the jurisdiction of Her Majesty's Consul under the provisions of the Consular Jurisdiction Act. Her

[25] Clarendon to March, Mar. 30, 1870; Encl. 8 in No. 6 (F.O.), ibid.
[26] C. 496, 1872.

179

Majesty's Government will give their consideration as to the means by which these difficulties can be met."[27]

The failure to accompany approval of March's regulations by legal change to give them the backing of British law greatly militated against their success. The operation of the regulations was discussed in a letter from the Emigration Commissioners to the Colonial Office in October, 1871.[28] The commissioners took the view that, despite the concurrence and participation of the native chiefs in making the regulations which gave them legal force, there had never been any administrative power adequate to enforce them. The submission of the planters was merely "voluntary" and might be "refused at any time." For all practical purposes they were "always a dead-letter." In so far as March had relied on British statutes and, more particularly, on the Merchant Shipping and Passenger Acts, his position was legally untenable.[29]

The necessity for legal change in the consul's position had been sufficiently recognised in Great Britain even in 1870 to prompt consideration of the possibility of conferring magisterial powers on the consul through British law. The problem of how to do so was complicated, not only by the difficulty of investing a consul with magisterial powers to be exercised on foreign soil, but also by the legal doubts which had arisen over the enforcement of 9 Geo. IV, c. 83, s. 4. This enactment had given the Supreme Courts of New South Wales and Tasmania power to try British subjects for offences committed on Pacific Islands not subject to any civilised Power.[30] The doubt arising was whether warrants could properly be issued in the Australian colonies for the arrest of persons still remaining in the islands.[31] Lord Belmore, the Governor of New South Wales, wrote to Earl Granville that:

"Though a prisoner on his arrival in the Colony may be amenable to the law, yet . . . until his arrival, his detention may be without warrant. What seems . . . to be required is this, if the Consuls are to continue to send persons as prisoners to Sydney, they should, in addition to taking depositions as was done in Morgan's case, have power to issue a warrant magisterially to legalize their custody and their conveyance to the place at which they are to be tried."[32]

27 Clarendon to Thornton, Sept. 2, 1869; C. 399, 1871.
28 C. 496, 1872; Encl. in No. 2 (F.O. and C.O.).
29 As to contemporary opinions of March's work, see, for favourable comment, H. Britton: *Fiji in 1870*; Melbourne, 1870; p. 17.
30 See above, Chapter VI.
31 Doubts arose from the *Young Australian* case. See Chapter XXI, below, and Belmore to Granville, Nov. 5, 1869; C. 399, 1871.
32 ibid.

The proposal to confer magisterial powers on the consuls was discussed intermittently up to 1874, but with little prospect of effective action being taken after 1872. In 1871, in reply to a statement by the Attorney-General of New South Wales, Sir James Martin, that the conferring of such powers would involve the exercise of sovereignty over Fiji, Lord Kimberley made it clear that it was some kind of extra-territoriality on the basis of agreement with the native chiefs, which was desired.[33] Brookes states that an Order in Council to enlarge the powers of the British Consul in Fiji was actually prepared and formally sanctioned by the Queen; but this became nugatory when a new Government, claiming international recognition, was established in Fiji in June, 1871.[34]

In 1874 it was made clear that Great Britain had abandoned any idea of expanding consular jurisdiction in Fiji, partly because of the establishment of the new government there in 1871. The instructions issued to Commodore Goodenough and Mr. Consul Layard when they were commencing their investigations in Fiji referred to March's proposals in these terms:

> "It would be difficult to justify the establishment of such Consular jurisdiction, unless it can be shown that the country in which it is to be exercised does not possess a Government capable of controlling those who reside within its limits."[35]

The Foreign Office anticipated that four main difficulties would confront any general attempt to extend consular jurisdiction.

1. It was doubtful how far the Fijian Government (established in 1871) would accept the principle. This difficulty had not arisen in March's case in 1870, as there the Consul had received his powers from the native chiefs.
2. It was doubted whether even British subjects would submit to the rule of the Consul.
3. There was the problem of other foreigners resident in Fiji. What would happen when these came into conflict with British subjects, or acted in opposition to laws which the British Consul was attempting to enforce? Mr. Consul Williams at Samoa had complained in 1870 of the "jealous" attitude of foreigners to "any inquiries made by the British Consul."[36]
4. What would be the status of vessels owned by British subjects in Fiji and transferred to the Fijian flag? Would these still be subject to the control of the Royal Navy?

[33] C. 509, 1872.
[34] Brookes, op. cit., p. 372.
[35] C. 983, 1874.
[36] C. 399, 1871; No. 62. As to possible disputes with consuls of other Powers, see C. 3814, 1883, p. 13.

In view of these doubts and difficulties the Foreign Office decided that no proposals for the establishment of extra-consular jurisdiction in Fiji should be entertained. So far as Fiji was concerned, the time for such expedients was passed.

In forming a final judgment on British policy towards the development of extra-consular jurisdiction in the South Pacific two points should be regarded as basic:

(i) The whole problem of consular jurisdiction was merely part of the wider problem of government. The peculiar position of the consuls as the official representatives of the Great Powers naturally led to their being regarded as suitable agencies of government in the islands.

(ii) The jurisdiction could be exercised in one of three ways: (a) as a form of extra-territoriality, requiring official British sanction, together with the consent of the native rulers; (b) as an informal extension of the consular powers resting on the concurrence of the native rulers, white residents and any other persons or states affected; and (c) through the act of the native rulers, endowing the consuls with legal powers, and making them, in effect, agents of the native government.

From the evidence discussed above it has to be concluded that Great Britain had no interest in the problem of government as such. Her interest in the extension of consular functions was confined to ways and means of regulating the labour trade in which the activities of British subjects were reviving all the former agitation against the slave trade, and embarrassing the British Government in its relations with the humanitarian movements at home. Considered as a means of controlling the labour trade, what were the merits and deficiencies of the three forms of extra-consular jurisdiction?

Extra-territorial jurisdiction involved few complications of legal principle, being an established procedure in backward countries. But reliance on this method opened the door to abuses through transfers of flags and nationalities and required specific action by Great Britain in conjunction with the native rulers to establish the extra-territoriality. Further, which native rulers were to be recognised as sovereigns? It might also have involved competitive foreign claims to extra-territorial privileges. Finally, as was observed by Smythe, such an extension of consular jurisdiction would place the onus on Great Britain of supplying the consul with means to enforce his authority.

An informal extension of consular powers (with the concurrence of the native chiefs and white residents and with some tacit acquiescence on the part of Great Britain) had much to recommend it. W. T. Pritchard, Thurston and March were all able to employ this method with some show of success. But its uncertainties and the experience of Williams in Samoa showed that any effective control over the labour trade would need a securer legal basis than this method could provide. Moreover, the consul's means of enforcing his decisions were limited.

Lastly there was the alternative of permitting the native rulers to endow the consuls with special powers. The experience of Pritchard and Williams sufficiently demonstrated that this method was unacceptable in Great Britain because of the risk of international complications and because of the invidious position in which it might place the consul. The ability of the native rulers to provide adequate sanctions for the consul's jurisdiction was also doubtful.

Summing up, it would appear that, even apart from the question of British policy, extra-consular jurisdiction, though an inevitable development from the lack of effective government in the islands, could not solve the basic problems of administration. It was a palliative produced by conditions on the spot, dependent for its successful operation on the continued goodwill of the native rulers, on the relations existing between the consuls and white residents, and in the last resort on the willingness of the Great Powers to support their consuls. British policy, because of indifference to the islands, because of unwillingness to accept extended commitments there and because of fear of foreign complications generally stood in the way of effective use of consular powers.[37] With the increasing trend in the islands to establish governments capable of meeting the new conditions and with the progressive annexation of one group after another to the Great Powers, extra-consular jurisdiction ceased to be a matter of importance to British policy. The excesses of the labour trade, which had given rise to British interest in this method of island government, found another remedy in the establishment of the Western Pacific High Commission[38] and, so far as Great Britain was concerned, extra-consular jurisdiction had ceased to be important by the end of the 'seventies.

[37] The abortive attempt to conclude an agreement with the U.S.A. over consular supervision of the labour traffic seems to have been as far as British policy was prepared to proceed in the direction of international agreement.
[38] Discussed below in Chapters XXIII et seq.

Chapter XVIII

COTTON AND MINIMUM INTERVENTION IN FIJI.
1855-1870

The first occasion on which an offer of cession fairly referable to the new problem of government, rather than to fear of French aggression or to missionary prompting, was made to Great Britain was in 1855. In that year Captain Fremantle, the senior naval officer on the Australian station, visited the main island groups in the South West Pacific and reviewed their situation thoroughly. While at Fiji he received a repetition of the offer made to Captain Denham (H.M.S. *Herald*) the previous year by Tui Levuka to cede Ovalau Island.

Tui Levuka, the principal chief of Ovalau, had offered the island to Queen Victoria with the approval of the other chiefs.[1] The 1855 offer made to Denham was largely instigated by the English Wesleyan missionary, James Calvert, who was fearful of French action in Fiji and dreaded an outcome similar to that in Tahiti.[2] Denham merely received Tui Levuka s offer, communicated it to the Admiralty and allowed the matter to stand over until the arrival of Fremantle, who considered the problem on the broadest possible basis.

Fremantle recommended that the offer should be accepted and that British rule should be extended throughout the whole of the Fijis.[3] White residents of every nationality, he argued, would welcome the establishment of British government in the group. The natives themselves were fearful of the French, whom they regarded as the spoliators of Tahiti. He reported that Thakombau, who had made himself King of Mbau and claimed to be King of Fiji,[4] was embarrassed by the American claim for $45,000 assessed

1 Fremantle to Admiralty, Dec. 12, 1855; F.O. 58/84B.

2 Derrick, op. cit., I, p. 136.

3 Fremantle to Osborne, Nov. 15, 1855; F.O 58/84· qu. Brookes, op. cit., pp. 237-238.

4 As to Thakombau's claim to the latter title see Smythe to Newcastle, May 1, 1861; *Corr. rel. to Fiji, 1862.*

against him by Commander Boutwell of the U.S.S. *John Adams.*
Thakombau had also to contend with the presence in Fiji of the
King of Tonga and his army, originally called in by himself to
help put down a rebellion in Mbau.

Fremantle went so far as to recommend a complete abandonment
of the existing British policy of minimum intervention. He argued
that Tonga, which had been constrained to conclude a treaty with
France in 1855,[5] would be glad to enter into a similar arrangement
with Great Britain. In fact King George of Tonga wrote to Queen
Victoria through the Governor of New South Wales in October,
1858, requesting that Great Britain guarantee the independence of
his kingdom and enter into a treaty of commerce and amity.
Fremantle also considered that Samoa, torn by the faction fighting
of petty chiefs, would be grateful for the establishment of British
government.

His case was founded on the changing conditions in the Pacific.
Pointing to the increasing trade between Australia and the islands
and to the opening up of the South Pacific by steam navigation,
Fremantle stressed the prospective gains of intervention in the
Pacific, while arguing that the French occupation of New Caledonia
had made essential the establishment of British protectorates over
Fiji, Tonga and Samoa. Each group, he thought, should be
under the control of a resident commissioner, subordinate to a
peripatetic governor-general.

Fremantle understood the Pacific situation well. But his recommendations were ignored in Great Britain. Despite the obvious
weaknesses of the policy, the British Government proposed to
concentrate its attention on extending consular representation in
the islands, rather than on tackling the fundamental problem of
island government. Great Britain was still unwilling to accept
responsibilities in the islands. Her concern was merely to wait
and to watch (rather desultorily) in the hope that the *status quo*
would be preserved.

In Fiji, Thakombau himself took the initiative in seeking
stronger government. The claim levied against him by the United
States authorities naturally disposed him to play off one foreign
government against another. He was encouraged in this policy by
the extraordinary degree of attention lavished on him by foreign
governments in the late 'fifties. In 1856 the French warship
Le Bonze had called at Levuka and friendly relations had been
cultivated by its officers with the chiefs. In March, 1857, there was

[5] See Chap. XIV, above.

a visit from the U.S.S. *Falmouth,* which hoisted a new ensign at the Rewa consulate. Three months afterwards a treaty was signed by Thakombau with the United States. After three more months the British Government sent W. T. Pritchard to be consul in Fiji. In June, 1858, another French warship, *La Bayonnaise,* came to Levuka and its commander negotiated a treaty with Thakombau.[6]

These incidents naturally disposed Thakombau to seek advantages from alliances with western Powers. Another factor influencing him in the same direction was his hope that a treaty between himself and Great Britain would set the seal on his claims to be recognised as Tui Viti.[7] The United States insistence that the American claims were levied against him personally and not against the chiefs in general had already increased his prestige in the group.[8] British recognition would guarantee him in the position of the paramount native ruler in Fiji.

Accordingly in October, 1858, Thakombau made—through William Pritchard, the newly appointed British Consul—an elaborate offer of the cession of the Fiji group to the British Crown.[9] From the terms of the offer it appeared that the desire to be relieved of his indebtedness to the United States and the ambition to be recognised as Tui Viti were the principal motives on Thakombau's part.

Only a week before the offer was made he had received an embarrassing visit from the U.S.S. *Vandalia,* as a result of which the American claim had been reassessed at $48,254.

Thakombau's offer of October, 1858, expressly stipulated that Great Britain should accept responsibility for the debt owed to the Americans and permit Thakombau to "retain the title and rank of Tui Viti, in so far as the aboriginal population is concerned." As consideration for the British payment of the American claims Thakombau promised to convey to Queen Victoria 200,000 acres of land in fee simple—an undertaking into which he had no legal capacity to enter.

The wider problems of government in Fiji and, perhaps, the interest and influence of the white population, were reflected in Thakombau's insistence that he wished:

> "to procure for our people and subjects a good and permanent form of government . . . and . . . due protection and shelter from the violence, the oppression and the tyranny of Foreign Powers."

[6] Derrick, op. cit., I, p. 136.
[7] See below, this page, for Thakombau's stipulations on this point.
[8] Cf. Goodenough and Layard Report; C. 1011, 1874; p. 2.
[9] *Corr. rel. to Fiji, 1862.*

This offer to Great Britain far exceeded Thakombau's legal powers but was ratified by other leading chiefs on December 14th, 1859.[10]

The role of the white settlers and of Pritchard, the British Consul, in presenting the offer of cession is not clear. Pritchard himself declared that Thakombau had come to him for advice about the American claims. "The result of our interview," he briefly added, "was the cession of Fiji to the Queen on the 12th day of October, 1858, on condition that the American claim was paid by the British Government."[11] Pritchard at that time had been at Fiji for not much more than a month. Like his father he was zealous for the extension of British rule in the Pacific and heedless of the considerations which restrained the Imperial Government from action.

The missionaries at first supported Pritchard in his transactions with Thakombau and his recommendations to Great Britain that the offer of cession should be accepted. According to Pritchard, it was the missionaries who encouraged him to believe quite wrongly that Thakombau was competent to make the original offer of 1858.[12] Later, however, the missionary attitude changed.[13]

On receiving the offer Pritchard immediately left for London greatly alarmed by the increasing French interest in Fiji[14] and fearful lest the British Government preserve its customary indifference to territorial offers from the South Pacific. Pritchard's reception in London was better than he had anticipated. Lord Malmesbury, the Secretary of State for Foreign Affairs, approved his having left Fiji to bring the offer of cession to London[15] and Pritchard found that the problem of Fiji was already under consideration because of the cotton-growing potentialities of the group and because of a despatch from the Governor of New South Wales, reporting an imminent cession.[16]

The Colonial Office had already reached views opposed to the acceptance of the cession. Merivale, the Permanent Under-Secretary, had declared that Great Britain need not fear France in the Pacific so long as the naval supremacy of Great Britain was maintained. "The embarrassment of the situation," Merivale admitted, "lay in the fact that the South Sea Islands, Christianised and partly

---

[10] ibid.

[11] W. T. Pritchard, op. cit; p. 216.

[12] ibid, p. 218.

[13] See below, page 194.

[14] The French frigate *La Bayonnaise* had visited Fiji shortly before this time and Thakombau had signed a treaty guaranteeing complete freedom to Roman Catholics in Fiji.

[15] Pritchard, op. cit., p. 221.

[16] Brookes, op. cit., pp. 243 ff.

colonised by Englishmen, longed for British protection against the advent of a different nationality and religion." But he opposed acceptance of Fiji, nevertheless.[17] Carnarvon relied on the familiar reluctance to acquire further colonies unless in case of clear immediate gain and summed the matter up by noting that, "it is painful to refuse, but there must be a limit somewhere to our protecting and governing duties, especially when we gain nothing by the acquisition." The Secretary of State for Colonies admitted that, in the event of war, the French could soon be swept out of any islands they might acquire in the South Pacific, but added that a French "quarrel with any English missionary in the South Sea Islands would suffice for a war in the English Channel."[18]

These opinions had been expressed before Pritchard's arrival in London. In view of their general tenor it is somewhat surprising that the offer of cession was not declined immediately. Similar offers from other groups and from Fiji had been rejected within the immediately preceding years. Great Britain had only just reaffirmed the policy of extending consular representation in the islands in preference to acquiring political responsibilities there. Nevertheless when Pritchard arrived, the offer of cession was referred to the Colonial Office and considered on a basis which clearly implied a contemplated departure from the minimum intervention policy in the case of Fiji.

The explanation of this attitude is to be found in the cotton-growing potentialities of Fiji. The growth of the British textile industries had led to the formation in Manchester in 1857 of a Cotton Supply Association which sought to develop new sources of supply of raw cotton. When the British Consul in Baltimore sent home samples of excellent cotton grown in Samoa and Tonga[19] the Foreign Office instructed British representatives in the South Seas to report on the capacity of the islands for cotton culture.[20] Fiji offered the largest area of arable land available in the Pacific islands. Pritchard himself in recommending the acceptance of the cession offer had written that:

"I would bring most prominently under your Lordship's notice the capability of this group to produce *Cotton*. In compliance with instructions from Lord Clarendon . . . I instituted enquiries and made personal observations, in search of information respecting the

17 ibid, p. 244.
18 ibid.
19 T. J. Bartlett to Sec. of State, June 23, 1867; N.S.W. (Leg. Council): *Cotton Produced in South Pacific Islands, 1857.*
20 Clarendon's Circular Despatches, No. 1 (July 20) and No. 2 (Sept. 12), 1857; ref. to in Pritchard to F.O., Feb. 8, 1859; *Corr. rel. to Fiji, 1862.*

production of this invaluable article: and I am convinced, my Lord, that as a cotton producing country Fiji is of the utmost value to Great Britain."[21]

Pritchard also mentioned the possibilities of coffee, sugar, nutmegs, turmeric, ginger, indigo, antimony and timber in Fiji, but his main emphasis was on cotton.

Powerful support for his claims regarding Fijian cotton was received from the Manchester Cotton Supply Association, which reported on the samples brought to Great Britain from Fiji by Pritchard. The Executive Committee of the Association passed a resolution:

"That the samples of Fiji cotton which have been submitted by the Foreign Office to the Committee . . . are found to be of qualities most desirable for the manufacturers of this country . . . such a range of excellent cotton is scarcely now received from any cotton-growing country which supplies this requisite raw material to Great Britain."[22]

The Association enquired of the Foreign Office "what steps Her Majesty's Government may be disposed to take for ensuring to this country abundant supplies of cotton from the Fiji Islands."[23] This enquiry and the Committee's findings on Fijian cotton were passed on to the Colonial Office by the Foreign Office.[24]

Some delay followed in reaching any decision. Merivale had become fairly favourable to the acceptance of the offer and had corresponded with the Admiralty concerning the strategic advantages of the Fiji group.[25] He had been informed that the annexation of Fiji would ensure to Great Britain "a great part of the available harbours in that part of the Pacific" and that Fiji was nearly on the direct route from Panama to Sydney, the deviation involved in calling at Fiji being only 320 miles.[26]

Admiral Washington, the Admiralty Hydrographer, stated that:

"On looking into this subject I have been struck by the entire want by Great Britain of any advanced position in the Pacific Ocean. We have valuable possessions on either side . . . but not an islet or a rock in the 7,000 miles of ocean that separate them. The Panama and Sydney mail communication is likely to be established, yet we have no island on which to place a coaling station."[27]

[21] Pritchard to F.O., Feb. 8, 1859; ibid.
[22] Resolution of Feb. 25, 1859; ibid.
[23] Sec. of Cotton Supply Assocn. to Malmesbury, Mar. 1, 1859; ibid.
[24] Hammond to Merivale, Mar. 5, 1859; ibid.
[25] Merivale to Admiralty, Mar. 9, 1859; ibid.
[26] Corry (Admiralty) to Merivale, Mar. 14, 1859; ibid.
[27] Washington's Report to the C.O., 1859; qu. in W. Seed to Julius Vogel, Sept. 23, 1873; N.S.W.: *Intercolonial Convention, 1883;* p. 91.

Merivale had also enquired from the Foreign Office whether any foreign Power had claims to Fiji and had been answered in the negative.[28]

These favourable reports, together with the recommendations of the Cotton Supply Association, very nearly swung Merivale to a view favourable to annexation,[29] but the Secretary of State, Bulwer-Lytton, had already ordered the matter to be shelved until Disraeli's Reform Bill of 1858 should have been disposed of.

The new Palmerston Government had the Duke of Newcastle at the Colonial Office and as no finality had yet been reached on Fiji it was decided to send a special commissioner to Fiji to investigate the offer of cession on the spot.

It is clear from the instructions issued to Colonel W. J. Smythe, R.A., who was chosen as the special British commissioner, that Great Britain was completely indifferent to the problem of government in Fiji and concerned merely with its strategic and commercial potentialities. The Duke of Newcastle wrote to Smythe that:

"The question . . . whether or not the Fijis ought to be added to the numerous colonial possessions of this country must be determined by the same motives of ordinary expedience which direct the general national policy. The principal reasons of this class which have been urged for accepting the sovereignty of the Fiji islands are these:— 1st, that they may prove a useful station for any mail-steamers running between Panama and Sydney; 2nd, that they may afford a supply of cotton; and 3rd, and in close connection with the first reason, that their possession is important to the national power and security in the Pacific Ocean."[30]

Smythe was also to report on the possibility of abolishing inhuman practices (such as cannibalism) in Fiji and on the system of land tenure, especially in its bearing on Thakombau's offer of 200,000 acres to Her Majesty.

It will be noted that on the first and the third points mentioned in the quotation from Newcastle's letter the Colonial Office had already received expert advice from the Admiralty. Why an artillery officer should have been instructed to check the official conclusions of the Admiralty Hydrographer is difficult to explain, save in terms of the mid-nineteenth century convention that an officer and a gentleman was competent to undertake any public

28 Hammond to Merivale, Apr. 21, 1859; *Corr. rel. to Fiji*, 1862.
29 Cf. Brookes, op. cit., p. 245.
30 Newcastle to Smythe, Dec. 23, 1859; *Corr. rel. to Fiji*, 1862.

duty. A similar difficulty arises in explaining the instructions given to Smythe to report on the cotton prospects of Fiji. Newcastle considered that difficulties encountered in West Africa, Queensland and Natal might arise also in Fiji and was far from convinced that, botanical matters apart, the economic prospects of cotton growing in Fiji were good enough to warrant annexation:

> "There seems to be no doubt that the Fiji Islands produce a good specimen of the cotton plant. . . . But, these are by no means the only considerations which the subject embraces. . . . You will, therefore, examine not merely the capacities of the soil and climate of the Islands, but the condition of labour and social economy under which the cotton can now be raised, or may in future be raised. The number of the labouring class; their probable fitness and willingness for continuous labour; their circumstances, how far independent and open to the European hirer, and how far dependent on their chiefs; the mode in which adherence to agreement may best be procured from them; . . . the amount of probability that regularity of production, which is so essential in commerce, may be counted on; all these are among the elements of the problem which your assistance is required in solving."[31]

The questions asked by Newcastle were eminently sensible. But it is not easy to see that Smythe was qualified to advise on such matters of commerce and island customs. It is true that a botanist, Dr. Berthold Seemann, was sent out with Smythe, in order to make special enquiries about cotton prospects, but his work was clearly regarded as subordinate, and although his conclusions contradicted those of Smythe, they were disregarded.[32]

In Fiji Smythe sided with the missionaries (whose opinions were by that time opposed to British annexation)[33] and was at loggerheads with Pritchard, the consul. His investigations in Fiji revealed no great understanding of the problems involved and very little tact in dealing with the natives.[34] His whole record in the group was such as to scout any suggestion that he was personally qualified to conduct a serious investigation into the matters entrusted to him. The Dictionary of National Biography comments that Smythe did good work on magnetical and meteorological

[31] ibid.

[32] As to Smythe's record see *D.N.B.*, article by R. H. Vetch on W. J. Smythe. Not the least peculiar aspect of Smythe's appointment is that the Foreign Office was neither consulted nor officially informed (Cf. F. Rogers to Wodehouse; *Corr. rel. to Fiji, 1862*; No. 9).

[33] See below, p. 194.

[34] For some account of Smythe's dealings with the natives, see S. M. Smythe: *Ten Months in the Fiji Islands;* London, 1864.

surveys in Fiji, but the weight of the evidence is against believing that any other parts of his investigation were competently undertaken.

The report[35] which Smythe submitted in 1861 was opposed on every point to the acceptance of the offered cession. Smythe admitted that the chiefs favoured British intervention, but he stressed the fact that Thakombau had not been competent to make his original offer (later ratified by other chiefs), nor to promise a grant of 200,000 acres of land. Smythe claimed that the shortest route from Panama to Sydney passed south of Fiji and that navigation in Fijian waters was difficult because of reefs, shoals and hurricanes. The supply of cotton from Fiji, he considered, could never be more than insignificant, partly because of the shortage of labour, partly because of the land problem. Not only was Fiji not required to preserve the British position in the South Pacific, but its possession, in the event of war, would merely add to British difficulties. Finally, Smythe contended that, despite the admittedly evil influence of the white residents, annexation was not really in the best interests of the natives:

> "Looking solely at the interests of civilization, the forcible and immediate suppression of the barbarous practices of the heathen . . . might appear a very desirable act; yet, in beneficial influence on the native character, it might prove less real and permanent than the more gradual operation of missionary teaching. . . . Judging from the present state of the Sandwich Islands and the former condition of Tahiti, it would seem that the resources of the Pacific Islands can best be developed, and the welfare of the inhabitants secured, by a native government, aided by the counsels of respectable Europeans."[36]

Smythe's report was accepted by the Government and the offer of cession was declined.

It is typical of the whole record of the Smythe investigation that his conclusions were contrary to expert opinion on almost every point. Dr. Seemann, the botanist who had been commissioned by the Colonial Office to report on the vegetable products of Fiji, pronounced judgment contrary to Smythe's opinions but was disregarded.[37] Seemann not only considered that Fiji was naturally suited for cotton growing but he disagreed with Smythe's gloomy view of the labour difficulty. Whether or not Seemann himself erred in his opinion of the suitability and availability of Fijian labour, the fact remains that, according to the available

[35] Report, encl. in Smythe to Newcastle, May 1, 1861; *Corr. rel. to Fiji, 1862.*
[36] ibid.
[37] Seemann's Report (Seemann to Elliott, June 17, 1861); ibid.

papers, the Colonial Office could have had no good reason for preferring Smythe's opinion to his. And it is true that the cotton exports of Fiji increased rapidly in the 'sixties, despite Smythe's opinion that they would never be more than insignificant. Cotton exports from Fiji were valued at £9,200 in 1865[38] and at £88,920 in 1871.[39] Fijian cotton in 1871 sold at Manchester for 3/- to 3/2 per lb. compared with 10d. and 1/- per lb. on ordinary cotton.[40]

On the two other main points referred to his attention—the position of Fiji on the Panama-Sydney route and the suitability of Fiji as a British base in the South Pacific—Smythe's opinion was contrary to that of the Admiralty Hydrographer, already quoted.[41] While it is true, as a matter of calculation, that it would be a longer deviation on the Panama-Sydney route to call at Fiji than it would be to call at Auckland, Smythe overlooked the fact that Auckland was less of a half-way house than, say, Suva or Levuka. He also disregarded the commercial value of calling at Fiji. Pritchard's argument on this point had quite rightly been that Fiji would become an important trade centre in its own right and would not remain a mere half-way house between Panama and Sydney, which is what Smythe seems to have envisaged. Smythe's argument that "reefs and shoals" endangered navigation in Fijian waters exaggerated a difficulty to which the expert opinion of the Admiralty gave far less weight.

Summing up, it is difficult to avoid agreeing with the opinion of Alderman McArthur expressed in a speech on Fiji to the House of Commons in 1872—that Smythe was either unfit for his task or went to Fiji with a prejudice against accepting the cession.[42] An official publication of the Colony of Fiji suggested in 1924 that Smythe might have been over-influenced by the Maori Wars, of which he had acquired knowledge while proceeding to Fiji.[43] It might have been added on this point that Smythe had fought in the Kaffir Wars and that his report stressed the probability of long conflict with the natives, if British rule were established.

The reasons why the Colonial Office accepted Smythe's report are suggested in minutes discussed on page 196. The terms of Smythe's instructions and the general tenor of British policy in the

[38] Thurston's Report on the Navigation, Trade and Social Conditions of the Fiji Islands; 1866; Appendix to *Corr. rel. to Fiji, 1871.*
[39] Speech by Alderman McArthur in H. of C.; June 25, 1872; *Parlty. Debates,* CCXII, 194.
[40] ibid.
[41] See page 189, above.
[42] McArthur's speech, June 25, 1872; loc. cit.
[43] Fiji: *The Colony of Fiji,* 1874-1924; Suva, 1924; p. 12

islands, however, seem to justify the conclusion that, throughout the whole affair, the British Government preserved its usual determination not to become involved in island problems. The promise of cotton made the prospects of Fiji as a possible exception to the usual rule of minimum intervention worth examination. But when Smythe reported unfavourably and drew attention to the difficulties likely to be encountered in the administration of Fiji, the Government gladly let the matter drop. No offer of cession which involved the certainty of weighty administrative problems and political complications had the slightest chance of acceptance unless accompanied by rich promise of commercial or strategic gain.

The decision to decline the Fijian offer was communicated to the Fijians through Sir John Young, the Governor of New South Wales.[44] The reasons set out in the official document for the Government's decision merely summed up Smythe's arguments,[45] and included these words:

"It would appear very uncertain whether the welfare of the natives would not be better consulted by leaving their civilization to be effected by causes which are already in operation."

The comment obviously has reference to the missionaries in Fiji, whose role in relation to the 1858 offer of cession was a varied one. In his *Polynesian Reminiscences* Pritchard declared that the Wesleyan missionaries had originally supported the proposed cession. They had acted as interpreters throughout the negotiations with Thakombau and had witnessed his signature.[46] As noted above, the missionaries, according to Pritchard, had also assured him that Thakombau was competent to make the offer.[47] "But," wrote Pritchard, "when I unwittingly stated that, in an interview with the late Duke of Newcastle, his Grace had asked me, 'What will the Wesleyan missionaries do when they see a bishop accompanying a governor, for the Church always goes where the State goes?' there was a sudden change. The cession was looked upon with suspicion—personal motives were imputed—and ultimately from cordial co-operation they passed to sullen opposition."[48]

Pritchard's relations with the missionaries were (on his own

---

[44] *Corr. rel. to Fiji, 1871*; No. 2 (N.S.W.).

[45] F. Rogers to E. Hammond, Sept. 7, 1861; qu. in Henderson, op. cit., p. 16.

[46] The witnesses were J. S. Fordham, Wesleyan missionary; J. Binner, Wesleyan Mission Trainer; R. S. Swanston, Hawaiian Consul at Fiji, and W. T. Pritchard, H.B.M. Consul; *Corr. rel. to Fiji, 1862*.

[47] See above, page 187.

[48] op. cit., p. 217.

account)[49] not such as to make his version of their role in the offer
of cession acceptable without some reservation. But it is certain
that the missionaries influenced Smythe against recommending
acceptance.[50] When the British decision not to accept the offer
was communicated to Fiji the missionaries regarded it as evidence
that Great Britain deemed the responsibility for civilizing Fiji to
be theirs alone and welcomed the trust.[51]

In 1870 two further appeals for the establishment of a British
protectorate over Fiji were forwarded to Great Britain. One was
from two hundred British subjects resident in the group and the
other from all the dominant chiefs of Fiji, including Thakombau
and Ma'afa.[52] The protectorate proposed in these appeals was to
extend for 10, 15 or 20 years until a Fijian Government based on
the Hawaiian model should have been firmly established. What
the appeals envisaged was British protection during the inter-
mediate stage prior to the establishment of a native government, as
recommended by Smythe.

Although the appeals stressed the favourable location of the
Fiji group and its trade relations with the Australasian colonies,
and although the danger of action by foreign countries was indicated at some length, their effectiveness was considerably reduced
by the fact that in the same year an appeal[53] had been made to the
United States to take possession of Fiji and been refused.[54] It was
certainly not to be expected that Great Britain would depart from
her minimum intervention policy when other Powers declined to
accept political responsibilities in Fiji. Furthermore (according to
a confidential memorandum prepared in the Colonial Office and
dated May 12th, 1874) an offer of cession had been made to
Germany and had also been refused.[55]

Great Britain neglected to reply to either of the appeals of 1870,
an omission which was strongly criticised by Alderman McArthur
in the Commons debate on Fiji in June, 1873.[56] The fact was that,

[49] ibid, pp. 217-218.
[50] Cf. C. M. Smythe, op. cit., and Smythe Report, loc. cit.
[51] Report of the Australasian Wesleyan-Methodist Missionary Society, 1862-63;
pp. 45-46.
[52] H. Robinson's "Summary of Events in Fiji," encl. in Robinson to Carnarvon,
Oct. 3, 1874; Corr. with Robinson, 1875. Also Thurston to Granville, Dec. 16,
1872; C. 435, 1874. Also C. 983, 1874.
[53] Encl. in N.S.W. (No. 5), Corr. with Robinson, 1875.
[54] Fish to Brower, Oct. 12, 1870; Dept. of State Despatches (U.S.A.), Vol. 60;
qu. Brookes, op. cit., p. 365.
[55] Confidential Memorandum on Fiji (C.O. Australia, No. 39), May 12, 1874.
[56] Parlty. Debates, 1873, CCXVI, 940. According to Thurston's despatch of
Dec. 16, 1872, Consul March also claimed that no reply had ever been received
(Thurston to Granville, Dec. 16, 1872; C. 435, 1874.)

not having been convinced of the strategic and commercial importance of Fiji, the British Government saw no reason for departing from the minimum intervention policy. British policy in Fiji continued to be limited to consular representation and naval visitation.

APPENDIX.

Some light is thrown on the attitude of the Colonial Office to Smythe's report through the minuting on the relevant despatches. On Smythe's letter enclosing his report, Rogers noted that, "I suppose it would be proper to write to the F.O. to say that Col. Smythe's statements joined to the warnings conveyed by the N.Z. war appeared to the Duke of Newcastle to establish conclusively the impolicy of appropriating the Fiji Islands—that any civilized power which made itself responsible for the government of these Islands must be content to incur large immediate expense with the probability of finding itself involved before long in native wars and possibly disputes with other civilized countries—and that it was very uncertain whether the welfare of the natives themselves would not be much better consulted by leaving their civilization to be effected by causes which appeared to be already in operation." Newcastle added, "A very creditable and interesting report and quite conclusive against the acceptance of sovereignty. Write to the F.O. as proposed above . . ." (C.O. 83/1.)

CHAPTER XIX

COLONIAL IMPERIALISM

THOUGH the appeals from Fiji were neglected in Great Britain, the British Government had to pay more attention to the strong demand from Australia and from New Zealand for British intervention in Fiji, Samoa and the other Pacific islands. The desire of the Australasian colonies for a British Oceania complicated the British response to the problem of government. When Great Britain was called upon to devise a policy towards offers of cession and still more when new island governments appeared seeking British recognition, the issue often had to be viewed in the light of the clamorous demand of the colonies that the whole of Oceania should be brought under the British flag.

The ambitions of Australia and New Zealand continued to be of importance long after the problem of government as it existed in the 'sixties and 'seventies had given way to new problems. But it is appropriate to examine at this point the general character of colonial imperialism and its early working. The Australasian wish for a British Oceania first became important in British policy as a complicating factor in determining policy towards the problem of government. (See Chapters XIII and XIV above for Australian protests against French aggrandizement.)

Expansionist sentiment in the colonies was compounded of the usual ingredients. Colonial merchants possessed a large share of the island trade; colonial investors had acquired assets in island plantations; colonial missionaries had special interests in groups like the New Hebrides; even many of the settlers in the islands had come from the colonies.[1] Most important of all was the colonial belief that the strategic safety of Australia and New

---

[1] British trade between the Australasian colonies and the South Pacific islands between 1871 and 1880 was as follows:—

Colony.	Vessels.	Imports. £stg.	Exports. £stg.	Total. £stg.
New South Wales	1,305	2,147,858	2,726,227	4,874,085
Victoria	187	162,095	110,647	272,742
Queensland	320	2,899	83,800	86,699
New Zealand	908	705,223	548,147	1,253,370
TOTALS	2,720	3,018,075	3,468,821	6,486,936

Source: C. 3814, 1883; pp. 9-10.

Zealand depended on Oceania becoming British, or at least not falling into hostile hands. This fear was fostered by the French domination of the trade routes with America and East Asia. Moreover, after 1863 New Caledonia was used as a penal settlement and escaping convicts began to cause alarm in Australia. French action in the South Pacific and the dread of a recrudescence of convictism gave the colonies a sense of urgency that the British Government was unable to share.

Lacking the resources and the legal power to seize the islands themselves, the colonies repeatedly urged the Imperial Government to intervene. From the standpoint of colonists who had everything to gain and nothing to lose from British rule in the islands, it seemed that the British Government was merely shirking its responsibilities when offers of cession were declined. "Like the dog in the manger," wrote that ardent expansionist, the Rev. John Dunmore Lang of Sydney, "Great Britain will neither undertake the great work of colonisation herself, nor permit it to be undertaken by her own people."[2]

In Australia the belief that Oceania should be British had always been strong. In the early years of settlement the British destiny of the islands was taken for granted. In the 'twenties Australian fears had been agitated by American activity. In the 'thirties both Americans and French were feared; later suspicion rested mainly on the imperial designs of France.

During the 'fifties expanding commercial interests in the islands and the rapid growth of Pacific communications led to insistent demands from Australia for a British Oceania. The Rev. Dr. Lang and Mr. (later Sir) Henry Parkes, who was to become one of the foremost figures in New South Wales political history, looked forward to the extension of British colonial interest throughout all the Pacific islands.[3] Parkes stressed the importance of the new Panama route to Australia[4] and in 1859 drew attention to the prospective menace to Australia involved in the French ownership of New Caledonia.[5]

By 1870, when the case for British intervention in Fiji was becoming very strong, Lang, the most fervent of the expansionists, was attempting to break off the legal fetters which prevented New South Wales from annexing the islands. In September, 1870, he petitioned the Legislative Assembly of New South Wales, arguing

[2] J. D. Lang: "New Guinea" (*Transactions of the Royal Society of N.S.W.*, 1871; p. 45).

[3] See Benians, loc. cit., p. 347.

[4] H. Parkes: *Speeches on Various Occasions*; Melbourne, 1876; pp. 86 ff. The speech referred to was delivered in 1858.

[5] ibid, Speech to the Legislative Assembly, Dec. 20, 1859, pp. 97-103.

that, as Phillip's original commission had extended to the "adjacent islands" in the Pacific Ocean, New South Wales might take possession of Fiji without further authority from Great Britain.[6] Lang contended that the Constitution Act of 1855 had transferred all the territorial rights of Great Britain under Phillip's commission to New South Wales. The Colonial Office, however, easily detected the fallacy in Lang's argument. Each Governor's commission revoked that of his predecessor, so that the vague claim to the "adjacent islands" had long ceased to have legal significance.[7] In any case, Lang's contention was absurd because Great Britain had time and again, both by statute and by official statement, denied that she possessed any sovereignty in the islands of the South Pacific.

In 1870 also Lang made another suggestion for the extension of British sovereignty to Fiji. In his book, *The Coming Event! or Freedom and Independence for the Seven United Provinces of Australia*,[8] he argued that, so soon as a union of the Australian colonies had been obtained, Australia "should immediately take possession of the Fiji Islands, of the New Hebrides group of Islands and of the Solomon Islands."[9] The occupation and settlement of New Guinea would naturally follow the establishment of a National Government for the colonies on the Pacific Ocean.[10]

Lang's rather speculative approach to the problem of extending British sovereignty in the South Pacific reflected a growing conviction in the colony that the southern portions of Oceania were commercially important, strategically vital and politically part of Australia.

The case put forward in Australia during the early 'seventies to establish the urgency of British action rested on two main points: first, that other powers were active in the islands and might seize all the favourable situations to the detriment of Australia and New Zealand before Great Britain had decided to act; and, second, that conditions in the islands were deteriorating so rapidly because of the lack of effective government there, that trade and commerce were being greatly impeded.[11]

[6] *Corr. rel. to Fiji, 1871*; Encl. in No. 7 (F.O. and C.O.).

[7] ibid, No. 9.

[8] London, 1870.

[9] p. 382.

[10] p. 466.

[11] Colonial rivalries also played a part in promoting expansionist sentiment. Thus Lang argued in 1875 that, because of the Victorian action in having Melbourne made the terminus of the P. & O. steamship route from Great Britain to Australia across the Indian Ocean, N.S.W. had a special interest in the Pacific routes. (J. D. Lang: *Brief Notes of the New Steam Postal Route . . . by San Francisco and New York;* Sydney, 1875.)

The second point was specially emphasised in the *Sydney Morning Herald,* which was prominent in the attacks on the lawlessness that had been allowed to develop in the islands. An interesting paragraph in August, 1870, for example, complained that defaulters from New South Wales, some of them liable to charges of embezzlement and theft, were finding refuge in Fiji and reverting to their corrupt practices in the trade of the group.[12] Official backing for the *Herald's* protests was frequently forthcoming, the most important instance being the despatch of January, 1873, from Sir Hercules Robinson (Governor of New South Wales) to the Colonial Office complaining of the lack of effective government in Fiji.[13] Robinson accompanied his report with the statement, that annexation of Fiji or some other assertion of British law there was urgently necessary. In 1874 the official Goodenough and Layard Report on conditions in Fiji stressed the need for local courts of law to permit the recovery of commercial debts and the repression of crime.[14]

The aspirations of the Australian colonies were formulated officially in 1870 when the Inter-Colonial Conference held in Melbourne adopted a resolution in favour of the establishment of a British protectorate over Fiji.[15] The resolution was forwarded to the Colonial Office by Viscount Canterbury (the Governor of Victoria) with an intimation that, "the establishment by a foreign government of supreme authority . . . [in Fiji] would naturally and necessarily be distasteful and prejudicial commercially in time of peace to the Australian possessions of the Crown and might be dangerous in time of war."[16]

Canterbury's despatch called forth from Kimberley a long statement on British policy towards Fiji and the aspirations of the colonies.[17] Kimberley admitted that conditions in Fiji had changed considerably since Smythe had prepared his report in 1860-61. He also admitted that the immediate problem in Fiji was one of establishing effective government. But the difficulties in the way of British action, Kimberley argued, remained as insuperable as ever:

"The Islands are under the jurisdiction of several chiefs, and, even if they all concurred in an Act of Cession to the Queen, the experience of other Colonies shows that disputes would be sure afterwards

12 *S.M.H.,* Aug. 13, 1870.
13 Robinson to Kimberley, Jan., 1873; repr. in Henderson, op. cit., pp. 58 ff.
14 C. 1011, 1874; p. 2.
15 *Corr. rel. to Fiji, 1871*; Encl. in No. 5 (Vict.).
16 Canterbury to Granville, Aug. 12, 1870; ibid, No. 6.
17 Kimberley to Canterbury, Mar. 16, 1871; ibid, No. 11.

to arise, especially as to the occupation of land by the settlers. It would be impossible for this country to undertake the responsibility of the government of the Islands without a sufficient force to support its authority and Her Majesty's Government are not prepared to station a military force for this purpose in Fiji."[18]

In conclusion Kimberley stated that Great Britain was willing to make some contribution towards good government in Fiji by increasing the powers of the British Consul. (This decision, which had special reference to the abuses of the labour trade, and was never properly carried into effect, is discussed in Chapter XVII.)

In addition to this official reply the Australian resolution also produced a counter-suggestion from the Colonial Office. Mr. Verdon, Agent-General of Victoria, advised the Colonial Office to the effect that Fiji should be placed under the joint protectorate of the Australian colonies. "Such a measure," Verdon considered, "would be very acceptable to them and would be a step towards federation."[19] Verdon was mistaken on both points, but the Colonial Office and the Foreign Office revived the idea more than once in the 'seventies and Gladstone regarded it with some favour. Before the Australian colonies were informed officially of the new suggestion, however, the outlook had been changed by the establishment of a government in Fiji with the participation of white residents.[20]

When the contents of Kimberley's letter to Canterbury became known to the Government of New South Wales, the Attorney-General of the State, Sir James Martin, wrote to the Governor, Lord Belmore, that having received unofficial advice from "reliable sources" that Great Britain would be prepared to confer special powers on New South Wales to set up a government in Fiji, the State Cabinet wished to indicate its objections to such a proposal.[21] New South Wales, the Cabinet considered, lacked the financial resources and the armed forces necessary to annex Fiji or to establish a protectorate there. Moreover, the acquisition of Fiji was thought to be a matter of imperial, rather than of colonial concern and hence to be the responsibility of Great Britain.

Martin's letter was transmitted by Belmore to Kimberley, reaching the Colonial Office in October, 1871. Kimberley replied to Belmore with a formal invitation to the Government of New South

[18] ibid.

[19] Minute on Canterbury to Granville, Aug. 12, 1870; C.O. 309/94; qu. Brookes, op. cit., p. 367.

[20] See next chapter.

Wales to annex Fiji.[21] The answer was apparently prompted by the willingness of the Colonial Office to listen to Charles Cowper, the Agent-General of New South Wales, who had great experience and knowledge of opinion in the colony, even when Cowper's advice was directly contrary to the official decisions of the New South Wales Government. According to a minute by Herbert on Belmore's despatch to Kimberley, Cowper had given it as his opinion, that "if a full statement of the readiness of this Government to facilitate the annexation of Fiji to New South Wales or another colony were laid before the Parliament and so made public there would be a strong public opinion in favour of that step."[22] For reasons unexplained, Kimberley accepted this advice and obtained a favourable decision from Cabinet on October 27 and 31, 1871. Cowper's opinion proved to have been totally mistaken; the New South Wales Government altogether declined to act and the British Government adhered to its own former decisions.[23]

By what process of reasoning the Colonial Office felt justified in acting on the advice of the Agent-General (newly appointed) in preference to that of the Premier and Attorney-General of the colony is far from clear. The political circumstances surrounding Cowper's appointment and his relationships with Martin[24] were such as to have suggested very strongly that advice of such a kind emanating from him should have been treated with reservation. Whether the Colonial Office placed much reliance on making the offer to New South Wales seems highly doubtful in view of the fact that, on the same day as he wrote to Belmore, Kimberley issued a circular despatch recognising *de facto* the new government set up by the white settlers in Fiji in conjunction with Thakombau.[25]

While Australian (especially New South Wales) interest had been concentrated mainly on Fiji and New Guinea, New Zealand interest was principally in Samoa. For twenty years after the beginning of official colonisation in New Zealand, the settlers there had been fully occupied with their internal problems. Only a few

[21] Martin to Belmore, Aug. 8, 1871, encl. in Belmore to Kimberley (No. 128), and Kimberley to Belmore, Nov. 3, 1871; C. 509, 1872.
[22] Minute by Herbert on Belmore to Kimberley, Aug. 9, 1871 (cit. sup.); C.O. 201/564.
[23] Cabinet decision in Gladstone Papers, 44639. N.S.W. decision in Stephen to Kimberley, Apr. 19, 1872; C.O. 201/569.
[24] As to political circumstances in N.S.W., see letters from E. Butler to C. Gavan Duffy, Jan. 1, 1871, in Duffy Correspondence (Public Library of Victoria, Melbourne). Also C. E. Lyne: *Life of Sir Henry Parkes*; Sydney, 1896; Chapters XXI et seq.
[25] Nov. 3, 1871; repr. in Henderson, op. cit., p. 56.

far-sighted enthusiasts like Selwyn and Grey had dreamed of a British Oceania. In the 'sixties, however, New Zealand merchants and shipowners began to come into their own in the islands.

The leader and publicist of the colonial movement in New Zealand during the early 'seventies was Julius Vogel, Treasurer and Postmaster-General from 1869 and Premier from 1872. Part of Vogel's motives in his policy of island imperialism was avowedly commercial. He recommended in 1874 that the New Zealand Government should arrange the formation of a company to develop the islands. Interest of five per cent. per annum would be guaranteed by the Government and the island trade would be organised so as to provide markets for New Zealand commerce as well as sources of tropical products.[26]

The memorials with which his Government bombarded the Colonial Office, however, laid greater emphasis on factors of imperial interest than on New Zealand hopes of profit from island trade. Control of Samoa was held to be vital to New Zealand safety. Meade's treaty with Chief Mauga for the use of Pago Pago Harbour by the United States was treated as proof of United States aggrandizement in Samoa.[27] The New Zealand Government also insisted that control of Samoa was essential to control of the island labour trade, whose abuses Great Britain was committed to removing.[28]

When other arguments were exhausted the New Zealand Government resorted to the extraordinary thesis that the colony, by reason of its mixed population, had a special aptitude for handling islanders. The assistance of New Zealand was generously offered in the great national work of extending the British dominion throughout the whole of Polynesia—a process which would produce benefits, so the New Zealand Government claimed, for the islands, their inhabitants, British settlers and generally for Great Britain and New Zealand themselves.

So much enthusiasm for new colonial ventures was coldly received by the British Government. Kimberley explained in 1872 that:

"Her Majesty's Government are not insensible to the fact that the increase of commerce in the Pacific, and the constant advance of European settlement in those regions, must render the South Sea

[26] Minist. Memorandum No. 5, Feb. 5, 1874; N.Z.: *Papers Relating to the South Sea Islands, 1874.* Also Fergusson to Kimberley, Mar. 11, 1874; ibid.

[27] Minist. Memoranda Nos. 2 and 3, June 5, 1872, and July 25, 1873; ibid; also Fergusson to Kimberley, Mar. 11, 1874; cit. sup, (n. 26).

[28] Minist. Memoranda No. 1 (Encl. 1) and No. 5, Nov. 24, 1871, and Feb. 5, 1874; ibid.

Islands of far greater interest than formerly. They are not, however, prepared to advise Her Majesty to take upon herself further assumption of sovereignty or of a protectorate over the Navigators Islands."[29]

The Foreign Office enquired of the United States Government whether there were any prospect of an American protectorate in Samoa and cheerfully accepted an answer in the negative. The Foreign Office and the Colonial Office together decided that the suggestions made in 1873 for government of Samoa through "colonial agencies" were too vague for serious consideration. Kimberley reminded Governor Fergusson once again that there was no prospect of sanction of "any steps which would lay this Government under obligations to interfere with the affairs of these islands."[30]

The New Zealand Government was not easily discouraged and the possibility that British action in Samoa might be induced by representations from New Zealand repeatedly complicated the problem of government in that group. One of the factors weakening the Steinberger Government was the belief that the strong New Zealand campaign for British annexation of Samoa might succeed.[31] The knowledge that New Zealand was pressing continuously for British rule in Samoa was a factor in inspiring appeals to the Colonial Office and to British authorities in the South Pacific for the establishment of a protectorate or the acceptance of a cession.[32]

The imperialistic notions of the New Zealand Government exercised little direct influence in Great Britain. But they did affect conditions in Samoa itself. At a time when the competing Samoan factions had come to the point of realising that some form of intervention by a Great Power was indispensably necessary if constant civil strife were to be avoided, the expansionist policy of New Zealand and the British acquisition of Fiji in 1874 seemed to offer some promise of British action in Samoa. This was one reason why Great Britain, despite the relatively small scale of British interests in Samoa, was amongst the Powers whose intervention was sought in the group. To this degree at least, British policy towards the problem of government in the South Pacific was influenced by the imperialism of the Government of New Zealand.

29 Kimberley to Bowen, Feb. 23, 1872; ibid.
30 See ibid, Despatches from the Secretary of State for Colonies, Nos. 2 (with enclosures), 3 and 4.
31 See next chapter.
32 See *Corr. resp. Affairs in the Navigators Islands, Part II.* See also G. H. Ryden: *The Foreign Policy of the United States in relation to Samoa;* New Haven, 1933.

Chapter XX

NEW ISLAND GOVERNMENTS
(1865—1876)

The problems of extra-consular jurisdiction and the offers of cession (which the Australasian colonies were so anxious to have accepted) both stemmed from the failure of the Great Powers to establish their own governments in islands opened up by their subjects. The impact of alien culture and economy on native society was destroying the foundations of order in the South Pacific. The establishment of permanent commercial settlements stirred up changes which deeply affected native societies. Sometimes the natives themselves became traders and wage-earners. Everywhere, from the growing settlements of Europeans to the isolated areas where natives and whites so often clashed in unrestrained violence, there was increasing need for those forms of law and order which only a western government could provide.

Extra-consular jurisdiction and offers of cession were amongst the earliest responses to the new problems. The third and most elaborate solution of all grew out of the attempts to form in the islands themselves new governments, based on European and American models. The inspiration behind these attempts was the desire of the white residents to introduce, not only essential law and order for the purposes of commerce, but also to obtain a balance of legal power in the islands which would favour their own interests.[1]

For example, the years after the refusal of Great Britain in 1862 to accept the government of Fiji saw several movements in that group to establish efficient administration. These attempts to provide a stronger government were in part a consequence of the increase of the European population which followed the commencement of plantation agriculture on a large scale and the rumours in 1860 that Great Britain intended to annex.

---

[1] The attempt of Benjamin Boyd, the New South Wales squatter, trader and merchant, to establish a government in the Solomons in 1851 is of quite a different character from the attempts to establish governments which are described in this section. Boyd's was to have been a personal government and only his murder by the natives prevented legal complications from arising. Cf. *B.S.I.P. Handbook;* Suva, 1923; p. 14.

"From about 1865, various attempts were made at different parts of the group, under the influence of whites, to establish the first principles of Government; and Cakobau, Maafu and one or two other Chiefs were assisted by English Secretaries—or, perhaps we should say instructed by English Secretaries—to draw up and issue Constitutions. Thus there were the Constitutions of Bau of 1865 and 1867, Laws of Tovata of 1867 and others; the Secretaries to these Chiefs being, in nearly every case, respectable, and in some cases, able men. There were, however, considerable districts beyond the boundaries of Bau or of the Tovata; and, as yet, no administration of justice had been attempted beyond the native magistracy of local Chiefs."[2]

To understand British policy towards these attempts to establish effective government in Fiji, it is necessary to consider their origins in some detail. There were five constitutions drawn up and adopted in various parts of Fiji between 1865 and 1871.[3] In 1865 the chiefdoms of Fiji were united in a confederation, of which Thakombau was elected President for two consecutive years. When his period of office expired, this constitution was allowed to lapse and the confederation dissolved. In 1867 the Lau Confederation of three chiefdoms was formed under Ma'afu, while in the same year Thakombau was crowned King of Fiji. In 1870, the Constitution of 1867 having expired, appeals were made to both Great Britain and the United States to establish a protectorate over Fiji. These appeals were declined.[4]

Affairs might then have drifted, had it not been for the energy of some of the whites, who were keenly aware of the difficulties of carrying on trade without law courts and who wanted a government dominated by themselves in order to control the natives. The formation of such a government was suggested in a pamphlet addressed by "Some Settlers in Fiji to the White Residents in Fiji." Holding that neither Great Britain nor the United States would intervene in the group unless their commercial and strategic interests would gain thereby, the authors of the pamphlet proposed that a Fijian Government should be established "as an independency," relying for assistance on the American willingness to protect "any self-governed community professing the same principles of liberty and justice which are respected in the United States." France, according to the pamphlet, already possessed all the island bases she needed. "Nor is it certain," the authors con-

---

[2] C. 1011, 1874. (Goodenough and Layard Report, 1874.)

[3] The relevant documents are reprinted in Henderson, op. cit., pp. 17, 19, 26, 28 and 43.

[4] See above, Chapter XVIII.

tinued, "that it would be desirable that the strong, and perhaps arbitrary, measures adopted towards the natives and original holders of the soil in New Caledonia, would be such as would be the most beneficial to a white population settling in Fiji."[5]

On November 21, 1870, the white residents of Levuka obtained a charter from Thakombau, authorising them to form a body corporate, with power to frame and pass police, municipal and other regulations and to recover such taxes and imposts as were necessary. This step, however, was completely inadequate as a solution to the main problem of government in Fiji. A Court of Law capable of commanding respect for its decisions was an indispensable requisite and effective administration certainly needed to be extended beyond Levuka.

In these circumstances, and anxious to remove from Fiji the stigma of disorder, so that Levuka might be made a port of call on the projected steamship route between Sydney and San Francisco, the merchant group in Levuka put pressure upon Thakombau to form a new government in association with them.[6] As a result Thakombau was proclaimed constitutional sovereign of Fiji in June, 1871, and Messrs. Burtt, Woods, Sagar and two other European residents, together with two native chiefs, were appointed Ministers under the lapsed 1867 Constitution until a new constitution could be prepared.[7] On August 18, 1871, a constitution on the Hawaiian model was adopted. The Government itself continued in power until the House of Assembly was dissolved by proclamation and a further new constitution prepared. (June-October, 1873.)[8]

Right from the first the new government established in 1871 was a more important and substantial organisation than any of its predecessors. During the two years of its life British policy towards it had to be defined on two points:

(a) Did Gt. Britain recognise this government as the lawful government of Fiji?

(b) Did Gt. Britain regard this government as a government in *de facto* control of Fiji?

The problem of whether or not to recognise the 1871 Government as the lawful government of Fiji was much more complicated than

[5] *Corr. with Robinson, 1875;* Encl. in (N.S.W.) No. 6.
[6] C. 1011, 1874.
[7] ibid.
[8] C.O., *Correspondence to the Governor of N.S.W. resp. the acknowledgment of the Government set up by a section of the white settlers . . . in Fiji; 1873.* Encl. in No. 1.

might have appeared. British policy had been to recognise the native rulers as sovereign in the territories they occupied. But there was no clear relationship between the various chiefs of Fiji and the Government established under the kingship of Thakombau.

Important legal issues were also involved. The new Government was dominated by British subjects. Indeed it was generally asserted at the time—and with virtually no contradiction—that the Government was one formed and controlled by Britons. The only question was whether the participation of Thakombau entitled the government to recognition by Great Britain.

The complication from the point of view of British policy arose from the principle in British law that no British subject may throw off his allegiance and form a new government. Further, the Foreign Enlistment Act (designed to prevent British subjects from taking part in wars between states at peace with Great Britain) made it a misdemeanour to enter the military or naval service of any foreign sovereign. March and other opponents of the Woods Government relied on these legal difficulties in opposing recognition of the Government and counselling disobedience of its edicts.

In strict law March was largely justified. The only answer to his case was that provided by Sir Alfred Stephen, the Administrator of the Government of New South Wales, who (in his personal capacity) wrote to March putting the case for recognition.

". . . can we think it within the prohibition that, in a country like the Fijis, a number of British subjects have associated themselves with the undoubted Sovereign to assist him in establishing order out of chaos for their own necessary protection . . . ?

"Then as to the second (i.e., the Foreign Enlistment Act), what moral offence really would it be, if a defence force were indispensable to sustain this new order of things, to repress outrages, and perhaps put down marauders, to aid by personal service or otherwise, so good a cause? Far be it from me to advocate even the technical breach of a statute; but we are to consider for what purpose it was made, and to look at the actual, probably unprecedented, state of things, in a new and half-settled country, where self-protection, in itself a necessity, may justify or excuse the breach."[9]

Stephen's views were founded on clear recognition of the fact that the overriding need of Fiji was for effective government. For all practical purposes, Stephen wisely considered, no legal complications should be placed in the way of British subjects participating in the new government. Stephen even went so far as to suggest that some of the British subjects in Fiji might be held to

[9] Stephen to March, Apr. 17, 1872; ibid.

208

have acquired Fijian nationality under the Naturalisation Act (33 Vict., c. 14, s. 6).[10] (This view was held very strongly by Charles St. Julian, who produced a pamphlet, *The International Status of Fiji*, in Sydney in 1872. St. Julian pointed out that the British subjects in the Woods Government had taken an oath of allegiance to Thakombau after the passage of the Naturalisation Act and argued that they were therefore entitled to the benefit of the Act.)

Stephen's views were eventually approved by the British Government. Commenting on the whole of the New South Wales correspondence relating to the recognition of the Woods Government, including Stephen's letter to March, Kimberley wrote that:

> "The views of Sir A. Stephen, as expressed in these Despatches and Papers, are in accordance with those of Her Majesty's Government, and I approve of the course taken by him."[11]

This decision was reached, however, only after many other complications had been disposed of between the governments of Great Britain, New South Wales and Fiji.

Apart from the legal difficulties discussed by Stephen, the problem of recognition was complicated by the marked hostility of several quarters in Fiji to the new government as a whole and to G. A. Woods, the Prime Minister, in particular. Woods officially complained in 1872[12] that March, the British Consul, had deliberately obstructed the government by denying its legality and "directly encouraging organised resistance of authority."[13] March was far from being alone in his opposition to the new government, which managed to incur the hostility of considerable sections of the white population of Fiji. One group, consisting predominantly of British residents, published a manifesto, described as a *Declaration of Freedom*.[14] On the grounds that the Woods Government was alleged to be illegally constituted, the Declaration recited that the signatories would not recognise the Government and that they

---

[10] Section 6 of this Act provided that: "Any British subject who has at any time before or may at any time after the passing of this Act, when in any foreign State, and not under any disability, voluntarily become naturalised in such State, shall, from and after the time of his so having become naturalised in such foreign State be deemed to have ceased to be a British subject, and be regarded as an alien."

[11] Kimberley to Robinson, Aug. 9, 1872; *Correspondence to the Governor of N.S.W. resp. the Govt. of Fiji; 1873.*

[12] Encl. 1 and 2 in No. 3, ibid.

[13] March received no intimation of the official British policy until June, 1873, and then only through unofficial channels. Cf. Brookes, op. cit., p. 375.

[14] Encl. in No. 3, *Correspondence to the Governor of N.S.W. resp. the Govt. of Fiji; 1873.*

pledged themselves to resist its laws and taxes. Some of the native chiefs, jealous of Thakombau's claims, also resisted the new Government. In April, 1873, Ma'afu and Tui Thakua threatened secession.[15] The political weaknesses of the Government's position were summed up in the Goodenough and Layard report in these terms:

> "The mistake . . . made, and which has led to many subsequent ones, was that the whole public, native and foreign, was taken by surprise. A General Government was started without the general consent; and, consequently, although the whites in all parts of the group were induced, by their strong desire for a Government of some sort or other, and by fair promises, to adhere at first to what was then started; yet both whites and natives have held themselves free to disown and oppose the Government so constituted whenever they thought fit, and to ask for its dissolution."[16]

Goodenough and Layard took the view that the Woods Government was concerned only to advance the personal interests of its members. The general lack of interest in any matters not directly affecting the whites resulted in wide discretionary powers (especially over natives) being left in the hands of Woods and his clique. Finally the New South Wales Government was opposed to Woods, an important consideration in view of the loans, which the new Government endeavoured to raise in Sydney.[17] Woods's commercial prospects in New South Wales were not good, for trading circles there generally opposed his government. The official attitude of the New South Wales Government was expressed when the Attorney-General, Sir James Martin, wrote to the Governor, Lord Belmore, stating that his Government was opposed to the new Government in Fiji as unprecedented and likely to produce "complications of such a character as to demand the interference either of the United States or of some European Power."[18] The Attorney-General added that Kimberley's proposal to increase British consular powers in Fiji was contrary to international law and to the recognition of Fijian sovereignty. The New South Wales Government, it was added, regretted the British decision[19] not to annex Fiji and was strongly opposed to British recognition of the new Fijian Government. It was in this letter that the Attorney-

15 C. 1011, 1874.
16 C. 1011, 1874.
17 Belmore to Kimberley (encl. Martin to Belmore, Aug. 8, 1871); C. 509, 1872. Woods failed to raise a loan in Sydney in Feb., 1872, but succeeded at the end of the year. (Corr. with Robinson, 1875; Encl. in No. 1.)
18 Martin to Belmore, Aug. 8, 1871; cit. sup.
19 Kimberley to Canterbury, Mar. 16, 1871; Corr. rel. to Fiji, 1872; No. 11.

General made it clear that New South Wales would not itself annex Fiji, even if special powers were granted for the purpose.[20]

The opposition of the New South Wales Government to the recognition of the Woods Government was fruitless. In a circular letter of November 3, 1871, Kimberley declared that, as the new Government was actually exercising authority in Fiji, it should be "dealt with . . . as a *de facto* government, so far as concerns the districts which acknowledge its rule."[21]

This decision was fully in accordance with international law and usage. *De facto* recognition was the obvious course to adopt in the case of a government of doubtful legitimacy which appeared to be exercising authority throughout a substantial part of Fiji. A further advantage of *de facto* recognition was that it relieved Great Britain from the necessity of pronouncing judgment on the British subjects who had inaugurated the new government. By recognising the Government and by treating its minister as Fijians, Great Britain avoided the legal problems relating to abandonment of British nationality, which might have obstructed recognition *de jure* and would have had to be solved if recognition were completely withheld.

The practical effect of the recognition was, of course, to absolve Great Britain from any obligation to intervene in Fiji in the interests of her subjects there, who were becoming increasingly resentful at the mounting disorder in the group. Recognition also had the advantage of freeing Great Britain from international responsibility for the conduct of her subjects in Fiji. In the same way as the recognition of native sovereignty had been used to justify a policy of minimum intervention, so the recognition of the Woods Government made continued adherence to the minimum intervention policy possible for Great Britain.

The British decision to recognise the Woods Government was bitterly resented in New South Wales, where commercial interests earnestly wished for a strong, stable government in Fiji. The Attorney-General wrote to the Administrator of the Government that New South Wales could not heed Kimberley's instruction to recognise *de facto* because "until the Government recently established in Fiji is recognised by Her Majesty, it cannot be properly recognised by the Government of this Colony."[22] As a legal argument, this contention was merely nonsense. The Adminis-

[20] See above, Ch. XIX.
[21] Repr. in Henderson, op. cit., p. 56.
[22] Martin to Stephen, Apr. 22, 1872; *Corr. to the Governor of N.S.W. resp. . . . Fiji*, 1873.

trator rightly pointed out to the Attorney-General that, whether Great Britain recognised *de facto* or *de jure,* "the recognition . . . is exclusively an Imperial question" and that any British decision was clearly binding on New South Wales.[23] A fortnight previously Kimberley had written to Stephen in similar terms.[24]

In August, 1872, the British Government itself made an important qualification to the original recognition *de facto.* The Colonial Office advised the Australian Governors that British subjects beyond the limits of Fiji were not to be accepted as citizens of Fiji, nor held to be exempt from British jurisdiction.[25] This meant that Great Britain admitted the existence of a Fijian nationality, but denied that persons formerly British subjects could retain Fijian nationality when not in Fiji. Further, despite the grant of *de facto* recognition, Great Britain claimed the right to retain jurisdiction over British subjects in Fiji, even if they claimed Fijian nationality. The qualifications imposed by Kimberley were necessitated mainly by the inability or unwillingness of the Fijian Government to control the island labour trade. Great Britain was by this time committed to a policy of regulating the labour traffic and was therefore concerned at the fact that ships under the Fijian flag and recruiters claiming Fijian nationality could evade the vigilance of British patrols. The practical effect of Kimberley's decision was to retain jurisdiction over British subjects who might shelter behind Fijian nationality in order to evade British law.

From the point of view of the Fijian Government the qualification of the recognition was little short of a disaster. The Fijian Attorney-General complained that the qualification "unnecessarily detracts from the legal position taken up by the Fijian authorities and nation."[26] Kimberley's action, the Attorney-General considered, encouraged resistance to the Government and was itself of doubtful validity in international law.

The real burden of the Attorney-General's complaint was that Great Britain remained indifferent to the problem of government in the islands (save in the case of the labour trade, which had political significance in Great Britain). The compromise finally adopted by the British Government absolved it from any legal obligation to intervene in Fiji for the sake of assisting the government there, while leaving British efforts to control the labour trade

[23] Stephen's Minute for Cabinet, Apr. 29, 1872; ibid.
[24] Kimberley to Stephen, Apr. 12, 1872; ibid.
[25] C.O. to Robinson, Aug. 14, 1872; N.S.W., *Fiji Islands,* 1872.
[26] Dec. 2, 1872; C. 983, 1874.

unfettered by the weakness or opposition of the new Fijian Government.

British policy towards the new governments formed in Samoa was similar in its fundamentals to the policy worked out in the case of Fiji. There were, however, marked differences in the way in which the problem came up for British consideration. The record of British policy towards the new governments in Samoa between 1873 and 1876 bears a clear imprint of the bungling of the consular and naval officers in that group.

The first of the new governments in Samoa was formed in 1873 at the close of a disastrous civil war. Some of the chiefs, with the assistance of the British, German and United States Consuls, the principal missionaries and Colonel Albert Steinberger, the informal Special Agent of the United States,[27] then drew up a constitution. The governing body was the Taimua, consisting of seven chiefs, whose appointment lasted for one year. British policy towards this government, which worked fairly well, was never defined, although Commodore Goodenough, R.N., treated it as the established authority in Samoa.[28]

In 1874, at the expiration of the first Taimua's year of office, a new constitution was proposed. During the discussions Steinberger returned to Samoa from the United States. On his first visit he had won golden opinions from both missionaries and natives. As he bore presents from the United States Government to the Samoan chiefs, his second visit was generally regarded in the group as being official and related to the prospect of an American protectorate. Actually, Steinberger held no official position. The United States Government was not prepared to intervene and Steinberger had had to return to Samoa at his own expense and armed only with an agreement with the German Godeffroy Company in which he

[27] This was Steinberger's first mission to Samoa. President Grant had been interested in the proposal to establish an American protectorate over Samoa. In order to obtain support in Congress, he had decided to send an agent to Samoa to report on conditions there. Meade's treaty with Mauga, the principal chief of Pago Pago, for the use of Pago Pago Harbour, had already been concluded and U.S. shipping interests were anxious to develop commercial activities in Samoa. Fish, the U.S. Secretary of State, was slow in acting on Grant's plan for sending Steinberger to Samoa. When he did finally write to Steinberger, he made it clear that the mission was one of limited scope. The Colonel was informed that he was not "a regular diplomatic agent, formally accredited to another government, but an informal one, of a special and confidential character, appointed for the sole purpose of obtaining full and accurate information in regard to the Navigator's [sic] Islands." (Fish to Steinberger, Mar. 29, 1873; U.S., *H.Ex.Dox. 161*, 44 Cong. 1 Sess.; qu. Ellison, op. cit., pp. 47-48.)

[28] Ellison, op. cit., p. 56 (n. 1).

undertook to procure for that firm trading privileges amounting almost to a monopoly in Samoa.[29]

Steinberger's influence was strong and the new constitution was very nearly his own work. There was to be a King elected for four years from either of the rival families of Malietoa and Tupua. There were to be two legislative bodies, the Taimua (House of Nobles) and the Faipule (House of Representatives). But there was also to be a Premier (Steinberger himself), who was practically irremovable and endowed with the most extraordinary powers. The Premier acted as sole counsellor to the King on all matters of State. The King could not act without his knowledge. The Premier was entitled to speak in either House at any time.

It is now accepted that Steinberger's administration was generally efficient. But he encountered serious opposition from the whites. His government was felt to be pro-native. As time went on, doubts as to his official connection with the United States Government began to undermine his authority. The growing interest of New Zealand in Samoa and the British annexation of Fiji in 1874 led to hopes amongst the whites that Great Britain might intervene in Samoa and set up a white man's government.

Matters came to a head in January, 1876, when Foster, the United States Consul, received word from Washington that Steinberger had no official backing from the American Government. After the arrival of H.M.S. *Barracoutta* (Captain Stevens) at the end of 1875 an open attack was made on Steinberger's position. The British and United States Consuls, long jealous of Steinberger's ascendancy, supported by some of the dissident whites, and aided by Captain Stevens, then succeeded in rousing white opinion to the point of active hostility to Steinberger. Ultimately they induced the King to order his arrest and deportation.[30]

The actions of the British representatives were so obviously illegal that they raised the problem whether compensation were due to Steinberger, or to the United States Government, for the acts of arrest and deportation. Stevens himself was immediately rebuked by his commanding officer, Commodore Hoskins, for having proceeded to Samoa without leave and for exceeding his authority there.[31] After prolonged correspondence between the British and American Governments the British view that, because Stevens had acted at the request of the United States Consul, he

29 Corr. resp. Proceedings of H.M.S. "Barracoutta," Encl. 1 in No. 6.
30 F.O.: Confidential Memorandum, No. 3375, 1877, summarises these developments.
31 Hoskins to Stevens, Mar. 1, 1876; Hoskins to Admiralty, Mar. 9, 1876; Corr. resp. H.M.S. "Barracoutta."

incurred no personal liability, was allowed to prevail. He was, however, reprimanded and dismissed from the service.[32]

This matter of compensation was really a minor issue. The major problem for British policy was that raised by the overthrow of the Steinberger Government and the claim made by the consuls at Samoa (and by Captain Stevens) that, since that Government had not been recognised by any of the Great Powers, it had no power to legislate for foreigners resident in Samoa. This claim was formally stated by the consuls and by Stevens in a proclamation dated January 13, 1876, after a conference held on H.M.S. *Barracoutta*. The proclamation attacked the Samoan Government for having set aside and obstructed the "legitimate jurisdiction and authority of the Representatives of foreign Powers in Samoa." Eight resolutions were reached at the conference and formally promulgated:

(1) "No subject or citizen of a nation which is represented by a Consul shall be arrested without the consent of the said authority, as previous to July, 1873."

(2) No Samoan laws relating to foreigners were to have any effect whatsoever.

(3) No Samoan was to put irons on any foreigner save with the consent of the foreigner's consul.

(4) All trials and condemnations previously made by the "present Government against a subject or subjects . . . of any of the nations as are represented by an accredited official" were to be pronounced null and void unless the consent and approval of the Consul concerned had been obtained.

(5) Foreigners in Samoa having no consul there of their own nationality might appeal to any consul they chose.

(6) Persons of foreign extraction residing in Samoa and held to contracts of service and labour "shall be subject to and governed by the laws of their employers, his or her nation."

(7) Lists of persons affected by resolutions (5) and (6) were to be furnished to the Samoan Government from time to time.

(8) "We finally withdraw our subjects and citizens from the jurisdiction and influence of this Government until the Samoan Government consent to foreign Representatives having due authority in the framing of their laws, and they, the subjects and citizens, are hereby withdrawn.[33]

These resolutions amounted to an attempt to restore not merely extra-consular jurisdiction as it had existed up to 1873 but also to

[32] Salisbury to Welsh, Aug. 4, 1879, cited in Ellison, op. cit., pp. 80-81. The Consuls, Williams and Foster, were also dismissed.

[33] *Corr. resp. H.M.S. "Barracoutta"*; pp. 22-23.

establish a system of extra-territoriality unauthorised by the Samoan Government, and, so far as Stevens and Williams were concerned, unauthorised by the British Government.

Although Great Britain was clearly committed to nothing by the making of such a proclamation, the circumstances in which it had been made and the disorders, which broke out after the deportation of Steinberger, raised immediate problems for British policy. The preliminary task of dealing with the situation produced by Stevens and the consuls fell to Commodore Hoskins, R.N., who arrived at Samoa in May, 1876. Hoskins recommended that the Samoans should return to the pre-Steinberger form of government.[34] This recommendation was merely a personal opinion and was not made as a matter of official British policy. The only declaration made by Hoskins in an official way was in the widest possible terms:

"It was not the intention of any civilized nation to annex or grant a protectorate to the islands, but the wish of Her Majesty's Government was that there should be a strong, independent Government."[35]

Any good influence which Hoskins's counsels might have exercised was largely nullified when he lost native sympathies by laying the blame on the Samoans for a skirmish which had taken place with Captain Stevens's men on March 13th. His attitude proved offensive to the Steinberger adherents (who turned out to be in the majority) and contributed little to the restoration of peace.[36]

British policy was never officially defined towards the Steinberger Government, but only towards the actions of the British representatives who helped in Steinberger's overthrow. After events in Samoa became known to the Foreign Office, the British Government decided to insist on British extra-territoriality in Samoa. The British Consul was instructed to withdraw British subjects from Samoan jurisdiction and eventually, as part of the new High Commission policy adopted in 1875-1877, a treaty establishing British extra-territoriality in Samoa was signed in 1879.[37]

The significant aspect of the British record in regard to the Samoan Government is the absence of intervention or expression of policy until the appointment of Liardet as the new British Consul and the withdrawal of British subjects from Samoan jurisdiction in October, 1876. Liardet was empowered to convey to the Samoan chiefs the British wish that they themselves would "form a strong

34 *Confid. Memorandum, No. 3375, 1877*, p. 3.
35 ibid, p. 7.
36 See Chapter XXIV below, for effects of these incidents on British policy.
37 C. 3905, 1884, and Chapter XXIV, below.

Government free from all foreign influence." "To this end," Liardet's instructions continued with great acumen, "it was essential that they should live in peace amongst themselves."[38] In other words, so far as British policy was concerned, the onus of forming a workable government in Samoa rested on the Samoans.

The decision to insist on British extra-territoriality in Samoa struck a heavy blow at the prospects of efficient government in the group. When Germany and the United States also washed their hands of any responsibility for good government in Samoa and insisted that their interests were confined to the protection of their own subjects, the establishment of favourable conditions for trade and the obtaining of naval bases, the cause of good government in Samoa suffered a fatal set-back.

The fundamental difficulty in Samoa was that conditions were too unsettled to give any locally formed government a chance of lasting success. Only a modern Power could have established efficient administration in Samoa. Steinberger succeeded for a short time, partly because of adventitious personal factors (such as the ascendancy achieved during his first mission), partly because he was believed to be supported by the United States.

The problem facing the British Government in Samoa was thus different from that raised in Fiji. In Samoa there was no prospect of the island government succeeding. In Fiji the government did succeed to a limited degree in purely internal matters.

British policy was, however, the same in each case. Great Britain would not intervene in the islands save for the limited purposes of controlling the labour trade, punishing the worst excesses of British subjects, restraining native depredations and maintaining the political *status quo*. Where a local government offered any prospect of achieving these ends, it would receive limited support from Great Britain—as in the case of Fiji. Where, however, the local government obviously stood in urgent need of external assistance, Great Britain would make no contribution towards its success.[39]

[38] F.O., *Confidential Memorandum No. 3375, 1877.*

[39] The case of Tonga is not discussed here as the native government formed there was of a different type from those discussed above and presented different problems of policy. See Chapters XXIV and XXIX, below.

CHAPTER XXI

THE KIDNAPPING PROBLEM

THE problem of government was complicated from the middle 'sixties by the rise of the labour trade. The planters, whose interests expanded so rapidly in Fiji, Samoa and Queensland in and after the 1850's, soon discovered that one of their gravest problems was the shortage of labour. Because white labour was held to be unsuitable for plantation work in tropical zones, it became the officially accepted view that whites should confine themselves to commerce and to the ownership or management of plantations, while natives supplied the necessary physical labour.[1] Financially, this division of labour had the additional advantage of low costs. When it was found in some of the most important plantation areas that indigenous native labour was unsuitable or unavailable (because of social prejudice or lack of economic incentive to accept plantation work), recourse had to be had to imported native labour. So began, as far as Queensland and the island plantations were concerned, the labour trade and the blackbirding of the South Pacific in the second half of the nineteenth century.

The famous Benjamin Boyd was the first British subject to use native labour from the islands on a substantial scale. In 1847 he imported into Australia natives from Tanna in the New Hebrides. Conversations with sandalwood traders had led him to believe that the natives would make good shepherds. His experiment failed.[2] Sixteen years later in 1863 the labour trade of the Western Pacific had its substantial beginning when Captain Towns imported sixty South Sea islanders into Australia,[3] to be employed in the Queensland cotton industry, which was then being stimulated as a result of the American Civil War.[4] Fiji was experiencing similar conditions and also began to import native labour. When the demand

1 Cf. *Memorandum on the Future of N.G. and Polynesia*, Nov. 7, 1883, by Sir W. des Voeux; C. 3863, 1884.
2 Fitzroy to Grey, Dec. 24, 1847; *H.R.A.*, I, xxvi, p. 119. See H. P. Wellings: "Ben Boyd's Labour Supplies"; (*J.R.A.H.S.*, Vol. 19, 1933; pp. 374 ff.).
3 A. H. Markham: *The Cruise of the "Rosario"*; London, 1873 (2nd ed.); p. 47.
4 The Peruvian labour trade began in 1862. The natives were used on plantations and in quarries in Peru. As a result of protest by the diplomatic corps at Lima, the trade was formerly abolished in 1863.

for cotton declined at the end of the American Wars, its place was taken by sugar so that the need for native labour continued unabated. By the late 'sixties the labour trade had attained great dimensions and considerable notoriety.

Official circles were soon informed of abuses in the trade. Doubts had existed even at the time of Boyd's 1847 experiment. In that year Governor-General Fitzroy reported to the Colonial Office that an investigation had been instituted by the Attorney-General at Sydney into Boyd's activities, in view of rumours that the natives had been brought to Australia against their will.[5] Boyd was cleared of the charges, although considerable suspicion remained.

The next year Earl Grey at the Colonial Office wrote to Fitzroy referring to reports that outrages had been committed by labour recruiters at Rotuma and stressing the "anxious desire of Her Majesty's Government to do all in their Power to prevent the illtreatment of the Natives of the Islands in the Pacific by British Subjects."[6] Grey suggested that, if every precaution were taken to ensure good treatment for the natives during their employment, "individuals will not entertain such expectations of advantage from bringing these Islanders to New South Wales as to induce them to pursue that object by improper means."

These early despatches show that the substance of the case against the trade had been carefully examined in Great Britain within five years of the first experiment. When, following on the success of Towns's venture, the labour trade suddenly expanded with the utmost rapidity, British policy towards it was already on record. The British Government had already expressed its belief that labour recruiting was likely to be fruitful of abuses and stand in need of rigid control. It was not the use of imported labour that was objected to (despite some fears that white men would lose their opportunities), but the strong probability that labour would not be recruited without violence, deceit and crime.

Within a few years of its commencement, the labour trade was distinguished for its abuses. The evidence against those engaged in it is not, however, as uniformly convincing as some of the missionary and official documents imply. The most judicious of contemporary observers frequently expressed doubts as to the allegations of abuses and, while not denying that abuses took

[5] Fitzroy to Grey, Dec. 24, 1847; H.R.A., I, xxvi, p. 119.
[6] Grey to Fitzroy, July 29, 1848; H.R.A., I, xxvi, p. 524. See also the despatch from Governor Grey of New Zealand, recommending regulation of the trade. (Grey to C.O., Mar. 10, 1848; Further Papers rel. to the Affairs of N.Z., 1848).

place, hesitated to condemn the recruiters and the planters root and branch.[7]

The precise degree of the abuses which developed is of little importance here. What is significant is the nature of the reports sent home to the British Government. These reports became the basis of British policy towards the labour trade.[8] Their common theme was the need for greater control of recruiting.

So far as British subjects were concerned, the labour trade was mainly used for the plantations of Fiji (and other islands) and of Queensland. Fiji was not British territory and the general British rule of declining responsibility for conditions in the islands appears to have been applied automatically for some years, save where naval officers and the British Consul intervened to restrain abuses.[9] Queensland was of course a different case. The British Government was confronted with four alternatives, one or other of which had to be followed: (a) to suppress the labour traffic to Queensland; (b) to attempt regulation by imperial legislation; (c) to allow Queensland to legislate for the regulation of the trade; or (d) to combine the second and third alternatives.

The difficulty in leaving the labour trade to the control of Queensland was that the gravest abuses alleged were occurring beyond the jurisdiction of the Queensland Government. Queensland was a self-governing British colony. Its legislative competence extended only to making laws for the peace, welfare and good government of Queensland. As a result the Queensland Parliament could not pass a law to regulate recruiting in the islands by British subjects. All that it could do was to legislate for the welfare of island labourers in Queensland and for the control of conditions on recruiting ships which sought to land their cargoes in Queensland. There could be no question of exercising control in the islands themselves (even in the cases of British subjects) nor of regulating the recruiters on the high seas.[10] Legal devices such as the requirement of bonds to be forfeited to the Government in the event of kidnapping or other breaches of the regulations might give the Queensland Government some control over the trade

[7] See the views of Lord Belmore, Governor of N.S.W., in Belmore to C.O., Sept. 8, 1871 (N.S.W. Leg. Ass., *"Kidnapping in the South Seas,"* 1871) and of Sir Alfred Stephen, the Chief Justice of N.S.W., in Stephen to Belmore, Sept. 2, 1871 (ibid).

[8] See Bibliography, Part IV (E).

[9] See A. H. Markham, op. cit., and G. Palmer: *Kidnapping in the South Seas*; Edinburgh, 1871.

[10] For use of the 1817, 1823 and 1828 Acts in labour control, see pp. 230

ѵutside its own territories. But difficulties of detection and proof would limit their value.

Despite the difficulties confronting colonial legislation on the subject, the first British step towards the control of the labour trade of the Western Pacific was taken by Queensland. In 1867 the Government of Great Britain sought explanations from Queensland concerning allegations of abuses in recruiting and sent warships to the Pacific islands in order to investigate conditions there. The naval commanders reported that the position was worse than had been realised in Great Britain and the Admiralty advised the Colonial Office that the matter was one for imperial, rather than for colonial, action. The naval officers also considered that mere legislation would not suffice to regulate the traffic and raised all the legal issues as to the limited extent of Queensland's legislative competence:

"... these islanders are incapable of understanding the nature of a written contract with an employer. ... Whatever regulations may be made for the well-being and liberty of these people, on their being brought nominally within reach of the laws and tribunals of Queensland, yet ... no proper and efficient control can be exercised over the manner in which these people are obtained. ... The task of their collection and shipment is from the nature of the work likely to fall into the hands of an unscrupulous and mercenary set, who, under pretence of persuading the natives into making engagements as labourers for a term of years, would not hesitate to commit acts of kidnapping, piracy and murder. Entertaining these views, my Lords are unable to concur in any recommendation with regard to framing an Act of the Colonial Legislature for the regulation of the introduction of these people into the Colony."[11]

Despite this adverse report, which after first-hand survey of the position specifically rejected any suggestion that Queensland legislation could discharge British responsibilities towards the labour trade, the Colonial Office approved the enactment of the Queensland Polynesian Labourers Act. The decision is the more surprising in view of the evidence previously collected as to the need for imperial action to control the labour trade. The Colonial Office also had to reach its decision in face of a petition forwarded through the Acting Governor of Queensland in January, 1868, to Her Majesty, praying that "the traffic in human beings" might be stopped.[12] The petition was unavailing and the royal assent was

[11] Admiralty to C.O., qu. in Brisbane Petition to H.M., Dec. 13, 1871; *South Sea Corr., 1873.*

[12] O'Connell to Buckingham and Chandos, Jan. 27, 1868; qu in Palmer, op. cit., p. 167.

given to the Queensland Bill which became law as 31 Vict., No. 47.

The provisions of the Act were simple—and obviously inadequate. They aimed at the control of recruiting South Sea islanders for labour in Queensland and at supervising conditions of employment in the colony. No island labourers were to be brought to Queensland except under licences granted in accordance with the Act and on the terms prescribed by the Act. Bonds were to be required of all persons proposing to import labourers. (Sections 1 and 6.) Bonds were also required of the masters of recruiting vessels. (Section 15.) Other sections prescribed conditions on recruiting vessels and provided for the supervision of the natives while in Queensland.

The most obvious limitation of the Act was that it left the way open for practically unrestricted abuses in the islands. As Commodore Stirling pointed out in 1872, the labour traffic in the Pacific supplied five different areas—Fiji, Tahiti, Peru, Queensland and several other groups and unfrequented islands, whose isolated planters used imported labour.[13] The Queensland Act attempted to control recruiting for only one of these areas, leaving the Peruvian and inter-insular traffic in a virtually unregulated state, so far as British legislation was concerned. The only control provided by the Queensland Act over recruiters outside the limits of Queensland was through the bonds.

The dangers of relying on the 1868 Act for the control of the labour trade were strikingly revealed in the famous *Daphne* case. The *Daphne* was a labour recruiting vessel licensed by the Queensland Government to procure 50 natives for the plantations of that State.[14] When examined by the British Consul, March, and the commander of H.M.S. *Rosario,* Commander Palmer, at Levuka in Fiji, the *Daphne* was found to be loaded with 100 natives, twice the permitted number. The vessel did not comply with the standards of the 1868 Act in the matter of accommodation. Its licences did not entitle it to visit Fiji at all while engaged in the labour trade. All the evidence pointed to the fact that, though licensed for the Queensland trade, the vessel was really being used to supply the more lucrative Fijian market.

When questioned by March and Palmer, the *Daphne's* officers alleged that the 100 natives were being returned from Queensland

[13] Stirling to Admiralty, Apr. 22, 1872; C. 496, 1872.
[14] The facts, which are not in dispute, are taken from G. Palmer, op. cit., and from Palmer to Belmore, May 22, 1869 in N.S.W., Leg. Ass., *"Kidnapping in the South Seas,"* 1871. The latter source consists of the documents dealing with Palmer's charge that the N.S.W. authorities did not press the prosecution in the *Daphne* case.

to their own islands and were still on board because they had signed re-engagement papers. But the re-engagement papers, when produced, were not in order and did not tally with the ship's log book. Moreover, one of the licences issued by the Queensland Government was in favour of the notorious Ross Lewin,[15] whose brutal excesses were well known in the islands.

Confronted with the fact that, although the vessel was licensed by the Queensland Government, it was not at the time within Queensland jurisdiction, nor even bringing labourers to Queensland, Palmer found himself unable to take action under the 1868 Act. Even if the *Daphne* had been recruiting for Queensland, Palmer could have taken no action beyond reporting the circumstances to the Queensland Government, which could then have forfeited the *Daphne's* bonds and refused permission to land the natives on board.

Palmer resolved to arrest the vessel on the ground that it was engaged in the slave trade within the meaning of the Acts 5 Geo. IV, c. 113, and 6 and 7 Vict., c. 98. This action was the only course open in the case of an offending British vessel so long as it was operated only in the inter-insular labour traffic or if licensed by the Queensland Government, so long as it remained out of Queensland jurisdiction. The *Daphne* was brought to Sydney and Palmer requested the Government of New South Wales to bring a slave trade prosecution against the master and supercargo.

The case created a furore. But no conviction could be obtained against the accused in the Water Police Court. Proceedings were then instituted in the prize jurisdiction of the Vice-Admiralty Court on behalf of the officers and men of the *Rosario* against the *Daphne* as a slaving vessel. But Sir Alfred Stephen, the Chief Justice, held that the natives were not slaves and found for the respondents. Palmer merely received a certificate under the Act that he had had "probable cause" for the seizure and prosecution of the *Daphne*.[16]

The significance of the case lay in three points:

(a) it was proved beyond doubt that British subjects engaged in the inter-insular labour trade had little to fear from Queensland law;

(b) the decision that natives, who had been lured on board and coerced into signing agreements, were not entitled to the benefits

---

[15] As to Ross Lewin, see A. H. Markham, op. cit., pp. 88-89.

[16] The Chief Justice gave the certificate with great doubt. Palmer's expenses were eventually paid by the Admiralty, which approved his actions.

of the slaving acts[17] sufficiently demonstrated that British law had no remedy for the wrongs of deceit and coercion inflicted on natives recruited in the inter-insular labour traffic;

(c) the action of the Queensland officials in granting a licence under the 1868 Act to such a person as Lewin in respect of a vessel which did not comply with the regulations made under the Act cast serious doubt on the willingness of the Queensland Government to exercise effective control over the labour trade.[18]

In the long run the *Daphne* case probably encouraged further excesses.[19] The hands of naval officers, who knew what was going on, were tied by the impossibility of obtaining a conviction against offenders and by the fact that the Admiralty had decided not to pay the expenses of any further prosecutions such as that against the *Daphne*. Even Markham, for all his crusading zeal, did not care to proceed again to decisive measures. When in 1872 he found the English schooners *Donald M'Lean* and *Helen* acting contrary to law, he would not seize them because of the precedent of the *Daphne*. Instead he merely obtained from the masters of the schooners (apparently without much difficulty) signed admissions of their illegalities.[20]

The restricted scope of the 1868 Act soon attracted attention in Great Britain, where the missionaries, in their fervent denunciations of blackbirding, tended to blame every excess—even in the inter-insular traffic—on the Queensland recruiters.[21] The Secretary of the London Missionary Society indignantly protested to Earl Granville at the Colonial Office that:

"It is surely intolerable that when Christian men, after great labours . . . have, under God's blessings, overcome the barbarism and cruelty of these savage tribes; have swept away their heathen vices; have brought them the blessings of Christianity and of civilization . . . that then lawless men among the stronger races, whether

---

[17] The ground of this decision was that Fiji, where the natives were being taken, was not a country whose institutions included slavery. (See Belmore to C.O., Oct. 5, 1871; N.S.W., Leg. Ass., *"Kidnapping in the South Seas,"* 1871.)

[18] The *Challenge* case was similar. Captain Montgomerie (H.M.S. *Blanche*) arrested the *Challenge* and had the captain prosecuted in Sydney for slave-trading. The conviction was merely for assault and Montgomerie was billed for the unlawful seizure and detention of the *Challenge* and for damage occurring on the voyage to Sydney. (A. H. Markham; op. cit., pp. 77-79.) See also G. Palmer, op. cit., p. 152, on the *Young Australian* case and documents thereon in N.S.W., Leg. Ass., *Corr. resp. conviction of Hovell and Rangi for the murder of a South Sea Islander,* 1869.

[19] Temporarily it may have checked the traffic. See H. Britton: *Fiji in 1870;* Melbourne, 1870; p. 18.

[20] A. H. Markham, op. cit., pp. 50, 192 and 258.

[21] Cf. 1868-69 articles in the *Leeds Mercury* and *The Times.*

Peruvians or Englishmen, should take advantage of their weakness and ignorance; should kidnap their persons; should carry them into unknown lands, and, under the name of contract labourers, should make them, to a great extent, their unwilling and helpless slaves."[22]

Objections of substance—apart from the extent of its operation—were also raised concerning the 1868 Act. In 1869 the Emigration Commissioners were requested to advise the Colonial Office on the efficacy of the Act in light of the *Lyttona* outrage, a case of "man-stealing" reported to Commodore Lambert in 1868 by the Rev McNair. T. W. C. Murdoch, writing on behalf of the Commissioners, informed the Colonial Office in April, 1869, that the Act, together with existing statutes, should provide all the legal measures necessary to control the Queensland labour traffic.[23] With reference to the *Lyttona* case, however, Murdoch had to admit that, if McNair's statements were correct, the Act, for all its legal merit, was insufficient to restrain abuses:

"Should it appear that the people were procured in the manner described, and that they have been landed in the colony without discovery of the fact, it will be difficult to avoid the conclusion that the Polynesian Labourers Act is a failure. But, if so, there seems no alternative, but to prohibit the trade altogether. . . . I do not see in what way the Act could be altered to make it more efficient to prevent kidnapping. . . . To give practical effect . . . to any Act that might be passed by Parliament, it would be necessary to employ vessels to cruise amongst the islands. It is sufficient to remark that even then the cruisers could only deal with British vessels. The American and French vessels engaged in trade among the islands would be beyond their cognizance."[24]

There are four conclusions to be drawn from this statement:

(a) In the opinion of the Emigration Commissioners, communicated to the Colonial Office, the 1868 Act was as good an Act as could be passed under existing general policy, that is, by a colonial government with limited legislative powers.

(b) In practice the 1868 Act was almost certainly a failure.

(c) The only alternatives to continued reliance on the Act were (i) to prohibit the labour trade altogether so far as British subjects were concerned, or (ii) to pass an Imperial Act to regulate the trade. Increased naval patrol work would be essential in either case.

(d) Whatever Great Britain might do, foreign vessels would

[22] L.M.S. to Granville, Apr. 6, 1869; *South Sea Corr., 1869.*
[23] Murdoch to Rogers, Apr. 14, 1869; ibid.
[24] Same to same, June 21, 1869; ibid.

remain uncontrolled unless parallel international action could be arranged. By implication, British subjects and ships might engage in the trade through concealment or change of their nationality.

Summing the matter up, it is to be concluded that, by April, 1869, British officials had advised their Government that, practically speaking, legislative attempts by a colony to control the labour trade had to be regarded as a failure.

In Australia also there was agitation for the more effective control of the labour trade, or, alternatively, for its complete suppression. The source of the agitation appears to have been mainly humanitarian sentiment, sedulously cultivated by missionary interests. A public meeting in Brisbane, the home of several of the commercial interests involved in the trade, resolved in March, 1869, that the 1868 Act was a failure. Holding that no colonial legislature could pass an adequate Act, the meeting petitioned for the repeal of the existing Act.[25] "Any further attempt to legislate upon this subject," ran the resolution, "will be useless and unproductive of good results." A month earlier a public meeting in Sydney, where many allegations were being made against the sincerity of Queensland attempts to control the trade,[26] had resolved to petition the Queensland Government to change its immigration policy and had concluded that:

> "No provisions in the Act can prevent the trade becoming one of kidnapping in the South Seas and of slavery in Queensland."[27]

The growing conviction in the colonies that mere colonial legislation could not rid the labour trade of its abuses was also reflected in the Earl of Belmore's letter to the Colonial Office in May, 1869, pointing out that only men-of-war could supervise the trade efficiently.[28] The same view was expressed by the zealous Palmer.[29]

The vehemence of the charges against the labour trade raised a new complication. Great Britain had left the task of control to the Government of Queensland, despite expert advice to the contrary. When the 1868 Act failed so badly as to produce a public outcry for the suppression of the trade, or, in the alternative, for imperial legislation, the Queensland Government was placed in a most

[25] Encl. 2 in No. 2 (Q'l'd), ibid.

[26] Island labourers were not then employed in N.S.W. plantations. (Belmore to C.O., Oct. 5, 1871: N.S.W., Leg. Ass., "*Kidnapping in the South Seas*," 1871.) But N.S.W. commercial interests were engaged in the labour trade. (A. H. Markham, op. cit., p. 52.) As to allegations against the sincerity of the Queensland Government, see *S.M.H.*, May 22, 1869.

[27] *S.M.H.*, Feb. 9, 1869.

[28] Belmore to Granville, May 17, 1869; *South Sea Corr., 1869.*

[29] Palmer to Belmore, May 25, 1869; C. 399, 1871.

difficult position. It denied the truth of the more extreme charges against the trade and upheld the principle of the control, rather than the suppression, of the trade.[30] It went farther and officially claimed that the matter was one for imperial legislation. In commenting on the Brisbane petition for the repeal of the Act, the Attorney-General, Lilley, declared that, if the Act were removed from the statute book, the islanders would have no legal means of ensuring their return to their own homes.[31] Lilley admitted that no colonial legislature could "take any active steps for the suppression of violence in the South Sea Islands." "Imperial force," he added, "will be required, should kidnapping, or any other kind of wrong, be shown to be carried on there." He did not consider the possibility of complete suppression of the labour trade, concerning whose abuses he still professed some scepticism.[32] His main recommendation was for the enactment of a new Imperial Passenger Act, conferring enlarged powers on the Queensland Government.

The Queensland attempt to place the responsibility for further remedial action on the British Government did not succeed. The Colonial Office had already decided early in 1869 that the Queensland Act should be supplemented with new safeguards and that more rigorous measures would have to be taken to ensure its proper enforcement. The numerous attacks in the English and Australian press on the excesses of the labour recruiters and the complaints from the French in the Loyalty Islands, that British recruiters were "stealing" natives, prompted the Colonial Office to send several despatches to Queensland enquiring into the working of the Act.[33] At no time did the Colonial Office hint at the possibility of imperial legislation to control the labour trade.

In April, 1869, Granville wrote to Governor Blackall that, while the Colonial Office recognised that the 1868 Act made "the best practicable provision for requiring that immigrants should not be introduced except by persons who had obtained a licence from the Government in case the immigrants are shown to be kidnapped or treated otherwise than as provided by law," was it certain that the Act was strictly enforced? What enquiries were made into the

[30] Blackall to Granville, Apr. 16, 1869; *South Sea Corr., 1869*.

[31] Lilley to Blackall, Apr. 13, 1869; ibid.

[32] Lilley's views as to the suppression of the trade were supported by the findings of the S.C. of the Leg. Council in Aug., 1869, that "no unnecessary obstacles should be placed in the way of . . . (the) introduction" of the labourers. (C. 468, 1871.) The Royal Commission appointed in N.S.W. to enquire into the French charges of kidnapping in the Loyalty Islands also reported in favour of continuance of the trade. (C. 399, 1871.)

[33] See *South Sea Corr., 1869*.

character and standing of licensees? Had any penalties yet been inflicted?[34] On the same day Granville wrote a second ·letter to Blackall arising out of articles in *The Times* and the *Leeds Mercury*[35] in which he stated that the honour of the British Crown was involved in the successful control of the labour trade.[36] In July the Foreign Office circularised the British Consuls in the Pacific requesting information as to how the trade was being conducted.[37]

The Queensland reply to Granville's queries was not a reassertion of the case for imperial legislation, but an expression of indignant amazement at what were described as the wickedly exaggerated accounts of labour trade abuses published in the press. Some specific accusations[38] were combated.[39] Granville's attention was drawn to the amendments to the 1868 Act proposed by the Select Committee of the Legislative Council.[40] The Committee had recommended that the Government should send out a recruiting agent with each vessel to supervise the engagement and transportation of the natives. Efficient interpreters were to be obtained in order that the contracts might be explained to the natives and their complaints be understood.[41] Similar arrangements had already been recommended by the Queensland Immigration Agent in a memorandum prepared early in 1869.[42]

The British Government accepted the new Queensland position and throughout 1870 the Colonial Office maintained strong pressure to have the recommendations of the Immigration Agent and Select Committee as to the appointment of government agents on all recruiting vessels put into force.[43] Granville even suggested that, in view of the wide interest in the problem, which involved other Australian States and also affected British relations with France, it might be desirable for the agents to be nominated by the Colonial Office itself.[44]

But it was not until the end of 1870 that the Queensland Govern-

[34] Granville to Blackall, Apr. 23, 1869; ibid.
[35] Apr. 21 and 16, 1869.
[36] Granville to Blackall, Apr. 23, 1869; C. 468, 1869.
[37] July 31, 1869; C. 399, 1871.
[38] In the *Leeds Mercury*.
[39] Blackall to Granville, July 11, 1869; C. 468, 1871.
[40] S.C. of L.C., Aug., 1869; C. 468, 1871.
[41] ibid.
[42] Encl. 4 in No. 2, C. 468, 1871.
[43] See Granville to Blackall, Feb. 18, 1870 (Nos. 9 and 10), Mar. 15, 1870; Kimberley to Blackall, Oct. 3, 1870, Mar. 24, 1871; ibid.
[44] Granville to Blackall, Mar. 15, 1870; ibid.

ment finally decided to appoint recruiting agents.[45] In April the Governor's speech at the opening of Parliament had stated that, "no further legislation" for the protection of Polynesian immigrants was necessary, but that attention would be given to the problem because ·of the wishes of Great Britain.[46] In June the Executive Council decided that the only remedial measures of any value would be to tighten up naval supervision of the trade.[47] But in December it was decided that recruiting agents should be appointed.

On the evidence it seems reasonable to conclude that only the persistent pressure of the Colonial Office induced the Queensland Government to take the elementary precaution of putting government agents on recruiting vessels. Whether from reluctance to regulate the trade, or whether from conviction that only imperial legislation and naval supervision could remedy the problem, the Queensland Government was certainly slow in remedying the deficiencies of the Act of 1868.

The British Government had not swerved from the policy of attributing the main responsibility for control of the Queensland labour trade to the colonial government. Instances of direct intervention by the British Government for the control of the trade were few. The increase of British participation in the inter-insular labour trade and the protests of the British Consuls and naval officers in the South Pacific led to an abortive attempt at remedial action in 1869-1870. In an endeavour to bring at least British subjects participating in the trade under some form of control[48] the Foreign Office permitted the British Consul in Fiji to exercise (or continue to exercise) extra-consular jurisdiction over the labour traffic in that group.[49] The British Government even examined the possibility of investing the Consul with magisterial powers for the purpose. This plan, however, was abandoned because of the legal complications involved.

In addition to the somewhat languid consideration given to the problem of increasing consular powers, Great Britain also made some efforts to secure joint international action to control the labour trade. It was hoped that Great Britain and the United States of America would be able to confer parallel powers on their

[45] Blackall to Kimberley, Dec. 27, 1970; O'Connell to Kimberley, Jan. 25, 1871; ibid.

[46] Apr. 26, 1870; ibid.

[47] Extract from Minutes of the Executive Council of Queensland, June 17, 1870; ibid.

[48] Cf. Clarendon to March, Aug. 3, 1869; C. 399, 1871.

[49] See above, Ch. XVII, as to extra-consular jurisdiction.

respective consuls, but the legal difficulties encountered by both countries prevented this plan from being carried into effect.[50] Subsequently the United States of America promised to co-operate with Great Britain in suppressing the abuses of the labour traffic.[51] But no action appears to have followed this agreement.[52]

These attempts to arrange international action for the control of the labour trade were plainly of secondary importance in British policy. Why was it that the British Government was so reluctant to pass imperial legislation, despite the constant missionary and official appeals? Why was the onus of controlling a trade for which its citizens were only partly responsible and to which its laws could extend only partly placed on the Government of Queensland?

The former problem is highly significant. Almost every circumstance of the development of the trade, apart from the single fact that some of the labour was used in Queensland, seemed to mark it out for imperial legislation. Both the recruiting and the use of native labour by British subjects extended beyond the limits of the self-governing British colonies. Repeated intimations had been made by the governments of New South Wales and Queensland that imperial legislation was necessary to control the trade.[53] International complications arising from the trade had already caused embarrassment with France[54] and necessitated plans for joint action with the United States to secure its suppression.

Moreover, the cases had proved that existing imperial legislation for the punishments of crimes committed in the islands had little or no effect in restraining the abuses of the recruiters. After the *Young Australian* case in 1869 Earl Belmore had to report that the Act, 9 Geo. IV, c. 83, giving power to the Supreme Court of New South Wales to try certain offences committed in the islands was difficult to apply:

"Although the Courts have power to try for such offences, it has lately been held by the Attorney General in the case of the alleged murders on board of the *Young Australian,* that warrants cannot properly be issued in this Colony for the arrest of persons still

[50] Clarendon to Thornton, Sept. 2, 1869; C. 399, 1871. Also Granville to Bowen, Sept. 16, 1869; ibid.

[51] Thornton to Clarendon, Sept. 23, 1869; ibid.

[52] See below, p. 261.

[53] See especially Belmore to Kimberley, Nov. 24, 1873; C. 496, 1872; and Lilley to Blackall, Apr. 13, 1869; C. 468, 1871.

[54] In 1868 the French Governor of New Caledonia complained that British ships were stealing natives from the Loyalty Islands. Official British enquiry found that the charges were unfounded. (C. 399, 1871.)

remaining in the islands, who were concerned in that offence. It will thus be seen that though a prisoner on his arrival in the Colony may be amenable to the law, yet that until his arrival, his detention may be without legal warrant."[55]

The ineffectiveness of the slave trade legislation has already been noted.[56] The fact was, as the cases themselves had proved, that no existing imperial legislation made any significant contribution towards the regulation of the labour trade.

Moreover, the great number of cases arising out of the inter-insular trade swept away the whole basis of the original attitude of the British Government towards the labour problem, that, because Queensland was the main British territory concerned, Queensland should be responsible for controlling the trade.

Despite all these reasons for direct imperial action, Great Britain up to 1871 had done nothing towards controlling the labour trade apart from acquiescing in the passage of the 1868 Act, pressing for its improvement, obtaining the appointment of a Royal Commission in New South Wales to enquire into the French complaints of illegal recruiting in the Loyalties, toying with the idea of extending the jurisdiction of the British Consul in Fiji and entering into abortive negotiations with the United States for joint action to control the trade.

The basic reason for the British reluctance to intervene directly and effectively is to be found in the continued adherence to the minimum intervention policy as a principle too vital to be sacrificed lightly. Without substantial departure from the policy, the scope of a British imperial enactment for the control of the labour trade could not have been made much more extensive than that of the Queensland Act. A British Act passed within the minimum intervention policy, passed, that is to say, with continued recognition of native sovereignty and continued non-acceptance of political responsibilities in the islands, would not only have been ineffective against foreigners and foreign vessels, but also would have been every whit as difficult to enforce out of British territories as the Acts of 1817, 1823 and 1828 had proved to be.

To have made an imperial enactment substantially more effective than the Queensland Act, Great Britain would have had to exercise jurisdiction in the islands themselves and to have instituted extensive naval patrols. From a legal point of view, the first step would have involved a clear departure from the doctrine of native

---

[55] Belmore to Granville, Nov. 5, 1869; C. 399, 1871.
[56] see above, pp 223 ff.

sovereignty (unless special agreements were made with the natives) and might even have necessitated annexation or the establishment of a protectorate over the islands concerned.

Action on these lines was necessarily repugnant to the Colonial Office and the Foreign Office, especially under the Liberal Government of Gladstone. The Liberals were opposed to further extensions of the governing responsibilities of Great Britain. In the Pacific there were special reasons for caution. British policy sought to maintain the *status quo*. Any action involving considerable intervention in the islands might have precipitated United States action in Hawaii or generated international rivalries in the South Pacific.

Treasury influence was—as usual—also opposed to intervention. The Treasury continued to exert great pressure on colonial affairs and opposed any extension of British responsibilities through which expenditure might be increased. In December, 1870, the Treasury announced that it would not sanction the expenditure of imperial funds to prosecute persons charged with kidnapping in the South Pacific.[57] Despite the objections of the Foreign Office and the Colonial Office, the decision, which was designed to force the Australian colonies to pay for all prosecutions against labour trade offenders, was carried into effect. According to Brookes, the Treasury's attitude resulted in delay to the preparation of a remedial Bill even after Great Britain had become convinced that imperial legislation had become inescapably necessary.[58]

In March, 1871, Earl Granville enquired of the Australian Governors whether their colonies would pay a share of the costs of prosecutions launched in Australian courts under a projected British Act.[59] New Zealand (which had not been invited to express an opinion) and every Australian state except Western Australia agreed to do so.[60] A month later the British Consuls in the Pacific were forbidden to incur expenditure in detaining offenders or sending them to the colonies for trial, unless the colonies had already intimated their willingness to meet all the costs.[61] While it may be possible to argue that Great Britain legitimately regarded the labour trade as an abuse in whose suppression the colonies should (and in fact did) share,[62] it is incon-

[57] Brookes, op. cit., p. 369.
[58] ibid.
[59] Circular to Australian Governors, Mar. 3, 1871; C. 399, 1871.
[60] C. 399, 1871.
[61] Granville to H.B.M. Consuls in the Pacific, Apr. 6, 1871; ibid.
[62] Cf. C. 496, 1872.

testable that the success of the Treasury's opposition demonstrated the extreme reluctance of the Government to take the steps necessary for effective control of the labour trade.

The attitude of British subjects in the islands made it easy to maintain the policy. Up to almost the end of 1871 they had not brought their demand for British intervention to the point at which Great Britain had either to accede to the demand for effective control or attempt to renounce all her interest in British subjects in the South Pacific. When some of the settlers of Fiji wrote to the Earl of Belmore requesting greater supervision of the labour trade (a request which Belmore treated at face value) their suggestion was merely that the British Consul should have power to inspect all ships arriving with foreign labourers and involved no implication of wider intervention.[63] The proposed arrangement, whose utility would have been limited to the labour trade in Fiji, would not have involved any significant departure from the minimum intervention policy. It could in fact have been introduced by agreement with the Fijian chiefs, sanctioned by Act of Parliament for extension of the consul's powers.

Even British officials resident in the islands were not asking at this stage for any intervention more extensive than that requested by the planters of Fiji. The consuls at Fiji merely sought an official extra-consular jurisdiction over the labour traffic. Williams, the British Consul in Samoa, sought an international commission to enquire into the trade, but otherwise did not press the matter of labour trade control.[64]

The conditions under which a Queensland enactment, supplemented by some naval supervision and encouragement to the consul's efforts to restrict abuses in Fiji, could be regarded in England as discharging British obligations towards the control of the labour trade were rapidly passing away in 1871. The long record of atrocities committed by British subjects in the inter-insular labour traffic had been crowned by the dreadful *Carl* massacre and by the murder of Bishop Patteson and his colleague, the Rev. Atkins, at Nukapu Island in the Swallow Group. The death of the famous missionary bishop, who was a personal friend of several leading British statesmen, was directly attributable to the acts of labour recruiters as the murders had been committed in revenge for outrages perpetrated by kidnappers a few months previously. As a result of the incident appeals were made from

[63] Memorial to Belmore from planters, &c., in Fiji; Encl. 2 in No. 8; C. 399, 1871.

[64] Williams to Clarendon Jan. 12, 1870; ibid.

Australia[65] and New Zealand[66] for imperial legislation to control the labour traffic. In Great Britain itself Patteson's death became the occasion for renewed pressure on the Government to legislate for the control of the labour recruiters.

The circular addressed by the Colonial Office to the Australian colonies in March, 1871, had intimated that a Bill was in prospect by which certain acts of preparation usually connected with kidnapping would be made felonies cognizable in the colonial courts. The attempt made in the circular to clear away the financial obstacles to British legislation for the control of the labour trade reflected the realisation of the Foreign Office and the Colonial Office, that imperial action was overdue and that the obstructive attitude of the Treasury could not be allowed to delay British action much longer.[67]

Even so, it was not until the murder of Bishop Patteson gave the labour trade problem an enhanced political significance that a Bill was introduced in the House of Commons. On February 15, 1872, Knatchbull-Hugessen moved the first reading of the Pacific Islanders Protection Bill in a speech which laid down the policy that the labour trade was unexceptionable in principle and required only proper regulation, not suppression. Quoting the words of Patteson, "I advocate the regulation and not the suppression of this traffic," Knatchbull-Hugessen declared that Her Majesty's Government had already strengthened the Australian naval squadron. All that remained to be done was to introduce legislation extending to British subjects engaged in the inter-insular labour traffic. The Bill proposed to make kidnapping of natives a felony cognizable in the Supreme Courts of the Australian colonies. Provision was made to secure the attendance of native witnesses and to facilitate the taking of evidence.[68]

When the Bill was debated at its second reading on March 7 and in Committee on April 22 the advocates of complete suppression put up a strong case. Admiral Erskine declared that the Bill would not afford adequate protection to labourers kidnapped for Queensland[69] and proposed an amendment which would virtually have suppressed open British participation in the trade save in the case of Queensland.[70] Erskine, whose great practical experience in the

---

65 *South Sea Corr.*, 1873.
66 N.Z., Parlt., *South Sea Papers, 1874.*
67 Cf. Brookes, op. cit., p. 369.
68 *Parlty Debates*, CCIX, 522-3.
69 ibid, col. 1615.
70 ibid, CCX, 1666.

Southern Pacific commanded respect for his views, received support from Sir Charles Wingfield and R. N. Fowler, who were both prominent in colonial matters.

But the Government's policy, that native labour was too valuable an asset to the colonies to be foregone by them and that, provided it were purged of its abuses, the labour trade was unexceptionable in principle, easily prevailed.[71] The royal assent was received and the Pacific Islanders Protection Act became law on June 27, 1872.[72]

The new Act was limited in its extent. Designed to deal with criminal outrages committed by British subjects upon natives of islands in the Pacific Ocean not within Her Majesty's Dominions nor within the jurisdiction of any civilized power, the Kidnapping Act (its short title, by which it was best known) had four main provisions:

(1) No British vessel was to carry native labourers of the islands (other than crew) unless the master had entered into one surety approved by the Governor of an Australian colony or by a British consular officer in the islands and had received a licence in the prescribed form. (Section 3.)

(2) The Supreme Court of any Australian colony was given power to try and to punish any British subject who enlisted or decoyed a native against his will. (Sec. 9.) The Courts might issue commissions for the taking of evidence. (Sec. 12.)

(3) British vessels offending against the Act, or reasonably suspected of so offending, were liable to seizure (Sec. 6) and to adjudication before a Vice-Admiralty Court in any of Her Majesty's dominions. (Sec. 12.)

(4) Vessels complying with the Queensland Act of 1868, or any like Act passed by any Australasian colony, were not liable to seizure under the Pacific Islanders Protection Act, 1872.

Five fast schooners[73] were provided to patrol the islands on the recommendation of Commodore Stirling,[74] senior naval officer on the Australian station.[75]

Within a year there were cases before the courts involving prosecutions under the new Act. Some offenders received heavy

[71] It is interesting to note that Sir C. Adderley complained that the Bill did not impose on the colonies the expense of carrying out the regulations.

[72] 35 and 36 Vict., c. 19.

[73] *Alacrity, Beagle, Conflict, Reynard* and *Sandfly*. The first and the last of these were specially famous.

[74] Stirling to Admiralty, Apr. 22, 1872; *South Sea Corr.*, 1873. The suggestion had emanated from the Marquis of Normanby, Governor of Queensland.

[75] Admiralty to Stirling, July 12, 1872; N.S.W., Circular Despatch re 1872 Act. (Mitchell Library, Public Documents, Misc. No. 4.)

sentences.[76] Nevertheless, the limitations of the Act soon became apparent. Apart from the provisions as to seizure and the requirement as to bonds the Act was no more than an extension to the specific case of the labour trade of the principles laid down in the Acts of 1823 and 1828, that is, provision for trial in an Australian colony of offences committed by British subjects anywhere in the Pacific, whether on sea or on land. The provision that a licence had to be obtained from an Australian Governor or a British consular officer was ludicrously ineffective. As other powers exercised no control over the trade, it was a simple matter for a master to change his flag (legally or illegally) and so evade British jurisdiction.

Moreover, the Act tacitly preserved the British recognition of native sovereignty and thus virtually excluded the possibility of effective control of labour recruiting in the islands themselves. The new legislation certainly made the task of the recruiter more difficult but it did not put him out of business. In point of fact the increasing degree of regulation carried with it a threat of scarcity in the plantation labour supply and so increased the value of the individual native. If the islands continued without effective government, considered Julius Vogel, the Prime Minister of New Zealand, the repression of slavery in the South Seas would mean "such an inducement to those who are successful in the trade as to couple with the efforts to check slavery an encouragement to promote it, and make necessary larger means of repression."[77]

The fundamental weakness in the Kidnapping Act was that, in accordance with general British policy towards the South Pacific, it ignored the main island problem. The lack of effective government in the islands themselves, of which the abuses in the labour trade were partly a consequence, was not taken into consideration in framing the Act. What the unsatisfactory working of the Act and the criticisms of Vogel and others alike made plain was that no attempt to control the inter-insular trade could succeed until the main condition making abuses possible had been removed. Efficient government had to be instituted in the islands. Not only Vogel, but also Admiral Erskine,[78] Alderman McArthur,[79] Sir Charles Wingfield[80] and several other members of the British and colonial Parliaments recognised this fundamental need.[81]

[76] Derrick, op. cit., I, p. 174.
[77] Memorandum by Vogel, Feb. 5, 1874; N.Z., Parlt., *South Sea Papers, 1874.*
[78] *Parlty. Debates,* CCX, 1666.
[79] ibid, CCXII, 192-197; CCXVI, 940 ff.
[80] ibid, CCXII, 201-2; CCX, 1669.
[81] See debates cited above and N.Z., Parlt., *South Sea Papers, 1874.*

The comments of all these observers drew attention to the fact that, in practice the labour problem and the problem of government had become almost indistinguishable. For its own political purposes the British Government had found it necessary to make attempt to regulate the labour trade independently of the problem of government. The ill-success of attempts so made sufficiently demonstrated the falsity of the conception on which they were based. British policy towards the South Pacific was in fact still in terms of minimum intervention. There was no wish on the part of the British Government to seek or see any territorial or political changes there. The problems of the islands were a matter of indifference save where they directly impinged on matters capable of inflaming public opinion in Great Britain.

On a realistic assessment, the distinction made between the regulation of the labour trade, which was a subject of political importance in Great Britain, and the institution of effective government in the islands, which was in general a matter of little political consequence in Great Britain, could be maintained only at the cost of failure to achieve the avowed purposes of the Acts of 1868 and 1872. But this fact was not permitted to influence British policy decisively.

The true nature of the island problem was most clearly understood in New Zealand, where the Government's wish for a British Oceania enabled it to see the problem of island government, not as an embarrassment of which British policy should steer clear, but merely as one more reason for British annexation of the islands. On the premise that the islands ought to be British, there was no difficulty in perceiving the true relationship between the labour trade and the problem of government.[82]

In Great Britain, on the other hand, no significant official interest was taken in the problem of island government, save in the case of Fiji, where British interests had multiplied rapidly and exceeded those of all other foreign powers. In the case of the other groups, the problem of island government was as much a matter of indifference to the British Government in the early 1870's as it had ever been. The only vital issue for British policy towards these islands was that of the labour trade. In this matter the established British policy was to intervene as little as possible in the islands, even at the cost of reducing the effectiveness of the desired control.

[82] Cf. Vogel's Memorandum of Feb. 5, 1875; cit. sup. (n. 77).

CHAPTER XXII

FIJI BECOMES BRITISH

FIJI was clearly a special case. The high proportion of British settlers amongst the Europeans in that group and its increasing commercial contacts with the Australian colonies ensured that its internal condition could not remain a matter of indifference to Great Britain much longer. Events were rapidly forcing Whitehall to consider the labour trade and the problem of government in their proper relations. Moreover, the new government set up in 1871 had been inspired and formed by British subjects, whose actions could not be a matter of indifference to Great Britain, if only because of their possible international complications.

The position in Fiji in 1872 was that the Woods Government was still in office, granted a qualified recognition *de facto* by Great Britain and in practice unable to govern effectively. With the growing complications of the labour trade and the increasing tendency of the government to govern only in the interests of its own leading members,[1] the internal condition of Fiji had become chaotic. The one encouraging feature for those who still sought good government was the appointment of J. B. Thurston, formerly Acting British Consul, as Chief Secretary. Thurston, an astute and experienced administrator, did his best to build up the prestige of the new government, but with little success.

The previous record of British relations with Fiji was sufficient to prove that the British Government would have no interest in the problem of Fijian government as such. But three factors came to invest the problem with a special significance for even the Gladstone Ministry. The first was the use of the Fijian flag to evade British jurisdiction under the 1872 Act. How this practice led to specific qualification of the British recognition *de facto* of the Woods Government has already been noticed.[2] Second, despite her indifference to the cause of good government in Fiji, Great Britain had already interfered there so often and to so great an extent through the work of her consuls and her naval commanders,

[1] Cf. Confidential Despatch from Robinson to C.O., Jan. 27, 1873; repr. in Henderson, op. cit., pp. 58 ff.
[2] See Ch. XX, above.

that she could not deny that the problems of government in Fiji were partly of her own making. This point was stressed in the 1873-1874 debates on Fiji in the House of Commons.[3] Moreover, the fact that British subjects were the principal movers in the formation of the Woods Government gave Great Britain a special interest in its activities, if only because of possible international complications and because March, the British Consul, regarded himself as the only legitimate British official in the islands and opposed the attempts of British subjects to establish a Fijian Government.[4] The third factor affecting the British attitude to the problem of government in Fiji was the extraordinarily rapid growth of British trade in the group. In 1873 Thurston reported to the Foreign Office that Australian colonists were investing substantially in Fiji. According to his reports, the export trade of Fiji was mounting rapidly and most of it was in British hands. The development of cotton was hindered only by inferior transport, lack of labour and inexperience. Copra was being sold at the good price of £8 per ton.[5]

Growing commercial interest was also reflected in the activities of the Polynesian Company[6] formed in Melbourne in 1868 by a group anxious to take advantage of Thakombau's embarrassment with his United States claims.[7] Thakombau granted this company a charter together with 200,000 acres of land, the exclusive right to carry on banking in Fiji and perpetual freedom from taxation in return for the Company's promise to pay in full the United States claim of £9,000. Only the vigilance of British officials prevented the Company from carrying its agreement into effect.[8] The real importance of the Company was that its schemes demonstrated the growth and nature of commercial interest in Fiji and themselves encouraged a new increase of settlement and investment in the group.

To would-be investors, investors, settlers and planters the disturbed internal conditions of Fiji were matters of deep concern. The New South Wales Government, presumably prompted by Sydney commercial interests, bitterly opposed the recognition of the

[3] Cf. McArthur's assertion in the House of Commons on Aug. 4, 1874, that British policy towards Fiji had not been neutral. (*Parlty. Debates*, CCXXI, 1264-1272.) Also Wingfield's speech on June 13, 1873; ibid, CCXVI, 941-942.

[4] *Fiji Times*, Feb. 5, 1873.

[5] H. Britton: *Fiji in 1870*; Melbourne, 1870; pp. 11-12, 16.

[6] Cf. *Corr. rel. to Fiji, 1871 (Victoria)*.

[7] During the visit of U.S.S. *Tuscarora* in July, 1867, Thakombau had had to sign a new agreement to discharge the U.S. claim within four years by annual payments. The islands of Koro, Batiki and Gau were seized as security. (Derrick, op. cit., I, pp. 177 ff.)

[8] Robinson to Carnarvon, Oct. 20, 1874; *Corr. with Robinson, 1875*.

Woods Government in Fiji on the ground that its members were not persons of good commercial credit able to make conditions in Fiji safe for investment. When in June, 1872, McArthur moved in the House of Commons his first motion in favour of the establishment of a British protectorate over Fiji, he himself laid emphasis on the bad effects for trade of the existing conditions in Fiji.[9] Speaking in support of McArthur's motion, Mr. Eastwick, M.P., declared that:

> ". . . an independent buccaneering government had been established which will attract all the desperate characters in Australia and the surrounding islands. It was already raising troops to coerce the peaceable settlers and overawe our Consul."[10]

Sir Charles Wingfield pointed out that, "the Fiji Group was fast becoming the refuge of scoundrels and fugitives of all descriptions."[11]

Though no satisfactory evidence was produced in rebuttal of his allegations, McArthur's motion was lost by 135 votes to 84. The Government's view was that the new legislation then before Parliament (the Pacific Islanders Protection Bill) would dispose of the labour problem. No other Fijian problem interested the Gladstone Government. As Gladstone himself wrote to Kimberley some months later, he did not wish "to be a party to any arrangement for adding Fiji and all that lies beyond it to the cares of this overdone and over-burdened Government and Empire."[12] In the debate itself Knatchbull-Hugessen on behalf of the Government pointed out that the Smythe Report had opposed any extension of British rule to Fiji. The Fijians, Knatchbull-Hugessen asserted, had not asked for British intervention. If the Australian colonies wished for a stronger government in Fiji, Great Britain would permit New South Wales to annex the group. But the problem of Fijian government was not one of importance to the British Government.

What the debate clearly revealed was that the members who voted in favour of the motion were more concerned with the ill-consequences of ineffective government to the trade and peace of the Pacific than with the continued failure of both the British and Fijian Governments to come to grips with the labour trade. The problem of the labour trade was mentioned in the debate, but it

[9] *Parlty. Debates,* CCXII, 192-197.
[10] ibid, col. 200.
[11] ibid, cols. 201-202.
[12] Feb. 26, 1873; qu. Knaplund, op. cit., p. 137.

was evidently regarded as a secondary issue, not itself sufficiently important to warrant a departure from minimum intervention. McArthur himself defined the true relationship between the problem of government in the islands and the problem of regulating the labour traffic when he made it clear that the latter was definitely subordinate to the former. Though McArthur and his supporters did not hesitate to draw the obvious conclusion, that British rule would have to be extended to Fiji, if the labour trade were to be controlled, the British Government still refused to admit that the problem of island government was a matter of concern to British policy. Only the Australian colonies, it was argued, really wished for or would gain from the establishment of British rule in Fiji.

Despite the Government's attitude on this point, the real issue for British policy towards Fiji was rapidly becoming one of the adequacy or inadequacy of the existing government in Fiji. Could it maintain law and order? Could it establish conditions favourable to trade? Could it suppress the abuses of the labour traffic in Fiji and on vessels flying the Fijian flag? If it could be proved that the Fijian Government could not discharge its principal functions effectively, so a growing body of commercial and political opinion in Great Britain and Australasia concluded, then the British Government should step in and establish British rule throughout the group.

Against this case for intervention, the British Government itself argued that British action in Fiji would precipitate United States action in Hawaii[13] and elsewhere, thus destroying the *status quo* in the islands on which the British policy of minimum intervention was based and which had already been threatened so seriously by French action in the preceding decades. So far as Fiji itself was concerned, the difficulty and expense of establishing law and order there would offset any compensating advantages in the way of increased trade and improved native welfare. If conditions in Fiji were as bad as the commercial interests claimed, the task of setting up British rule would be long, costly and possibly prodigal of British blood. These points were stated quite clearly by Lord Kimberley to the Aborigines Protection Society and the Royal Colonial Institute when those bodies sent deputations to him in May, 1873, requesting the annexation of Fiji.[14] Kimberley pointed to the experience of the Maori wars in New Zealand as sufficient reason for hesitation in the case of Fiji. He argued that, if the

[13] Memorandum on Fiji, Apr. 30, 1873; F.O. 58/139; qu. in Brookes, op. cit., p. 380.
[14] This interview is reported in the *Fiji Times*, July 26, 1873.

case put forward by the commercial and the humanitarian interests were basically correct, then similar conditions could be expected to arise sooner or later in all the Pacific islands. Was Great Britain expected to annex the whole of Polynesia? If Fiji were annexed on the grounds set out by the Royal Colonial Institute and the Aborigines Protection Society, there would be no limit to the governing duties which Great Britain would have to accept in the Southern Pacific, until all the groups had passed under the control of one or other of the Powers. Nor would Kimberley concede the urgency of the humanitarian case for British intervention. Whenever British settlers appeared in large numbers, he pointed out, the natives began to disappear. Were these "unhappy creatures" to be "improved off the face of the earth" by the humanitarian intervention of the British Government?

Kimberley's rather mixed bag of arguments could not conceal the fact that he himself had doubts as to the justice and even the expediency of continued refusal to annex Fiji. Evidence was pouring in to prove that conditions in Fiji were rapidly deteriorating and to show that peaceable trade, security of person and property and reasonable conditions in the labour traffic could not be expected under the Fijian Government.

The challenge to minimum intervention was taking much the same form in the case of Fiji as it had in the case of New Zealand thirty-five years previously. British interests could no longer take advantage of their country's policy of minimum intervention to trade and settle in the islands as they pleased. Planters especially had fixed stakes in the islands and earnestly wished for political security. The disruption of native society and the unsettling effects of the opening up of Fiji to western traders and planters had produced a situation in which strong government was needed, not merely to suppress the somewhat spectacular abuses of the labour trade, but also to guarantee that modicum of law and order without which neither the persons nor property of the British subjects in Fiji could be safe.

The year 1873 opened with striking proofs of the collapse of administration in Fiji. On January 27th Sir Hercules Robinson, the Governor of New South Wales, wrote to the Colonial Office concerning the imminent failure of the Woods Government and stressing the need for remedial British action, even if annexation were impossible.[15] Robinson's despatch was founded on reports[16] received from J. B. Thurston, the Chief Secretary of Fiji, which

[15] Robinson to Kimberley, Jan. 27, 1873; repr. in Henderson, op. cit., pp. 58 ff.
[16] Thurston to Robinson, Dec. 20, 1872; cf. Brookes, op. cit., pp. 377 ff.

revealed the danger of civil war in the group. Thurston's despatch to Robinson also enquired whether it would be feasible to telegraph to London to ascertain what reception would be accorded to a further offer of cession from Fiji, were one to be made.[17] On January 31st Thurston himself cabled to the British Government at the request of Thakombau in these terms:

> "Will H.M. Government entertain a proposal from the Government of Fiji to cede the Kingdom to Her Britannic Majesty, if its King and people once more and through the King's responsible advisers express a desire to place themselves under Her Majesty's rule?"[18]

The conditions which led to these developments were set out in Robinson's despatch to the Colonial Office and in Thurston's confidential letter to Robinson. Fiji, it was revealed, was on the brink of civil war. Robinson, who analysed the situation in a shrewd and careful way, laid most of the blame on the Government itself, condemning it as a mere device for keeping power in the hands of a scheming minority of the whites.[19] Taxation was high and official expenditure extravagant. Robinson considered that there was no hope of success for any democratically constituted government in Fiji. "The conditions essential to the success of free institutions do not exist in Fiji," he wrote. The best interests of Fiji, he thought, would be served by the erection of the group into a British Crown Colony. Rejecting this solution as politically impracticable in view of previous decisions to the contrary, and holding that there was no prospect of either New South Wales or Victoria accepting responsibility for the government of Fiji, Robinson concluded that "the maintenance of a Local Government of some sort" appeared to be "the only possible means of rendering life and property secure in that country, and of preventing bloodshed between the different races which now inhabit it." Robinson suggested that the British Government should co-operate with Thakombau to that end. If necessary, the extra-territoriality of British subjects could be provided for and consular courts established.

The root difficulty of the Fijian Government was that it had lost the support of the majority of the white settlers, by whose representatives it had been established, who had elected the Legislative Assembly and in whose interests the expensive superstructure

[17] Ibid.

[18] Repr. in Henderson, op. cit., p. 65. This is the "February offer," so called because it was not received by the British Government until February.

[19] See paras. 6, 7 and 8 of Robinson to Kimberley, Jan. 27, 1873; cit. sup.

of highly-paid officials, judges and members of Parliament was ostensibly maintained. This is made clear from the files of the *Fiji Times* for 1872-1873. Instance after instance was reported of angry protests from white settlers at the extravagance of the Government. The *Fiji Times* frequently opened its columns to correspondence of a most vituperative character, condemning the Government root and branch.

A substantial body of the white settlers, alarmed by the increasing disorder in Fiji, and by the rapidly mounting public debt, which would soon destroy the Government's credit, earnestly desired annexation by Great Britain. From the middle of 1872 onwards these settlers openly plotted the destruction of the Government, which, they felt, governed only in its own interests and was making Fiji uninhabitable by the planting class.

Reports of McArthur's 1872 motion were welcomed by this group and led to the formation of the Fiji Reform League, whose objects were to abolish "the present bungling, inoperative and expensive Government machinery" and either to replace it by efficient Government or to secure the annexation of Fiji to Great Britain.[20] A public meeting held at Levuka on October 26th resolved to circulate a petition for annexation[21] and received the tacit support of Thurston, the Chief Secretary, who at that stage was without hope of making the Fijian Government work effectively.[22] Thakombau was also understood to favour annexation.[23] A month later Thurston sent his cable to the Colonial Office enquiring whether Fiji would be accepted by Great Britain in the event of a further offer of cession being made.

Early in 1873 the annexation fever in Fiji was growing apace. It flourished on the extravagant expenditure and mounting indebtedness of the Government. When Woods, the Prime Minister, arrived at Levuka with the proceeds of a loan raised in Sydney one section of the white settlers proposed to seize the specie and send it back so as to avoid further increase of the Fijian debt.[24] Several districts requested their representatives in the Legislative Assembly to resign. In December, 1872, the British Subjects Mutual Protection Society was revived by its President, White, "with a view to destroying the present Government."[25] The

[20] *Fiji Times,* Oct. 16, 1872.
[21] Derrick, op. cit., I, p. 222.
[22] Thurston to Hope, Oct. 12, 1872; *Letter Journals of Capt. G. W. Hope of H.M.S. "Brisk"*; Turnbull Library, Wellington.
[23] ibid.
[24] March's Memo. on Fijian Affairs, May 7, 1873; C. 983, 1874.
[25] Encl. in *Corr. rel. to H.M.S. "Dido."*

settlers at Ba resisted the Government and clashed with its troops. Two of the settlers, White and DeCourcey Ireland, were deported to Sydney by Captain Chapman (H.M.S. *Dido*), who investigated the disturbance.[26]   In June, 1873, the Legislative Assembly, in which there was a two to one majority against the Government, was precipitately closed.[27]   Meeting after meeting was held by the dissident whites, whose opposition developed into a refusal to pay taxes when the ministers suspended the constitution and proceeded to enfranchise the natives.[28]

These developments could only be described as a collapse of government. Efforts made during 1873 to bring the Government under Thurston's control failed.   By the end of the financial year in 1873 the debts of the Government amounted to £87,000. Matters were worsened by a slump in trade, especially cotton, as a result of which the planters were impoverished and became discontented and rancorous.

Finally, the Government had failed to control the labour trade.[29] Legislation for the purpose had been introduced in the Fijian Parliament as early as December 14th, 1871, with the Act to Regulate the Hiring and Service of Foreign and Native Labourers. (Fiji, Cakobau Rex, No. 8.)   This set up a form of control not legally inferior to that established in Queensland.   Two further Acts were passed in July, 1872, known as an Act to Regulate the Hiring and Service of Fijian Labourers (Cakobau Rex, No. 27) and an Act to Regulate the Hiring and Service of Immigrant Labourers (Cakobau Rex, No. 34).   The benefits of this legislation were destroyed by the open hostility of the white settlers in Fiji, who regarded the group as their own and treated the natives, whether imported or indigenous, as merely a convenient source of labour.   Further, the taxing legislation of Fiji imposed such a burden of poll tax on the natives that many of them fell victims of an arrangement by which their labour was sold at fixed rates to any settler able to pay their tax.   Where taxation arrears had been allowed to accumulate, settlers acquired what was virtually penal labour for long periods at rates as low as 1/- a day for adult males.[30]

That the abuses of the labour trade could not be removed or even alleviated in any substantial way by the Fijian Government was

[26] ibid.
[27] Encl. in No. 1, *Corr. with Robinson, 1875.*
[28] C.O.: *Confid. Memo. on Fiji, 1874.*
[29] C. 1011, 1874; p. 4.
[30] Robinson to Carnarvon, Oct. 16, 1874; *Corr. with Robinson, 1875.*

L

abundantly clear. The testimony of March[31], Stirling[32] and Thurston[33] was quite agreed on this point.

So far as conditions inside Fiji were concerned the case for annexation put forward in the House of Commons in June, 1872, had become unanswerable by June, 1873. The "independent, buccaneering government," whose ability to maintain law and order and favourable commercial conditions had been challenged in the earlier debate, had practically ceased to be a government at all. There was no longer—on any realistic view—any question as to whether or not the Government could work. It was obvious that no satisfactory administration could be expected from the Woods Ministry or any other locally established government. The problem for Great Britain by June, 1873, therefore, was in the old familiar terms of assessing whether the manifest interests of British subjects in the group and the necessity of suppressing British misdeeds in the groups could be held to outweigh the expense and complications of a new addition to the Empire.

In Great Britain the arguments of the Royal Colonial Institute, that trade would follow the flag, and of the Aborigines Protection Society, that Fiji was becoming the centre of a new slave trade, had failed in May to convince the Government of the need for British intervention in Fiji. In June McArthur renewed the demand in Parliament for the extension of British rule to Fiji[34] and received strong support from both commercial and humanitarian advocates of annexation.[35] McArthur's speech, which was published with emendations by the Aborigines Protection Society in 1874,[36] was an uncompromising attack on British policy towards Fiji from the time of the Smythe report onwards. Smythe's report was dismissed with the assertion that its author had since changed his opinions.[37] The recognition of the Woods Government *de facto,* the permission given to New South Wales to annex Fiji and the desultory attention given to the problems of the British Consul in the group were attacked as evidence of a shuffling policy of indifference and

[31] March's Memorandum, May 7, 1873; cit. sup.

[32] Stirling's despatches in *South Sea Corr., 1873.*

[33] n. 22, above.

[34] McArthur's motion was: "That, as the Chiefs of Fiji and the white residents therein have signified their desire that Great Britain should assume the protectorate or sovereignty of those Islands, it is desirable that H.M. Government, in order to put an end to the condition of things now existing in the Group, should take steps to carry into effect one or other of these measures."

[35] *Parlty. Debates,* CCXVI, 934-959.

[36] See Bibliography, Part VI (B) (7).

[37] In his 1872 speech McArthur had imputed either prejudice or personal unfitness to Smythe; *Parlty. Debates,* CCXII, 193-4.

ignorance. The failure to answer the 1871 memorial from Fiji was attributed to the unjustifiable neglect of the Foreign Office. With a telling blend of commercial and humanitarian appeal, McArthur contended that Fiji would prove a magnificent field for British investment and would provide for Great Britain an opportunity of putting down the slave trade in the Pacific while making a clear profit on the administration of Fiji. This double-barrelled argument was a direct attack on Manchester School supporters, who held that the Empire was a useless source of expense and political friction. Great Britain, McArthur concluded, should no longer delay in extending her rule to Fiji. The conditions laid down by the Prime Minister, Gladstone, in his speech on Fiji in 1872, "that Her Majesty's Government would not annex any territory great or small without the well-understood and expressed wish of the people to be annexed, freely and generally expressed and authenticated by the best means the case will afford,"[38] had been amply met by the appeals made in 1872 (and also in January and May of 1873).

The supporters of McArthur's motion made it clear that the character of the Fijian Government was still the main source of their anxiety as to the well-being of British interests in Fiji. Sir Charles Wingfield[39] attacked the reputations of members of the Fijian Cabinet. Referring to the *Nukulau* case,[40] he doubted whether Ministers would work to suppress the labour trade. "The policy of treating the Fijian Government as an independent *de facto* Government," Wingfield concluded, "had tied the hands of our naval commanders, had weakened the authority of our Consul and had lowered the dignity of Her Majesty's Representative in New South Wales."[41]

In reply to what was undoubtedly a strong case for annexation to protect British interests and to control British subjects, Gladstone was driven back on a long and mostly irrelevant defence of the Government's treatment of March, the former British Consul, who had been transferred suddenly from Fiji to Brazil. As Great Britain already had more trade opportunities than she could use, the Prime Minister continued, the acquisition of Fiji could not be regarded as a matter of prime commercial or political importance. That Gladstone, the Prime Minister who had come to power in

[38] ibid, col. 217.

[39] *Parlty Debates*, CCXVI, 941-2.

[40] This was the *Unkulau* referred to in March to Belmore, Dec. 18, 1871; *South Sea Corr., 1873*.

[41] Wingfield also bitingly attacked the removal of Consul March to an unhealthy post in Brazil, accusing the Government of being discomfited by March's zealous repression of labour trade abuses.

December, 1868, at the head of the Liberal Party on a policy of "peace, retrenchment and reform," should be somewhat indifferent to the problem of government in Fiji and somewhat too ready to permit a nice legality[42] to obstruct the action of his Government was not surprising. He had won the elections to the accompaniment of a record number of promises and in office was too preoccupied with the Irish question, with agrarian discontent, with educational reform and ballot reform to be in favour of extending an Empire whose ramifications, in the opinion of his Party, were already an embarrassment rather than a source of strength.

The peculiar mixture of economic and humanitarian considerations raised in the debate was typical of colonial discussions in Great Britain during the 'seventies. The Conference on Colonial Questions held at Westminster Hotel in July, 1871, for instance, revealed a general readiness to believe that "the sons of England . . . will in all times have the ineradicable disposition to trade with England," so that the annexation of colonies in the interests of trade was unnecessary. At the same time the conference produced protest after protest against the "wrongs inflicted on unhappy Polynesians by Englishmen."[43] The 1873 debate on Fiji revealed a similar interplay of arguments.

Although Gladstone had opposed McArthur's motion in favour of British intervention in Fiji, he was constrained, nevertheless, to admit the possibility of need for some change in British policy. In the course of his speech he declared that an enquiry on the spot was necessary and on August 15, 1874, E. L. Layard, who was to proceed to Fiji as the new British Consul, and Commodore Goodenough, senior naval officer on the Australian station, were appointed as commissioners to report on "various questions connected with the Fiji Islands."[44]

The main task assigned to the Commissioners was to report on four suggested alternatives in British policy towards Fiji. These alternatives were:

"(1) To invest the British Consul with magisterial power over British subjects settled in the Islands.

(2) To recognise the Government, which now exists in the Islands, and which has already been dealt with as a *de facto* Government.

(3) To establish a British Protectorate over the Islands.

(4) The assumption by Her Majesty of a territorial Sovereignty over

[42] See *Parlty. Debates*, CCXII, 217.
[43] *Discussions on Colonial Questions*, Conference at Westminster Hotel, July, 1871; London, 1872.
[44] C. 983, 1874.

the Islands, and, as a necessary sequence, the constitution within them of some form of Colonial Government."[45]

Why a Commission of enquiry was necessary to determine which of these alternatives should govern British policy for the future, Gladstone did not explain. On the evidence of reports from Robinson, Thurston, March, Chapman and Stirling, the collapse of administration in Fiji and the risk of serious disorder and injury to British interests there were established beyond a doubt. The Colonial Office had received long and detailed reports of the activities of the Government of Fiji right from the time of its inception and could have been in no doubt as to the friction which had developed between the majority of white settlers and the Government, nor as to the impossibility of establishing efficient government under a Fijian constitution.

The evidence of Sir Hercules Robinson, the Governor of New South Wales and a most highly trusted servant of the Crown, should have been regarded as conclusive on these points. In January, 1873, Robinson had passed on to the Colonial Office Thurston's recommendation that "a British ship of war should, for a time be stationed at Fiji so as to deter British subjects from open acts of violence."[46] In transmitting this recommendation, Robinson expressly stated that he saw no reason to doubt Thurston's assessment of the situation within Fiji. He went on to declare that the existing constitution of Fiji was unsuitable to conditions in the group, adding that it was hopeless to expect any government established on such principles "to protect from oppression and spoliation the native population of the country."

This was the official opinion, unequivocally stated, of the highest British representative in the South Pacific. It was fully corroborated by the evidence of Stirling, Chapman, March and Thurston. Where, then, was the need for a commission of enquiry into such alternatives as those that were submitted to Goodenough and Layard as the proper objects of their investigation?

Again, if it were desired to obtain an independent and authoritative summing up of the situation, why were Goodenough and Layard chosen for the task? Goodenough, a commodore in the navy, was a gunnery expert of good family and connections. He had had wide naval experience and won a reputation for conspicuous gallantry. But the only apparent reason for his selection to report on Fiji was that he was the senior naval officer in the South

[45] ibid.
[46] Robinson to Kimberley, Jan. 27, 1873; repr. in Henderson, op. cit., pp. 58 ff.

Pacific.[47] His conduct of the investigation in Fiji was painstaking but revealed a lack of that political astuteness, which was pre-eminently required in any independent investigator.[48] Despite his undoubted ability and his distinguished naval record, his qualifications as a commissioner to report on conditions in Fiji cannot be rated highly. Layard was the new British Consul to Fiji and a marine biologist of some distinction.[49] How it could have been thought that either he or Goodenough, or even the two of them in conjunction, could have much to add to existing knowledge of Fiji is not easily explained. They were selected, it would seem, merely because they were the men on the spot and neither in fact possessed the special qualifications and experience necessary to form the basis of a new investigation into British policy towards Fiji. The only expert assistance they received while in Fiji was that of T. Horton and C. L. Sahl, who prepared a useful analysis of the financial position of the Fijian Government and drew attention to many abuses.

Doubts as to whether the commission of enquiry were anything more than a means of staving off an unwelcome issue, on which the Government was in danger of embarrassment in the House, are reinforced by the nature of the detailed instructions issued to Goodenough and Layard. The tenor of these instructions was completely in accordance with the issues debated in Parliament on June 13, 1873. The main substance of the debate had been whether the absence of effective government in Fiji (a circumstance itself partly attributable to the entry of British capital and British settlers and to the interference of British Consuls and naval officers) created such a peril for British subjects and British trade and so encouraged the labour traffic as to outweigh the obvious objections to incurring expense and trouble by adding to an Empire already regarded as too large. The practical issue had been simply whether the Fijian Government should continue to be recognised or whether Great Britain should annex.

The instructions issued to Goodenough and Layard were brought into line with the debate by the expression of opinion in the instructions against two of the alternatives on which the Commissioners were supposed to report. The extension of consular powers recommended by March in his memorandum of May 7, 1873, was explicitly ruled out by the instructions on the ground that it was

[47] Cf. *D.N.B.*, Vol. 22.
[48] Note, for example, the tone of his letter to Thurston on Jan. 10, 1874. (Repr. in Henderson, op. cit., p. 78.)
[49] Cf. Derrick, op. cit., I, p. 238.

unsuitable to legal conditions in Fiji and likely to prove difficult in administration.[50] Any suggestion of a protectorate was also ruled out[51] on the ground that it would impose undefined responsibilities on Great Britain and probably necessitate greater intervention because "many things would be done or tolerated by the local authorities which this country could not as a protecting Power pass over in silence without discredit."[52]

The two remaining alternatives, after extended consular jurisdiction and the establishment of a protectorate had both been rejected, were recognition *de lege* of the Fijian Government and the erection of Fiji into Crown Colony. These were the alternatives which had been discussed in the June debate and they were discussed in the instructions in such a way as to reveal the Government's realisation that the main concern of the advocates of annexation was the protection of British settlers, British investment and British trade. The Commissioners were to ascertain:

(1) To what extent the existing Government was acknowledged throughout the group by whites and natives.

(2) Whether recent resistance to the Government had been founded on doubts as to its proper constitution or objections to its principal members.

(3) Whether any Fijian Government locally constituted had a reasonable chance of success.

(4) What securities the Fijian Government, if recognised by Great Britain, would give for the suppression of slavery and kidnapping.

(5) Whether the Fijian Government would guarantee to British subjects most-favoured nation treatment in Fijian trade and commerce.

Whether the British Government really considered it possible that answers favourable to the recognition *de jure* of the Fijian Government could be made to these questions is unknown. The whole tenor of previous advices from Fiji certainly excluded the possibility. The inclusion of this list of queries in the official instructions was, however, without doubt politically necessary in view of Gladstone's assertion that the Government would have to enquire further into the Fijian situation before committing itself to action.

The instructions issued to Goodenough and Layard were merely to report on the questions and alternatives recommended to them. They were not authorised to do more. So far as their instructions

[50] See Ch. XVII, above, on extra-consular jurisdiction.
[51] C. 983, 1874; p. 6.
[52] *Parlty. Debates*, CCXVI, 934-959.

went, they were merely a fact-finding mission charged to report on local conditions as they affected British policy towards Fiji.

On arrival in Fiji in December, 1873, Goodenough found that Thakombau and Thurston had considerably abated their anxiety for a British annexation. After the dissolution of the Legislative Assembly in June, the Ministry had felt less embarrassed than previously, while the work of Captain Chapman and Commodore Stirling seemed to prove that the Royal Navy could be relied upon to check the worst extremities of seditious action amongst the resident whites. Indeed, for some months before the arrival of Goodenough and Layard the officers of the Royal Navy had been responsible in the last analysis for maintaining basic law and order in Fiji.[53]

Thakombau and Thurston showed a marked disposition to permit this state of affairs to continue. They apparently hoped that the new constitution promulgated in October, 1873, would prove workable. On his arrival Goodenough was informed by Thakombau and Thurston that there had been and there was no intention of asking for annexation. Thurston's cable of January 31, 1873, it was pointed out, had merely asked whether an offer of cession, if made officially, would be considered. No such offer had been made by the Fijian Government nor was one in contemplation.[54] Thakombau and Thurston were, no doubt, the more strongly entrenched in this attitude because Goodenough had gone out of his way to denounce the new constitution and to threaten British subjects in the Fijian forces with trial in Sydney, if they shed blood in its defence. Apart from doubts as to the legality of the new constitution, the existence in it of an immutable clause prohibiting the cession of Fiji would have rendered it obnoxious to Goodenough.

The attitude of Thakombau and Thurston took Goodenough and later Layard by surprise. If the Fijian Government were determined not to cede Fiji, then, from the standpoint of its avowed purpose, their mission was obviously useless as no alternatives would remain for British policy. The Colonial Office itself having excluded every possibility but British recognition of the Fijian Government and British annexation of Fiji, a Fijian decision not to cede to Great Britain would mean that only the former alternative would remain. At most the mission could merely report

---

[53] Goodenough to Admiralty, Nov. 27, 1873, qu. in C.O., *Confid. Memorandum on Fiji*, May 12, 1874. Also Goodenough to Thurston, Jan. 10, 1874; repr. in Henderson, op. cit., p. 78. Cf. Brookes, op. cit., p. 287.

[54] Derrick, op. cit., I, 238 ff.

whether the existing recognition *de facto* should be extended to recognition *de jure*.

Confronted with this position, the Commissioners determined to recommend to the chiefs the cession of the group to Great Britain. Accordingly an open letter was sent to Thakombau and the chiefs of Fiji in January, 1874, asking them whether they wished Great Britain to annex and suggesting to them that British rule would be for the general benefit.[55] Acting as if they themselves had authority to negotiate for a cession, Goodenough and Layard informed the chiefs that:

> "It is no new thing for England to govern islands like Fiji. She owns and governs—in several parts of the world—a great number of similar islands to Fiji, and it will be very easy for her to govern Fiji also, and preserve its peace, and promote the welfare and prosperity of its people."

The chiefs were exhorted to remember that the continued influx of whites would make it more and more difficult for a native government to rule in Fiji.

This frank advocacy of an offer of cession was quite beyond the scope of the instructions issued to the Commissioners, who had been sent out merely on a mission of enquiry. There was no obligation whatsoever imposed on Goodenough and Layard by their instructions to keep the way open for cession. So soon as they wrote to Thakombau and the chiefs advising a course of action, they exceeded their official functions.

There is no conclusive answer to the question, why Goodenough and Layard should have acted in the way they did. But considerable stress should be laid, first, on the opinion formed by Goodenough almost immediately on his arrival—that the Government of Fiji depended on the Royal Navy to maintain order amongst its British residents and, second, on the shocking financial position which was revealed by the investigations of Horton and Sahl. In November, 1873, Goodenough had explained to the Admiralty the conditions under which government was functioning in Fiji:

> "A constitution enacted by consent of white delegates with the authority of Thakombau has been suspended through the instrumentality of white men acting under it as Ministers, and the taxes imposed by an Assembly elected under the Constitution up to last September have been exacted since that date by the aid of British naval forces

[55] Government of Fiji, *Official Correspondence,* Letter from Commodore Goodenough, R.N., and Mr Consul Layard to the King and Chiefs of Fiji; Jan. 12, 1874.

on this station, and could have been collected in no other way short of the employment of Fijian soldiers, armed and commanded by Englishmen, against the majority of white settlers of whom five-sixths are also Englishmen."[56]

The sorry story of maladministration in Fijian finances was fully revealed in the Horton and Sahl report of March 16th, 1874.[57] Unauthorised payments, corruption and an enormous rise in the national debt were the outstanding revelations. Of the whole debt of £87,000 only £1,127 had been spent on reproductive works. Current expenditure was nearly three times as great as current revenue.

In light of what they themselves had observed concerning the political situation of Fiji and in light of what had been reported to them concerning the wretched financial situation of the Fijian Government, it is readily comprehensible that Goodenough and Layard felt justified in acting in the way they did by the necessity of protecting British interests in the group and safeguarding the Fijian Government's Australian and British debenture-holders.

Finally, it is certain that Goodenough, at least, personally held the opinion that Great Britain had already intervened so much in Fijian affairs that she was morally bound to insist on annexation. In a private letter written about the time of his mission to Fiji[58] Goodenough used these words:

"I cannot but look upon annexation as a positive duty, putting aside the great advantage of having Fiji as a central station in Polynesia, in which respect the situation is the very best which can be found. It seems to me to be a duty in several ways. In old times we constantly lectured the chiefs about good government, we have interfered right and left with their affairs, and we have thus caused them to look to us for support with some confidence and to distrust themselves.

"Then our settlers have come, and, on the presumption that they were all great people enjoying the help of the British Consul, they were received, and land was given them on terms which they would not have got, if the natives had not trusted us. . . .

"The state of things is a good deal owing to our neglect also. There is no doubt in my mind that had magisterial powers been given to a Consul as recommended by Colonel Smythe, much of the trouble and annoyance of the last few years would have been avoided,

[56] Goodenough to Admiralty, Nov. 27, 1873; C.O., *Confidential Memorandum on Fiji*, May 12, 1874.
[57] Appendix 6 in C. 1011, 1874.
[58] So described by Goodenough's widow, V. H. Goodenough, in *Journal of Commodore Goodenough, &c.*; London, 1876.

and the Consul would have enjoyed the respect due to him. . . .
Now it is altogether too late, and annexation is imperative."[59]

This statement of Goodenough's personal views explains why he
felt that the Fijian Government should be induced to offer a cession.
It also throws a revealing light on the degree to which previously
the British Government had simply ignored information concerning
the situation in Fiji. The conditions which led Goodenough and
Layard to exceed their instructions were in general no worse than
those which Thurston, March, Stirling, Robinson and the Government of New South Wales had been reporting to Great Britain
since 1871, and which in fact had already led Great Britain to
qualify her *de facto* recognition of the Woods Government.

In the circumstances it argued an indifference to the whole
problem of government in Fiji to send out a commission of enquiry
into conditions which had already been sufficiently reported to the
British Government and in respect of which recommendations had
already been made. What was obviously required—and this is
proved by the record of the Goodenough and Layard mission—was
not a commission of enquiry but a commission endowed with
powers to negotiate with the Fijian Government either for cession
or some other arrangement to protect and control British interests
in the group. Such a course of action, however, was not within
the realms of possibility under the Liberal Gladstone Government.

After the exercise of persistent pressure, Goodenough and Layard
wrung from Thakombau and the chiefs of Fiji an offer of cession
on March 21, 1874.[60] The offer contained numerous conditions,
some of a highly particular character.[61] Its legal extent was not
well defined, but it was expressed to extend to the sovereignty of
the group (Article 2) and to the government of Fiji.[62] Elaborate
provision was made as to the position and remuneration of Thakombau and the chiefs and the existing land system of Fiji was
carefully preserved.

The Goodenough and Layard Report[63] recommended acceptance
of this offer of cession. The Report itself was so strongly biassed
in favour of annexation that it over-simplified its account of
conditions in Fiji in order to build up a case for British intervention. Having stated quite correctly that, "there is no reasonable ·

[59] ibid.
[60] Thakombau to Goodenough and Layard; Appendix 1 in C. 1011, 1874.
[61] Encl. in Thurston to Goodenough and Layard, Apr. 11, 1874; Appendix No. 2,
ibid.
[62] Thakombau to Goodenough and Layard, cit. sup.
[63] Apr. 13, 1874; C. 1011, 1874.

255

prospect that a native government can continue to preserve order," the Report went on to assert that the chiefs were willing for British annexation and that the settlers and traders were anxious that Fiji should be erected into a Crown Colony. This statement completely overlooked the hesitation of the chiefs before making the offer of cession and completely disregarded the fact that the Government of Fiji was not without support amongst the white residents, some of whom openly opposed British annexation on the ground that it would mean the end of the labour trade.[64]

The case for an extension of consular jurisdiction was surveyed in the report at some length, although the Colonial Office had indicated that this alternative was not acceptable:

"If Her Majesty's Government do not finally determine to annex these islands, the only course to be pursued is, in our opinion, to give to Her Majesty's Consul the large discretionary powers and assistance . . . with which he would have no difficulty in controlling the employment of Polynesian labourers, as Her Majesty's Consul is now endeavouring, but without magisterial powers, to do."

The best grounds for hope of a successful outcome from an extension of consular powers lay in the general readiness of British settlers to submit to the consul's jurisdiction.

That they regarded extra-consular jurisdiction as only an inferior alternative to annexation was made clear in the Commissioners' report. Their main conclusion was in these terms:

"We beg to assure your Lordship that we can see no prospect for these islands, should Her Majesty's Government decline to accept the offer of cession, but ruin to English planters and confusion in the native Government.

"As a Crown Colony, we think that Fiji would certainly become a prosperous settlement."

Specific recommendations were made in the Report as to the retention of the chiefly system of Fiji and the Fijian social system, the presumption being in each case that Great Britain would in fact annex.

It was suggested (no doubt with reference to the query raised in the instructions whether British annexation of Fiji might not shift the labour trade to the unannexed islands) that the British Governor of Fiji should have authority over British subjects in the New Hebrides and the Solomons and islands not under French control south of the equator and west of 168° W. This would

[64] *Fiji Times*, Dec., 1873.

enable British subjects in these islands to have recourse to the courts of Fiji and to engage in the labour trade in a regular way through licences taken out in respect of vessels registered in Fiji. It apparently escaped the notice of the Commissioners that the granting of such jurisdiction to the Governor of Fiji would raise complicated legal problems and might also be resented by other Powers. "Authority over the persons and acts of British subjects" in the islands concerned clearly implied more than a mere power to try in Fiji British subjects charged with offences committed in the islands. What Goodenough and Layard contemplated was that Great Britain should exercise her own jurisdiction in the islands.[65]

Speaking in the House of Commons on August 8, 1874, Gladstone declared that the Goodenough and Layard Report was a chaotic document and that McArthur's proposals for a British Fiji flowed from a deluded philanthropy.[66] New native wars and increased government expenditure on a group which was really of no concern to the British Government would follow any act of annexation, Gladstone declared. But Gladstone was no longer Prime Minister. Having dissolved Parliament before the effluxion of time, the Liberal Government had suffered a heavy reverse at the polls and been replaced by a Conservative Ministry under Disraeli. Control of the Foreign Office had passed to Lord Derby, while the Colonial Office had come into the hands of the Earl of Carnarvon. The Conservatives, who had a majority of more than fifty in the House of Commons, had strongly attacked the foreign and imperial policy of the Liberal Government. Instead of looking askance at the pro-annexation tenor of the Goodenough and Layard Report, the Conservative Government received it with some favour.

The policy of the new Government towards Fiji was announced by Carnarvon in the House of Lords on July 17, 1874.[67] Carnarvon adopted the principles of the Goodenough and Layard Report in rejecting all the alternatives in British policy save straight-out annexation. Fiji, he said, was a fertile region, strategically situated, with good harbours and vital for Pacific commerce and the control of the labour traffic. From the humanitarian point of view there was a duty imposed on the British Government "of protecting a region invaded by English capital and by English lawlessness." Her Majesty's Government favoured acceptance of an offer of

[65] A similar principle was adopted in the establishment of the Western Pacific High Commission in 1875-77; see below, Chapter XXIII.
[66] *Parlty. Debates*, CCXXI, 1282-1292.
[67] ibid, cols. 179-196.

cession from Fiji, but the offer must be made unconditionally. The cession of March 21, which was clogged with many restrictions and conditions, was not acceptable to the British Government.

Two days before making this speech Carnarvon had informed Sir Hercules Robinson, the Governor of New South Wales, that the March offer could not be accepted. Robinson was advised that Her Majesty's Government would recommend acceptance of the offer of cession provided that it were made in accordance with the principles of Para. 52 of the Goodenough and Layard Report, "that the Chiefs, withdrawing all conditions, would trust to the generosity and justice of Her Majesty."[68]

Robinson was instructed to proceed to Fiji so soon as public business would permit in order to negotiate an unconditional cession and to establish a provisional government. A deed of cession was signed on October 10, 1874, by Robinson, Thakombau and the chiefs.[69] This transferred the sovereignty of the whole Fijian Group to Great Britain, with reservations only as to the rights and interests of Thakombau as Tui Viti and of the other high chiefs and the proper adjustment of financial liabilities and land claims.

New South Wales laws were adopted in Fiji until British administration could be established.[70] The Queensland Polynesian Labourers Act, 31 Vict., No. 47, was adopted also.[71] Fiji was made a Crown Colony by Charter dated January 2, 1875, passed under the Great Seal of the United Kingdom for erecting the group into a separate colony and for providing a system of government.[72]

The real points at issue for British policy in relation to the annexation of Fiji had been debated in the House of Commons on August 4th.[73] McArthur had then moved that the House was gratified to learn that the Government had yielded to the "unanimous" request of the inhabitants of Fiji so far as to direct Sir Hercules Robinson to proceed to the group with a view to procuring a cession.

The debate itself showed clearly that the decision to annex was based, not so much on new developments in Fiji, as on a changed policy towards colonial problems. Throughout the debate only one of the facts on which McArthur and the annexationists relied was

[68] Cmd. 1114, 1875; No. 1.
[69] Repr. in Henderson, op. cit., pp. 88-9.
[70] *Corr. with Robinson*, 1875; Encl. 3 in No. 5.
[71] ibid, Encl. 4 in No. 1.
[72] Copy in the Public Library, Sydney, in the *Statutory Rules and Orders Revised to December 31, 1903*.
[73] *Parlty Debates*, CCXXI, 1264-1301.

seriously disputed: the question being whether or not the offer of cession transmitted by Goodenough and Layard really reflected the wishes of the chiefs of Fiji. McArthur held that the March offer had been made voluntarily and was entitled to acceptance at its face value.[74] But Gladstone held that there had been no unanimous request[75] and Sir Francis Goldsmid pointed out that the whole question of the validity of the offer really depended on the degree to which the chiefs were competent to bind the other natives.[76]

As the Government had no intention of accepting the offer, the question of its validity was not fundamental. Nor was it treated as such. The real question was, whether or not, on a certain set of facts (not themselves seriously disputed) annexation were justified.

The annexationists pointed out that the welfare and prosperity of British subjects in Fiji depended on the prompt erection of an effective British Government in Fiji. To refuse to establish such a Government would be to shirk clear responsibilities since British policy towards Fiji had long since ceased to be neutral. Great Britain had interfered in Fijian affairs over and over again, especially through the activities of the Royal Navy. British policy, indeed, had done much to produce the problem of government in Fiji and Great Britain could not reasonably decline to intervene there. Moreover, the problem of the labour trade, it was argued, demanded effective British intervention on humanitarian grounds.

The annexationist case, based on the necessity of protecting British interests, of controlling the labour trade and of accepting responsibility for a situation which British policy had done so much to produce was considered by many speakers to be too weak to justify the expense and difficulty of establishing British Government in Fiji. Gladstone frankly declared that the prospective ruin of British planters in Fiji was no ground for annexation. With Sir Charles Dilke he held, that to intervene in Fiji in order to put down the labour traffic was absurd, because Goodenough and Layard themselves had had to recommend that the "undefined serfdom" of thousands of Fijians should be maintained. This serfdom, Gladstone held, was a form of domestic slavery to which Great Britain could not be a party. Both Gladstone and Dilke considered that a long series of wars with the natives would follow the annexation of Fiji just as they had followed the annexation of New Zealand. They referred also to the bad financial position of the Fijian Government, for whose debts, including the debt to the

[74] ibid, cols. 1264-1272.
[75] cols. 1282-1292.
[76] cols. 1279-1282.

United States, Great Britain would have to become responsible.

None of these facts was seriously disputed. It was simply a question of relating policy to them; and each side to the debate decided the question in terms of general principles, rather than of particular questions relating to Fiji.

In the last analysis the decision to annex Fiji must be interpreted partly in terms of a change in the fundamentals of British colonial policy. With the entry into power of the Conservative Government a new era in colonial policy became possible. The accession to power of the Disraeli Government in 1874 cleared the way for a period of right-wing ascendancy in colonial matters and for the further expansion of the Empire. The new policy did not mean, however, that minimum intervention had ceased to be the main characteristic of the British attitude towards the South Pacific.

Fiji was regarded by the Disraeli Government as a special case. The decision to annex the group was dictated by conditions which had at that time no parallel in other islands of the South Pacific. In no other case were conditions in the islands able to induce the Conservative Government to annex. The general tenor of British policy in the South Pacific remained one of minimum intervention, although it was clear that the Conservative Government would intervene to the fullest possible extent where a case of necessity or advantage arose.

CHAPTER XXIII

THE WESTERN PACIFIC HIGH COMMISSION

In the 'seventies the only island group in which British interests not only predominated over those of all other Powers, but were themselves considerable, was Fiji. There was little inducement to expand the Empire by adding to it other islands of the distant South Pacific. Colonial attention was concentrated instead on Asia and Africa. So far as governing responsibilities were concerned, the Conservative Ministry of Disraeli was well content to follow the policies of its predecessors and to adhere to minimum intervention as the main principle of British policy in the South Pacific.

The only problem that urgently demanded a more extensive treatment was that of the labour trade. One of the avowed reasons for the British annexation of Fiji had been the hope of putting down the "nefarious traffic in human flesh" which that group supported. But even in the instructions issued to Goodenough and Layard, the fear had been expressed that the establishment of British rule in Fiji would merely drive the labour traffic into the surrounding, unannexed groups. Goodenough and Layard had recommended that:

> ". . . the Commission of the Governor of Fiji should give him authority over the persons and acts of British subjects in the New Hebrides and the Solomon Islands, or the islands of the Pacific south of the equator and west of 168 degrees West (except New Caledonia and the Loyalty Islands, which are under the French flag)."[1]

The difficulties anticipated in the instructions to the Commissioners and for which their report had endeavoured to provide a remedy rapidly became apparent in practice.[2] The British Government was soon compelled to seek means of tightening up its control of the labour traffic.

In 1873 Great Britain had endeavoured to negotiate with the United States of America for an extension of the Slave Trade Treaty of 1862 to Pacific waters. The negotiations had broken

[1] C. 1011, 1874.
[2] Cf. *Parlty. Debates*, CCXXII, 1388 and 1857 ff.

down because of the British refusal to outlaw the traffic in Chinese coolies.[3] When the question was raised again in May, 1874, it was held over until the problem of Fiji had been settled.

At the time at which Fiji was annexed British efforts to control the labour trade were limited to the Queensland Act of 1868 and the Kidnapping Act of 1872 as enforced by the Royal Navy, the Government of Queensland and the Courts of the Australian Colonies. The Acts of 1817, 1823 and 1828 and the slave trade Acts were of little practical usefulness. The inadequacy of the existing law as an attempt to regulate the inter-insular traffic had been established within a few months of the commencement of the 1872 Act.[4]

After the annexation of Fiji had given Great Britain a territorial interest in what was geographically the central and economically the most important group in the South Pacific, the case for further measures to regulate the labour traffic became overwhelming. Even the cause of law and order within Fiji itself demanded effective control over the labour trade in all its aspects. Public opinion in Great Britain also favoured a tightening up of the whole system of control. The annexation of Fiji had been hailed by missionary interests as a step in the right direction and further action had been recommended.[5]

The obvious step for remedial British legislation to take was the establishment of British law capable of effective application to the labour trade in the islands from which the inter-insular traffic was conducted. The difficulties in the way of taking this step were, however, very considerable. A mere change in the law without a radical change in general policy would have been futile. The existing Acts of Parliament had been proved to be practically useless.[6] The basic need was obviously for an improved machinery of justice, for readier means of bringing offenders to trial, for surer means of detecting wrongful acts. Above all else, it was necessary that British law should follow British subjects into the unannexed islands where native rulers still retained their sovereignty.

To establish adequate machinery throughout the extensive island groups, many of them still little known, and separated in some cases by thousands of miles of ocean, was obviously a matter of the greatest difficulty. But the challenge to the British Government

[3] Brookes, op. cit., p. 385.

[4] See above, Ch. XXI.

[5] See the interesting excerpt from the *Methodist Recorder* published in the *Fiji Times*, Oct. 11, 1873. Also Encl. 1 in No. 3, *Corr. with Robinson, 1875*.

[6] See Chapters VI, XVII and XXI, above.

to prevent British subjects from perpetrating outrages in islands adjoining Fiji and the Australasian colonies was too clear and too powerful to permit any difficulty to stand in the way of further efforts at control.

In March, 1875, the Earl of Carnarvon introduced the Pacific Islanders Protection Bill,[7] a measure which all political parties appear to have taken for granted.[8] In its original form the Bill was of severely restricted character. As Carnarvon himself stated in moving the second reading,[9] the object was merely to extend and amend the Kidnapping Act of 1872, the principles of which the Government had no desire to change. Fiji, which had been annexed five months earlier, was to be regarded as one of the "Australian colonies" for the purposes of the 1872 Act so as to give its courts jurisdiction over labour trade offences. The natives of Fiji would have the benefit of both the 1872 Act and of the new Bill; liberty was reserved to the Fijian legislature, however, to enact Fiji out of this provision. The Bill also extended the Kidnapping Act to fisheries by stipulating that licences should be obtained for the use of Polynesians as seamen on fishing vessels. Power was given in the Bill to condemn cargoes as well as ships in cases of offences against the Act and powers similar to those exercised by the Supreme Courts of the Australian States were given to the High Court of Admiralty and the Vice-Admiralty Courts for the trial and condemnation of vessels detained under the Act.

Carnarvon admitted that even these amendments would not solve the whole problem. Alluding to the practice of changing flags in order to evade British jurisdiction, he declared that only by agreement amongst the European Powers could a measure for the control of the labour traffic be made effective.

The prospective effectiveness of the Bill was much less than Carnarvon admitted. Nothing had been done to improve the control over the inter-insular labour traffic apart from the new powers vested in the courts of Fiji. The recommendations in the Goodenough and Layard Report for the establishment of some official control over British subjects in the unannexed islands had been completely disregarded. In fact, the Bill constituted only a slight advance beyond the provisions of the Kidnapping Act, which both Carnarvon and Kimberley, with obvious indifference to

[7] *Parlty. Debates*, CCXXII, 1388.

[8] Kimberley, the Sec. of State for Colonies in the previous administration, spoke in favour of the Bill. See *Parlty. Debates*, CCXXII, 1857.

[9] ibid, 1857-1860.

South Pacific problems as such, persisted in regarding as effective.

In March the Bill was treated as a non-contentious measure and received the full support of the Liberals.[10]   In May, however, Carnarvon introduced a vital new clause to the Bill, which revolutionised its main principles and completely transcended the bounds of the general policy followed in the 1872 Act.   On May 4th he moved in the House of Lords[11] for permission to insert a new Clause 5 in the Bill:

> ". . . to empower Her Majesty to exercise jurisdiction over British subjects in islands of the Pacific Ocean not within the jurisdiction of any civilized Power; by Order in Council to create and constitute the office of High Commissioner in and over such islands, with authority to make regulations for the government of British subjects therein; to erect a Court of Justice for British subjects with civil, criminal and Admiralty jurisdiction, corresponding with the authority of the High Commissioner; giving power to Her Majesty in Council to make ordinances for the government of British subjects being within those islands; and conferring on the High Commissioner certain powers."

Once again Kimberley gave his unstinted support, praising the amendment as likely to prevent the development in other islands of conditions similar to those which had led to the annexation of Fiji.[12]   Kimberley's remark at least had the merit of linking up the clause with the main trend of British policy in the South Pacific —the avoidance of political responsibility.   But neither he nor Carnarvon explained why the new clause was considered necessary in a Bill which both sides of the House had united in accepting only two months previously.

It would seem that the decision to extend the legislation beyond the scope of a mere amendment to the 1872 Act was taken partly because of the continued growth of the inter-insular labour trade, which had merely been driven out of Fiji by the British acquisition of that group, and partly because of the increasing activity in which the Royal Navy had had to engage in the islands.[13]   Fear that the activities of British subjects in the islands might proceed from producing disturbances with the natives to embarrassing British relations with the Great Powers, whose subjects were trading and settling in the islands, also strongly suggested that British law should follow British subjects wherever they went.

[10] Cf. *Parlty. Debates*, CCXXII, 1860.

[11] ibid, CCXXIV, 2-3.

[12] ibid, col. 3.

[13] Note Mr. Ashley's question in the House of Commons on Mar. 11, 1875; *Parlty. Debates*, CCXXII, 1605.

In its revised form the Bill became law on August 2 as the Pacific Islanders Protection Act, 1875.[11] The new Act not only tightened up the system introduced by the 1872 legislation. It also established judicial and administrative authority throughout the islands. Section 6 provided that:

> "It shall be lawful for Her Majesty to exercise power and jurisdiction over Her subjects within any islands or places in the Pacific Ocean, not being within Her Majesty's dominions, nor within the jurisdiction of any civilised power, in the same and as ample a manner as if such power or jurisdiction had been acquired by the cession or conquest of territory and by Order in Council to constitute the office of High Commissioner in, over and for such islands and places, or some of them, and by the same or any other Order in Council to confer upon such High Commissioner power and authority in Her name and on Her behalf, to make regulations for the government of Her subjects in such islands and places and to impose penalties, forfeitures or imprisonments for the breach of such regulations."

The section further provided that a Court of Justice with civil and criminal jurisdiction over Her Majesty's subjects in the islands under the High Commissioner might be created by Order in Council.

The main powers to be conferred on the High Commissioner for the Western Pacific were (i) exclusive control over British subjects throughout the High Commission area; (ii) the superintendence of the labour traffic; and (iii) control of intercourse between British subjects and the natives of the Western Pacific.[15] The High Commissioner and any Deputy Commissioners (under the direction of the High Commissioner) were given full consular powers in addition to powers to be conferred by Order in Council under the Act.

The innovations of the Act were considerable. The British Government was at last breaking through some of the most jealously guarded ramparts of the minimum intervention policy. British law was to follow British subjects wherever they went in the islands. Instead of a system of remote control over British subjects in the islands, institutions very like those of extra-territoriality were to be established.[16]

From a wider point of view it was the old policing policy, as implemented by men-of-war and consuls, which was to be replaced

[14] 38 and 39 Vict., c. 51.
[15] Cf. A. H. Gordon to Kimberley, Jul. 16, 1881; C. 3641, 1883.
[16] See next chapter.

by the new institutions of the High Commission. The attempts made by consuls and naval officers to institute law and order by semi-official and unofficial extension of their prescribed duties were to be replaced by the official institutions of British law, adopted as nearly as possible to conditions in the islands.

The circumstances which led to the decision to appoint a supreme official to control British subjects in the unannexed islands were those which the British Government had been doing its best to ignore for fully half a century. The progress of white settlement in the islands, the increasing ramifications of British trade, the rapid decay of native law and custom, and the entry into the South Pacific of the nationals of other Powers, who might come into conflict with British subjects, were the factors underlying the establishing of the new British legal system in the South Pacific.

The immediate cause for the creation of the High Commission was the need for controlling the labour trade, whose growth in the unannexed islands threatened the development there of conditions likely to demand extensive British intervention. The High Commission was established as an alternative to annexation.[17] Its creation was in full accordance with the traditions of previous British policies and was designed to preserve the conditions which made continued adherence to the basic concepts of minimum intervention possible.

[17] The speeches of Carnarvon and Kimberley in the House of Lords made clear their opinion that one of the main reasons for the establishment of the High Commission was the desire to prevent a recurrence of events like those in Fiji, which might lead to further demands for annexation. (*Parlty. Debates*, CCXXIV, 2-3.)

CHAPTER XXIV

TREATIES OF EXTRA-TERRITORIALITY

FROM a legal point of view the Pacific Islanders Protection Act, 1875, raised some interesting problems. Section 6 made it clear that the High Commissioner's powers were to be exercised only in islands not in the possession of Her Majesty, "nor within the jurisdiction of any civilised power." The authority thus conferred on the High Commissioner was plainly inconsistent with any British recognition of native sovereignty in the islands referred to in Section 6. Hence it followed that the Act could not be extended to any islands the sovereignty of whose rulers had been recognised by Great Britain.

Section 7 made it plain that, although Great Britain proposed to exercise some sovereign powers in the islands to which the Act was extended, no British sovereignty was claimed therein:

"Nothing herein or in any such Order in Council contained shall extend or be construed to extend to invest Her Majesty, her heirs or successors, with any claim or title whatsoever to dominion or sovereignty over any such islands or places as aforesaid, or to derogate from the rights of the tribes or people inhabiting such islands, or of the chiefs or Rulers thereof, to such sovereignty or dominion."

To recapitulate, the 1875 Act could apply only to territories whose sovereign independence Great Britain did not recognise. Further, just as in the cases of the earlier Acts, the 1875 Act stipulated that Great Britain herself claimed no sovereignty in the islands.

The Western Pacific Order in Council, which brought the Act into operation, was not issued until 1877. The details of the Order are discussed in the following chapter. What is relevant to note here is the list of island groups to which the Order was made to extend: the Friendly Islands, the Navigators, the Union, Phoenix Ellice, Gilbert, Marshall, Caroline, Solomon and Santa Cruz Islands, together with Rotuma, New Guinea (east of 143 degrees), New Britain, New Ireland, the Louisiade Archipelago and "all other islands in the Western Pacific Ocean not being within the limits of Fiji, Queensland or New South Wales and not being within the jurisdiction of any civilised Power."

Difficulties arose over the Friendly Islands (Tonga) and the Navigators (Samoa), because developments in each of them made it difficult to hold that they were not "civilised Powers." In the cases of the other islands there was no suggestion of native sovereignty ever having been recognised by the British Government, or of there being any other reason for regarding them as "civilised."[1]

Tonga in 1877 was a comparatively well-ordered community. It possessed its own courts of law, creditably conducted. In view of the signing of the German treaty with Tonga in 1876, Sir Arthur Gordon, the first High Commissioner of the Western Pacific, suggested that Great Britain also should enter into treaty relations with Tonga.[2] The general principle of his suggestion was agreed to in March, 1877, when Lord Derby suggested that "it would be prudent to take steps at once to obtain from the Tongan authorities a recognition of the right of Her Majesty to exercise exclusive jurisdiction, civil and criminal, over her own subjects in those islands."[3]

The Colonial Office, however, perceived the difficulty involved in these suggestions. If a treaty were signed with Tonga, could Tonga be regarded as an uncivilised state, to which the 1875 Act and the Order in Council might apply? As Tonga had just signed a treaty with Germany, was it reasonable to deny the sovereignty of Tonga any longer?[4] Gordon was invited to submit suggestions for an "arrangement," which, "while respecting the rights of the existing authorities, may avoid the danger to which . . . attention has been drawn."[5]

The problem in the case of Samoa was more complicated. "Practically, the islands of that group have no Government whatever," reported Gordon. "The so-called Courts are . . . a grotesque burlesque on the administration of justice, and the exclusive jurisdiction of the High Commissioner's Court in every case in which a British subject is concerned should be peremptorily insisted on, with or without the recognition of the Samoan chiefs."[6]

---

[1] Naval officers treated many native rulers as sovereigns. But their actions were inconclusive. See Ch. VII, above.

[2] See Herbert to Gordon, Oct. 3, 1878; *Further Corr. resp. the Navigators, Part III.*

[3] Derby (Mar. 24, 1877) qu. in Gordon to Hicks Beach, Oct. 28, 1878; ibid.

[4] C.O. to F.O., Dec. 20, 1878; ibid.

[5] Herbert to Gordon, Oct. 3, 1878; cit. sup. (n. 2).

[6] Gordon to Hicks Beach, Oct. 28, 1878; cit. sup. (n. 3).

Actually the British Government had already withdrawn its subjects from compulsive Samoan jurisdiction. The new British Consul, Liardet,[7] appointed in 1876, had been instructed not to permit British subjects to be made subject to the local jurisdiction without his express permission, save in certain cases of serious crimes and embroilment with the natives:

> "Mr. Liardet was also instructed to represent that, pending the issue of an Order in Council for bringing British subjects in Samoa under British jurisdiction, Her Majesty's Government could not allow British subjects to be amenable to the local jurisdiction without his consent as Consul; but at the same time there was no wish to shelter British subjects from just punishment for any crimes they might have committed, and from the consequences of their acts if they mix themselves up in native quarrels and commit crimes which would entail punishment in a civilised State."[8]

These instructions were issued before the 1875 Act had been brought into operation by the issue of the Order in Council. Samoa was one of the groups to which the Act extended and Liardet's instruction to withdraw British subjects from Samoan jurisdiction is to be construed as an attempt to fill the hiatus between the collapse of government in Samoa and the issuing of the Order in Council.

The decision to extend the principles of the Act to Samoa before it came into operation is to be attributed to the reports reaching Great Britain of the lamentable state of affairs in the group after the downfall of Steinberger and the deportation of the king. Power having passed into the hands of jealous chiefs, scheming whites and despotic consuls, it was obviously wise to withdraw British subjects in Samoa from the competing factions claiming political authority there.

The proposal to sign a treaty with some Samoan authority proceeded therefore, not as in the case of Tonga, from respect for a well-governed island community, in whose affairs it would be absurd to intervene, but from the multiplicity of foreigners in Samoa, the competing claims of the Powers there and the common desire of Great Britain, the United States and Germany to obtain special privileges internationally recognisable. Moreover, Great Britain had been petitioned to provide protection for Samoa,[9] by

---

[7] Liardet replaced the Acting Consul, S. F. Williams, who had taken a leading part in the overthrow of the Steinberger Government and whose removal had been recommended by Commodore Hoskins. (See Ch. XX, above.)

[8] F.O.: *Confidential Memorandum No. 3375, 1877;* page 8.

[9] ibid.

which was meant intervention to prevent further civil anarchy.[10]

Just as in the case of Tonga, the prospect of a treaty with Samoa raised problems as to whether the High Commissioner's jurisdiction could be extended to states enjoying treaty relations with Great Britain and other civilised powers. At the request of the Foreign Office the problems involved were submitted to expert legal opinion.

The legal position was a complicated one. Apparently there was no attempt to justify the exercise of High Commissioner's jurisdiction under the 1875 Act in states having treaty relations with Great Britain. Administrative and legal opinion agreed that that Act applied only to "uncivilised" communities. The question was whether the jurisdiction in Tonga and Samoa could be supported under the Foreign Jurisdiction Acts, 1843-1875, which were part of the legal basis of the 1877 Order in Council.

The Foreign Jurisdiction Acts had been passed to meet the needs of law and order amongst British subjects in backward territories. The rapid opening up of new territories in the nineteenth century had produced case after case in which British subjects had penetrated into regions whose laws and customs were such that their application to British subjects could not be regarded in Great Britain as satisfactory from any point of view. The Foreign Jurisdiction Act, 1843 (6 and 7 Vict., c. 94), had provided that Her Majesty might by Order in Council exercise jurisdiction in foreign countries where jurisdiction had been obtained by treaty, capitulation, grant, usage or sufferance. Such jurisdiction might be exercised in the same and as ample a manner as if it had been acquired by conquest or cession of territory.[11]

The attention of the legal advisers was specially drawn to the Foreign Jurisdiction Acts as providing a possible basis for jurisdiction in Samoa and Tonga. It is not clear either how far they examined or rejected this suggestion. All that their opinion states is that a new Order in Council would be necessary to permit the exercise of High Commission jurisdiction in Tonga and Samoa, if the proposed treaties were signed. Apparently the law advisers held either that the 1877 Order in Council could not apply to some islands by virtue of the 1875 Act and to other islands by virtue of the Foreign Jurisdiction Acts, or that, as there had been no treaty, capitulation or similar arrangement in the cases of Tonga and Samoa, the Foreign Jurisdiction Acts, 1843-1875, were inapplicable.

[10] Gordon to F.O., Apr. 25, 1877; *Corr. resp. Affairs in the Navigators Islands, Part I.*

[11] The amending Acts of 28 & 29 Vict., c. 116, (1865) and 38 & 39 Vict., c. 85, (1875) are irrelevant.

The second interpretation is probably correct. It is supported by the enactment in 1878 of a Foreign Jurisdiction Amendment Act (41 and 42 Vict., c. 67) extending the Acts to countries having no regular government from which jurisdiction might be obtained by the methods referred to in the Act of 1843. The 1878 Act clearly extended the Foreign Jurisdiction Acts to cases like those of Samoa, where there was no government recognised by Great Britain in 1876-77, and of the great majority of the islands in the High Commission area. Tonga, having a government from which jurisdiction might be obtained by the methods of the earlier Acts, remained unaffected by the amending Act of 1878.

The position after 1878 was, therefore, that High Commission jurisdiction could be supported in all the islands of the High Commission area under the combined effects of the Act of 1875 and the Foreign Jurisdiction Acts.[12] No treaties were legally necessary save in the case of Tonga, and, after the United States-Samoan Treaty of 1877-78, in the case of Samoa also.

In Samoa, where the British treaty followed closely on similar treaties concluded by the United States of America and Germany, Sir Arthur Gordon proceeded to negotiate with the dominant Malietoa party.[13] His negotiations were aided by the German and American Consuls, a British-Samoan Treaty being concluded on August 28, 1879. The treaty granted British subjects wide extra-territorial rights in Samoa, so as to permit the exercise of High Commissioner's jurisdiction there. Provision was also made for the peaceful pursuit of trade, the settlement of land disputes and the right of Great Britain to establish a naval station and coaling depot on any Samoan harbour, excepting Apia, Saluafatu and Pago Pago where Germany and the United States had prior rights. The

[12] A new Order in Council was issued on August 14, 1879, based on the Acts of 1872 and 1875, on the Foreign Jurisdiction Acts, 1843-1878, and on any other enabling powers. It increased the regulation-making power of the High Commissioner to include "the maintenance (as far as regards the conduct of British subjects) of friendly relations between British subjects and all kings, chiefs and other authorities in those islands, and persons subject to them." The High Commissioner also received extended judicial powers. Four Acts were extended to the High Commission area as though it were a colony, viz., the Fugitive Offenders Act, 1843, the Admiralty Offences Colonial Acts of 1849 and 1860, and the Merchant Shipping Act, 1867, s.11.

[13] The United States and German treaties had been signed with the opposing faction. Gordon's instructions were to negotiate with whichever faction was dominant when he arrived. See Salisbury to Gordon, July 4, 1879; *Further Corr. resp. the Navigators Islands, Part III.* As to requests from Samoa for British protection and the nature of the protection required, see above Ch. XX and Gordon to F.O., Apr. 25, 1877; *Corr. resp. the Navigators Islands, Part I.*

Samoan Government also promised Great Britain most favoured nation treatment.[14]

The treaty between Great Britain and Tonga was signed on November 29, 1879. It exchanged promises of most favoured nation treatment and made British subjects in Tonga subject to the High Commissioner's Court for offences under British law while remaining subject to Tongan courts in respect of Tongan law.[15]

[14] For treaty, see *Further Corr. resp. the Navigators Islands, Part III.* The treaty was comparable with those signed by the U.S.A. and Germany, except that Great Britain received more extra-territorial rights than did either of the other Powers and that, unlike the U.S.A., Great Britain offered no help to Samoa.

[15] C. 3400, 1882.

Chapter XXV

THE HIGH COMMISSION AT WORK

No Order in Council was issued under the 1875 Act until August, 1877. The only explanation of the delay is that both the Foreign Office and the Colonial Office needed time to consider the position created by the sudden change of policy made in the Act. During the intervening two years doubts arose as to the expediency of some of the legal and administrative changes contemplated in the Act.

The degree of control to be vested in the High Commissioner over the foreign relations of Great Britain in the South Pacific was considered to be too extensive for an official not under the control of the Foreign Office. Accordingly, when the Order in Council was issued, the High Commissioner was given control over only British subjects. The conduct of relations with native states and tribes was to be confided to the Consul-General for the Pacific, under the authority of the Foreign Office.[1] As in practice the offices of High Commissioner and Consul-General were vested in the same person (the Governor of Fiji), the change from the original plan was less important than might have seemed. It referred to the allocation of policy responsibility in Great Britain rather than to administrative changes in the South Pacific.[2]

A more extensive change than that relating to consular powers appeared in the alteration of the plans for control of the labour trade. Originally one of the main objectives in establishing the High Commission had been held to be the institution of effective control over the labour trade. But, almost immediately after the 1875 Act the powers of superintending the labour traffic granted to the High Commissioner were partly taken away by powers granted to the Governors of the Australian colonies.[3]

[1] Gordon to Kimberley, July 16, 1881; C. 3641, 1883.
[2] ibid and C. 3905, 1884; para. 168.
[3] Gordon to Kimberley, July 16, 1881; cit. sup. It is not clear what powers are referred to. Gordon's despatch is stated to have been written in great haste. The only relevant statutes appear to be the Foreign Jurisdiction Amendment Act, 1875 (38 & 39 Vict. c. 85), giving power to order deportation of British subjects from foreign territories where H.M. exercised jurisdiction to places where they might be tried, and the Territorial Waters Jurisdiction Act, 1878 (41 & 42 Vict., c. 73), giving all British Courts of Admiralty and Vice-Admiralty power to try offences committed by persons of any nationality in any ship within British territorial waters. Queensland passed a new and more extensive labour trade act in 1880 (44 Vict. No. 17).

The Order in Council issued on August 13, 1877,[4] and which came into force in 1878 was thus narrower in its conception than had been contemplated when the enabling Act was passed two years earlier. Not only were the powers conferred on the High Commissioner less extensive than those originally intended, but the Order used the powers in a highly technical way. Consisting of 321 articles, it devoted only six of them to the duties of the High Commissioner and his deputies. These six articles provided for the appointment of the High Commissioner (Article 7), for an official seal (Article 8), and for the appointment of Deputy Commissioners by the High Commissioner (Article 10), who were liable to suspension or removal by him (Article 11). The High Commissioner was authorised to make regulations for the government of British subjects in the Western Pacific (Article 24), to prohibit any British subject from living in any part of the Pacific (Article 25) and to remove him, if necessary, from any island on which he might be residing (Article 26). Of the remaining 315 Articles in the Order, most related to the powers and procedure of the High Commissioner's Court and of the Chief Judicial Commissioner.

As already noted, a further important Order in Council was issued in August, 1879.[5] This Order increased the judicial powers of the High Commissioner when away from his headquarters (so as to avoid the necessity of conveying accused and witnesses to Fiji). It also gave him an extended power of making regulations "for the government of British subjects in the Western Pacific Islands and for securing the maintenance (as far as regards the conduct of British subjects) of friendly relations between British subjects and all kings, chiefs and other authorities in those islands and persons subject to them." The High Commissioner's powers were further increased by the extension of certain Acts to the High Commission area as though it were a British colony.[6]

Whatever the merits of the two Orders in Council from the standpoint of the functioning of the High Commissioner's Court, and the avoidance of legal complications in the islands, it soon became obvious, after the Orders were brought into operation, that the general legal system set up under the Act and Orders had important deficiencies. The position of the High Commissioner

[4] *Hertslet's Commercial Treaties*; Vol. XIV.
[5] See Chapter XXIV, above. For Order in Council see F.O.: *Further Corr. resp. the Navigators Islands, Part III* (Appendix).
[6] As to High Commission area, see Chapter XXIV above. The Acts referred to were the Fugitive Offenders Act, 1843; the Admiralty Offences Colonial Acts, 1849 and 1860; the Merchant Shipping Act, 1867, s. 11.

and his Court in relation to the Royal Navy was insufficiently defined; the legal powers vested in the High Commissioner were inadequate for the objects of his appointment; there were no sufficient means provided through which the High Commissioner might exercise authority in the far-flung islands of his jurisdiction; the division of authority in the control of the labour trade was fatal to efficient administration.

The most important of the administrative difficulties encountered by the High Commission was that of its relations with the Navy. In its widest aspects, this problem had to be considered as part of the main task of exercising High Commission authority throughout the widely scattered islands. The problem of relations between the High Commissioner and the Navy also included the problem of making High Commission justice as effective a deterrent against wrong-doing as "commodore justice" administered by men-of-war had proved to be.

Up to 1877 the Royal Navy had kept order in the islands in its own way:

"When a British subject was guilty of any serious crime, or became generally obnoxious, he was either taken to Australia for trial, or more often deported to some other islands, or to a neighbouring Colony. The powers, such as they were, exercised by British naval officers had a strong deterrent effect, and the traders were, as a rule, quite ready to bow to their decision in matters of dispute which came before them. In like manner when outrages were committed by the natives, the captain of the next ship visiting the place, after a careful investigation on the spot, dealt with the case as he thought fit."[7]

That naval officers frequently acted in excess of their legal powers is obvious.[8] But it is equally obvious that the rough justice they meted out had been preferable to the absence of any authority at all and that most British residents in the islands were fairly well satisfied with the judicial work of naval officers.

The 1875 Act and the 1877-79 Orders in Council, however, if fully applied, would have destroyed the whole of this more or less informal jurisdiction exercised by the Navy over British subjects. The justice administered by naval officers would have had to be suppressed in favour of a complicated legal system, depending in

[7] C. 3905, 1884; para. 60.
[8] For example, in relation to "Acts of War"; strictly, these were to be undertaken only when natives had first committed acts of war. But naval officers used their vague powers under the heading to justify the hanging of natives for murder, etc.

the last resort, however, on naval forces for its administration. The difficulty was apparently considered in Great Britain during 1875-77 without any clear principle being evolved to lay down the respective functions of the Navy and of the High Commissioner.[9]

The principal effect of the establishment of the Western Pacific High Commission, so far as the Navy was concerned, was to exclude British subjects from naval jurisdiction. After the issue of the 1877 Orders in Council British subjects could be reached only by legal process. The long distances over which the High Commissioner had to extend his authority and the precise legal forms which had to be complied with at every stage from the commencement of an enquiry to the launching of a prosecution, meant that High Commission justice was less effectively administered than the old "commodore justice" of the Navy had been. The High Commissioner was obstructed, not only by lack of means of communication with the islands under his control, but also by the inadequacy of the staff at his disposal. In 1884 it was reported that, although the High Commission area extended 3,500 miles from east to west and 2,500 miles from north to south, only two resident Deputy Commissioners had been appointed and these were in Tonga and Samoa, where the labour trade presented few problems to British administration.[10] On occasion naval officers had been given temporary commissions as Deputy Commissioners in order that they might represent the High Commissioner in a distant place. At the time of the 1878 gold discoveries in New Guinea, for example, the Australian Commodore despatched H.M.S. *Sappho* to Port Moresby, after obtaining for her commander from the High Commissioner (who was in Sydney) authority to act as a Deputy Commissioner.[11]

Even when the arm of the law could be made to reach offenders, it could only rarely hold them to account. Under island conditions the requirement that all proceedings in respect of offences had to be commenced within three months of the alleged offence secured immunity for many bad characters. "We have shown how much the great legal powers of the High Commissioner are rendered inoperative by the want of an executive to enforce its orders," concluded the Commission appointed in 1883 to enquire into the working of the Western Pacific Orders in Council. "Whilst it has extinguished the assumed jurisdiction of the Navy," the Report

[9] C. 3814, 1883; p. 6.

[10] C. 3905, 1884; p. 7.

[11] A.C.V. Melbourne: "Relations between Australia and New Guinea up to the establishment of British Rule in 1888"; *J.R.A.H.S.*, Vol. XII, p. 293.

continued, "its own powers, especially amongst the more remote islands, remain in abeyance from the impossibility of exercising them."[12]

The establishment of the Western Pacific High Commission had not only reduced effective control over British subjects in the islands. It had also affected adversely the informal jurisdiction exercised by the Navy over natives. The High Commission itself had no jurisdiction over natives. Although there was power in the High Commissioner and Consul-General to control British relations with natives, there was no power over individual natives. In practice, moreover, there was no power in the Consul-General or the High Commissioner to deal with native tribes which had been guilty of attacks on British subjects.

The difficulty which arose was that, while the High Commission itself had no power over natives, it did have power over naval officers, as British subjects, in their relations with the natives. The High Commissioner and his Court could restrain naval officers from performing any acts beyond their legal powers.[13] As most of the jurisdiction exercised by the naval officers over natives had been of doubtful legality, the establishment of the High Commission with a responsibility for preserving law and order, hindered the Navy in its work with the natives.

Two questions were involved. First, there was the problem of naval jurisdiction in cases where accusations were brought against individual natives. Could the Navy continue to punish the offenders, demand restitution of property and exact compensation for wrongs as it had done in the past? Second, there was the problem of acts of war such as the bombardment of villages in punishment of "outrages."

The High Commissioner claimed (as he was bound to claim) that he had the right and even the duty of restraining naval officers from exceeding their legal powers. Moreover, as Consul-General, it was for him to decide whether "acts of war" against offending native tribes were necessary. Both these points were pressed by the Chief Judicial Commissioner during his office as Acting High Commissioner in 1878-1879.[14]

The senior naval officer on the Australian station, however, pointed out that the High Commissioner would in any event have

[12] C. 3905, 1884; p. 10.
[13] ibid.
[14] See A. H. Gordon to Kimberley, July 16, 1881; cit. sup. Also Gordon's Memorandum, July 16, 1882; C. 3641, 1883.

M

to rely on·the Navy to carry out his decisions and contended that the punishment of outrages was a matter for the Navy alone.

The British Government ruled that the naval officers were exclusively responsible for the undertaking of acts of war against native tribes and for determining whether such acts were necessary. Where practicable, and where there would be no serious delay, the High Commissioner was to be consulted before action was taken.[15]

The effect of the decision to leave the naval officers in possession of the field was, of course, still further to restrict the powers of the High Commissioner. In the final apportionment of authority between the High Commission and the Navy it was established, not only that relations with the natives were in most cases to be the responsibility of the Navy but also that the High Commissioner had no authority to call on the Navy for support:

". . . the High Commissioner has no control whatever over the movements of the Australian Squadron, nor can he direct the course, or hasten or retard the sailing, of a single vessel."[16]

In view of these decisions it is surprising that relations between the Navy and the High Commission were so free from friction. Little help was received from Great Britain. Indeed, the 1884 Report stated that the instructions sent out to the Commodore touching his relations with the High Commissioner were invariably ambiguous and such as to throw on the naval officers concerned the sole responsibility for disciplinary action against natives. The Report itself, after pointing out that the Navy in practice could not confine itself to "acts of war," attributed the continued good relations of the High Commissioner and the Commodore to adventitious personal factors.[17]

The proviso that the High Commissioner was to be consulted wherever possible before action was taken against natives was fairly well observed. Usually, however, the High Commissioner was not in a position to prescribe the details of punishment. He merely indicated his approval of proposed action in general terms and was informed later of what punishment had been inflicted. The High Commissioner usually approved what had been done.[18]

The refusal to invest the High Commissioner with either independent means of visiting the islands so as to hold his own enquiries or with power to order the Navy to make a ship available

[15] Gordon to Kimberley, July 16, 1881; C. 3641, 1883.
[16] Gordon's Memorandum, Feb. 26, 1881; ibid.
[17] C. 3905, 1884; p. 10.
[18] C. 3641, 1883; No. 29

me.int that, despite the good intentions of the 1875 Act, the quality of justice administered in the islands was probably no better in 1880 than it had been in 1870.

This point was emphasised in the Australian press. The *Sydney Morning Herald,* for example, on December 28, 1880, quoted from an issue of the *Daily News,* commenting on the duties originally imposed on the High Commission and the hopes of better conditions in the South Pacific that were still entertained in England:

> "Heretofore it has been left to our naval officers to decide what punishment should be inflicted upon Polynesians who take the lives of white men. Such discretion is, we believe, for the future to be exercised by Her Majesty's High Commissioner in the Pacific, Sir Arthur Gordon, and no longer by naval officers on their own responsibility. The story of the *Dauntless* is a sufficient justification of the new order.[19] So many lawless Europeans roam among the islands of Polynesia, that when any of them fall by the hands of the Natives, some kind of judicial enquiry should manifestly precede any act of retaliation."[20]

The *Sydney Morning Herald* then proceeded to contrast the existing practice with what had been intended under the 1877 Order in Council:[21]

> "These [naval] ships have been travelling police stations, and experience has shown that it is only by machinery of this kind that justice can be administered at all. Her Majesty's High Commissioner has also been Governor of Fiji. It is hardly possible that the Governor of a Colony can spend his time visiting distant islands whenever an atrocity report reaches him and it is less possible to bring red-handed savages to Fiji. As a matter of fact, the High Commissioner has done little or nothing in the way of bringing the savages to justice and events have shown that the High Commissioner alone has been proved to be quite insufficient for this purpose. If Her Majesty's ships do not do the work, it will not be done."

No advance in fact had been made on the position of six or seven years previously. Even before the British Government finally apportioned the respective responsibilities of Navy and High Commission it was the Navy which was doing the work and carrying out its duties in substantially the same way as before the establishment of the High Commission.

[19] The *Dauntless* case occurred at Api, in the New Hebrides, in Aug., 1880.
[20] *S.M.H.*, Dec. 28, 1880.
[21] This comment was written before the final apportionment of authority between the High Commission and the Navy, but after it had become obvious that only the Navy could undertake effective action.

The absence of power in the High Commission to punish offences by natives against British subjects led to an unsuspected and troublesome result. British subjects discovered that, while the operation of the High Commission tended to prevent them from imposing their will in the islands in the old rough fashion, no protection would necessarily be accorded to them, if they involved themselves in difficulties with the natives. The whole complicated apparatus of the imperial and colonial acts was available in law, if not in practice, to punish British offenders, while natives and other foreigners, who might be implicated in the same misdeeds, stood a very good chance of escaping scot-free so far as the British Government was concerned. There was no jurisdiction over foreigners without the written consent of their "competent authority."

In the circumstances it was no matter for surprise that British residents in the islands protested strongly against the inequities which had grown up under the High Commission system.[22] Sir Arthur Gordon, the High Commissioner for the Western Pacific, himself pointed out in February, 1881, that, because he could punish British subjects for offences committed against natives, but could not punish natives for offences committed against British subjects, unrest was increasing amongst even the best class of British residents in the islands.[23]

In July, 1881, Gordon recommended that, where native chiefs were willing to concede such a power, the High Commissioner should be given jurisdiction over natives committing offences against British subjects.[24] The Colonial Office, however, was unwilling to depart from the principle of minimum intervention already laid down, that:

"... the British Government disclaim all obligation to protect or interfere on behalf of persons voluntarily placing themselves in positions of danger in a savage country and that those who enter on such enterprises do so at their own risk."[25]

It was not surprising that the British Government should have laid down such a principle at a time when British subjects were involving themselves in conflict with native peoples all over the world. But in the case of the South Pacific the rule of no responsibility for the safety of British subjects, however much it was mitigated by naval action against offending natives,[26] was capable

[22] Cf. C. 3905, 1884; pp. 4 ff.
[23] C. 3814, 1883; p. 6.
[24] ibid.
[25] Quoted in Gordon's memorandum of Feb. 26, 1881; cit. sup.
[26] See Gordon to Kimberley, July 16, 1881, cit. sup.

of operating with special severity. The exacerbation of white-native relationships through the labour traffic, the growing commercial contacts of the islands with the Australasian colonies[27] and the complications developing from the more privileged position in relation to the natives obtained by the nationals of some other Powers combined to make the position of British subjects difficult.[28] The official report on the Western Pacific Orders in Council, presented in 1884, declared that there were precedents which would justify the exercise of the jurisdiction sought by the High Commissioner over the natives.[29] The general opinion amongst British subjects in the islands was that the working of the High Commission resulted in hardship to themselves and no substantial benefit to the natives.[30]

A similar point of view was taken by the Australasian colonies. Queensland, New South Wales and New Zealand, especially, saw in the High Commission policy an unsatisfactory alternative to their own schemes of British annexation of all the islands of the Western Pacific. When the first two High Commissioners opposed Queensland's plans for the annexation of Eastern New Guinea and condemned the crimes of colonial labour traders, real bitterness developed between the colony and the High Commission.

At the Intercolonial Conference held in Sydney in 1881 resolutions were passed condemning the laxity which characterised British official relations with the natives of the South Pacific. The powers conferred on the High Commissioner, it was considered, were "ineffectual for the protection of the lives and property of the whites as against the natives, mainly owing to the absence of sufficient authority for the punishment of the latter for outrages committed by them."[31] The colonial concern with internal conditions in the islands reflected not only the growing Australasian interest in island trade but also the fear that chaotic conditions within the islands would be made a pretext for annexation by some foreign Power.[32]

In July, 1883, the Agents-General for New South Wales, New Zealand, Queensland and Victoria took up the attack on the High Commission at the instruction of their respective Governments. They wrote to Lord Derby that:

[27] See Chapter XIX, above.
[28] For example, in Samoa.
[29] C. 3905, 1884; para. 13.
[30] Cf. S.M.H., Dec. 28, 1880.
[31] *Intercolonial Conference, Sydney, 1881;* Minutes of proceedings.
[32] See Ch. XIX, above.

"If there was serious trouble by reason of there being no jurisdiction over foreigners, another trouble was growing up even more serious, because there was none over natives. So far from outrages diminishing after the Order in Council was promulgated, they increased. . . . The newspapers teemed with accounts of outrages; it was said that no week passed without the announcement of another massacre in the islands."[33]

Corroborative evidence of these assertions is readily available.[34] The abuses perpetrated by labour recruiters, the evil influences of the arms and liquor traffics and the unscrupulous methods of white traders and planters combined with the collapse of the normal restraints of native society to produce a particularly brutal series of outrages. The massacres of crews from the *Sandfly*, the *Ripple*, the *Esperanza*, the *Borealis* and the *Anne Brooks* marked the outbreak of excesses even worse than those of pre-High Commission days.

For these attacks on British vessels the Navy exacted a terrible revenge. In 1880 H.M.S. *Emerald* (Captain Maxwell) was sent from island to island burning villages, cutting down trees and destroying canoes. Even the officers involved recognised the futility of such crude acts of retribution. But because of the general tenor of British policy towards the South Pacific, only one kind of punitive action against natives was legally possible and that was the commission of "acts of war." In the circumstances there is real poignancy in Maxwell's comment that:

"There was no more to be done in the way of hunting these wretched people . . . they have been hunted and worried till it will be long before they settle down. . . . I regret that my whole voyage in these islands has been one of apparently ruthless destruction; but no other course has been possible."[35]

These punitive voyages not only proved that the Navy was really unsuitable for the delicate task of establishing peace between whites and natives. They also demonstrated the terrible consequences which could develop from the permission given to naval officers by the British Government to initiate "acts of war" and to threaten declarations of war in order to punish guilty tribes or to secure the apprehension of guilty natives. A striking example is afforded by the visit of H.M.S. *Cormorant* to the Floridas in 1881

[33] Agents-General for N.S.W., N.Z., Q'l'd. and Vict to Derby, July 21, 1883; C. 3814, 1883; p. 7.
[34] See *Reports concerning the State of Affairs in the Western Pacific . . . August, 1884*; C. 4126, 1884.
[35] Qu. in C. 3814, 1883; p. 7.

to punish the *Sandfly* murderers. Commander Bruce of H.M.S. *Cormorant* issued the following proclamation to the natives:

"In consequence of an English officer and boat's crew having been murdered by Florida men, the Queen of England declares war with the whole tribes of Floridas, unless the actual murderers are given up in 14 days."[36]

The murderers were given up and hanged. The Agents-General in their letter to Derby cited this case with strong disapprobation, adding that, "Surely, it was not this which could ever have been looked for as the outcome of the scheme of 1875 for the government of the Western Pacific."[37]

The unctuousness of the colonial protests against the High Commissioner's record had little to justify it in Queensland's case. By 1880 the Colonial Office was in doubt as to the willingness of the Queensland Government to stamp out the arms traffic. (It had become customary in both Fiji and Queensland to pay natives for their labour partly in rifles and ammunition of an inferior type. On return to their islands, the natives used their new weapons to spread death and disorder.) In August, 1879, John Gorrie, the Acting High Commissioner, had recommended to the Colonial Office the complete prohibition of the arms traffic.[38] The Colonial Office had agreed and had written to the Governor of Queensland, Sir A. E. Kennedy, and the High Commissioner, Sir Arthur Gordon, recommending action on the lines suggested by Gorrie. Little result followed in Queensland, although the Colonial Office continued its attempts to prod the Queensland Government into taking action.[39] The High Commissioner was more responsive and issued a regulation under the extended powers vested in him by the 1879 Order in Council.[40] This regulation, however, extended only to Samoa, because there was no satisfactory means of enforcing such a regulation anywhere save in Samoa.[41] (There was no labour trade in Tonga.) Control of the labour trade was mainly in the hands of the colonies at that stage and, if they did not take legislative action, there was little use in the High Commissioner's attempting a general prohibition of the traffic.[42]

No satisfactory action was taken until a change of government

[36] C. 3641, 1883.
[37] C. 3814, 1883.
[38] Gorrie to C.O., Aug. 18, 1879; C. 3641, 1883.
[39] See despatches of Jan. 16, 1881, June 17, 1881, Oct. 1, 1881, and Feb. 27, 1882; ibid.
[40] C.O. to Gordon, Jan. 17, 1881; ibid.
[41] Gordon to C.O., Apr. 21, 1881; ibid.
[42] See Gordon to Kimberley, July 16, 1881; cit. sup.

in Queensland in 1884 permitted the desired action to be taken there. Thurston, the Acting High Commissioner, then issued a regulation forbidding the arms and explosives traffic throughout the Western Pacific.[43] Thurston's action was endorsed by the High Commissioner, Sir William Des Voeux, and approved by the Colonial Office.

The incident showed the inability of the High Commissioner to use his legal powers to achieve an end desired by himself and approved by his superiors in London. The sorry position in which Gordon, Gorrie, Thurston and Des Voeux found themselves reflected not only the administrative weaknesses of the High Commissioner but also the ill-effects of the continued division of responsibility for the control of the labour traffic in the South Pacific.

Even the regulations issued in 1884 were unsatisfactory because they did not extend to foreigners in the islands. Many British subjects, in fact, were punished on the information of foreigners for engaging in practices at which the foreigners themselves were adept. After the British colonies and the High Commissioner had made their contribution to the solution of the problem, the British Government felt able to approach France, Germany and the United States to secure joint international action.[44] Russia and Austria joined in the conversations, which, however, produced no positive remedial measures.[45]

The root cause of the inefficiency in practice of the High Commission was the refusal of the British Government to give it powers adequate to balance its commitments, as originally intended. If established on the basis laid down in 1875 and given adequate facilities, the High Commission could have been made to work satisfactorily, at least until the Great Powers commenced the partition of the Southern Pacific. Instead, the conception of the High Commission held by the British Government was progressively narrowed, so as to leave control of the labour trade in the hands of the Australian colonies, partly because, after the annexation of Fiji, the only British territory substantially engaged in the kanaka traffic was Queensland, partly because of unwillingness to incur trouble and expense in setting up the necessary administrative establishment throughout the unannexed islands. As a result the

---

[43] C. 4273, 1885; pp. 30-31. Also C. 5240, 1889; pp. 11-12.

[44] Cf. Kimberley to Loftus, Apr. 3, 1881; C. 3641, 1883.

[45] The problems of the labour traffic and the arms traffic were greatly eased after Queensland abandoned recruiting in 1890, although that State temporarily resumed recruiting in 1892.

good intentions which had prompted the substantial reforms envisaged in the 1875 legislation were allowed to slip into oblivion, while, between 1878 and 1884, the High Commission failed to improve conditions in the labour trade and effective authority remained vested in the hands of naval officers alone.

It is to be admitted, of course, that the primary objective of the High Commission was not the punishment of atrocities or the regulation of the labour traffic. As established in 1877, the High Commission was designed principally to bring law and order to British subjects in the islands.[46] Having regard, however, to the degree to which the problems of the labour trade were inextricably mixed with those of bringing law and order to the whites and of instituting effective government in the islands, it is to be concluded that the Orders in Council of 1877-80 embodied a narrow and restricted conception of the functions of the High Commission. Little advance had been made on the position proved to be untenable so long before as in the 'twenties when experience showed that it was useless to set up any form of control over British subjects, while exercising no effective supervision over natives and foreigners in the islands. The British fear of extended commitments in the islands stood as surely opposed to effective implementation of a policy of control in the 'seventies as it had previously in the 'twenties and 'thirties. No effective attempt was made either by agreement with other Powers or with the native states, or by mere extension of British political authority in the islands, to put the High Commission on the broad basis demanded by island conditions.

That an international agreement was not out of the question at the time and in the circumstances is strongly suggested by the fact that Sir Arthur Gordon, the first High Commissioner, who had a most exceptional knowledge of island problems, recommended the conclusion of such an agreement in his memorandum of June 16, 1882,[47] as a practical policy. Gordon there advocated the establishment of an international commission on the lines of the old Mixed Commission Slave Trade Courts, to control all persons resorting to the South-west Pacific, whatever their nationality. Such a commission could be established, Gordon considered, by agreement between Great Britain, the United States of America, France and Germany. The legal difficulty involved in exercising jurisdiction over natives would be resolved by parallel international action withdrawing recognition of native sovereignty. Although

[46] Gordon's memorandum, Feb. 26, 1881; cit. sup.
[47] C. 3641, 1883.

Gordon did not press this recommendation, as he doubted whether the United States would co-operate, the fact that he considered international action in such detail was sufficient to prove that such action was not politically out of the question. The British Government, however, appears to have confined international action until the middle 1880's to· fruitless attempts to conclude a labour trade agreement with the United States.[48]

Up to that time the High Commission principle remained the official British policy. Nevertheless, the High Commission was starved for funds,[49] and the powers conferred upon it were inadequate. For example, it was doubtful under Article 45 of the 1877 Orders whether Deputy Commissioners had power to imprison. Accordingly in 1879 the Acting High Commissioner ordered the Deputy Commissioners to inflict fines only. As fines were unenforceable in the lawless islands without the sanction of imprisonment, offenders frequently escaped punishment. Again, for many offences coming under the cognizance of Deputy Commissioners the law provided no other punishment than that of imprisonment without the alternative of a fine. In these cases the Deputy Commissioners were powerless. It was useless to refer cases to the High Commissioner, in the majority of instances, because of the provision that all proceedings in respect of offences had to be commenced within three months of the date of the alleged offence. A further difficulty was that, although the High Commissioner was given a wide power to make regulations, he could not attach to them any penalty greater than £10 or imprisonment for three months. As a result important regulations had to operate without adequate sanctions.[50]

From an administrative point of view, the union of offices of High Commissioner of the Western Pacific and Governor of Fiji imposed grave restrictions on the High Commissioner's ability to visit the islands under his control.[51] The emphasis placed right

[48] See Ch. XXI, above.

[49] C. 3905, 1884.

[50] ibid.

[51] ibid. An extraordinary administrative difficulty complicated the early years of Sir William Des Voeux's work as High Commissioner and Governor of Fiji. Des Voeux was the second High Commissioner, succeeding the famous Sir Arthur Gordon. So high was the confidence of the Colonial Office in Gordon that, when he was transferred to the position of Governor of New Zealand, he was asked to retain the supervision of native affairs in Fiji and to retain his office as High Commissioner. Des Voeux's appointment was Governor of Fiji and Assistant High Commissioner, with a dormant appointment as High Commissioner to take effect when Gordon vacated that office. The arrangement was not to the liking of either man and worked creakily, but without personal friction, until 1882. (Des Voeux: *My Colonial Service*; 2 vols., London, 1903; Vol. II, pp. 4-5.)

from the first on the necessity of establishing a legal system in the South-west Pacific for the benefit of British residents led to the concentration of the High Commission's executive power in Tonga and Samoa, although there was no labour trade in Tonga and in Samoa the labour trade was in the hands of the Germans. Deputy Commissioners were appointed in these two groups immediately on the proclamation of the Orders in Council by special instructions of the Secretary of State and the High Commissioner was instructed to appoint no other resident or salaried Deputy Commissioners in other parts of the Pacific.[52] These Deputy Commissioners were able to discharge their duties in Tonga and Samoa fairly well, but, as the Commission appointed in 1883 to report on the working of the Western Pacific Orders in Council pointed out:

> "Tonga and Samoa are only very small groups, not in any way comparable as to size or population with most of those enumerated as within the jurisdiction of the High Commissioner, and certainly not as likely as many other localities to be the scene of illegal proceedings on the part of British subjects."[53]

The Commission did not hesitate to reach the conclusion that:

> ". . . the Order in Council is, as regards the greater part of the Pacific, practically powerless for good, while its provisions have laid restraints on the action of Her Majesty's Naval force which did not previously exist."[54]

[52] C. 3905, 1884; para, 38. In 1878 a Deputy Commissioner was appointed at Darnley and Murray Islands at the request of the Queensland Government. He was withdrawn a year later at the request of the same Government, on the ground of administrative difficulties arising from an officer of the Queensland Government holding an appointment from another source; ibid.

[53] C. 3905, 1884; paras. 42-44.

[54] ibid, para. 46.

Chapter XXVI

PLANS OF REFORM

The Commission which so roundly condemned the functioning and structure of the High Commission was one of considerable authority. It had been appointed in 1883 at the instance of Sir Arthur Gordon, the High Commissioner for the Western Pacific.[1] Gordon had suggested a full enquiry into the working of the Western Pacific Orders in Council when he prepared his memorandum on the functioning of the High Commission in June, 1882.[2] The other members of the Commission were Rear-Admiral Sir Anthony Hoskins, K.C.B., Admiral Superintendent of Naval Reserves, and Rear-Admiral Wilson, each of whom had had first-hand experience of Western Pacific conditions. Wilson, while in command of H.M.S. *Wolverene,* had himself administered "commodore justice."

Gordon in his 1882 memorandum had submitted specific suggestions for the reform of British policy in the South West Pacific. If no fundamental changes in policy could be made, he considered that the number of civil Deputy Commissioners in the islands should be increased and that officers in command of cruisers should also possess powers of Deputy Commissioners whilst in the islands. Naval officers, however, except in summary cases should have only the powers of committing magistrates, not those of judges. In this way Gordon sought to preserve the practical usefulness of having Deputy Commissioners visiting the islands regularly, while avoiding the worst features of "commodore justice." He went on to recommend that offences committed by natives against British subjects should be equally cognizable with those committed. by British subjects against natives. To assist in detecting offences and to increase the efficiency of the High Commission, a vessel (not a man-of-war) should be permanently in the service of the High Commissioner.

These suggestions were put forward on the assumption that no

[1] C.O. to Admiralty, Jan. 22, 1883; Admiralty to C.O., Feb. 5, 1883; both C. 3641, 1883.
[2] June 16, 1882; ibid.

fundamental change in policy would be made by the British Government. But Gordon did not conceal his opinion that far more extensive readjustments than these mere variations of existing arrangements would be necessary. He submitted six alternative plans:

(1) Total abolition of the Western Pacific High Commission and reversion to the system of "commodore justice." This alternative was rejected because it would have involved a return to the very conditions which the Orders in Council had been framed to meet.

(2) Transfer to the High Commission of all the existing powers of the Navy in the islands. But to do this would not solve the problem of the need for reconstitution of the High Commission with more effective powers, especially over natives and foreigners.

(3) "Another course would be to render the High Commissioner what he was originally intended by the Imperial Government to be. In this event the High Commissioner ought not to be the governor of a colony, or hold any other office and should reside chiefly in the islands. With numerous deputies, and a despatch boat at his service and an extended jurisdiction over natives committing offences . . . the work required might thus be very fairly, if not completely, done, so far as regards British subjects. It would, however, involve a considerable expenditure . . ." This was the alternative favoured by Gordon.

(4) The establishment of a Mixed Commission by international arrangement so as to secure control over foreigners and natives in the islands. (See previous chapter.)

(5) Direct annexation of many of the island groups would be to everyone's advantage but was an improbable event.

(6) A chartered company might be formed to control the whole area. Gordon felt, however, that this suggestion was already anachronistic and, in any event, likely to produce international difficulties owing to the great diversity of nationalities already present in the islands.

The gist of all these recommendations was, first, that the existing High Commission was a failure, and second, that only really extensive intervention on the part of Great Britain could achieve the true objectives of the 1875 Act. Gordon's memorandum made it clear that, in his opinion, the third of his six alternatives came nearest to the real needs of the situation and to what had been intended by the British Government when the enabling legislation had been passed.

Actually, Gordon's memorandum had no other result than the

appointment of the 1883-4 Commission, as already noted.[3] The recommendations of this Commission were similar to those made in the Gordon memorandum. The same alternatives were considered, although they were discussed more fully. In particular, the Commission opposed the scheme for abolishing the High Commission and reverting to commodore justice on the ground that "the abandonment of control over the acts of British subjects in the Pacific would not be tolerated by foreign Powers having large interests there." The scheme for transferring the High Commission's powers to the Navy was shown to involve risk of collision between the Navy and the judicial officers of the High Commission. Moreover, it was pertinently asked, would British subjects in the South West Pacific accept regulations made by a naval officer?

The Commission, after considering all six alternatives,[4] strongly favoured that recommending reform of the existing system. Their preference was expressly based on a wish to implement the main objective of the 1875 Act—to bring British law within the reach of all British subjects. The High Commission principle, it was held, had always offered a means of achieving this end. All that was required was a broader conception of the conditions under which the High Commission would have to function and a livelier appreciation of the practical difficulties of its administration.

The Commission's recommendations, however, were merely directed to removing the administrative difficulties of the High Commission. They showed no attempt to solve the major problem of the lack of effective jurisdiction over natives and foreigners, no appreciation of the true nature of the problem of government. But specific recommendations were made for the removal of most of the difficulties which had been encountered in exercising the desired degree of control over British subjects. The Orders in Council were to be revised carefully with a view to simplification. The positions of High Commissioner for the Western Pacific and Governor of Fiji were to be separated and the headquarters of the High Commissioner removed to New Guinea, where the largest body of uncontrolled whites then existed. Improved representation of the Commission in the islands was to be established by dividing the islands west of Fiji into five districts, in each of which a

---

[3] The findings of this Commission have already been discussed in the examination of the work of the Western Pacific High Commission. For report, see C. 3905, 1884.

[4] Five alternatives are specifically enumerated in the Report, but one of these contains Gordon's suggestion for joint international action, already considered.

Deputy Commissioner was to be stationed.[5] Deputy Commissioners would have the use of the High Commissioner's steam yacht to visit the whole of their districts annually and would also possess small sailing boats of from five to twenty-five tons.. The Western Pacific Orders in Council were to be modified so as to enable naval officers to bring offenders before the High Commission Court and to arbitrate in civil cases. Previous provision made for this purpose in 1881 by rules of Court had been held to be *ultra vires* the Orders in Council. The High Commission was to be given full control over recruiting in the islands and a superior class of labour agents was to be nominated and paid by the Imperial authorities with contributions from the owners of the trading vessels.[6]

While it is not to be disputed that these recommendations struck at many of the main weaknesses of the existing organisation of the High Commission, it is obvious that the viewpoint of those who framed them was nearly as restricted as that of the lawyers who had drafted the 1877 Order in Council. The fundamental island problem, that is, the lack of effective government in the islands themselves, was ignored almost as much in 1884 as it had been when the High Commission policy was first adopted. The force of the minimum intervention policy still prevented any thorough attack on the basic problems of British administration in the islands.

The limited scope of the recommendations of the Gordon memorandum and of the Commission was the more remarkable in that both referred to the rapid expansion of foreign interests in thé islands. Both pointed out that there was no reason why international action should not be undertaken in order to preserve law and order amongst the incoming whites who were dislocating

[5] The Line Islands, the Gilberts, the Ellice Islands and the Marshalls and Carolines were to be visited annually by a ship of war, whose commander would have a temporary commission as a Deputy Commissioner. Resident Deputy Commissioners were to be stationed at Port Moresby, Duke of York Island, Havannah Harbour (in the New Hebrides), the South Solomons and the North Solomons (with the Admiralty Group).

[6] The Report recommended that every colonial vessel starting out on a labour cruise should be compelled to report to the Deputy Commissioner of the District where it was proposed to recruit and to receive from him a recruiting agent and a licence, stating at what islands and for what number of men the licence was good. When recruiting had been completed, the vessel was to return to the Deputy Commissioner to discharge the labour agent and to report. It was then bound under heavy penalties to proceed direct to its destination. A similar procedure was to be followed when labour was being returned. The recruiting of women was to be limited to the wives and close relatives of the men recruited. This recommendation revealed the recognition of British officials on the spot that, from a practical point of view, it was useless to entrust the supervision of the labour trade to the Australian States.

government and perpetually disturbing the peace and in order to regulate relationships between whites and natives generally. Alternatively, the common interest would be preserved, the report and the memorandum declared, by annexation of the main island groups to the major Powers.

Despite these admissions, Gordon and the Commission felt constrained by the overwhelming pressure of what was regarded as probable in British policy, to report against any of the wider attempts to solve Pacific problems and to concentrate on a mere patching-up of the existing High Commission principle. As a result their recommendations were unrealistic in so far as they did not take adequate account of the new problems and new possibilities produced by the rapid expansion of foreign interests in the South Pacific. The major Powers had already carved out substantial economic interests in the islands and had commenced the final process of political partition. To discuss patching-up the High Commission as an alternative to annexation or international action was in the circumstances merely anachronistic.

A recommendation which did take somewhat greater account of the changing island conditions was made a few months before the Commission's Report by Sir William Des Voeux, the High Commissioner for the Western Pacific. Des Voeux submitted a "Memorandum on the future of New Guinea and Polynesia with reference to the Question of Australasian Annexation or Protectorate" to the Intercolonial Convention held in Sydney at the end of 1883.[7] The memorandum assessed the prospects of future economic development of the islands and discussed the bases of British policy in the South Pacific. In its main recommendations it constituted an alternative to the schemes proposed in the Commission Report and the Gordon memorandum.

It is important to note that Des Voeux's memorandum, though professedly a personal document, possessed a much more significant character. Despite his insistence that his participation in the Convention would be unofficial, the nature of the views expressed in the memorandum, touching as they did on his official duties as High Commissioner, prevented their being regarded as merely personal. Moreover, Des Voeux attended the Convention with the consent of the Colonial Office, which knew that he proposed to correct certain misapprehensions as to the role and policy of the High Commission and to comment on the suggestion that Fiji should be included in a larger colony of Australasia. It is true

[7] The memorandum was dated Nov. 7, 1883. (C. 3863, 1884.)

that no specific approval was given beforehand to his detailed proposals. But he attended the Convention with official sanction and spoke on matters within the scope of his official duties. His memorandum is to be regarded, therefore, as representing at least a view which the British Government was not unwilling to have discussed.[8]

Des Voeux's starting point was his admission that Great Britain was still reluctant to extend her political responsibilities in the islands. He stressed his own view that the potential economic advantages of the islands were slight. Their only staple product was copra, and plantation labour was lacking. Great Britain could not reasonably be expected to act in the islands without the financial and material backing of her Australasian colonies. Returning to the kind of argument which had so appealed to Gladstone in 1871-72, Des Voeux recommended that, if Great Britain had to acquire any of the islands, the costs of administration should be shared by the Australasian colonies along with the mother country. The ultimate objective should be to transfer the administration of the islands to the colonies, which had a closer interest in their welfare and development than had Great Britain.

Where Des Voeux's arguments were substantially new was in his insistence that British intervention, when judged to be necessary, should be limited to "control over persons of all nations in their relations not only with natives but with one another." Straight-out annexation, followed by the establishment of an ordinary colonial government, Des Voeux considered to be undesirable because it would make the natives British subjects and force on them the whole apparatus of British law in a sudden change which could not fail to be injurious to native life and society.

Detailed administration in the annexed islands he believed to be unnecessary. As he did not believe that the islands had any substantial economic future, he did not hesitate to press his view that economic development should not be allowed to overshadow native interests or to endanger the process of adjusting native life to new conditions. All that was required in the way of administration, in his opinion, was a general supervision by from 12 to 20 Commissioners, stationed in the more important places, empowered to try cases involving whites or whites and natives and assisted by police guards. No more than a system of arbitration should be established to deal with disputes between natives. Where complaints were made against whole native tribes, recourse would have

[8] See Nos. 84, 89 and 106, C. 3863, 1884.

to be had to "acts of war." Complete over-all authority would be vested in a Chief Commissioner, stationed in Australia, probably in Melbourne, away from the vested interests which would oppose such a policy.

Des Voeux in effect invited the colonies to submit to Great Britain a plan for annexation of the islands (other than the New Hebrides and Samoa)[9] on the basis of sharing the costs with the mother country, the reversion of the political responsibilities to belong to the colonies. His plan would have relieved the colonies of their strategic fears regarding the islands and was also calculated to cost as little as possible. Commercially, of course, it was pessimistic, but as the colonies had emphasised all through the aspects of finance and defence, there was little ground for complaint in Des Voeux's insistence that administrative policy in the islands should be partly determined by their unpromising economic future.

Neither the Commission's Report nor Des Voeux's memorandum appears to have received much attention in Great Britain. The former in its recommendations (though not in its observations of fact) failed to take account of the rapid increase of international interest in the South Pacific. The latter in effect recommended to the Australasian colonies an island policy which would have met the objections of Great Britain to intervention in the South Pacific while relieving the fears of the colonies as to foreign aggression in islands near to their shores. Des Voeux's memorandum was for colonial rather than home consumption. Its reception in Australia and New Zealand is discussed in the next chapter.

[9] As to the New Hebrides, Great Britain was adhering to a convention with France, establishing non-intervention as the policy of both Powers in the group. As to Samoa, Des Voeux himself stressed the prior claims of Germany which he regarded as likely to be admitted by the British Government. (Des Voeux to Jervois, Oct. 26, 1883; C. 3863, 1884.)

Chapter XXVII

JOINT MINIMUM INTERVENTION[1]

The reports made by the Gordon Commission and by Sir William Des Voeux, apart from Des Voeux's comments on Australian and New Zealand ambitions, made no recommendation of any fundamental change in British policy. The Gordon Commission planned in terms of the conditions of 1877. Des Voeux gave limited recognition to the changes transforming island affairs but did not attempt to assess their full implications for British policy.

The first and greatest change in the South Pacific was the fact that the growing foreign populations of the islands were receiving increased backing from their governments. The process of commercial development, which had increased so rapidly since the 'fifties, had come to the point at which official intervention was attracted. Valuable investments in the islands, claims to land, the growth of regular shipping routes and the settled interests of the planter class and the missionaries all required the protection of the Powers. The presence of rival groups of foreigners, especially in cases where competing land claims developed (as in Samoa and the New Hebrides), was a further reason for official intervention. The problem of government remained not only unsolved, but complicated by the presence of such large numbers of foreigners of diverse nationalities that the expedients of extra-consular jurisdiction and local attempts to form effective governments were faced by increasing difficulties.

The most important instance in which Great Britain was faced with such an aggravation of earlier problems was Samoa, where Great Britain, Germany and the United States of America all had substantial interests. The British role was complicated by the

---

[1] The subject matter of this chapter and the following chapter has been discussed extensively in several recent works. The treatment here is kept as brief as possible. For detailed accounts, see S. H. Roberts: *History of French Colonial Policy* (London, 1929); A. C. V. Melbourne: "Relations between Australia and New Guinea up to the establishment of British Rule in 1888" (*J.R.A.H.S.*, XII, XIII); S. Masterman: *The Origins of International Rivalry in Samoa, 1845-1884* (London, 1934); G. H. Ryden: *The Foreign Policy of the United States in relation to Samoa* (New Haven, 1933); M. E. Townsend: *The Rise and Fall of Germany's Colonial Empire, 1884-1918* (New York, 1930).

incessant demand from New Zealand for annexation of the group.

In the 'seventies none of the Powers concerned had wished to rule Samoa. The United States had considered the idea but had dropped it, despite the Samoan appeals for American intervention. Great Britain, in accordance with her established policy, had declined invitations to accept a protectorate.[2] German policy was still in the anti-colonial stage. Accordingly, the tendency was to apply what amounted to a common policy of minimum intervention in the form of treaties of extra-territoriality with guarantees of the protection of foreign commercial rights. There were individual differences in the policies of the Powers (for example, the British reliance on the High Commission system in respect of British subjects in Samoa), but generally the Powers agreed on a policy of seeking, not territorial gain, but only protection of the interests of their subjects and citizens.

This policy was soon elaborated into a system of joint action by the consuls. Internal disorder in Samoa made consular rule the only practicable alternative to complete chaos. Just as British indifference to the problem of government earlier in the century had produced extra-consular jurisdiction, so the failure of any of the three Powers to accept political responsibilities in Samoa produced joint extra-consular jurisdiction in the late 'seventies.[3]

Some formality was given to consular rule as a result of the visit of Sir Arthur Gordon to Samoa in 1879. After concluding the Anglo-Samoan Agreement of that year, Gordon had received an offer of cession of the group to Great Britain.[4] This obviously had to be refused, as had also the proposal for a joint protectorate by Great Britain, Germany and the United States, which was submitted to the consuls a few days later. But, perceiving the strength of the European support in Samoa for a system of joint control by the Powers, Gordon secured the co-operation of Captain Chandler (U.S.S. *Lackawanna*) and Captain Mensing (H.I.G.M.S. *Albatross*), together with the British, United States and German Consuls, in signing on September 2, 1879, the well-known Apia Convention. Agreement was made by the three foreign governments with the Malietoa faction for the placing of the town of Apia (on Upolu) under the control of the consuls of the three nations. A municipal board, consisting of the consuls, was to have

[2] As to offers of cession to Gt. Britain, see F.O.: *Confidential Paper No. 3372, Nov., 1877.*

[3] For earlier examples of consular jurisdiction, including joint consular jurisdiction in Fiji and Samoa, see Ch. XVII, above.

[4] Ellison, op. cit., p. 105.

power to make and enforce regulations, including the right of taxing houses and land for the purpose of defraying public expenditure. The board also had power to appoint a magistrate to try offences against its regulations. Apia was to be neutral territory in the event of a civil war in Samoa. Four years after its date, the convention was to be revised; if conditions then justified the step, Apia was to pass back to the control of the Samoan Government.[5]

The Apia Convention, taken in conjunction with the three treaties, represented a deliberate return to the principle of extra-consular jurisdiction. The only substantial changes from the original version were the formal treaty provisions for extra-territoriality, the neutralisation of the Apia district and the agreement for joint consular action.

British policy favoured the Apia Convention, which was regarded as a means of preserving reasonable order amongst Europeans of all nationalities in Samoa, while also giving them the means of withdrawing from civil strife amongst the natives.[6] The British view apparently was that the Convention and the treaty of 1879 made it possible for British subjects to remain in Samoa without involving themselves in the faction disputes of the group, while doing something to ensure that they remained at peace with the other foreign residents.

The system of joint minimum intervention evolved in Samoa had a counterpart later in the New Hebrides. European settlement in this group began in an extensive way during the 'seventies. Cotton, coffee, maize, cocoa, cocoanuts and bananas were the principal crops. British interests, consisting mainly of missionaries (Presbyterians from Australia in most of the islands), predominated. The visits of British warships soon proved to be insufficient to maintain law and order and the missionaries and the more respectable British settlers (fearful also of French intervention) inspired several unsuccessful appeals for British annexation.[7] There were also appeals from the Presbyterian Church in New South Wales, Victoria, South Australia and Tasmania and from the Free Church of Scotland. France also received a few appeals for annexation, some of them from British settlers, mainly because of the proximity

[5] "Convention for Government of Town and District of Apia"; Apia, Sept. 2, 1879; C. 2748, 1881. Also *Further Corr. resp. Affairs in the Navigators Islands, Parts II and III.*

[6] Gt. Britain treated the Convention as a treaty; ibid; and Ellison, op. cit., p. 106.

[7] For appeals prior to 1862, see Chapter XIV, above. For appeals from 1862 to 1875, see Paton to Service, Jun. 8, 1883; C. 3814, 1883.

of the New Hebrides to New Caledonia and the growing French interests in the New Hebrides.

The Australian colonies strongly supported the requests for British annexation.[8] The presence of the French in New Caledonia was regarded as a strategic threat, which would be worsened if France seized the New Hebrides also. The use of New Caledonia after 1863 as a penal colony stimulated fears that the New Hebrides, if annexed by France, would be put to a similar use, and that escaping convicts would contaminate Australia with the dregs of the French gaols.

Neither the British nor the French Governments had any wish to press claims to the New Hebrides during the 'seventies. Great Britain still adhered to the minimum intervention policy and considered that the interests of the Australian colonies would be met, provided that the independence of the group was preserved. France at that juncture was also prepared to acquiesce in a policy of "hands-off" in the New Hebrides, being herself engaged in a policy of consolidation in Europe, and of territorial aggrandizement in the Congo, Madagascar and Tonkin. Accordingly, in January, 1878, despite the protests of Sir George Grey and other fervent annexationists in Australia, New Zealand and the islands themselves, the two Powers agreed to respect the independence of the New Hebrides.[9]

So far as British settlers were concerned, the policy of the 1878 agreement proved more acceptable than had been expected. The establishment of the Western Pacific High Commission brought them within the jurisdiction of a British Court and made it possible for them to acquire recognised titles to land.[10] As against this benefit there had to be weighed the familiar disadvantage, that the High Commission afforded white settlers very little protection against natives.

The great difficulty facing the British settlers and missionaries in the New Hebrides was still their fear of France. In March, 1883, two of the Australian missionaries wrote to the Colonial Office, complaining of French spoliation of British property. They declared that a company had been formed in New Caledonia to colonise the New Hebrides with Frenchmen and thus to "force

[8] See esp. Palmer to Derby, Jun. 10, 1863; C. 3863, 1884.

[9] For text of negotiations, see Scholefield, op. cit., pp. 316 ff. Comment on the agreement in C.O. to Agents-General, Aug. 31, 1883; C. 3814, 1883.

[10] The New Hebrides were omitted from the list of islands specially enumerated in the 1877 Order in Council. The High Commissioners mainly disregarded suggestions that the 1878 Agreement with France precluded their exercising jurisdiction there; C. 3814, 1883; pp. 11, 39.

France to take possession of the group as Britain has had to do in Fiji."[11] The missionary protests were fully in accord with a joint representation made by the Agents-General of New South Wales, New Zealand, Queensland and Victoria to the Colonial Office in July, 1883. The Agents-General stressed that the colonies, despite their important interest in the New Hebrides, were only vaguely aware of the 1878 Agreement, while they were constantly being alarmed by reports of imminent French aggrandizement in the group.[12] In June, 1883, all the Australian colonies and New Zealand expressed opinions in favour of annexation, protectorate or some other form of intervention.[13]

Towards the end of 1883 an Intercolonial Convention met in Sydney and considered the island problem in detail, Victoria taking the lead so far as the New Hebrides were concerned. The Convention urged[14] the annexation of New Guinea and expressed fears that the New Hebrides would be occupied by France and made a convict settlement. The Recidivist Bill, which was then before the French Chamber, was mentioned with great anxiety, as experience of escaped convicts from New Caledonia had already been both painful and difficult. The prospect of relapsed criminals being sent to the South Pacific was hotly resented. There was also alarm over the fact that France had already commenced a new forward movement in the islands.[15] It was resolved that the 1878 Agreement should be replaced by some more specific understanding preventing the New Hebrides from being acquired by a foreign Power. Great Britain, the Convention considered, should take the first opportunity of obtaining control of the group.

The British Government supported the colonies in their protests against the recidivist proposals and the Foreign Office discussed with the French Government the prospect of discontinuing transportation to the Western Pacific altogether.[16] For the rest, however, the Foreign Office declined to believe in any threat of French action in the New Hebrides. The French Government had already reiterated its intention of adhering to the agreement of 1878,[17] which was in fact formally renewed in 1883.[18] In the circumstances

[11] Wilson and Paton to C.O., Mar. 1, 1883; C. 3863, 1884. The company was the Compagnie Calédonienne formed by John Higginson. See below, p. 300.
[12] July 21, 1883; C. 3814, 1883.
[13] Nos. 1-11; ibid.
[14] For details of resolutions, see next chapter.
[15] See below, p. 301.
[16] C.O. to F.O., Dec. 15, 1883; C. 3863, 1884. Also Nos. 2-15, 23-33, 35-36, 38 ff., etc.; C. 3839, 1884.
[17] Encl. in No. 22; C. 3814, 1883.
[18] ibid.

the British Government was not prepared to accept the extensive responsibilities, which the Australian Governments would have forced upon it.

Despite the reaffirmation of 1883, expanding trade and settlement in the group made it plain that the 1878 Agreement was merely temporary. Alarmed by the increase of French commercial activity in the New Hebrides (believed to be a deliberately planned prelude to French annexation), Australian interests in 1884 formed the Anglo-Australian Company, with its headquarters at Malekula. The Company's venture was obstructed by French action in the form of heavy land purchases in the desired area and an agreement entered into by representatives of the French company and the Government of New Caledonia with the chiefs. (The agreement exchanged the mutual promises of protection of the chiefs and the Company and France.)[19] The Australian missionaries at once petitioned the Colonial Office to proclaim a protectorate and the Australian Governments, perturbed by reports that France was about to send convicts from New Caledonia to the New Hebrides, informed the Colonial Office that they were prepared to pay the cost of taking possession of the archipelago. The colonies had to be content with Lord Derby's undertaking, that no proposal for French annexation of the New Hebrides would be considered in Great Britain without consulting them and securing conditions deemed satisfactory by them.[20]

Matters in the New Hebrides were eventually brought to a head by French action.[21] French settlers in the group had complained that they were being forced out by British interests, supported by the Western Pacific High Commission. Seeking French annexation, they claimed that the New Hebrides had been included by implication in New Caledonia when possession was taken of that group in 1853. John Higginson, a naturalised French subject of British birth,[22] continued his vigorous agitation for French annexation of the New Hebrides. Frenchmen in the group began to complain that their lives and property were left unprotected. From 1882 to 1886 over twenty Europeans, including several agents of the Compagnie Calédonienne, had lost their lives and pillage and destruction had become rife. In 1886 the Government of New Caledonia decided to intervene, acting apparently on its own initiative. Troops were landed in three places to punish natives,

19 F.O.: Historical Section Handbooks, No. 147, *New Hebrides*; pp. 11-12.
20 Derby to Jervois and same to Loch, May 18, 1885; C. 4584, 1885.
21 See F.O.: *New Hebrides*, cit. sup., p. 12.
22 Higginson had been resident at Noumea since 1859; ibid, p. 10.

who had destroyed French lives and property, and to protect French settlers.

The intervention from New Caledonia led to fresh discussions between the Governments of Great Britain and France, feeling in Australia, New Zealand and New Caledonia making it difficult for either Power to withdraw (even if France had wished to do so.) Annexations in the Pacific had already raised important questions under the Declaration of London, 1847,[23] which had restricted French and British action in the Societies. The negotiations were made the occasion of settling all outstanding differences between Great Britain and France in the South Pacific. In 1880 France had annexed Tahiti and its dependencies (including the Tuamotus and some of the Austral Islands), a year after the death of Pomare IV. Rapa (Aparo), the remainder of the Australs and the Mangareva Group (the Gambiers) were annexed in the immediately following years. A protectorate was established over Raiatea in 1882 and over Uvea (Wallis Island) and Futuna in 1887.

The French Government admitted the illegality of the French proceedings in the New Hébrides, but it did not withdraw the troops. British relations with France were already complicated by the Suez Canal question, the Somaliland boundary delimitation problem, German threats against France (and allegations as to French intentions against Germany), the Moroccan question and the ancient quarrel over the fishing rights off Newfoundland. Plainly it was no time for rigid insistence on the terms of the 1878 Agreement. But such an insistence was demanded by the Australian and New Zealand delegates to the Imperial Conference held in London in 1887. It required the personal intervention of Lord Salisbury, the British Prime Minister and Foreign Secretary, to prevent the colonial delegates from embarrassing Anglo-French relations.

Salisbury's handling of the New Hebrides question proceeded on the familiar lines of give and take, which the British policy of "hands-off" in the Pacific made possible. The two Governments dealt with the Suez Canal question and the New Hebrides question in reciprocity. While Salisbury was being badgered by the House of Commons about his acquiescence in the French occupation of the New Hebrides[24] the French Ministry was being pressed on the Canal question. Salisbury himself was amazed at the delaying tactics of the French, whose relations with Germany were ominous,

[23] See Ch. XIII, above.
[24] See *Parliamentary Debates*, 1887; CCCXI, 298; CCCXIV, 682, 946; CCCXV, 247; CCCXVI, 1164, 1309; CCCXVIII, 529, 675, 1701; CCCXIX, 218.

but agreed to an arrangement under which the Canal and New Hebrides problems were disposed of together. The New Hebrides settlement, embodied in the Convention of 1887, was far from popular—in either Great Britain or the colonies, Salisbury being charged with having conceded too much to the law-breaker.

By the Convention of 1887[25] the Declaration of London was abrogated. Under the Convention and the accompanying Declaration and Regulations of 1888 Great Britain and France applied a joint policy of minimum intervention in the New Hebrides. The two Powers agreed to set up a Joint Naval Commission of British and French officers to control the interests of their nationals in the group. No questions of sovereignty were raised and there was no attempt to set up an administration nor to proclaim a protectorate. In effect the two Powers regularised a system of joint naval jurisdiction in the group as a means of staving off the more troublesome questions of annexation and government.

The joint minimum intervention system proved satisfactory to neither Power. The impotence of the Commission, which could function only when British and French warships happened to be in the New Hebrides at the same time, was quickly revealed. To supplement the Commission's work, Great Britain in 1888 appointed a consul and vice-consul in the New Hebrides, while the French settlers, in order to provide some measure of law and order, organised the municipality of Franceville at Vila in 1889. The British representatives were withdrawn in 1890 and the French experiment was subsequently abandoned as contrary to the Convention. Heavy strain continued to be imposed on the joint policy of minimum intervention until in 1906 the hardly more satisfactory Anglo-French Condominium was established in the New Hebrides.[26]

In underlying principle there were marked resemblances in the Apia Convention (or, at least, British participation in the Convention) and the New Hebrides Agreement of 1878 and the Convention of 1887. So far as Great Britain was concerned, the basic principle of policy was still to avoid political responsibilities, whilst maintaining some control over British subjects and affording some protection to British and colonial interests in the islands. In both Samoa and the New Hebrides the British policy was made difficult to apply by the presence of foreign interests, supported by foreign Powers. The principle of joint policies of minimum inter-

[25] C. 5256, 1888. See also E. Jacomb: *France and England in the New Hebrides*; Melbourne, 1914; Appendix.
[26] Cd. 3288, 1907.

vention was evolved easily enough to meet conditions in which no Power was willing for any other to annex.

The workability of a policy of joint minimum intervention depended on three factors: (i) that no Power should be prepared to disregard the opposition of its rivals and proceed to annexation: obviously this factor tended to disappear at times when the Great Powers were negotiating questions of rival interests, so that a Pacific territory might be bartered for a concession elsewhere; (ii) that minimum intervention should be capable of maintaining an acceptable degree of law and order amongst whites and of keeping the ·peace between whites and natives; and (iii) that no Power should obtain such interests and commercial dominance as would lead it to exercise political influence contrary to the spirit of the policy.

During the eighteen-eighties all of these factors disappeared in Samoa.[27] By 1883 it was clear that Germany had determined to obtain a special place there. German interests in Samoa predominated over those of Great Britain and the United States of America.[28] While not then prepared to dispute the position of the other Powers in the group, German policy was directed to wringing further concessions from the Samoans. The commercial and political aspirations of Germany in the Pacific had begun to coincide.

The internal situation in Samoa was such that strong government was impossible. Malietoa Laupepa, the ruling king, was bullied into making concession after concession to the Germans, led by Weber and Stuebel. In November, 1884, Malietoa and 48 chiefs petitioned Queen Victoria for annexation to Great Britain or New Zealand.[29] When the request was disclosed the Germans extracted a further agreement from the Government of Samoa (November 10, 1884). Expressed to be negotiated "for the purpose of securing the benefits of good government to Germans residing in Samoa and in execution of Article XI of the German-Samoan Treaty of Friendship of January 24, 1879," the new treaty provided for the appointment of a German-Samoan Council to make laws for the mutual benefit of the Government of Samoa and of the German residents. The Council was to consist of the German Consul with two German representatives and two Samoans, one each appointed by the king and the vice-king. There was also to be a degree of extra-territoriality for German subjects.

[27] See also Chapter XX, above.

[28] Thurston's Reports on Samoa; C. 5269, 1889; also Bridge's Report, C. 4584, 1885.

[29] C. 4273, 1885.

This agreement together with the request for annexation brought Samoan affairs once again into the hands of the Foreign Offices. Bismarck protested against any possible plan for British intervention in Samoa and was assured that the British Government would not intervene in either Samoa or Tonga, provided that the German Government gave reciprocal guarantees.[30] This settlement, so well in accord with established British policy, was threatened by the conduct of the New Zealand Ministry, of W. B. Churchward (British Acting-Consul) and of Malietoa Laupepa himself. The New Zealand Ministry received the petition of 1884 with enthusiasm and cabled to the Colonial Office, offering to pay the expenses of annexing both Tonga and Samoa, and to take over the Government of Fiji, if so desired.[31] The Ministry proposed to send to Samoa immediately in order to ascertain the true state of native feeling.[32] Churchward wrote to the Foreign Office, reporting a complaint from Malietoa of German pressure brought on him to sign the 1884 treaty. He enclosed a note of his own sent to the British Consul-General, referring to reports that the Germans were anxious to pick a quarrel with the Samoans for the purposes of annexation—a prospect at which, he stated, the natives were alarmed and resentful.[33]

The interests involved on the British side in this conflict were numerous. Official British policy was clear; it had been stated to Bismarck in December, 1884; it was being revealed in the Anglo-German dealings over New Guinea; it was restated to Governor Jervois of New Zealand in January, 1885, when Derby wrote that Great Britain would annex neither Tonga nor Samoa. The British and German Governments, he added, were determined on an international régime for Samoa, so that:

> "Her Majesty's Government hope that New Zealand Government will not preclude internationalisation of the islands, which is obviously best course for British interests at present juncture."[34]

The Anglo-German agreement was easy to reach, the two Powers having claims to adjust elsewhere, which were of sufficient im-

[30] F.O. to C.O., Dec. 4, 1884, and F.O. to Malet, Dec. 4, 1884; C. 4273, 1885.

[31] Jervois to Derby, Dec. 31, 1884; ibid. The Royal Assent had already been withheld from the New Zealand Confederation and Annexation Bill, 1883, which would have opened the way to acquisition of island colonies by New Zealand.

[32] Only four months previously Jervois had written to Derby doubting whether the Samoans really wished for annexation to New Zealand. He was referring to the 1883 offer; C. 4273, 1885.

[33] Churchward was later instructed not to countenance any offer of annexation; No. 187, ibid.

[34] No. 109; C. 4273, 1885.

portance to outweigh the claims of their Samoan interests. But it was more difficult to satisfy the New Zealand Government and the British and colonial settlers and investors in Samoa. Only a few months before these events, the Intercolonial Convention of November-December, 1883, had resolved that:

> "the further acquisition of dominion in the Pacific south of the equator by any foreign power would be highly detrimental to the safety and well-being of the British possessions in Australasia and injurious to the interests of the Empire."[35]

The New Zealand Government found further grounds for keeping the Samoan question open both in the 1884 treaty, forced on Malietoa after the offer to New Zealand became known, and in German activity over New Guinea. If New Guinea were to become German, contended the New Zealand Government, Great Britain should seize Samoa and Tonga and ensure that France adhered to her agreements over the New Hebrides.[36] British interests in Samoa were also dissatisfied with the growing German predominance there. Contending that they themselves were impeded by High Commission restrictions on the use of imported labour and entry into the arms and liquor traffics, British subjects in Samoa attacked any suggestion that Germany's special interests gave her a special place.[37]

These considerations counted for little with the British Government. In 1885-6 British and German interests in Africa and in the Pacific were in process of readjustment and the situation in both areas was considered as a whole. (See next chapter.) As part of the process a British and a German representative were asked to report on the situation in Samoa, the British representative being J. B. Thurston, the Colonial Secretary of Fiji.

The 1885 report achieved little so far as Samoan conditions were concerned. The Commissioners favoured administration by one of the Treaty Powers, with security guaranteed to the position of the others. The "mandate" so conferred would expire when Samoa became capable of self-government. Alternatively, the native government might be strengthened by introducing a European element and supporting it with necessary external aid, or an Anglo-Samoan Council might be set up[38] on the lines of the German-Samoan Council. Thurston accompanied his report with a summary of conditions in Samoa in which he made clear his

[35] N.S.W.: *Intercolonial Convention, 1883*; Report, p. 8.
[36] No. 114, ibid.
[37] See Thurston's Report of Oct. 1, 1886; C. 5269, 1889.
[38] C. 5269, 1889.

opinion that Samoa should be under German administration, with safeguards of Samoan autonomy and of the interests of Great Britain and the United States.

Before action was taken on the 1885 report, further disturbances were precipitated by the Germans in Samoa. Regarding Malietoa Laupepa as an Anglophile and claiming that his obligations to them had not been discharged, the Germans drove him from the seat of government and the German Consul hauled down the king's flag.[39] In face of British and American objections, Bismarck explained that the German representatives in Samoa had acted on their own initiative and promised that the German Government would adhere to the *status quo* until some other arrangement had been decided upon by the Treaty Powers.[40]

Despite all that had happened in Samoa, British policy was still conciliatory. Having to reach a general *modus vivendi* with Germany in Europe, in the Pacific and in Africa, the British Government agreed to the appointment of another commission of enquiry. J. B. Thurston, "known for his fair-minded appreciation of the German case," was again the British commissioner. The United States was also to participate, it being agreed that no Power would attempt to annex, or claim special predominance, or hinder the peaceful government of the group by the natives, and that a status of neutrality would be maintained. Each commissioner reported to his own government.

Thurston and the United States commissioner both concluded that there should be a native government—strengthened and aided by the Powers. Apia would remain neutral territory. The administration of justice to foreigners would be mainly in foreign hands. While the German commissioner, Travers, was still in Samoa, Dr. Krauel, of the German Foreign Office, called on the British Foreign Office and again pressed for the grant of a mandate to one of the Treaty Powers to rule Samoa for a period of years. Krauel suggested that, as German interests predominated, Germany should be the first mandatory. Consular jurisdiction would be retained for foreigners and perfect trade equality preserved for all nations. Alternatively, administration might be divided between a native government (not under Malietoa) for native affairs and a Mixed Foreign Commission (on which Germans would predominate) for matters affecting foreigners.[41]

The 1886 reports were considered at the Washington Conference

[39] Nos. 3 and 5; C. 5269, 1889.
[40] No. 4, ibid.
[41] Nos. 85 ff., ibid.

of 1887, where Great Britain and Germany made common cause on the point that the preponderance of German commercial interests in Samoa conferred on Germany the right to governmental control, subject to the maintenance of Samoan autonomy and the interests of the other Powers. The British attitude was largely conditioned by problems affecting Anglo-German relations outside Samoa. There were problems in East Africa, over Egypt and over British relations with France and Russia. On November 30, 1886, Lord Salisbury had written to Sir Philip Currie, urging the necessity of "sitting upon the Colonial Office":

> "We shall get into a new Angra Pequena trouble, if we do not look out. That is to say we shall force him [Bismarck] into a menacing position upon a matter upon which we are not prepared to resist him to the end and the result will be a discreditable 'skedaddle.' "[42]

The United States, however, adhered to the principles of Samoan autonomy and the absolute equality of the Treaty Powers in Samoa. No agreement was reached at the Conference, the major issue being whether Samoa should be subject to tripartite or single mandate control.

Soon after the adjournment of the Conference, Germany began a series of encroachments in Samoa. When these led to an abortive attempt to form an Hawaiian-Samoan alliance, Germany threatened war against Hawaii, whereupon the Hawaiians were dissuaded from entering into the alliance by the American interests thus involved. Disputes in Samoa itself soon led to a German declaration of war against Malietoa Laupepa. As a result Malietoa was defeated, exiled and replaced by Tamasese, whose claims had received intermittent support from the Germans in Samoa ever since the Apia Convention. For a time Tamasese, assisted by the German, Captain Brandeis, maintained order fairly well, but the régime had to contend with the jealousy of most of the whites and of Malietoa's following. In September, 1888, there was a serious revolt under Mata'afa of the Malietoa family. Several Germans lost their lives and the German position was maintained only by vigorous naval intervention. Dr. Knappe, the German Consul-General in Samoa, seized sovereign rights for himself and placed the whole of Samoa, with its white residents, under martial law. The German action aroused hot resentment in the United States where Congress voted money for the defence of American rights. Feelings in Great Britain, Germany and the United States cooled

---

[42] G. Cecil: *Life of Robert, Marquis of Salisbury*; London, 1922-32; Vol. IV, p. 36.

somewhat, however, after the famous Apia hurricane of March, 1889, had destroyed all the foreign warships in Apia harbour save the single British representative, H.M.S. *Calliope*. Seeing the turn that events were taking, Bismarck proposed the resumption in Berlin of the Conference held at Washington in 1887. He disowned Dr. Knappe's proceedings and opened the Conference in a conciliatory spirit.[43]

The Conference made it clear that once again the British and German representatives were in general agreement. Recognising that the system of multiple white control had broken down and, having regard to the adjustment of their conflicting interests elsewhere, the two Governments supported a plan for making one of the Treaty Powers (preferably Germany) a mandatory for the other two. Alternatively, separate "spheres of influence" might be established in Samoa and the surrounding groups. In either case native affairs would be left as far as possible to a native government.

The Anglo-German position was opposed by the United States. Washington adhered rigidly to the three-power concept of government in Samoa. Great Britain and Germany acquiesced, for reasons which were frankly stated by Lord Salisbury in a despatch to Sir Edward Malet, who represented the British Government at the Conference:

"I have seen one of the American Plenipotentiaries and gather that your deliberations will not be long or difficult and will result in a victory for the Americans. But as a settlement of the question, this issue will be quite valueless. The fundamental difference between their view and that which we and the Germans have supported is that we think some one European power must lead in the Government of the islands, whilst the Americans think that all three Governments must be on a precisely equal footing. I understand that on this point the Germans mean to give in. We cannot fight it alone, but the Government by three equal consuls will not work smoothly for three years together.

" They are talking of having a majority arrangement by which two of the Consuls shall outvote the other. To this I have a strong objection. Samoa matters very little to us, and I strongly demur to an arrangement under which, for Samoa's sake, we shall quarrel either with the Germans or the Americans once a month. . . .

"The greatest reform of all would be to lay a cable from Auckland to Apia. So, and so only, we should get rid of the *furor consularis*."[44]

[43] Ryden, op. cit., p. xv.
[44] G. Cecil, op. cit., Vol. IV, pp. 127-128.

The combined operation (by which British policy was dominated) of indifference and subordination of island problems to the wider problems of foreign policy elsewhere was as clearly stated in Salisbury's instructions to Malet as in Gladstone's famous letter to Granville.[45]

As a result of the British and German willingness to give in to the American claim, the General Act of the Berlin Conference reinstated Malietoa and declared Samoa to be a neutral state. But the group was subjected to a condominium of the three Powers, which claimed the right to nominate a number of the highest officials. Apia was to have a municipal government of which the consuls of the Treaty Powers should be members. Finally, there was to be a land commission to adjudicate land claims (which exceeded in extent the total area of the group).[46]

This reassertion of joint minimum intervention was the last effort of the Powers to avoid a more direct intervention in Samoa. The condominium policy was regarded by the British Government in 1889 as already outmoded. Its collapse was anticipated by Salisbury, who, if he did not perceive its glaring contrast to the needs of good government in Samoa, certainly did realise that a joint policy of "hands-off" had become a thing of the past.

The record of Samoa in the 'eighties was one of disintegration of the policy of joint minimum intervention when confronted by German expansionism, by the fact that government in Samoa was reduced to the level of *furor consularis et navalis* through the conflict of the native factions and the presence of the privileged Powers and by the divergence of the political interests of Great Britain and Germany and of the United States.

Events after 1889[47] proved that the condominium administration was no better able to stave off the movement towards annexation than had been the joint policy of the 'eighties. By 1898 the Samoan administration stood condemned in the judgment of all observers. After the death of King Malietoa Laupepa that year, the German Government proposed the partition of the group. Germany would take Upolu and Savai'i, while the United States would receive Tutuila (with Pago Pago) and the Manu'a group. In return for renouncing her claims, Great Britain would be compensated else-

[45] See next chapter.

[46] Such a Commission had been recommended by Thurston in 1886; Encl. in No. 96, C. 5269, 1889.

[47] The subject matter of this paragraph is strictly beyond the scope of the present work; it is included because of its bearing on the interpretation of policy before 1893.

where. British entanglements in the Fashoda Incident, South Africa and the Sudan outweighed the objections of Australia and New Zealand. When civil war in Samoa was followed by the report of three commissioners (sent out by the Powers) emphasising the need for annexation, the tripartite convention of December 2, 1899, was signed on the lines of the original German proposals.[48] The compensation of Great Britain took the form of renunciation by Germany of her rights in Tonga, the cession of German islands in the Solomons to the south of Bougainville and various concessions in Africa.[49]

Developments in Samoa and the New Hebrides during the last quarter of the nineteenth century had brought about significant changes in British policy. Throughout the period of joint minimum intervention, the British Government's attitude to the islands had been basically one of indifference. But the inertia that otherwise might have dominated British policy was constantly dissipated by two important factors: the commercial, strategic, missionary and political interests of Australia and New Zealand in the islands and, cutting across these interests, the expanding claims of France, Germany and the United States of America, all of them Powers with which Great Britain had vital interests to settle.

At almost every stage the interest of British Governments in the islands was indirect. Island policy was decided, not in terms of what Great Britain proposed to do in the South Pacific, but in accordance with the changing needs of British foreign policy and the necessity of preserving the interests of the two British Dominions in the South Pacific. Basically, British policy towards the islands themselves had not passed beyond the minimum intervention stage in either the New Hebrides or Samoa. But adjustments of policy had to be made in terms of British interests elsewhere.

[48] Cd. 38, 1900.
[49] See next chapter as to 1886 agreement between Great Britain and Germany. (C. 4656.)

Chapter XXVIII

THE PARTITION PROCESS—NEW GUINEA

New Guinea presented a very different case from Samoa. In 1867, when the first Australian company was formed to develop New Guinea, the eastern half of the island was unclaimed by any European Power, although pearlfishers and missionaries had established themselves on the south-east coast a short time previously. (The Dutch had held New Guinea west of 141° E. since 1828.) In 1884, when the British Government proclaimed a protectorate over South-eastern New Guinea, the scale of settlement and investment was still slight. At no stage in the relevant period were there established foreign interests (as there were in Samoa), whose conflicting claims might open the way to a policy of "internationalisation" and joint minimum intervention. New Guinea was undeveloped territory; so soon as it became a prize, there was nothing to prevent it from being involved in the general grab for colonial territories which grew up in the 'eighties.

In one important respect New Guinea was typical of the South Pacific islands: Great Britain had several times declined to accept any responsibilities there. In 1846 the British Government had refused to ratify the action of Lieutenant Yule (H.M.S. *Bramble*) in taking possession of the south coast.[1] Similarly, Captain Moresby's taking possession of Eastern New Guinea in 1874 was allowed to lapse.[2] In 1867 the Colonial Office declined to sanction the Sydney project of the colonisation of New Guinea by a public company.[3] Eight years later the New Guinea Colonising Association, formed in London, encountered the fatal opposition of the Colonial Office and of the Anti-Slavery Society, which feared the consequences to the natives of unregulated settlement by rough and adventurous men.[4]

Germany also had had few contacts with New Guinea before 1875. Despite her commercial activity elsewhere in the Pacific, Germany was the last of the Powers interested in the islands to

[1] Admiralty to C.O., Oct. 14, 1873; C. 1566, 1876.
[2] See No. 28, ibid.
[3] Melbourne, loc. cit., XII, p. 288. Also *S.M.H.*, Aug. 14, 1875.
4. Nos. 22 and 24 ff., C. 1566, 1876.

send ships and men to New Guinea. Although during the 'seventies some German firms established factories in the contiguous group of New Britain,[5] Bismarck in 1878 repudiated the annexation of the group by the commander of H.I.G.M.S. *Ariadne*.[6] According to official British papers, there were no German factories or plantations in mainland New Guinea even in 1884.[7]

During the late 'seventies British and Australian interests made repeated attempts to break down the opposition of the British Government to intervention in New Guinea. Every possible argument was used: the strategic importance of New Guinea in the defence of Australia, the commercial advantage of seizing so rich a territory, the necessity of protecting the natives from labour trade recruiters and the growing importance of the sea routes via Torres Strait.

These arguments were put forward in 1874-1875 by Mr. F. P. Labilliere, an Australian living in London, in correspondence with the Foreign Office and the Colonial Office.[8] Labilliere asserted that any settlements in New Guinea would soon become self-supporting and claimed that the Australian colonies would be willing to undertake their management.

In view of the known wish of the colonies for a British New Guinea, Carnarvon circulated Labilliere's correspondence amongst the Governors of the Australian colonies and New Zealand, asking for comment. The most determined Australian view was that expressed by Mr. (later Sir) Henry Parkes, as Colonial Secretary of New South Wales:

> "There probably is no country in the world which offers so fair and certain a field for successful colonisation as this great island, as there certainly is none so rich and attractive, and at the same time so close to British rule."[9]

Parkes suggested the granting of an imperial charter to permit an Australian company to colonise Eastern New Guinea without expense to Great Britain, but under British supervision.

The Government of New South Wales in the following year recommended a complete reversal of British policy in the South

[5] S. W. Reed: *The Making of Modern New Guinea*; Philadelphia, 1943; p. 79.

[6] F.O.: Historical Section Handbooks, No. 146, *Former German Possessions in Oceania*; p. 16.

[7] C. 4290, 1885; p. 9.

[8] C. 1566, 1876. Labilliere was a barrister and a prominent member of the Royal Colonial Institute. He was the author of *Federal Britain* (London, 1894) and other works on colonisation.

[9] Encl. 1 in No. 10, C. 1566, 1876. Queensland favoured annexation.

Pacific. A public meeting in Sydney had passed resolutions asking that Great Britain should annex New Guinea in the interests of Australia and the Empire.[10] Great Britain was urged by the New South Wales Government to annex immediately several islands to which New South Wales trade extended, including New Guinea, New Britain, New Ireland and the islands lying north-east and east of these as far as the Solomons, the New Hebrides, the Gilberts and the Ellice Islands.[11] The New South Wales Government prudently added, however, that the colonies possessed neither the resources nor the authority for such an undertaking and suggested that Great Britain should govern this far-flung island empire through the administration of Fiji.

The New South Wales recommendations received strong support in England from the Royal Colonial Institute and from Mr. Labilliere. The Institute believed that German policy towards colonies was about to change. The Hon. Arthur (later Lord) Kinnaird said that "Germany was determined to be a great naval power, and would look to colonisation as the principal means to that end, and if she looked to New Guinea, we may lose a very important colony."[12]

The Colonial Office answered all the appeals on two grounds: (a) there was no "present indication" of foreign action in New Guinea and provision had just been made for the control of the labour trade; hence it was unnecessary and inexpedient for Great Britain to annex New Guinea; (b) in the circumstances annexation would benefit only Australia and, as the colonial governments were unwilling to contribute towards the cost of administration, there was no good reason for British intervention.[13] The British Government bore in mind the refusal of the Australian colonies to contribute towards the cost of administration in Fiji (whose annexation they had repeatedly advocated) and was most reluctant to incur new charges in the South Pacific, which could bring only an indirect and speculative benefit to Great Britain herself.[14]

In general the more reasonable Australian politicians and newspapers agreed with the Imperial Government. Germany was taking no action in New Guinea; France was feared mainly in the New Hebrides. For two or three years the New Guinea question was allowed to rest.

[10] S.M.H., May 20, 1875.
[11] No. 15, C. 1566, 1876.
[12] No. 12, ibid; and Encl. in No. 45, C. 3617, 1883.
[13] Carnarvon to Robinson, Dec. 8, 1875; C. 1566, 1876.
[14] See Carnarvon to Governors, July 9, 1875, and Robinson to Carnarvon, Nov. 2, 1875; C. 1566, 1876. (Former in Appendix).

Rumours of gold discoveries in 1878, however, soon reawakened colonial interest. A new class of adventurers seemed likely to flock to New Guinea and the missionaries of the London Missionary Society feared the consequences of gold-seekers coming into contact with natives in communities destitute of law and order.[15] Here was a problem of a type with which the British Government was familiar and for which British administration in the South Pacific was geared. The Colonial Office requested the Admiralty to send a man-of-war to Port Moresby.[16] The Australian Commodore, acting on his own initiative, sent H.M.S. *Sappho* to Port Moresby, after obtaining for her commander from the High Commissioner (who was in Sydney) authority to act as a Deputy Commissioner.[17] In July, 1878, the Colonial Office stated to the London Missionary Society that the situation in New Guinea could be kept under control by the appointment of the resident Queensland magistrate at Thursday Island as a Deputy Commissioner at Port Moresby.[18]

Naval and High Commission jurisdiction were thus promptly in action. But the need for intervention proved to have been exaggerated. There was no substantial influx of white men, the missionaries' fears having been ill-founded. Preparations made by Queensland (without imperial sanction) to establish administration in New Guinea, if the gold-rush continued, were abandoned.[19] The representations of the Royal Colonial Institute and of Labilliere in favour of annexation were fruitless.[20]

The visit of the High Commissioner, Sir Arthur Gordon, to England in 1878 allowed first-hand discussions to take place between the principal British representative in the islands and the Colonial Office. Gordon was invited to report on the desirability of appointing a Deputy Commissioner in New Guinea.[21] His answer sums up the problem of extending High Commission justice to New Guinea. After pointing out that many nationalities would be involved in the opening up of New Guinea, Gordon stated:

"The jurisdiction of the High Commissioner would extend . . . only . . . to British subjects; but it is not to be supposed that any of the settlers, whatever their nation, would allow murders, thefts, and assaults to be committed (as against themselves) with impunity,

15 L.M.S. to C.O., June 3, 1878; C. 3617, 1883.
16 June 28, 1878; C. 3617, 1883.
17 Adm. to C.O., July 4, 1878; ibid.
18 July 13, 1878; ibid.
19 Melbourne, loc. cit., XII, 294 ff.
20 Nos. 8 and 16; C. 3617, 1883.
21 C.O. to Gordon, Oct. 5, 1878; C. 3617, 1883.

solely because the perpetrators did not happen to be Englishmen.

"In the absence therefore of any legal tribunal, which all would alike recognise, a sort of rough Court would undoubtedly be set up among the settlers themselves for the trial of such cases. . . .

"There would be an utterly illegal Court acting alongside that of the High Commissioner. . . . Under such circumstances the Court established by H.M.'s Order in Council could hardly, with decency, continue to discharge its functions."

Gordon's view was that annexation "by Great Britain of at least certain parts of New Guinea will speedily become inevitable, even if the necessity for such a step has not already arisen." He suggested that he himself should be given a reserve power to annex New Guinea, should events make it necessary to do so. Meanwhile, a Resident Commissioner should be appointed.

Reports that the gold-seekers had mostly abandoned their search apparently led the Colonial Office to cease consideration of Gordon's rather extraordinary advice.[22] British policy throughout the whole incident had resembled that which has been called minimum intervention and the representations of Gordon against relying on High Commission justice in New Guinea were later forgotten.

The New Guinea problem came to the fore again in 1882. The great increase in the colonial interest of Germany had caused much propaganda to be directed in that country towards the annexation of New Guinea. In 1880 a group of Berlin bankers and merchants formed Die Deutsche Seehandelsgesellschaft, a company intended to colonise New Guinea. A memorial on colonisation in the South Seas was laid before Bismarck on behalf of the Company. But the Chancellor, whose scheme to rehabilitate the finances of the Samoan company had just been rejected by the Reichstag, answered that the attitude of the Reichstag made any vigorous action in the South Seas politically impracticable.

The new German company was not dissuaded by its early rebuff, but proceeded to marshal the support of all German firms already doing business in New Guinea or likely to be interested there. News of the German activities (especially the reports in the Augsburger *Allgemeine Zeitung*)[23] caused the problem of New Guinea to be placed before the Colonial Office once again. On December 11, 1882, Labilliere wrote that Germany or France would take New Guinea, unless Great Britain established a stake there.[24] The

[22] There is no indication in the available papers as to how the Colonial Office viewed Gordon's advice.

[23] Nov. 27, 1882. See No. 44, C. 3617, 1883.

[24] Dec. 11, 1882; ibid.

occupation of a few points would secure for Great Britain at a low price a rich, strategically vital area. The Colonial Office simply answered that it was not prepared to act. When the Royal Colonial Institute advanced similar arguments the Colonial Office replied that there was no need to fear German action.[25]

The Australian colonies, being less scrupulous of offending Germany and more directly concerned with New Guinea than was Great Britain, took strong action. Lord Loftus, the Governor of New South Wales, drew the attention of the Colonial Office to the relentless activity of France in the New Hebrides and of Germany in Samoa and New Guinea. Even rumours of Russian activity were mentioned with alarm.[26] The *Sydney Morning Herald* argued that, if Great Britain would not take New Guinea (which was the best possible alternative), then the island should go to Germany, but in no circumstances should the French (with their penal colony schemes) be allowed to take possession.[27] Queensland argued even more strongly than New South Wales. The growing importance of traffic through Torres Strait, the increase of gold mining, pearl-diving and bêche-de-mer fishing in and near New Guinea and the strategic threat to Australia of foreign occupation of the island were all represented to the Colonial Office by the Queensland Government as justifying immediate intervention.

Despite the protests of the Australian colonies, Great Britain refused to be stampeded into action.[28] The key point of her policy in the South Pacific was still to avoid acceptance of political responsibilities. Faced with prolonged inaction on the part of the Colonial Office, the Queensland Government on April 4, 1883, took possession at Port Moresby of New Guinea between 141° and 155° E.[29]

Although the Colonial Office had previously suggested in a general way that the Australian States should annex islands for themselves, this action by the Queensland Government was irregular, inoperative in international law and impolitic.

The British Government took its stand on the illegality of the Queensland action, on the lack of evidence that any Power intended to intervene in New Guinea, on the undesirability of offending Germany and on Queensland's rather mixed record in relation to

[25] Dec. 9, 1882; answered Jan. 4, 1883; ibid.
[26] Loftus to C.O., Feb. 19, 1883; ibid.
[27] *S.M.H.*, Feb. 26, 1883.
[28] See C. 3617, 1883.
[29] No. 55, ibid.

native peoples.[30] Great Britain refused to ratify the Queensland action, despite the fairly general support accorded to it by the other Australian colonies[31] and the Queensland offer to pay the expenses of administration.

The despatch in which Lord Derby communicated the decision of the British Government indicated that a policy of Pacific expansion would have to await Australia's effective collaboration. Sir Thomas McIlwraith, the Queensland Premier, recognised that the British Government would not intervene in the islands unless the Australian colonies acted in unison, or took steps towards federation. He proposed that an intercolonial convention be held to discuss federation and at which future British policy towards the islands might also be considered.

The Convention was held in Sydney in the following December. Three resolutions affecting the New Guinea question were adopted:

(1) That further acquisition of dominion in the Pacific south of the Equator, by any foreign power would be highly detrimental to the safety and well-being of the British Possessions in Australasia, and injurious to the interests of the Empire.

(2) That having regard to the geographical position of the Island of New Guinea, the rapid extension of British trade and enterprise in Torres Strait, the certainty that the island will shortly be the resort of many adventurous subjects of Gt. Britain and other nations and the absence or inadequacy of any existing laws for regulating their relations with the native tribes, this Convention while fully recognising that the responsibilities of extending the boundaries of the Empire belongs to the Imperial Government, is emphatically of the opinion that such steps should be immediately taken as will most conveniently and effectively secure the incorporation within the British Empire of so much of New Guinea and the small islands adjacent thereto as is not claimed by the Government of the Netherlands.

(3) That the Governments represented at this Convention undertake to submit and recommend to their respective Parliaments measures of permanent appropriation, defraying in proportion to population, such share of the cost incurred in giving effect to the foregoing resolutions as H.M. Government, having regard to the relative importance of Imperial and Australasian interests. may deem fair and reasonable.[32]

During the progress of the Conference Lord Derby had under-

[30] July 11, 1883; C. 3863, 1884. Missionary influences especially opposed the Queensland action on the ground that Queensland might be seeking further sources of native labour.
[31] C. 3863, 1884.
[32] No. 68, C. 3863, 1884.

taken that he would give "early and careful consideration" to its resolutions.[33] But it was not until May 9, 1884, that he sent a circular despatch to the Australian Governors reiterating his belief "that no foreign power contemplated interference with New Guinea."[34] Part of the delay had been due to protests from Germany, which declined to believe that the resolutions had been passed solely on the motion of the colonies, and expressed fear that Great Britain was endeavouring to introduce a Monroe Doctrine into the South West Pacific. In January, 1884, Sir Julian Pauncefote, the Under-Secretary for Colonies, had had to assure the German Ambassador that there was no intention of acquiring further territories in the Pacific. The despatch sent by Derby in May attempted to meet the wishes of the colonists half-way while not departing from the undertakings given to Germany. Derby still contended that there was no danger of foreign annexation, but he admitted that "it is always possible that the subjects of a foreign power might require the protection or intervention of their Government." In order to provide protection for British subjects he proposed the appointment of a High Commissioner, or a Deputy Commissioner, "with large powers of independent action, stationed on or near the eastern coast of New Guinea."[35] The colonies were asked to contribute towards the cost of establishing the High Commissioner's jurisdiction.

All that Derby really proposed was a variation of the minimum intervention policy by which British subjects would be protected and a watch kept on the New Guinea situation. Gordon's earlier recommendations were overlooked. There would be no political intervention as reliance would be placed on the January conversations with the German Ambassador and on the belief that Germany had no intention of proceeding to annexation.

The Australian colonies at once promised to contribute the amount required for the establishment of the High Commission in South East New Guinea.[36] The colonies acted the more readily as they had been alarmed by the formation in Berlin in May, 1884, of the Neu-Guinea Kompagnie, which had immediately sent out Dr. Otto Finsch, a man well acquainted with the South Seas, to proceed to the north-east coast of New Guinea and also to New

---

[33] See P. Knaplund, op. cit., pp. 107 ff., for correspondence between Derby and Gladstone. The latter was strongly opposed to intervention.

[34] C. 3839, 1884.

[35] C. 3839, 1884.

[36] Nos. 40-44, ibid. Queensland and Victoria undertook to guarantee the whole cost. The New Zealand Parliament was not in session and no definite answer was made at this stage.

Britain in order to acquire on behalf of the company such territories as were to be had.[37]

The German Government formally gave its support to the Neu-Guinea Kompagnie on August 20. Earlier in the same month Count Munster, the German Ambassador in London, informed Lord Granville, of the Foreign Office, that his Government "wished to take steps to protect more efficiently those islands, and those parts of islands in the South Sea Archipelago, where German trade is largely developed and is daily increasing." Munster admitted that the Australian colonies had a claim to settle in the south-east of New Guinea, but contended that German enterprise should be allowed to develop on the north side and in New Britain.

The available documents are not conclusive, but it seems that Munster's representations, together with the news of the activities of the Neu-Guinea Kompagnie and the renewed alarm of the Australian colonies, determined the British Government to intervene in New Guinea. On the first day of the discussions with Munster Lord Granville had stated that, whereas Germany had no settlement in New Guinea, communications had been taking place between the Home and Colonial Governments, which "were nearer conclusion than is as yet known to the public." On the following day Munster was informed that Great Britain would not oppose the extension of German colonisation in islands of the South Pacific, which were unoccupied by any civilised power, and Granville added that the extension of British authority in New Guinea, which was shortly to be announced, would embrace only "that part of the island which specially interests the Australian Colonies, without prejudice to any territorial questions beyond those limits."[38]

The words actually used were important. Their plain interpretation is that Great Britain would confine her first intervention to the south-east portion of New Guinea, leaving other areas to be considered later. On August 28th the Colonial Office suggested to the Foreign Office that the protectorate should be established over "all the coasts of the island not in the possession of the Dutch Government, with the exception of that part of the northern coast comprised between the 145th degree of east longitude, and the eastern boundary of the territory claimed by the Dutch."[39] This proposal was more extensive than that envisaged in Granville's discussions with Munster when, apparently from a desire not to alarm the German Government, Granville had let it be understood

[37] Reed, op. cit., p. 81.
[38] Encl. in No. 5; C. 4273, 1885.
[39] No. 6, ibid.

that the protectorate would be established in the first instance only over the southern coast. On hearing of the British decision,[40] the German Government immediately protested and suggested that the regions on the northern coast in which both Powers were interested should be the subject of enquiry and report by a joint commission at Levuka.[41]

The German protest succeeded in restricting the British plan. On October 8, when Lord Derby requested the Admiralty to take the steps necessary for establishing the protectorate, British authority was confined to the "southern shore of New Guinea . . . from the 141st meridian of east longitude . . . eastward as far as East Cape, including any islands adjacent to the mainland in Goschen Strait, and to the southward of the said strait, as far south and east as to include Kosman Island."[42]

The protectorate was proclaimed in accordance with these instructions by H. H. Romilly, a Deputy Commissioner for the Western Pacific, on October 23, and by Commodore Erskine on November 26.[43]

Having succeeded in inducing Great Britain to reduce her claim in New Guinea, the German Government itself took action. In October the Neu-Guinea Kompagnie raised the German flag in New Britain and Northern New Guinea, apparently with Bismarck's acquiescence. Great Britain was officially informed in December that the German flag had been hoisted in Northern New Guinea.[44] Bismarck had taken a cool advantage of the British change of front in October and presented the Foreign Office with a most exasperating *fait accompli*. Having informed the Australian colonies throughout the New Guinea affair that no foreign action was to be anticipated, the British Government had to face a storm of fiery criticism in Australia.[45] Steps were promptly taken to protest against the German action and to extend the British protectorate right up to the German boundary.[46] Prolonged negotiations with Germany followed.

[40] No. 7, ibid.

[41] No. 8, ibid. The British Government acceded to the plan for a joint consideration of Anglo-German interests in the Pacific but recommended that the matter should be first discussed diplomatically. (No. 11.) Germany agreed. (No. 19.) Accordingly, New Guinea was amongst the subjects discussed by Meade, the Assistant Under-Secretary for Colonies, and Busch of Bismarck's staff in Dec., 1884. (*PP.* 1884-5, LIV, 653.)

[42] C.O. to Admiralty, Oct. 8, 1884; C. 4217, 1884.

[43] As to the proclamations, see Melbourne, loc. cit., XIII, pp. 153-154. Also see Nos. 41 and 55, C. 4273, 1885.

[44] See C. 4290, 1885; p. 9.

[45] C. 4273, 1885.

[46] ibid.

In the final adjustments between Great Britain and Germany over New Guinea the major factors in policy became very clear. Great Britain had no wish to rule New Guinea; her sole interest there was represented by the strategic and commercial needs of the Australian colonies. Germany was embarking on a policy of commercial and colonial expansion in which New Guinea seemed to play a small, though potentially valuable, part. The consequence of these attitudes was that Great Britain was never willing to seize New Guinea while she had the opportunity of doing so without challenge. So soon as Germany wanted New Guinea, Great Britain had to act.

But her interests were indirect interests. Accordingly policy in New Guinea was continually overshadowed by other factors—the claims of the Australian colonies, the necessity of good relations with Germany and the partition of colonial territories in which Great Britain had more immediate interests than any she possessed in New Guinea. For these reasons the final settlement over New Guinea was profoundly affected by the Angra Pequena and Cameroons disputes. On the evidence of Angra Pequena, the Cameroons and New Guinea, Bismarck did not hesitate to argue that Great Britain was adopting a dog-in-the-manger attitude. Great Britain, he said, was following a policy of raising legal technicalities to defeat the legitimate ambitions of Germany.

Bismarck's main argument, however, related to Egypt. Great Britain in the early part of 1885 was in the throes of the Egyptian question and Gladstone as Prime Minister exerted all his influence on the side of concession. Writing to Lord Granville on March 6, 1885, Gladstone declared:

> "I do hope that you are pressing forward the Pauncefote settlement of the north coast of New Guinea. . . . It is really impossible to exaggerate the importance of getting out of the way the bar to the Egyptian settlement. . . . If we cannot wind up at once these small colonial controversies, we shall before we are many weeks older find it to our cost."[47]

On the basis of giving way over New Guinea for the sake of German goodwill in Egypt, Great Britain was able to reach a settlement in April, 1885. Germany took the northern portion of New Guinea between 141° E. and 8° S. with half of the unexplored interior and all the islands lying off the north coast, together with New Britain. Great Britain took the remainder of Eastern New

[47] Fitzmaurice, E.: *Life of Lord Granville*, Vol. II, pp. 431-2; qu. Benians, loc. cit., p. 459.

Guinea.[48] The division followed approximately the line of the watershed.

A year later Great Britain (and France) gave further recognition to German expansion in the Pacific. By the declaration of 1886 Great Britain and Germany demarcated respective spheres of influence. The settlement excluded Samoa, Tonga and Niue (Savage Island), which were to be regarded as "neutral." The general effect of the declaration was to exclude Great Britain from the northern Solomons, the Carolines and the Marshalls, while giving her a free hand in the Gilberts and islands farther south, including the southern Solomons.[49] The Anglo-German Declaration of Reciprocity, which followed within a few days, established reciprocal freedom of trade in British and German possessions in the Western Pacific. Disputed land claims arising before the establishment of British or German rule were to be examined and decided by a mixed commission. No penal establishments were to be established in the Western Pacific by either Power.[50]

The settlement with Great Britain was part of a wider process in which Germany's new role in the Pacific won recognition from the Powers. France also participated at this stage. By the Franco-German Agreement of 1885, France recognised Germany's acquisitions and Germany disclaimed interest in the New Hebrides and the Society Islands (including Raiatea, specifically mentioned). Inside the French sphere of interest, France promised to protect German subjects in any groups that she might annex.[51]

The declarations of 1886 and the record of British policy towards New Guinea up to 1885 show how determined was the British Government to resist the partition process in the South Pacific. At a time when backward territories all over the world were being divided amongst the Powers, Great Britain, having no territorial ambitions of her own in the South Pacific, was forced into the position of opposing annexation because of the interests of Aus-

[48] C. 4441, 1885.

[49] Anglo-German Declaration Demarcating British and German Spheres in the Western Pacific, April 6, 1886. (C. 4656, 1886.) The conventional line of demarcation ran from Mitre Rock (8.0 S. on coast of New Guinea) to 8.0 S. 154.0 E., then to 7.15 S. 155.25 E., to 7.15 S. 155.35 E., to 7.25 S. 156.40 E., to 8.50 S. 159.50 E., to 6.0 N. 173.30 E., to 15.0 N. 173.30 E. The Western Pacific was defined for the purposes of the Agreement as bounded by 15.0 N., 30.0 S., 165.0 W. and 130.0 E. Germany was to keep north and west of the conventional line, and Gt. Britain to keep to the other side. By the Convention of 1899 (Cd. 38, 1900) Germany ceded to Gt. Britain the Solomon Islands previously on her side of the line except Bougainville and Buka.

[50] Anglo-German Declaration of Reciprocity, Apr. 10, 1886. (C. 4656, 1886.)
[51] F.O.: *Former German Possessions in Oceania*, cit. sup., pp. 19-20.

tralia and New Zealand. British policy still sought to preserve the *status quo* in the island world as the best means of guaranteeing the safety of Australia and New Zealand without incurring the expenditure and trouble of additional colonial responsibilities. When British efforts to arrest partition in New Guinea failed, Great Britain intervened half-heartedly and inefficiently. Her interest in New Guinea being only one of many imperial interests, the affairs of that island were out-balanced by the more urgent calls on British statesmanship elsewhere.

CHAPTER XXIX

THE NEW HIGH COMMISSION

By the early 'nineties the majority of the islands in the South Pacific had either been acquired by one or other of the Powers, or had become the subject of a joint agreement precluding annexation. The process had, as it were, become self-energising: each new annexation, each new agreement for a condominium or a joint policy of minimum intervention, served to stimulate interest in the islands still available for acquisition.

Great Britain had played a large, if reluctant, role in the partition process.[1] Her stake in the island world had grown considerably since 1877 when the High Commission was established. Moreover, it was obvious that the partition process would continue until all the islands had been acquired by one or other of the Powers, or had become subject to long-term agreements for condominium or minimum intervention.

The new political conditions in the South Pacific made it plain that a High Commission designed to take law and order to British subjects in the unannexed islands was fast becoming an anachronism. The virtual extinction of the Queensland labour trade after 1890 (despite the revival of 1892) also contributed to the obsolescence of the High Commission.

As the number of unannexed islands decreased, the British problem became less and less one of controlling British subjects in "uncivilised" islands. Instead, the problem for British policy was becoming more like one of colonial administration in the ordinary sense of the term. In groups where special treaty arrangements had been made special functions devolved on the High Commission. In Samoa after 1879 the High Commission had to recognise and work in conjunction with the Apia Municipality. In the New Hebrides after 1887 there was the duty of co-operating with the Anglo-French Joint Naval Commission. In Tonga the High Commissioner had a specially complicated role. Under the constitution of 1875 Tonga was a limited monarchy and was recog-

[1] In addition to acquisitions already noted, Great Britain had declared a protectorate over the Cook Islands in 1888-1892 and over the Southern Solomons in 1893.

nised as such (with reservations as to extra-territoriality) in the German treaty of 1876 and in the British treaty of 1879.[2] The difficulty in the way of treating Tonga as an independent state was that its rulers naturally lacked experience in running a constitutional monarchy. The problem was made the more difficult by the position in Tonga of the Rev. Shirley W. Baker, a British subject and former Wesleyan missionary, who had become Premier in 1881.

The troubles in which Baker was involved first came to a head in 1885. In that year there were serious disturbances in Tonga, ostensibly as a result of the decision of King George Tubou I to found a free Wesleyan Church, independent of the Wesleyan Church of Australia.[3] Baker was suspected of aggravating the vigour with which the new ecclesiastical policy was pushed through and even of having precipitated the King's decision. Baker's influence was undoubtedly strong and his importance to the King (himself a notable personality) was very great, in view of the extraordinary duties imposed on George Tubou as a constitutional monarch in relation with the Powers. That some part of the disturbances was to be attributed to resentment at Baker's own position was strongly suggested in 1886 when an attempt was made to assassinate him and was followed by strict and terrible penalties exacted by the law.

The allegations against Baker, the application of penal laws against those who declined to support the free Church and repeated outbreaks of violence produced a visit from the famous J. B. Thurston, then Assistant High Commissioner and Acting Consul-General. Thurston counselled moderation on both sides. His advice was either misrepresented to the King or misinterpreted by him. No improvement followed.

Sir Charles Mitchell, the High Commissioner, was then instructed by the British Government to visit Tonga and to report on the disturbances. The basis of the enquiry into the affairs of an independent native kingdom was the necessity for investigating

---

[2] The position of British subjects in Tonga was redefined in 1891 as a result of an agreement signed at Nukualofa between Gt. Britain and Tonga. Articles III (b) (c) of the 1879 Treaty were cancelled. For the future, British subjects in Tonga who were charged with offences against Tongan laws relating to customs, taxation, or public health, or against the local police regulations, might be tried in Tongan Courts. The provision operated only where the offence was not an offence against British law and there were stipulations as to the publicity of the proceedings. (C. 6594, 1892.)

[3] The Tongan Church had been removed from Board of Missions Control in May, 1881; C 5106, 1887.

the position of British subjects and (more especially) of Baker. Mitchell found that the Tongan constitution had been violated and he advised the King to restore liberty of worship. Although he concluded that Baker's influence had been an aggravating factor, the High Commissioner did not order his deportation, recognising his value to the King and the contribution that he could make towards orderly government in Tonga.[4]

The Tongan problem continued, however, down to 1890, with constant embarrassment to the High Commissioner. By that time events had come to the point at which the Tongan authorities themselves were glad of British intervention. Sir J. B. Thurston, who had become High Commissioner, visited Tonga and ordered the deportation of Baker. A relative of the King, Siaosi Tuku'aho, was made Premier with Mr. (later Sir) Basil Thomson as Assistant Premier for nine months. Thomson's appointment was made at the request of the King and the Chiefs, who had found it necessary to invite the High Commissioner's assistance in establishing government on a firm basis. As a result of Thomson's work, Tongan finances were reorganised and Tongan laws were embodied in a new Code of 1891.[5]

The complications in the work of the High Commissioner which were produced by the special status of Tonga did not differ fundamentally from those encountered in Samoa and in the New Hebrides. Western control was being extended in the islands, in the form of governments set up by the Powers or of governments supported or dominated by them. As a result the original conception of the High Commission was becoming outmoded. There was less and less need for a High Commissioner to control British subjects in unannexed territories and more and more need for a centralising agency to control and supervise all British interests, territorial or otherwise, in the South Pacific.

What was happening in the South Pacific was merely the counterpart of similar developments in backward territories all over the world. Especially in Africa, expedients like those used in the Pacific to retard extreme intervention or to divide up control of territories were being employed. The problem of taking law and order to British subjects in the newly acquired territories had already led to the passage of the British Settlements Act, 1887. The preamble of this Act described the situation which had necessitated its enactment:

[4] C. 5106, 1887.
[5] See A. H. Wood: *History and Geography of Tonga*; Nukualofa, 1938. As to 1891 treaty with Gt. Britain, see n. 2. above.

"Whereas divers of Her Majesty's subjects have resorted to and settled in and may hereafter resort to and settle in divers places where there is no civilised government, and such settlements have become or may hereafter become possessions of Her Majesty [and] it is expedient to extend the power of Her Majesty to provide for the government of such settlements."

The Act empowered the Crown in Council to establish laws and set up courts and administration in any British settlement. (Section 2.) "British settlement" was defined as any British possession, not acquired by cession or conquest, which did not possess a legislature of its own. (Section 6.)

The new Act was applied to the South Pacific by the Pacific Order in Council, 1893,[6] which was specifically extended to Tonga, Samoa, the Union Islands, Phoenix Islands, Ellice Islands, Gilbert Islands, the Marshalls, the Carolines, the Solomons, Santa Cruz, Rotuma, New Guinea (East of 143° E.), New Britain, New Ireland and the Louisiade Archipelago, so far as they were not within the jurisdiction of any civilized Power. "All other islands in the Western Pacific Ocean not being within the limits of the colonies of Fiji, Queensland or New South Wales, and not being within the jurisdiction of any civilized power" were also included in the new High Commission area.

The Order thus extended to acquired and unacquired territories, and to territories in which Great Britain had a special treaty position. In respect of the former, it provided throughout the area of the Western Pacific High Commission a centralised framework of government, able to administer all British islands in the South Pacific save Fiji and those controlled by the Australian colonies.[7] In respect of unacquired territories the Order preserved the old High Commission functions on an improved basis and made provision for extension to them of a British Government so soon as they should have been added to the British Crown.

The administrative and legal machineries set up by the Order were essentially those of a colonial government. English law, in both civil and criminal jurisdictions, was to be applied in High Commission Courts as nearly as possible. (Article 20.) Jurisdictions, both original and appellate, were established at common law and in equity, admiralty and probate. The jurisdiction of High

[6] The Order in Council was based also on the Acts of 1872 and 1875, and on the Foreign Jurisdiction Act, 1890.

[7] Further Orders in Council were in fact necessary. See the Gilbert and Ellice Islands Order in Council, 1915, and the New Hebrides Order in Council, 1906 (and 1922).

Commission Courts extended over the whole of the Western Pacific. Provision was made for court registries and for the ordinary legal incidents to births, deaths and marriages and commercial transactions. Legislative power resided mainly in the High Commissioner, who under Article 108 might enact local legislation in the form of Queen's Regulations, save where his authority was specifically restricted. Administration was placed in the hands of the High Commissioner, an Assistant Commissioner (if appointed) and Deputy Commissioners.

The substantial effect of the 1893 Order in Council was to set up a framework of colonial administration for British territories in the South Pacific. British policy had in fact been reversed. After over a century of avoidance of political responsibility, the British institutions in the South Pacific were reconstructed on the basis of what amounted to establishing a new colony in Southern Oceania.

The fundamentals in the development of British policy are clear. The first British interest in the islands (after the period of exploration had ended) was purely the consequence of their contiguity to Navy, the lack of external challenge to the British colony in sources of supplies for the penal colony. Otherwise there was no official interest in the island world at all. So long as other Powers did not settle in the islands, British Governments were content to base a policy of non-intervention on the ascendancy of the Royal Navy, the lack of external challenge to the British colony in Australia and the fact that distance, the ferocity of the inhabitants and the paucity of resources prevented the islands from offering any strong inducement to British trade.

The policy of non-intervention broke down. There were enough resources in the islands and in South Pacific waters to attract trade and commerce from Great Britain and New South Wales. Though not extensive, the contacts of early whalers, sealers and traders with native peoples and rival Americans raised important administrative problems. Moreover, Great Britain was from the end of the eighteenth century a great proselytizing nation. Missionary influence and prestige stood high in British political life. When missionaries demanded protection in the islands or complained that British subjects were being allowed to commit crimes with impunity, the British Government was under strong compulsion to act. Minimum intervention was the first consequence in British policy of trading and missionary activity.

Important as these factors were, they were overshadowed by the British interest in Australia. From the earliest times the New

South Wales settlement was the most important base for the development of island trade and provided a kind of forward headquarters for missionaries in the islands. It was mainly investment and trade from New South Wales which so transformed conditions in New Zealand as to destroy the policy of minimum intervention there. The Australian (and New Zealand) interest remained a factor in British policy throughout the first period of French aggrandizement. The British possession of these two countries, together with the need to protect British missionaries, was a key factor in the attempts made after about 1840 to preserve the political *status quo* in the islands. Political change might have proved adverse to Australia and New Zealand and have led to the embarrassment of the Protestant missionaries, thus necessitating British intervention. It was easiest—and quite consistent with the interests to be protected—to maintain a policy opposed to any change at all.

With economic conditions in the islands being transformed after the 'fifties, the new problem of government began the long, gradual process of reversing British policy. Expedients such as extra-consular jurisdiction and the formation of island governments under the influence of Europeans were first frowned upon by the British Government. But, especially after Australia had involved herself in the labour trade and British, Australian and New Zealand interests had invested heavily in island commerce, British Governments had to readjust the minimum intervention policy so as to permit British officials and British subjects in the islands to take some share in their government. The culmination of this process came in the annexation of Fiji and the establishment of the first Western Pacific High Commission.

In British policy Fiji was regarded as the exception and the High Commission (designed to take law and order to British subjects in backward island territories) as the general rule. But the whole trend of events was opposed to this assumption. The world-wide process of partitioning undeveloped territories amongst the Powers had spread to the South Pacific by 1880. Throughout the next decade, British policy had fought a rearguard action to maintain the old conditions and the existing policy, but, as Gordon, Des Voeux and Thurston had perceived, the battle was a hopeless one.

In the last resort Great Britain had to join in the partition process. Her interests in Australia and New Zealand and the not inconsiderable growth of her interests in the islands prevented her from withdrawing from the South Pacific. A great maritime

Power, concerned to maintain her position in the seas everywhere, she could not allow France, Germany and the United States to divide the islands amongst themselves. A colonial Power, with vital, expanding interests in other parts of the world, Great Britain was compelled to take bargaining advantage of her opportunities in the South Pacific. Despite British resistance, the South Pacific was becoming a colonial area. The High Commission had to be reconstituted accordingly and the policy of minimum intervention finally abandoned.

NOTES ON THE SOURCES

So little research has been done into the general history of the islands (apart from their diplomatic history) that, in writing the present work, two main lines of investigation have had to be followed. What were conditions in the islands? What was British policy? Time and time again the first question has had to be investigated in detail from original sources before the second question could even be framed in terms appropriate to the particular conditions of time and place.

The bibliography reflects this basic difficulty. It has been designed to show all the major sources used and, as a result, extends far beyond the range of British policy as such. Leading references, including the secondary sources, are given on general island history and on the history of particular island groups, in addition to references on British policy.

In the main the research was based on Sydney and Canberra sources. The documents available in the Mitchell Library, the Supreme Court Library, the Fisher Library and the Public Library in Sydney, and in the National Library, Canberra, comprise by far the greater part of the material needed for research into the operation of British policy in the unannexed islands between 1786 and 1893. Moreover, they contain material (such as the Brabourne Papers and the Tahiti Consulate Papers in the Mitchell Library, and the Dalrymple Collection and the Petherick Collection in the National Library, and various papers relating to early contacts between New South Wales and the islands in both these libraries) which are either unavailable, or not readily available, elsewhere. On the other hand has to be set the fact that, although British Parliamentary Papers have been available, there have been some periods for which unprinted Colonial Office, Foreign Office and Admiralty papers were not available. Fortunately the most important documents were generally to be found in the Mitchell Library as printed copies, transcripts or photostats. But in some cases reference has had to be made to such documents either through the agency of colleagues in London or through secondary writings. In a few cases references to newspaper reports (especially to *The Times*) have had to take the place of direct consultation of the primary source.

The modern secondary sources need special comment. The best general account of British policy in the South Pacific is that by E. A. Benians in the *Cambridge History of the British Empire*, Vol. VII, Part I, Chapter XII ("The Western Pacific, 1788-1885"). Despite its brevity, this chapter offers a most useful guide to British policy. G. H.

Scholefield's *The Pacific, Its Past and Future,* for long the principal secondary work on general island history, does not discuss the main outlines of British policy, but is useful for general reading on the diplomatic aspects of the record. The island background tends to be excluded. In the period up to 1875 there is now another diplomatic history in *International Rivalry in the Pacific Islands, 1800-1875,* by Jean I. Brookes. This work is founded on a wide range of sources, British, United States and Australian. It is felt, however, that the factor of international rivalry is somewhat over-emphasised and in matters where Miss Brookes's book and the present work are on common ground the conclusions reached are sometimes at variance.

Of secondary sources on particular island groups the most useful have been R. A. Derrick's *A History of Fiji,* Volume I of which was available in the form of an advance copy in the Mitchell Library, S. Masterman's *The Origins of International Rivalry in Samoa, 1845-1884,* and G. H. Ryden's scholarly work on *The Foreign Policy of the United States in relation to Samoa.* The works of J. S. Marais (*The Colonisation of New Zealand*) and A. J. Harrop (*England and New Zealand*) are referred to in Chapters IX and X, which, however, present a view considerably at variance with the respective opinions of these authors.

SELECTIVE   BIBLIOGRAPHY

SELECTIVE BIBLIOGRAPHY

PART I.   BIBLIOGRAPHIES.
PART II.   MANUSCRIPT SOURCES.
PART III.   PUBLISHED COLLECTIONS OF DOCUMENTS.
PART IV.   OFFICIAL SOURCES.
             (A) Acts of Legislatures.
             (B) Bills before Legislatures.
             (C) Orders in Council.
             (D) Debates in Parliaments.
             (E) Other Parliamentary Sources and Printed Official Papers.
PART V.   NEWSPAPERS AND JOURNALS.
             (A) Newspapers.
             (B) Journals, Periodicals, &c.
PART VI.   OTHER WORKS.
             (A) British Policy.
             (B) History of the Islands.
                 (1) General Descriptions and Narratives.
                 (2) The Policies of the Powers.
                 (3) Trade and Settlement.
                 (4) The Royal Navy.
                 (5) The Labour Trade and the Western Pacific High Commission.
                 (6) Missions.
                 (7) Regional Bibliographies.

ABBREVIATIONS

B.M.: British Museum.
D.C.: Dixson Collection, Sydney.
F.C.: Ferguson Collection, Sydney.
M.L.: Mitchell Library, Sydney.
N.L.: National Library, Canberra.
P.R.O.: The Public Record Office, London.

PART I—BIBLIOGRAPHIES

ALLEN, P. S.: *Bibliography of the Pacific Islands*. (See Stewart's *Handbook of the Pacific Islands*; Sydney, 1922.)

Allied Geographical Section: *Annotated Bibliography of S.W. Pacific and Adjacent Areas*; 4 vols., S.W.P.A. Headquarters, 1944.

BARTON, G. B.: *History of New South Wales from the Records*; Sydney, 1899. (Contains Bibliography of Terra Australis, New Holland and New South Wales. Cf. Chapter I of text.)

Cambridge History of the British Empire; Bibliographies in Vol. II and Vol. VII (Parts I and II); Cambridge, 1940 and 1933.

DAVIDSON, J. W.: "The Literature of the Pacific Islands"; *The Australian Outlook* (Sydney); Vol. I, No. 1, pp. 63-79.

FERGUSON, J. A.: *Bibliography of Australia*; Vol. I (1784-1830) and Vol. II (1830-8) issued to date; Sydney, 1941.

FERGUSON, J. A.: *Bibliography of the New Hebrides and a History of the Mission Press*; 3 vols., privately printed, Sydney, 1917-1943.

335

GIUSEPPI, M. S.: *A Guide to the MSS. preserved in the Public Records Office*; 2 vols., London, 1923-1924.

HOCKEN, T. M.: *Bibliography of the Literature relating to New Zealand* (Supplement, compiled by A. H. Johnstone); 2 vols., Wellington and Auckland, 1909-1927.

JORE, L.: *Essai de Bibliographie du Pacifique*; Paris, 1931.

PETHERICK, E. A.: Unpublished bibliography of Australian historical material. (National Library, Canberra.)

Samoa: *Handbook of Western Samoa*; Wellington, 1925. (For bibliography of Western Samoa from 1798 to 1924.)

United States of America: Library of Congress: *List of Books (with references to Periodicals) on Samoa and Guam* (compiled by A. P. C. Griffin); Washington, 1901.

> *Note*: Several of the works cited in Part VI contain good bibliographies. For island bibliographies, see especially, R. A. DERRICK: *A History of Fiji*; S. W. REED: *The Making of Modern New Guinea*; J. S. MARAIS: *The Colonisation of New Zealand*; G. H. RYDEN: *The Foreign Policy of the United States in relation to Samoa*.

PART II—MANUSCRIPT SOURCES

The following manuscripts were consulted in the Mitchell Library, Sydney. Numbers shown are M.L. file numbers.

1. *Despatches from the Governor of New South Wales to the Colonial Office, 1790-1797 and 1813-1879.*

    > Up to 1856 these comprise duplicates of the originals sent to England. Subsequently they comprise typewritten transcripts of the Governors' Letter-Books.

2. *Despatches to the Governor of New South Wales from the Home Office and the Colonial Office, 1787-1806 and 1831-1878.*

    > Up to 1853 these comprise duplicates of the originals sent to New South Wales from England. Subsequently they comprise type-written transcripts of the originals in the Governor's Office, Sydney.
    >
    > In addition there are copies of enclosures to despatches from the Governor of New South Wales, 1823-1860, being transcripts from papers in the Public Record Office, where no copy was kept in New South Wales of papers sent as enclosures to London.

3. *The Bonwick Transcripts.*

    > Transcripts in manuscript of documents in the P.R.O., B.M. and the C.O., London, dealing with Australian history from 1769 to 1830. The Transcripts contain the Governors' despatches inward and outward, and other papers such as the Cook Papers and Bligh Papers. Many of the transcripts have been printed in the *Historical Records of New South Wales*, and the *Historical Records of Australia*.

4. Correspondence of the Governors of New South Wales relating to New Zealand, 1840-1841, and Fiji, 1874-1875.

5. The Banks Papers.

    (a) *The Brabourne Papers*, Vols. III, IV and V.

    (b) Transcripts of Banks Papers in the B.M., included in the Bonwick Transcripts (supra).

    (c) Other Banks Papers.

6. The Tahiti MSS.

    > These comprise the Tahiti British Consulate Papers, 1827-1874.

7. Foreign Office Papers.

    > Documents of the F.O. on the Pacific Islands (F.O. 58/14 to F.O. 58/33) are available in the Mitchell Library in the form of photostats. They consist mainly of official correspondence with British consuls and naval officers in the Pacific.

8. Log of H.M.S. *Herald* from May 26, 1852, to Feb. 10, 1859. (Capt. H. M. Denham; log kept by R. H. Napier.) Mitchell Library MSS. A. 1783-1785. (See Chapter XIV of text.)
9. In addition, documents (mainly Board of Trade papers) were consulted on my behalf in the P.R.O.

PART III—PUBLISHED COLLECTIONS OF DOCUMENTS.

BELL, K. N., and MORRELL, W. P. (editors): *Select Documents on British Colonial Policy, 1830-1860*; Oxford, 1928.

HENDERSON, G. C. (editor): *The Evolution of Government in Fiji*; Sydney, 1935.

Historical Records of Australia. (Published by the Library Committee of the Commonwealth Parliament.)
Series I, III and IV; Sydney, 1914-
Series I: Despatches between Secretary of State and Governor of N.S.W. to 1848, 26 vols.
Series III: Settlement of the States, 1803-1830, 6 vols.
Series IV: Legal Papers, 1786-1827, 1 vol.

Historical Records of New South Wales (1762-1811). (Published by the Government of N.S.W.); 7 vols., Sydney, 1893-1901.

Historical Records of New Zealand. (Edited by R. McNab); Vol. II, Wellington, 1908.

Hertslet's Commercial Treaties.

KEITH, A. B.: *Selected Speeches and Documents on British Colonial Policy, 1763-1917*; 2 vols., Oxford, 1918.

ONSLOW, S. M.: *Some Early Records of the Macarthurs of Camden*; Sydney, 1914.

PART IV—OFFICIAL SOURCES

(A) ACTS OF LEGISLATURES.
(B) BILLS BEFORE LEGISLATURES.
(C) ORDERS IN COUNCIL.
(D) DEBATES IN PARLIAMENT.
(E) REPORTS, RETURNS, &C., including Parliamentary Papers and other official publications.

(A) ACTS OF LEGISLATURES.

(1) Imperial:

24 Geo. III, c. 25. (East India Company.)
24 Geo. III, c. 56. (Transportation.)
26 Geo. III, c. 32. (E.I.C.)
26 Geo. III, c. 50. (E.I.C. monopoly and whaling.)
27 Geo. III, c. 2. (N.S.W. Criminal judicature.)
28 Geo. III, c. 20. (E.I.C. monopoly and whaling.)
33 Geo. III, c. 52. (The same subject.)
33 Geo. III, c. 58. (Whaling bounties.)
34 Geo. III, c. 45. (Norfolk Island Criminal Jurisdiction.)
35 Geo. III, c. 92. (Southern Whale Fishery.)
38 Geo. III, c. 57. (The same subject.)
42 Geo. III, c. 18. (The same subject.)
43 Geo. III, c. 90. (The same subject.)
46 Geo. III, c. 54. (More speedy trial of offences committed upon the sea.)
53 Geo. III, c. 34. (E.I.C. monopoly and whaling.)
53 Geo. III, c. 155. (E.I.C. Act, 1813.)
54 Geo. III, c. 34. (Trade between the U.K., the E.I.C. area and intervening ports.)

57 Geo. III, c. 1. (See Chapter III, n. 61.)
57 Geo. III, c. 53. (Punishment of offences in the islands and on the seas of the South Pacific.)
59 Geo. III, c. 52. (Duties on colonial produce.)
59 Geo. III, c. 113. (Southern Whale Fishery.)
59 Geo. III, c. 114. (Legalising customs duties in N.S.W.)
59 Geo. III, c. 122. (E.I.C. monopoly.)
1 Geo. IV, c. 90. (Offences committed at sea.)
3 Geo. IV, c. 45. (British ships trading with British colonies.)
3 Geo. IV, c. 96. (Continuing 59 Geo. III, c. 114.)
4 Geo. IV, c. 96. (The New South Wales Act.)
5 Geo. IV, c. 113. (Slave Trade Consolidation Act.)
7 Geo. IV, c. 38. (Committing for trial in U.K. in respect of offences committed at sea.)
9 Geo. IV, c. 31. (Trial of murder and manslaughter committed abroad.)
9 Geo. IV, c. 83. (Australian Courts Act.)
3 & 4 Vict., c. 62. (Dependencies of N.S.W. might be erected into separate colonies.)
6 Vict., c. 13. (Foreign Jurisdiction.)
6 & 7 Vict., c. 94. (Foreign Jurisdiction.)
12 & 13 Vict., c. 96. (Trial within the colonies of offences committed within the jurisdiction of the Admiralty. This did not affect 9 Geo. IV, c. 83.)
28 & 29 Vict., c. 116. (Foreign Jurisdiction.)
33 Vict., c. 34. (Naturalisation Statute.)
33 & 34 Vict., c. 90. (Foreign Enlistment Act.)
35 & 36 Vict., c. 19. (Pacific Islanders' Protection Act, 1872. Not to affect 9 Geo. IV, c. 83.)
38 & 39 Vict., c. 51. (Pacific Islanders Protection Act, 1875.)
38 & 39 Vict., c. 85. (Foreign Jurisdiction.)
39 & 40 Vict., c. 80. (Merchant Shipping Act.)
41 & 42 Vict., c. 67. (Foreign Jurisdiction.)
41 & 42 Vict., c. 73. (Territorial Waters Jurisdiction Act.)
50 & 51 Vict., c. 54. (British Settlements Act.)
53 & 54 Vict., c. 37. (Foreign Jurisdiction.)

(2) Queensland:

25 Vict., No. 11. (Masters and Servants Act.)
31 Vict., No. 47. (Polynesian Labourers.)
33 Vict., No 9. (Immigration Act, 1869.)
44 Vict., No. 17. (Pacific Island Labourers.)
47 Vict., No. 12. (Amending 44 Vict., No. 17.)
49 Vict., No. 17. (Pacific Island Labourers.)
50 Vict., No. 6. (Pacific Island Labourers.)
55 Vict., No. 38. (Pacific Island Labourers.)

(3) New South Wales:

(For early Government and General Orders, see Chapter IV of text and references there cited. Also *Laws and Ordinances of New South Wales, 1824-1829* (Sydney, 1829) and *Acts and Ordinances, 1824-1856* (Sydney, 1856).
41 Vict., No. 23. (Exports of Arms and Warlike Stores.)
43 Vict., No. 6. (Islanders' Shipping Engagements Act.)

(4) Fiji:

(The following statutes are filed in the Mitchell Library, Sydney.)
Cakobau Rex, No. 8 of 1871. (Regulation of foreign labourers.)
Cakobau Rex, No. 27 of 1872. (Regulation of Fijian labourers.)
Cakobau Rex, No. 34 of 1872. (Regulation of immigrant labourers.)

SELECTIVE BIBLIOGRAPHY

(B) Bills before Legislatures.

(1) *Imperial*:
Bill for the Provisional Government of Settlements in New Zealand, 1838. (M.L.)
Kidnapping Bill, 1872; PP., 1872, III, 497, 503.
Pacific Islanders Protection Bill, 1875; PP., 1875, IV, 455, 465.

(2) *New Zealand*:
The Confederation and Annexation Bill, 1883. (Reserved for the Royal Assent, Sept. 8, 1883, which was withheld. See C. 3863, 1884; Encl. in No. 31.)

(C) Orders in Council.

The Western Pacific Orders in Council, 1877, 1879, 1880 and 1893. (In *Hertslet's Commercial Treaties*. For 1879 order see also *Further Corr. rel. to the Navigators*, Part III, Appendix.)

(D) Debates in Parliament.

(All references are to British *Parliamentary Debates*, 3rd series.)

1. Sir William Molesworth's motion of no-confidence in Lord Glenelg, Mar. 6 and 7, 1838. XLI, 495 ff.
2. The New Zealand Bill, June 20, 1838. XLIII, 871 ff.
3. Appointment of S.C. to report on New Zealand, July 7, 1840. LV, 523 ff.
4. French occupation of Tahiti, 1843 and 1844. Several references in LXVIII, LXIX, LXXI, LXXIII and LXXVI.
5. Question by Mr. McFie on Fiji, Feb. 12, 1872. CCIX, 207.
6. Question by Mr. Dixon on Fiji, Feb. 13, 1872. CCIX, 289.
7. Alderman McArthur's motion for a British protectorate in Fiji, June 24, 1872; CCXII, 192 ff.
8. Pacific Islanders Protection Bill, Feb. 15, Mar. 7, Apr. 22, 1872. CCIX, 522 ff., 1615 ff.; CCX, 1665 ff.
9. Question by Admiral Erskine. CCIX, 1154.
10. Alderman McArthur's motion for British rule in Fiji, June 13, 1873. CCXVI, 917 ff.
11. Earl of Carnarvon's statement on government policy towards Fiji, July 17, 1874. CCXXI, 179 ff.
12. Alderman McArthur's motion approving annexation of Fiji, Aug. 8, 1874. CCXXI, 1264 ff.
13. Pacific Islanders Protection Bill, Mar. 8, Mar. 16, May 4, 1875. CCXXII, 1388, 1857 ff.; CCXXIV, 2-3.
14. Mr. Ashley's question on H.M.S. *Sandfly* massacre, Mar. 11, 1875. CCXXII, 1605.
15. H.M.S. *Emerald* in the Solomon Islands, 1881. CCLXI, 1650; CCLXII, 471, 1095, 1821; CCLXIII, 1124; CCLXV, 722.
16. Debate on the Western Pacific, 1881. CCLXII, 1115; CCLXIII, 1454; CCLXIV, 1018.
17. Future Policy in New Hebrides, 1886. CCCVII, 63.
18. Affairs of Tonga, 1887. CCCXI, 168, 875; CCCXIII, 1104; CCCXIV, 955, 1268, 1817; CCCXVI, 1162, 1770, 1777; CCCXVIII, 547.
19. The New Hebrides, 1887. CCCXI, 298; CCCXIV, 682, 946; CCCXV, 247; CCCXVI, 1164, 1309; CCCXVIII, 529, 675, 1701; CCCXIX, 218.
20. Affairs in Samoa, 1888. CCCXII, 1838; CCCXXIV, 847; CCCXXV, 1234, 1471, 1819; CCCXXXI, 508; CCCXXXII, 866.
21. Affairs in Samoa, 1889. Several references in CCCXXXIII, CCCXXXV, CCCXXXVII.

(E) OTHER PARLIAMENTARY SOURCES AND PRINTED OFFICIAL PAPERS.

British Parliamentary Papers were consulted mainly in the form of copies bound by subject in the Mitchell Library. For this reason (and also to assist other students working in the Library) the Parliamentary Papers have been listed by title, followed by the session during which the given paper was printed, the sessional or command number of the paper, the volume of papers into which it has been bound and the page within the volume where it can be found.

(*a*) *GENERAL:*

(1) *British PP.*

Bigge's Instructions; 1823 (532), XXV, 633.

Bigge's Reports on the judicial establishments of N.S.W. and V.D.L. and on the trade and agriculture of N.S.W.; 1822 (448), XX, 539; and 1823 (33), (136), X, 515, 607.

(2) *Royal Navy.*

Australian Station: Station Orders for H.M. Ships and Naval Establishments on the Australian Station. 1884. (M.L.)

(3) *N.S.W. Papers.*

Legislative Council: Cotton in the South Pacific Islands, 1857.

(*b*) *AUSTRALIA AND NEW ZEALAND:*
  (See also under names of island groups.)
New Zealand: Papers relating to the South Sea Islands, 1874.
Victoria: Western Pacific High Commission (Intercolonial Conference, 1881); despatches from the Sec. of State rel. to the Resolution of the Intercolonial Conference resp. the State of Affairs in Polynesia and the Office and Functions of the High Commissioner.
New South Wales: Intercolonial Convention. 1883. Minutes and Reports.

(*c*) *FIJI:*

(1) *British PP.*

Correspondence rel. to the Fiji Islands; 1862 (2995), XXXVI, 701.

Correspondence and Documents rel. to the Fiji Islands; 1871 (435), XLVII, 777.

Reports by H.M. Consul on Trade of the Fijian Islands, 1869 and 1870; 1871 (in C. 343 and C. 429), LXV and LXVI, 225 and 178.

Further Correspondence rel. to Fijian Islands; 1872 (C. 509), XLIII, 469.

Correspondence between Governor of N.S.W. and Earl of Kimberley respecting certain statements in "Kidnapping in the South Seas"; 1872 (C. 479), XLIII, 685.

Despatches to Governor of N.S.W. respecting acknowledgment of government set up by white settlers; 1873 (124), XLIX, 431.

Despatch as to dispute between Fiji Government and White Settlers of Ba; 1873 (337), XLII, 577. (Cited as Corr. rel. to H.M.S. *Dido*, 1873.)

Instructions sent to naval officers concerning the so-called government of Fiji; 1873 (76), XLII, 589.

Instructions to Commodore Goodenough and Consul Layard; 1874 (C. 983), XLV, 297.

Report of Goodenough and Layard; 1874 (C. 1011), XLV, 323.

Correspondence (with Robinson) as to Cession of Fiji; 1875 (C. 1114), LII, 153.

Correspondence respecting Fiji; 1875 (C. 1337), LII, 227.

(2) *Other British Papers.*

F.O.: Proposed Annexation of Fiji Islands, 1873. (Confidential, for Cabinet only.)
F.O.: Confidential Memorandum by Mr. Consul March. May 16, 1873.

F.O.: Confidential Communications with Mr. Consul Layard, August, 1873. (Cited as Confid. Corr. rel. Fiji, 1873.)

C.O.: Confidential Memorandum on Fiji, May 12, 1874.

F.O.: Correspondence between Mr. Consul Layard and the Earl of Derby, Aug. 3, 1874. (Confidential, printed for Cabinet.)

(d) THE LABOUR TRADE:
  (See also under Fiji and Western Pacific High Commission.)

(1) British PP.

Correspondence rel. to the importation of South Sea Islanders into Queensland; 1867-68 (391), XLVIII, 537.

Further correspondence in continuation of No. 391; 1867-68 (496), XLVIII, 623.

Further correspondence rel. to importation of South Sea Islanders into Queensland; 1868-69 (408), XLIII, 1005.

Further correspondence (the same subject); 1871 (468), XLVIII, 155.

Further correspondence (the same subject); 1871 (C. 399), XLVIII, 297.

Correspondence between the Admiralty and the Commanders on the Australian and S. Pacific Stations in regard to the Deportation of South Sea Islanders; 1871 (79), XLVIII, 515.

Further correspondence in continuation of C. 399, 1871; 1872 (C. 496), XLIII, 711.

Report of Proceedings of H.M.S. Rosario among the Pacific Islands; 1872 (C. 542), XXXIX, 543.

Correspondence respecting natives of the Western Pacific and the Labour Traffic; 1883 (C. 3641), XLVII, 411.

Report of Commissioners on working of Western Pacific Orders in Council; 1884 (C. 3905), LV, 781.

Reports concerning state of affairs in the Western Pacific, 1884 (C. 4126), LV 817.

Correspondence rel. proposals for international agreement regulating the supply of arms, ammunition, alcohol and dynamite to natives of the Western Pacific; 1887 (C. 5240), LVIII, 663.

(2) N.S.W. Papers

Report of Royal Commission into alleged cases of kidnapping, 1869.

(e) NEW GUINEA:

British PP.

Correspondence respecting New Guinea; 1876 (C. 1566), LIV, 779.

Further correspondence respecting New Guinea; 1883 (C. 3617), XLVII, 37.

Further correspondence respecting New Guinea; 1883 (C. 3691), XLVII, 187.

Correspondence respecting natives of Western Pacific and the labour traffic; 1883 (C. 3641), XLVII, 411.

Correspondence respecting New Guinea, New Hebrides and other islands in the Pacific; 1883 (C. 3814), XLVII, 611.

Further correspondence respecting New Guinea and other islands and the Convention at Sydney of the Australian Colonies; 1884 (C. 3839 and C. 4217).

Further correspondence respecting New Guinea and other islands in the Western Pacific; 1885 (C. 4273 and C. 4584).

Memoranda of Conversations at Berlin between Mr. Meade and Prince Bismarck and Dr. Busch; 1885 (C. 4290).

Arrangements between Great Britain and Germany rel. to their respective spheres of action in New Guinea; 1885 (C. 4441).

Declarations between the Govts. of Gt. Britain and the German Empire rel. to demarcation of spheres of influence in Western Pacific (Berlin, 1886); 1886 (C. 4656), LXXIII, 479.

(f) NEW HEBRIDES:

British PP.

Reports on punishment of natives of Api (N.H.) implicated in murder of mate of *Dauntless*; 1881 (355), LX, 573.

Papers rel. to punishment of natives for outrages in Solomons and elsewhere; 1881 (284), LX, 521.

Correspondence respecting New Guinea, New Hebrides and other islands in the Western Pacific; 1883 (C. 3814). XLVII, 611.

Anglo-French Relations in the Pacific; 1888 (C. 5256), CIX, 61.

(g) NEW ZEALAND (to 1840):

(1) British PP.

Report from the S.C. of the H.L. on New Zealand; 1837-38 (680), XXI, 327. (Cited as H.L. Cttee. on N.Z., 1838.)

Despatch from Gov. Bourke to Lord Glenelg. with four enclosures, Sept. 8. 1837; 1837-38 (122), XL. 209.

Report from S.C. into petition of London merchants respecting colonization of New Zealand; 1840 (582), VII, 447.

Correspondence with Sec. of State relative to New Zealand, 1840; 1840 (238). XXXIII. 587.

Despatches from Gov. of N.S.W. rel. to N.Z.; 1840 (560), XXXIII, 575.

(2) Other British Papers.

C.O.: Communications rel. to an expedition sent from N.S.W. to N.Z. . . . for recovery of British subjects, September, 1835.

(3) N.S.W. Papers.

The New South Wales Act and Proposed Judicial and Legal Improvements, 1840. (Includes Normanby to Gipps. Aug. 29, 1839, on new legal establishment in N.Z.) (M.L., MSS. A. 1224.)

(h) PITCAIRN:

British Papers.

C.O.: Correspondence on removal of inhabitants of Pitcairn's Island to Norfolk Island, 1857.

C.O.: Pitcairn Island, General Administration Report. 1938.

(i) SAMOA:
(See also under New Guinea as to Germany.)

(1) British PP.

Convention for Apia between Her Majesty and King and Government of Samoa (Sept. 2, 1879); 1881 (C. 2748). XCIX. 383.

Treaty of Friendship between H.M. and King of Samoa (Aug. 28, 1879); 1881 (C. 2747), XCIX, 389.

Convention between Gt. Britain, Germany, U.S.A. and Samoa as to revision of Convention of Sept. 2, 1879 (Sept. 29, 1883); 1884-5, LXXXVII, 601.

Declarations between the Govts. of Gt. Britain and the German Empire rel. to demarcation of spheres of influence in Western Pacific (Berlin, 1886); 1886 (C. 4656). LXXIII, 479.

Correspondence respecting affairs of Samoa, 1885-1889; 1889 (C. 5629). LXXXVI. 295.

Further correspondence respecting Samoa; 1890 (C. 5907). LXXXI. 855.

Final Act of Conference on Samoa, Berlin, 1889; 1890 (C. 5911), LXXXI, 955.

(2) *Other British Papers.*

F.O.: Correspondence respecting affairs in the Navigators' Islands, Part I, 1867-78; Part II, 1877-78; Part III, 1878-79.

Confidential Paper, 3372, Nov. 1877.

Confidential Paper, 3535, March 19, 1878. (Memo. respecting Mr. Liardet's recent proceedings.)

Confidential Paper, 2849, June, 1878. (Corr. respecting H.M.S. *Barracouta* at Samoa.)

Confidential Paper, 3846, Dec., 1878.

Confidential Paper, 4467, July, 1881.

Further Correspondence respecting affairs in the Navigators' Islands, Part IV, 1880.

(3) *U.S.A. Papers.*

State Department: Message from President communicating to Senate information relative to Samoa, 1879. (M.L.)

State Department: Letter from T. F. Bayard to G. H. Pendleton at Berlin rel. to attitude of American and German representatives in Samoa, 1888. (M.L.).

(j) *THE SOCIETIES:*

Correspondence relative to proceedings of the French at Tahiti; 1843 (473), LXI, 363.

Correspondence relative to the Society Islands; 1844 (529), LI, 95.

Correspondence relative to removal of Mr. Pritchard; 1845 (603), LII, 287.

Papers relative to Tahiti and Leeward or Society Islands; 1847 (841), LXX, 63.

Correspondence respecting expulsion of Rev. J. Jones from Mare (Loyalty Islands) by the French authorities; 1888 (C. 5581), CIX, 75.

Declaration for abrogation of Declaration of 1847 between Great Britain and France; 1888 (C. 5372), CIX, 71.

(2) *Other British Papers.*

Correspondence relative to the Society Islands, 1822-47. (Parts I, II and III.) (Private and Confidential, printed solely for the use of Cabinet.)

F.O.: Memorandum on the Society Islands as distinct from the Georgian, together with French memorandum relative to the independence of Raiatea, Huahine and Borabora, 1846.

(k) *THE SOLOMONS:*

British PP.

Papers relative to the Solomon Islands; 1881 (284), LX, 521.

Papers relative to operations of H.M.S. *Opal* against natives of the Solomon Islands; 1887 (58), LII, 617.

(l) *TONGA:*

British PP.

Treaty of Friendship between Gt. Britain and Tonga (Nukualofa, Nov. 29, 1879); 1882, LXXXI, 575.

Report by High Commissioner of the Western Pacific on Tonga; 1887 (C. 5106), LVIII, 491.

Report in continuation of C. 5106; 1887 (C. 5161), LVIII, 507.

Agreement with Tonga on trial of British subjects by Tongan Courts (Nukualofa, June 2, 1891); 1892 (C. 6594), XCV, 749.

(m) *WESTERN PACIFIC HIGH COMMISSION:*

(See also under Labour Trade.)

(1) *British PP.*

Correspondence respecting New Guinea, New Hebrides and other islands in the Pacific; 1883 (C. 3814), XLVII, 611.

Correspondence respecting natives of Western Pacific and the labour traffic; 1883 (C. 3641), XLVII, 411.

Correspondence respecting convention at Sydney of the Australian Colonies; 1884 (C. 3863), LV, 487.

Report of Commissioners on working of Western Pacific Orders in Council; 1884 (C. 3905), LV, 781.

Reports concerning state of affairs in the Western Pacific; 1884 (C. 4126), LV, 817.

Correspondence rel. proposals for international agreement regulating the supply of arms, ammunition, alcohol and dynamite to natives of the Western Pacific; 1887 (C. 5240), LVIII, 663.

(2) Other British Papers.

W.P.H.C.: Public Services Reorganisation Report, 1937 (Suva).

PART V—NEWSPAPERS AND JOURNALS.

(A) NEWSPAPERS.

The Australian (1824-1848).

The Fiji Times (1869-1873).

The Sydney Gazette (1803-1842).

The Sydney Morning Herald (from 1831 to 1842, the *Sydney Herald*); (at relevant dates only).

The Times. (At relevant dates only.)

(B) JOURNALS AND PERIODICAL PUBLICATIONS.

The number of relevant periodicals available in full series has been small. The most important have been:

English Historical Review; London, 1886 to date.

History; London, 1916 to date.

Journal and Proceedings of the Royal Australian Historical Society; Sydney, 1901 to date. (J.R.A.H.S.)

Journal of Modern History; Chicago, 1929 to date.

La Revue du Pacifique; Paris, 1924-37.

L'Océanie française; Papeete, 1844-45

Pacific Islands Monthly; Sydney, 1931 to date.

Polynesian Society Journal (the Polynesian Society, New Zealand); New Plymouth, 1892 to date.

Revue de l'histoire des colonies françaises; Paris, 1913 to date.

References to other periodicals and journals have been mainly through special collections of articles, such as those in the Petherick Collection (N.L.) and the newspaper cutting books of the Mitchell Library, Sydney. Journals, articles from which have been consulted in this way, include *New Zealand Journal, Blackwood's, Edinburgh Review, Australian and New Zealand Magazine, La Revue Maritime et Coloniale, Westminster Review.*

In addition there were particular references to other journals as follows:

Australian Geographer; Vol. III, No. 4. (J. Shepherd: *"Austral-Asia."*)

Queensland Review, June, 1886. (C. F. Clarke: "The Pacific and the New Hebrides.")

Australian and New Zealand Assocn. for the Advancement of Science (1937). (A. B. Chappell: "James Busby, British Resident in New Zealand, 1833-1840.")

New Zealand Institute, Transactions; Vol. LII. (J. C. Andersen: "The Mission of the *Britomart* at Akaroa in August, 1840.")

Royal Geographical Society Journal; Vol. XXI (1851). (J. E. Erskine: "Proceedings at the South Sea Islands.")

Royal Historical Society, Transactions; Vol. XXVIII, 1946. (W. P. Morrell: "The Transition to Christianity in the South Pacific.")

SELECTIVE BIBLIOGRAPHY

PART VI—OTHER WORKS.

(A) BRITISH POLICY.

Discussions on Colonial Questions, Being a Report of the Conference held at Westminster Palace Hotel, July, 1871; London, 1872.

Statement of the Principles and Objects of a Proposed National Society for the Cure and Prevention of Pauperism, by Means of a Systematic Colonisation; London, 1920.

ADDERLEY, C. B. (Lord Norton): *Review of "The Colonial Policy of Lord John Russell's Administration"*; London, 1869.

BANNISTER, S.: *Humane Policy; or Justice to the Aborigines of New Settlements, etc.*; London, 1830.

British Colonization and Coloured Tribes; London, 1838.

BEECHAM, J.: (See under New Zealand.)

BENTHAM, J.: *Panopticon versus New South Wales, &c.*, London, 1812.

BROUGHAM, H,: *An Inquiry into the Colonial Policy of the European Powers*; 2 vols. Edinburgh, 1803.

BUCKLE, G. E.: *The Life of Benjamin Disraeli, Earl of Beaconsfield*; 6 vols., London, 1920.

BULLER, C.: *Responsible Government of Colonies*; London, 1840.

CALLANDER, J.: *Terra Australis Cognita*, etc.; 3 vols., Edinburgh, 1766-1768.

Cambridge History of the British Empire; Vol. II (The New Empire, 1783-1870), Vol. VII (Australia and New Zealand); Cambridge, 1940 and 1933.

CECIL, A.: *British Foreign Secretaries, 1807-1916*; London, 1927.

CECIL, G.: *Life of Robert, Marquis of Salisbury*; 4 vols., London, 1922-32.

COATES, D.: (See under New Zealand.)

Colonial Society Prospectus; London, 1837. (M.L., MSS., A. 272.)

CURREY, C. H.: *British Colonial Policy, 1783-1915*; Oxford, 1916.

Dictionary of National Biography.

EGERTON, H. E.: *Short History of British Colonial Policy, 1606-1909*; London, 1897 (ed. 1932).

FAY, C. R.: *Imperial Economy and its place in the Formation of Economic Doctrine*; Oxford, 1934.

FIDDES, G. V.: *The Dominions and Colonial Offices*; London, 1926.

FITZPATRICK, B.: *British Imperialism and Australia, 1783-1833*; London, 1939. *The British Empire in Australia, 1834-1939*; Melbourne, 1941.

FOX, R.: *Colonial Policy of British Imperialism*; London, 1933.

GREY, Earl: *Colonial Policy of Lord John Russell's Administration*; 2 vols., London, 1853.

GRIFFITH, G. T.: *Population Problems of the Age of Malthus*; Cambridge, 1926.

HALL, H. L.: *Australia and England*; London, 1934.

HASLUCK, P:. *Black Australians*; Melbourne, 1942. (For references to C.O. and native policy.)

HINDS, S.: (See under New Zealand.)

HUSKISSON, W.: *The Huskisson Papers* (ed. by L. Melville); London, 1931. *Speeches . . . with a Biographical Memoir supplied to the Editor from Authentic Sources*; 3 vols., London, 1831.

JENKS, L. H.: *The Migration of British Capital to 1875*; London, 1927.

KNAPLUND, P.: *Gladstone and Britain's Imperial Policy*; London, 1927.

KNORR, K. E.: *British Colonial Theories, 1570-1850*; Toronto, 1944.

LABILLIERE, F. P.: *Federal Britain; or Unity and Federation of the Empire; with chapter on Imperial Defence by Major Sir G. S. Clarke*; London, 1894.

LANG, J. D.: (See under New Zealand and Missions.)

The Coming Event! or Freedom and Independence for the Seven United Provinces of Australia; London, 1870. (Also Sydney, 1870.)

Brief Notes of the New Steam Postal Route from Sydney to England by San Francisco to New York, &c.; Sydney, 1875.

345

LEWIS, G. C.: *The Government of Dependencies*; London, 1841.

LINDLEY, M. F.: *The Acquisition and Government of Backward Territory in International Law*; London, 1926.

LUCAS, C. P.: *Historical Geography of the British Colonies*; Oxford, 1907.

MERIVALE, H.: *Lectures on Colonisation and Colonies*; London, 1861.

MILLS, R. C.: *The Colonisation of Australia, 1829-1842*; London, 1915.

MOLESWORTH, W.: *Speech in the House of Commons on March 6, 1838, on the State of the Colonies*; London, 1838.

MORRELL, W. P.: *British Colonial Policy in the Age of Peel and Russell*; Oxford, 1930.

MOTTE, S.: *Outline of a System of Legislation for securing protection to the Aboriginal Inhabitants of all Countries colonised by Great Britain*; London, 1840.

O'BRIEN, E.: *The Foundation of Australia, 1786-1800*; London, 1937; Sydney, 1950.

PARKES, H.: *Speeches on Various Occasions connected with the Public Affairs of N.S.W., 1848-1874*; Melbourne, 1876.

RAM, V. S.: *Comparative Colonial Policy with special reference to the American Colonial Policy*; Patna, 1925.

REES, W. L. and L.: *The Life and Times of Sir George Grey, K.C.B.*; London, 1892. (3 ed., n.d.)

SCHUYLER, R. L.: *The Fall of the Old Colonial System, a Study in British Free Trade, 1770-1870*; New York, 1945.

VOGEL, J.: *Great Britain and her Colonies*; London, 1865.

New Zealand and the South Sea Islands; London, 1878.

WAKEFIELD, E. G.: (See under New Zealand.)

WILLIAMSON, J. A.: *The Ocean in English History*; Oxford, 1941.

WILLSON, B.: *The Paris Embassy, 1814-1920*; London, 1927.

WRONG, E. M.: *Charles Buller and Responsible Government*; Oxford, 1926.

(B) HISTORY OF THE ISLANDS.

(1) GENERAL DESCRIPTIONS AND NARRATIVES COVERING THE PERIOD FROM 1770 TO 1893.

(See also under Trade and Settlement, Sec. 3, below.)

Anon.: *A Serious Admonition to the Publick on the Intended Thief Colony at Botany Bay*; London, 1786. (D.C., N.L.) Reprinted by G. Mackaness in *Australian Historical Monographs* (No. 7).

Anon.: *An Historical Narrative of the Discovery of New Holland and New South Wales, containing an account of the inhabitants, soil, animals, and other productions of those countries; and including a particular description of Botany Bay*; London, 1786. (2 ed., consulted, London, 1786.) (1 ed., D.C.; 2 ed., M.L.)

Anon.: *Copious Remarks on the Discovery of New South Wales; with a Circumstantial Description of Botany Bay, and the Islands, Bays and Harbours, &c., lying near it. . . . To which are added, Prefatory Observations . . . on Transportation, &c.*; London, 1787. (N.L.)

Anon.: *The History of New Holland, from its first discovery in 1616 to the present Time. . . . To which is prefixed an Introductory Discourse on Banishment*; London, 1787. (There were 2 edd. in 1787; copies in D.C., F.C., M.L., N.L. As to attribution of this work to William Eden, Lord Auckland, see E. O'Brien, op. cit., pp. 183-185.)

Anon.: *The South Sea Islander; Containing Many Interesting Facts Relative to the Former and Present State of Society in the Island of Otaheite*; New York, 1820. (M.L., N.L.)

ABBOTT, J. H. M.: *The South Seas*; London, 1908.

BURNEY, J.: *A Chronological History of the Voyages and Discoveries in the South Sea or Pacific Ocean*; 5 vols., London, 1803-17.

SELECTIVE BIBLIOGRAPHY

COLLINS, D.: *An Account of the English Colony in New South Wales . . . to which are added Some Particulars of New Zealand . . .* ; London, 1798. (A second volume was issued in 1802.) 2 ed., abridged to one volume, by Maria Collins; London, 1804.

COLQUHOUN, A. R.: *The Mastery of the Pacific*; London, 1902.

COOTE, W.: *The Western Pacific*; London, 1883.

DILLON, P.: *Narrative and Successful Result of a Voyage in the South Seas; . . . to ascertain the actual fate of La Perouse's Expedition. . . .*; 2 vols., London, 1829.

HAWKESWORTH, J.: *An Account of the Voyages undertaken by the order of His Present Majesty for making discoveries in the Southern Hemisphere, and successively performed by Commodore Byron, Captain Wallis, Captain Carteret, and Captain Cook . . .* ; 3 vols., London, 1773.

HOOKER, J. D.: (Ed.) *Journal of the Right Hon. Sir Joseph Banks during Captain Cook's first Voyage in H.M.S. "Endeavour"*; London, 1896.

PARKINSON, S.: *A Journal of a Voyage to the South Seas in H.M.S. "Endeavour" . . .* ; London, 1773 (2 ed., 1784).

PHILLIP, A.: *The Voyage of Governor Phillip to Botany Bay*; London, 1789. (There were several subsequent edd. and translations into French and German.)

REEVES, E.: *Brown Men and Women*; London, 1898.

RIVERS, W. H. R.: *The Melanesian Society*; 2 vols., Cambridge, 1914.

RIVERS, W. H. R.: (ed.) *Essays on the Depopulation of Melanesia*; Cambridge, 1922.

ROBERTS, S. H.: *Population Problems of the Pacific*; London, 1927.

RUSSELL, M.: *Polynesia, or an Historical Account of the Principal Islands in the South Sea*; London, 1842.

THOMAS, J.: *Cannibals and Convicts*; London, 1886.

TURNBULL, J.: *A Voyage round the World in the years 1800-1804; in which the author visited the principal Islands in the Pacific Ocean*; 3 vols., London, 1805. For 2 ed., see under New Zealand.

WHARTON, W. J. L.: (ed.) *Captain Cook's Journal of his first Voyage Round the World, made in H.M. Bark "Endeavour"*; London, 1893.

WILKES, C.: *Narrative of the U.S. Exploring Expedition during the years 1838-1842*; 5 vols., Philadelphia, 1845; ed. 1852.

WILLIAMSON, R. W.: *The Social and Political Systems of Central Polynesia*; 3 vols., Cambridge, 1924.

(2) THE POLICIES OF THE POWERS.

BENOIT, P.: *L'Océanie Française*; Paris, 1933.

BROOKES, J. I.: *International Rivalry in the Pacific Islands, 1800-1875*; Berkeley and Los Angeles, 1941.

BRYAN, E. H.: *American Polynesia*; Honolulu, 1941.

CAILLOT, E.: *Histoire de la Polynésie Orientale*; Paris, 1910.

DAWSON, W. H.: *The German Empire*; 2 vols., London, 1919.

DESCHANEL, P.: *La Politique Française en Océanie*; Paris, 1884. *Les Intérêts Français dans l'Océan Pacifique*; Paris, 1888.

DESCHARME, P.: *Compagnies et Sociétés coloniales allemandes*; Paris, 1903.

DULLES, F. R.: *America in the Pacific, A Century of Expansion*; Boston, 1932.

FLETCHER, C. B.: *The New Pacific: British Policy and German Aims*; London, 1917. *The Problem of the Pacific*; London, 1920. *Stevenson's Germany; The Case against Germany in the Pacific*; London, 1920.

GREAT BRITAIN AND IRELAND (Foreign Office): Historical Section Handbooks, 1920. (Edited G. W. Prothero.) No. 42: *German Colonisation*. No. 139: *Discoveries and Acquisitions in the Pacific*.

No. 144: *British Possessions in Oceania.*
No. 145: *French Possessions in Oceania.*
No. 146: *Former German Possessions in Oceania.*
No. 147: *New Hebrides.*
GREENWOOD, G.: *Early American-Australian Relations*; Melbourne, 1944.
LANESSAN, J. L. de: *L'Expansion Coloniale de la France*; Paris, 1886.
LEROY-BEAULIEU, P.: *De la Colonisation chez les Peuples Modernes*; 6 ed., Paris, 1908.
MAGER, H.: *Le Monde Polynésien*; Paris, 1902.
PERBAL, R. P.: *Les Missionaires français et le nationalisme*; Paris, 1939.
RAM, V. S.: *Comparative Colonial Policy, with special reference to the American Colonial Policy*; Patna, 1926.
REGELSPERGER, G., PELLERAY, E., and FROMENT-GUIEYESSE, G.: *L'Océanie Française*; Paris, 1922.
ROBERTS, S. H.: *History of French Colonial Policy*; 2 vols., London, 1929.
RUSSIER, H.: *Le Partage de L'Océanie*; Paris, 1905.
SCHNEE, H.: *German Colonisation Past and Future*; London, 1926.
SCHOLEFIELD, G. H.: *The Pacific, Its Past and Future*; London, 1919.
SCOTT, E.: *Terre Napoléon*; London, 1910.
SOUTHWORTH, C.: *The French Colonial Venture*; London, 1931.
STEPHENS, H. M.: *The Conflict of European Nations in the Pacific.* (From "The Pacific Ocean in History"; Papers and Addresses presented at the Panama-Pacific Historical Congress, San Francisco; Berkeley and Palo Alto, California, 1915.)
TOWNSEND, M. E.: *The Rise and Fall of Germany's Colonial Empire, 1884-1918*; New York, 1930.
Origins of German Colonialism, 1871-1885; New York, 1921.
ZIMMERMAN, A.: *Geschichte der Deutschen Kolonialpolitik*; Berlin, 1914.

(3) TRADE AND SETTLEMENT.

ANDERSON, A.: *Historical and Chronological Deduction of the Origin of Commerce from the earliest accounts*; 4 vols., London, 1787. (N.L.) (Refers to background of the N.S.W. settlement and the southern whale fishery.)
ARNAUDTIZON, M.: *Exploration Commerciale dans les Mers du Sud et de la Chine*; Rouen, 1854.
AUBE, T.: *Entre deux Campagnes*; *Notes d'un Marin*; Paris, 1881.
BARTLEY, N.: *Opals and Agates*; *being memories of fifty years of Australia and Polynesia*; Brisbane, 1892.
BERNATZIK, H. A.: *Sudsee: Travels in the South Seas*; trans. by V. Ogilvie; London, 1935.
BROWN, G.: *Melanesians and Polynesians*; London, 1910.
CHEEVER, H. T.: *The Whaleman's Adventures in the Southern Ocean*; ed. W. Scoresby, 3 ed., London, 1859. (The present title is the sub-title of what appears to be ed. 1 in the M.L., 1850: *The Whale and his Captors*.)
COGHLAN, T. A.: *Labour and Industry in Australia from the first Settlement in Australia to 1901*; 4 vols., Oxford, 1918.
COLLINS, D.: (See under General Descriptions and Narratives.)
COOPER, H. S.: *The Islands of the Pacific*; *their Peoples and their Products*; London, 1888.
DAKIN, W. J.: *Whalemen Adventurers*; Sydney, 1934.
DELANO, A.: *A Narrative of Voyages and Travels in the Northern and Southern Hemispheres . . .* ; Boston, 1817.
DUNBABIN, T.: *Slavers of the South Seas*; Sydney, 1935.
ELLIS, A. F.: *Ocean Island and Nauru*; *their story*; Sydney, 1935.
EVATT, H. V.: *Rum Rebellion*; Sydney, 1938.

FITZPATRICK, B.: (See under British Policy, Part VI (A).)
GREENWOOD, G.: *Early American-Australian Relations*; Melbourne, 1944.
HALL, H. D.: *Immigration in the Pacific; Analysis of Acts and Administration*; Honolulu, 1925.
HOHMAN, E. P.: *The American Whaleman; a Study of Life and Labour in the Whaling Industry*; New York, 1928.
HUNTER, J.: *An Historical Journal of the Transactions at Port Jackson and Norfolk Island, including the Journals of Governors Phillip and King . . .* ; London, 1793. (See especially for flax trade and whaling.)
JARMAN, R.: *Journal of a Voyage to the South Seas in the "Japan"*; London, 1838. (M.L. has also an ed. without date.)
LAWSON, W.: *Pacific Steamers*; Glasgow, 1927.
LOCKERBY, W.: *Journal of William Lockerby, Sandalwood Trader in the Fijian Islands, 1808-9*; ed. im Thurn and Wharton (Hakluyt Society); London, 1925.
LUBBOCK, B.: *The Colonial Clippers*; Glasgow, 1921.
McNAB, R.: *Murihiku*; Wellington, 1909. (See under New Zealand for full title.)
The Old Whaling Days; Christchurch, 1913.
From Tasman to Marsden; Dunedin, 1914.
MACONOCHIE, A.: *The Pacific Ocean*; London and Edinburgh, 1818.
MACPHERSON, D.: *Annals of Commerce, Manufactories, Fisheries, and Navigations*; 4 vols., London, 1805.
MANN, D.: *The Present Picture of New South Wales*; London, 1811.
MORSE, H. B.: *The Chronicles of the East India Company trading to China, 1635-1834*; Harvard, 1926.
New South Wales Society for affording Protection to the Natives of the South Sea Islands, and Promoting their Civilisation. (Printed record of formation of the Society in 1813. M.L., MSS. A. 877 at p. 355.)
PARKINSON, C. N.: *Trade in the Eastern Seas, 1793-1813*; Cambridge, 1937.
PHILIPS, C. H.: *The East India Company, 1784-1834*; Manchester, 1940.
PORTER, D.: *Journal of a Cruise in the Pacific, 1812-1814*; New York, 1822.
PRITCHARD, W. T.: (See under Fiji.)
RHODES, F.: *Pageant of the Pacific*; 2 vols., London, 1937.
RODRIGUES, J. C.: *The Panama Canal; its History, its Political Aspect and its Financial Difficulties*; London, 1885.
ST. JULIAN, C.: *Official Report on Central Polynesia*; Sydney, 1857.
SHANN, E. O. G.: *An Economic History of Australia*; Cambridge, 1930.
Southern Whale Fishery Company: Report to Directors, 1850. (M.L.)
STEWART, C. S.: *A Visit to the South Seas in the U.S.S. "Vincennes" during the years 1829 and 1830*; 2 vols., New York, 1832.
THOMPSON, L. G.: *History of the Fisheries of New South Wales*; Sydney, 1893.
VILLIERS, A. J.: *Vanished Fleets*; London, 1931.
WILLIAMS, E. C.: *Life in the South Seas*; New York, 1860.

(4) THE ROYAL NAVY.
(See also under The Labour Trade.)

BEECHEY, F. W.: *Narrative of a Voyage to the Pacific . . . performed in H.M.S. "Blossom"*; 2 vols., London, 1831. (M.L., N.L.)
BELCHER, E.: *Narrative of a Voyage round the World . . . in H.M.S. "Sulphur," 1836-1842*; 2 vols., London, 1843.
BLIGH, W.: *A Narrative of the Mutiny on board H.M.S. "Bounty," and the Subsequent Voyage of Part of the Crew in the Ship's Boat . . . to Timor*; London, 1790.
A Voyage to the South Sea, undertaken by command of His Majesty, for the purpose of conveying the Bread-fruit-tree to the West Indies in H.M.S. "Bounty," commanded by Lieut. William Bligh. Including an account of the Mutiny . . . to Timor; London, 1792.
Bligh and the "Bounty." (The above, ed. by L. Irving; London, 1936.)

BRENCHLEY, J. L.: *Jottings during the Cruise of H.M.S. "Curacoa" amongst the South Sea Islands in 1865*; London, 1873.

DARWIN, C. R.: *Narrative of the Surveying Voyage of H.M.S. . . . "Beagle" between the years 1832-1836*; Vol. III; London, 1839.

ERSKINE, J. F.: *Journal of a Cruise among the Islands of the Western Pacific in H.M.S. "Havannah"*; London, 1853.

GOODENOUGH, J. G.: *Journal of Commodore Goodenough, during his last Command as Senior Officer on the Australian Station, 1873-1875*; ed. with a memoir, by his widow; London, 1876.

HAMILTON, G.: *A Voyage round the World in H.M. Frigate "Pandora" (1790-1792)*; Berwick, 1793.

(The same.) Edited by B. Thomson; London, 1915.

HOOD, T. H.: *Notes of a Cruise in H.M.S. "Fawn" in the Western Pacific in the year 1862*; Edinburgh, 1863.

JUKES, J. B.: *Narrative of the Surveying Voyage of H.M.S. "Fly" . . . 1842-1846*; 2 vols., London, 1847.

MACGILLIVRAY, J.: *Narrative of the Voyage of H.M.S. "Rattlesnake" commanded by . . . Capt. Owen Stanley . . . 1846-1850*; 2 vols., London, 1853.

MORESBY, J.: *Discoveries and Surveys in New Guinea . . . a cruise in Polynesia . . . of H.M.S. "Basilisk"*; London, 1876.

WALPOLE, F.: *Four Years in the Pacific in H.M.S. "Collingwood," 1844-1848*; 2 vols., London, 1849.

(5) THE LABOUR TRADE AND THE WESTERN PACIFIC HIGH COMMISSION.

CHURCHWARD, W. B.: *"Blackbirding" in the South Pacific*; Swan Sonnenschein, 1888.

DUNBABIN, T.: *Slavers of the South Seas*; Sydney, 1935.

GORDON, A. H.: *Fiji: Records of Private and Public Life, 1875-1880* (Private and Confidential); 4 vols., Edinburgh, 1897-1910.

HOPE, J. L. A.: *In Quest of Coolies*; London, 1872.

LUCAS, T. P.: *Cries from Fiji*; n.d., n.p., circa 1880.

LUKE, H.: *The British Pacific Islands*; Oxford (O.P.W.A.), 1943.

MARKHAM, A. H.: *The Cruise of the "Rosario" amongst the New Hebrides and Santa Cruz Islands*; 2 ed., London, 1873.

MAUDSLAY, A. P.: *Life in the Pacific Fifty Years Ago*; London, 1930.

PALMER, G.: *Kidnapping in the South Seas*; Edinburgh, 1871.

PATON, J. G.: *Slavery under the British Flag; Correspondence and Protest against the Kanaka Labour Traffic*; Woodford, 1892.

ROBERTS, S. H.: *The Squatting Age in Australia*; Melbourne, 1935. (Refers to early use of imported labour.)

Population Problems of the Pacific; London, 1927.

ROMILLY, H. H.: *The Western Pacific and New Guinea*; London, 1886.

im THURN, E.: *Thoughts, Talks and Tramps*; ed. with a memoir by R. R. Marett; Oxford, 1934.

des VOEUX, G. W.: *My Colonial Service*; 2 vols., London, 1903.

WAWN, W. T.: *South Sea Islanders and the Queensland Labour Trade, 1875-1891*; London, 1893.

WILLARD, M.: *History of the White Australia Policy*; Melbourne, 1923.

(6) MISSIONS.

(Only general works with some bearing on British policy are listed here. See also regional bibliographies.)

ARMSTRONG, E. S.: *The History of the Melanesian Mission*; London, 1900.

ARTLESS, S. W.: *The Church in Melanesia*; London, 1936.

BEACH, H. P.: *Missions as a Cultural Factor in the Pacific*; Honolulu, 1927.

BLISS, E. M.: *The Encyclopaedia of Missions*; 2 vols., New York, 1891.

BROWN, G.: *Autobiography*; London, 1908.

COLWELL, J. A.: (ed.) *A Century in the Pacific; A Review of Missions throughout the Islands*; London, 1914.

ELLIS, J. E.: *Life of William Ellis*; London, 1873.

ELLIS, W.: *Polynesian Researches*; 2 vols., London, 1829; 2 ed., 4 vols., London, 1832-1836.

A Vindication of the South Sea Missions; London, 1831.

FINDLAY, G. C., & HOLDSWORTH, W. W.: *The History of the Wesleyan Missionary Society*; 5 vols., London, 1921-1924.

HOWITT, W.: *Colonisation and Christianity*; London, 1838.

HUIE, J. A.: *History of Christian Missions*; Edinburgh, 1842.

LANG, J. D.: *Popery in Australia and the Southern Hemisphere, and How to Check it Effectually*; Edinburgh, 1847.

LOVETT, R.: *The History of the London Missionary Society, 1795-1895*; 2 vols., London, 1899.

MARSDEN, J. B.: *Memoirs of the Life and Labours of the Rev. Samuel Marsden*; London, 1857.

MARSDEN, S.: *Letters and Journals of Samuel Marsden, 1765-1838*; ed. J. R. Elder; Dunedin, 1932.

MARTIN, K. L. P.: *Missionaries and Annexation in the Pacific*; Oxford, 1924.

MOISTER, W.: *A History of Wesleyan Missions*; 2 ed., London, 1871.

PATON, J. G.: *Autobiography*; Edited by his brother; Vol. I, London, 1890; Vol. II, London, 1899.

POMPALLIER, J. B. F.: *Early History of the Catholic Church in Oceania*; trans. by A. Herman; Auckland, 1888.

STOCK, E.: *The History of the Church Missionary Society*; 4 vols., London, 1899-1916.

TUCKER, H. W.: *Life and Episcopate of George Augustus Selwyn*; 2 vols., London, 1879.

TURNER, G.: *Nineteen Years in Polynesia*; London, 1861.

WILKS, M.: (See under Societies, Marquesas and Gambiers.)

WILLIAMS, J.: *A Narrative of Missionary Enterprise in the South Sea Islands . . .* ; London, 1837.

The Missionary's Farewell; *Valedictory Services of J. W.*; London, 1838.

YONGE, C. M.: *Life of John Coleridge Patteson*; 2 vols., London, 1874.

YOUNG, W. A.: *Christianity and Civilisation in the Southern Pacific*; Oxford, 1922.

(7) REGIONAL BIBLIOGRAPHIES.

FIJI (to 1875).

BRITTON, H.: *Fiji in 1870*; Melbourne, 1870.

BURTON, J. W.: *The Fiji of To-day*; London, 1910.

CHAPPLE, W. A.: *Fiji, Its Problems and Resources*: Auckland, 1921.

COOPER, H. S.: *Fiji, Its Resources and Prospects*; London, 1879.

DERRICK, R. A.: *A History of Fiji*, Vol. I. (Advance copy in the Mitchell Library, Sydney, dated 1942.)

FIJI, Colony of: *The Colony of Fiji, 1874-1924*; Suva, 1924.

FORBES, A. L.: *Two Years in Fiji*; London, 1875.

HENDERSON, G. C.: *Fiji and the Fijians, 1835-1856*; Sydney, 1931.

HORNE J.: *A Year in Fiji*; London, 1881.

McARTHUR, Alderman: *The Annexation of Fiji and the Pacific Slave Trade*; *Speech in the House of Commons, June 13, 1873*; London, 1874.

PATTERSON, S.: *A Narrative of the Adventures, Sufferings and Privations of Samuel Patterson, A Native of Rhode-Island, experienced by him in several voyages to various parts of the world*; Providence, 1825. (M.L.)

PRITCHARD, W. T.: *Polynesian Reminiscences; or Life in the South Pacific Islands*; London, 1866.

ROSS, C. S.: *Fiji and the Western Pacific*; Geelong, 1909.

ROWE, G. S.: *James Calvert of Fiji*; London, 1893.

St. JULIAN, C.: *The International Status of Fiji, &c.*; Sydney, 1872.

SMYTHE, S. M.: *Ten Months in the Fiji Islands, with an Introduction and Appendix by Col. W. J. Smythe*; London, 1862.

WILLIAMS, T, and CALVERT, J.: *Fiji and the Fijians and Missionary Labours among the Cannibals*; ed. by G. S. Rowe, 2 vols., London, 1858; and subsequent eds.

NEW CALEDONIA (to 1853).

BERNARD, A.: *L'Archipel de la Nouvelle-Calédonie*; Paris, 1905.

CALDWELL, J.: *Report on New Caledonia*; n.d., n.p. (M.L.)

CAMPBELL, F. A.: *A Year in the New Hebrides, Loyalty Islands and New Caledonia*; Geelong, 1873.

CAVE, P.: *La France en Nouvelle Calédonie*; Paris, n.d.

GARNIER, J.: *La Nouvelle Calédonie*; Paris, 1876.

HARDY, G.: *Histoire de la colonisation française*; Paris, 1928.

LEMIRE, C.: *La colonisation française en Nouvelle-Calédonie et ses dépendances*; Paris, 1877.

PARQUET, J.: *La Nouvelle-Calédonie*; Alger, 1872.

de SALINIS, P. A.: *Marins et Missionaires: Conquête de la Nouvelle-Calédonie, 1843-1853*; Paris, 1892.

SAVOLLE, C.: *Histoire de la Nouvelle-Calédonie et de ses Dépendances*; Noumea, 1922.

SULLIVAN, B.: *A Prospectus for forming a British Colony on the Island of New Caledonia . . . by a Company under Royal Charter*; Sydney, 1842. (M.L.)

NEW GUINEA (to 1884).

CHALMERS, J., and GILL, W.: *Work and Adventure in New Guinea, 1877-1885*; London, 1885.

CHALMERS, J.: *Pioneer Life and Work in New Guinea, 1877-1894*; London, 1895.

COOKE, C. Kinloch: (ed.) *Australian Defences and New Guinea; Compiled from Papers of the late Sir Peter Scratchley*; London, 1887.

KLEIN, W. C.: (ed.) *Nieuw Guinea*; 3 vols., Amsterdam, 1935-1938.

LYNE, C.: *New Guinea: an account of the Establishment of the British Protectorate*; London, 1885.

MURRAY, J. H. P.: *Papua, or British New Guinea*; London, 1912.

NIAU, J. H.: *Phantom Paradise; the story of the expedition of the Marquis de Rays*; Sydney, 1936.

REED, S. W.: *The Making of Modern New Guinea*; Philadelphia, 1943.

WICHMANN, A.: *Entdeckungsgeschichte von Neu-Guinea*; 2 vols., Leiden, 1909-1912.

NEW HEBRIDES (to 1887).

BRUNET, A.: *Le Régime International des Nouvelles-Hébrides*; Paris, 1908.

CAMPBELL, F. A.: *A Year in the New Hebrides, the Loyalty Islands and New Caledonia*; Geelong, 1873.

DAVILLE, E.: *La Colonisation française aux Nouvelles-Hébrides*; Paris, 1895.

DOUCERE, V.: *La Mission Catholique aux Nouvelles-Hébrides*; Paris, 1934.

HARRISSON, T.: *Savage Civilisation*; London, 1937.

JACOMB, E.: *France and England in the New Hebrides*; Melbourne, 1914.

STEEL, R.: *The New Hebrides and Christian Missions, with a sketch of the labour traffic*; London, 1880.

SELECTIVE BIBLIOGRAPHY

NEW ZEALAND (to 1840).

Anon.: *Important Information relative to New Zealand.* (*Written by a Gentleman who has been a Resident Fourteen Years at Hokianga; with an Appendix comprising the Latest Official Documents relating to that interesting Country*); Sydney, 1839. (N.L.)

BEAGLEHOLE, J. C.: *Captain Hobson and the New Zealand Company*; Northampton, 1927-1928.

BEECHAM, J.: *Colonisation; being remarks on Colonisation in General, with an examination of the proposals of the Association which has been formed for Colonising New Zealand*; London, 1838.

Remarks upon the Latest Official Documents Relating to New Zealand with notice of a Pamphlet by Samuel Hinds, D.D.; 2 ed., London, 1838.

BRODIE, W.: *The State of New Zealand*; London, 1845.

BUICK, T. L.: *The Treaty of Waitangi*; Wellington, 1914.

Sovereignty in New Zealand. (Paper read before Historical Section of A. & N.Z. Assocn. for Adv. of Science, Auckland, 1937; typescript copy in M.L.).

BUSBY, J.: *Authentic Information relative to New South Wales and New Zealand*; London, 1832.

Colonies and Colonisation; Auckland, 1857.

Our Colonial Empire and the Case of New Zealand; London, 1866.

CHURCH MISSIONARY SOCIETY (COATES, D.): *Documents Exhibiting the View of the Committee of the C.M.S. on the New Zealand Question*; London, 1839.

COATES, D.: *Notes for the Information of the Deputation to Lord Glenelg respecting the New Zealand Association, &c.* (Signed Dec. 28, 1837; n.d. on publication in London.)

The Principles, Objects and Plan of the New Zealand Association Examined in a Letter to the Rt. Hon. Lord Glenelg; London, 1838.

The Present State of the New Zealand Question considered in a letter to J. P. Plumptre, Esq., M.P.; London, 1838.

COATES, D., BEECHAM, J., and ELLIS, W.: *Christianity the Means of Civilisation*; London, 1837.

DALRYMPLE, A. and FRANKLIN, B.: *Scheme of a Voyage to Convey the Conveniences of Life, Domestic Animals, Corn, Iron, etc., to New Zealand, with Dr. Benjamin Franklin's Sentiments upon the subject*; London, 1771. (See *New Zealand Journal*, 1843, p. 42, for reprint. The original and Petherick's reprint (London, 1882) were consulted in N.L.)

DILLON, Peter: *Extract of a Letter from Chevalier Dillon to an influential character here, on the advantage to be derived from the establishment of well-conducted Commercial Settlements in New Zealand*; London, 1832.

ELLIS, W.: *Polynesian Researches during a Residence of nearly Six Years in the South Sea Islands*; 2 vols., London, 1829.

FITZROY, R.: *Remarks on New Zealand*; London, 1846.

GODERICH, Lord, and BUSBY, J.: *Letter to the Rt. Hon. Lord Viscount Goderich, and Address of James Busby, Esq., British Resident, to the Chiefs of New Zealand*; Sydney, 1833. (English and Maori versions.)

HARROP, A. J.: *England and New Zealand, from Tasman to the Taranaki War*; London, 1926.

HINDS, S.: *The Latest Official Documents Relating to New Zealand with Introductory Observations*; London, 1838.

HOCKEN, T. M.: *The Early History of New Zealand*; London, 1885.

LANG, J. D.: *New Zealand in 1839*; London, 1839. (Translated into French and included in du Petit-Thouars: *Voyage autour du Monde*; Paris, 1845; Vol. IV, pp. 54 ff.) As to 1873 ed., see Hocken, cit. sup., p. 72.

McDONNELL, T.: *Extracts from Mr. McDonnell's MS. Journal containing Observations on New Zealand*; London, 1834.

McNAB, R.: (See under Trade and Settlement; and Published Collections of Documents.)

McNAB, R.: *Murihiku; a history of the South Island of New Zealand and the Islands adjacent and lying to the south*; Wellington, 1909. (This includes *Murihiku and the Southern Islands*; Invercargill, 1907.)

MARAIS, J. S.: *The Colonisation of New Zealand*; Oxford, 1927.

MARSHALL, W. B.: *A Personal Narrative of two visits to New Zealand in H.M.S. "Alligator"*; London, 1836.

MORRELL, W. P.: *New Zealand*; London, 1935.

RAMSDEN, E.: *Busby of Waitangi*; Wellington, 1942. (Favourable to Busby.)

RUSDEN, G. W.: *History of New Zealand*; 3 vols., London, Melbourne and Sydney, 1883; 2 ed., London, 1895.

SCHOLEFIELD, G. H.: *Captain William Hobson*; Oxford, 1934.

Scottish Colonial Investment Company: *Notices of New Zealand*; n.p., 1839. (N.L.) Hocken (p. 75) cites only the prospectus of the Scots New Zealand Company (1838).

TURNBULL, J.: *A Voyage round the World, in the years 1800-1804; in which the Author visited the principal Islands in the Pacific Ocean*, &c.; 2 ed., London, 1813. (Contains an account of the *Boyd* massacres.)

WAKEFIELD, E. G., *A Letter from Sydney*; London, 1829.
The British Colonisation of New Zealand; London, 1837. (With John Ward.)
A Statement of the Objects of the New Zealand Association; London, 1837. (With John Ward.)
Mr. Dandeson Coates and the New Zealand Association in a Letter to the Rt. Hon. Lord Glenelg; London, 1838.

WALTON, J.: *Twelve Months' Residence in New Zealand*; Glasgow, 1839. (Pro-colonial.)

WARD, J.: *Supplementary Information relative to New Zealand Company; Despatches and Journals of the Company's Office of the First Expedition, and the First Report of the Directors*; London, 1840.

YATE, W.: *An Account of New Zealand*; London, 1835. (2 ed., 1835.)

PITCAIRN AND SURROUNDING ISLANDS.

BAARSLAG, K.: *Islands of Adventure*; New York, 1940.

BRODIE, W.: *Pitcairn Island and the Islanders in 1850*; London, 1851.

CASEY, R. J.: *Easter Island*; Indianopolis, 1931.

LUCAS, C. P.: *The Pitcairn Island Register Book*; London, 1929.

MURRAY, T. B.: *Pitcairn; The Island, the People and the Pastor*; London, 1853; 3 ed., London, 1854.

SCHAPIRO, H. L.: *Heritage of the "Bounty"*; London, 1936.

SAMOA (to 1889).

CHURCHWARD, W. B.: *My Consulate in Samoa*; London, 1887.

ELLISON, J. W.: *Opening and Penetration of Foreign Influence in Samoa to 1880*; Corvallis (Oregon), 1938.

KEESING, F. M.: *Modern Samoa, Its Government and Changing Life*; London, 1934.

KELLY, J. L.: *South Sea Islands: Possibilities of Trade with New Zealand*; Auckland, 1885.

KRAMER, A. K.: *Die Samoa-Inseln*; 2 vols., Stuttgart, 1902.

MASTERMAN, S.: *The Origins of International Rivalry in Samoa, 1845-1884*; London, 1934.

MEADE, H.: *A Ride through the Disturbed Districts of New Zealand: together with some Accounts of the South Sea Islands*; London, 1870.

NEAL, J. U.: *Report on the Pacific Islands*; Napier, 1885.

RYDEN, G. H.: *The Foreign Policy of the United States in relation to Samoa*; New Haven, 1933. (Especially for period ending in partition of the group.)

STAIR, J. B.: *Old Samoa*; London, 1897.

SELECTIVE BIBLIOGRAPHY

STEVENSON, R. L.: *Footnote to History*: *Eight Years of Trouble in Samoa*;
London, 1892. (Repr. 1893.)
TURNER, G.: *Samoa, A Hundred Years and Long Before*; London, 1884.
WATSON, R. M.: *History of Samoa*; Wellington, 1918.

THE SOCIETIES (to 1847), THE MARQUESAS (to 1842)
and THE GAMBIERS (to 1871).

Anon.: *History of the Otaheitean Islands, from their first discovery to the present
time*; Edinburgh and London, 1800. (N.L.)
ARAGO, J.: *L'Occupation des Marquises et de Taïti*; Paris, 1843.
CHRISTIAN, F. W.: *Eastern Pacific Lands*; *Tahiti and the Marquesas Islands*;
London, 1910.
DU PETIT-THOUARS, A. A.: *Voyage autour du monde sur la fregate la Venus,
pendant les années, 1836-1839*; 4 vols., Paris, 1840-1843.
ELLIS, W.: *A History of the London Missionary Society*; London, 1844.
GOYAU, G.: *Premier demi-siècle de l'apostolate des Picpuciens aux Iles Gambier*;
Braine—le-Comte, 1928.
GRACIA M.: *Lettres sur les Iles Marquises*; Paris, 1843.
HENRY, T.: *Ancient Tahiti.* (B.P. Bishop Museum Bulletin, No. 48, 1928.)
(For Pomare dynasty.)
JORE, L.: *George Pritchard, L'Adversaire de la France à Tahiti*; Paris, n.d.
(1940?).
LONDON MISSIONARY SOCIETY: *Brief Statement of the Aggression of the
French on the Island of Tahiti*; London, 1843.
ROLLIN, L.: *Les Iles Marquises*; Paris, 1929.
RUSSELL, S.: *Tahiti and French Oceania*; Sydney, 1935.
TUROT, J.: *Du Petit-Thouars dans la Polynésie*; Paris, 1844.
VINCENDON-DUMOULIN et DESGRAZ: *Les Iles Marquises*; Paris, 1843.
Les Iles Taïti; 2 vols., Paris, 1844.
WILKS, M.: *Tahiti: containing a review . . . of French Roman Catholic efforts
for the destruction of English Protestant Missions in the South Seas*; London,
1844.

THE SOLOMONS (to 1893).

ARMSTRONG, E. S.: *The History of the Melanesian Mission*; London, 1900.
GUPPY, H. G.: *The Solomon Islands and their Natives*; London, 1887.
KNIBBS, S. G. C.: *The Savage Solomons as They Were and Are*; London, 1929.

TONGA (to 1891).

BAKER, B.: *Memoirs of the Rev. Dr. Shirley Waldemar Baker*; Dunedin, Christ-
church and Wellington, 1927.
BLANC, Bishop: *A History of Tonga or Friendly Islands*; *trans. from the Tongan
by C. S. Ramsay*; Vista, 1934.
FARMER, S. S.: *Tonga and the Friendly Islands*; London, 1855.
im THURN, E.: *Report on Tonga*; London, 1905.
MARINER, W.: *An Account of the Natives of the Tonga Islands* (*compiled by J.
Martin*), 2 vols., London, 1817.
MAUDSLAY, A. P.: *Life in the Pacific Fifty Years Ago*; London, 1930.
THOMSON, B.: *Diversions of a Prime Minister*; London, 1894.
WOOD, A. H.: *History and Geography of Tonga*; Nukualofa, 1938.

INDEX

INDEX

Names of islands are given in the text in the modern spelling of the name used in the documents. Changes of name and usage are set out in the index.